W9-CHA-555

Guiding Children's Language Learning

Guiding Children's

Contributing Authors

JOSEPH L. FROST
University of Texas
Austin, Texas

HELEN HEFFERNAN
State Department of Education
Sacramento, California

RALPH E. KELLOGG
County Department of Education
San Diego, California

ROBERT M. BLOOM
John Winthrop School
Dorchester, Massachusetts

H. BERESFORD MENAGH
John Kennedy Center
Washington, D. C.

DONALD R. FERRIS
Purdue University
West Lafayette, Indiana

POSE LAMB
Purdue University
West Lafayette, Indiana

EDITH CROWELL TRAGER
San Jose State College
San Jose, California

RUTH HOCHSTETLER
Ball State University
Muncie, Indiana

ELIZABETH H. RATTÉ
Purdue University
West Lafayette, Indiana

MARY MONTEBELLO
Capitol University
Columbus, Ohio

Language Learning

Planning Editor

POSE LAMB
Purdue University
West Lafayette, Indiana

WM. C. BROWN COMPANY PUBLISHERS
DUBUQUE, IOWA

BROWN

EDUCATION SERIES

Edited by

LOWRY W. HARDING, PH.D.
The Ohio State University
Columbus, Ohio

Copyright © 1967
by
Wm. C. Brown Company Publishers

Library of Congress Catalog Card Number: 67–21309

All rights reserved. No part of this book may be reproduced in any form or by any process without permission in writing from the copyright owner.

Manufactured by WM. C. BROWN CO., INC., Dubuque, Iowa
Printed in U. S. A.

Introduction

The major purpose of this text is to present to prospective teachers, and in-service teachers as well, a group of independent yet related chapters dealing with instruction in the language arts.

No area of the elementary curriculum is more important than the language arts – speaking, listening, reading and writing (including handwriting, "creative" writing and spelling). The authors of this text feel very strongly that the elementary teacher needs to be particularly well prepared in this field. It is because the publishers of this book and especially their Education Editor, Lowry W. Harding, share this concern that this book came to be.

Why the rather unconventional collection of related chapters rather than the more traditional textbook written by one or two authors? The reader is almost certainly aware of the growing trend toward specialization in every field, including education. There are a number of obvious benefits which result from specialization, the most significant being the additional competence which should accrue to an individual who can devote his energies and intellectual abilities to one field of endeavor rather than several. This book is the product of the thinking and the writing of eleven "specialists," each contributing in one area of particular competence and interest. It is hoped that the major pitfall of specialization, narrowness, has been avoided through the use of two strategems. First, although each author has an area of particular interest within the language arts field, he is also conversant and familiar with the other areas. Chapters have been written by college instructors of language arts courses, curriculum directors and school administrators. Each author is forced, in pursuing his regular duties, to see the language arts as interrelated and, ultimately, inseparable.

The second strategem was assigning to an editor the task of correlating and integrating the several chapters, as well as editing them.

The writing styles of the various authors differ and no attempt has been made to disguise this. Acceptance of this difference in style in a college text may help a prospective teacher become more accepting of differences in the writing styles of the children he teaches. There are also slight philosophical differences among the authors, and this has influenced the arrangement of the chapters.

The authors do not differ in their belief that they are writing about a most significant area of children's learning in the elementary school. They are also in agreement with reference to the importance of utilizing the findings of researchers in the fields of curriculum, child growth and development of linguistics.

The study of language *can* be and *should* be challenging, rewarding and pleasant for children. The authors of this textbook hope they have been successful in presenting to teachers some suggestions for achieving these goals.

POSE LAMB
Planning Editor

Contents

Chapter Page

1. **Language Development in Children** 1
Dr. Joseph L. Frost

Language Development During Infancy 2
Language Development During the Preschool Period 4
Language Development in Nursery School and Kindergarten 9
Interrelationships Among Various Aspects of Language Development 11
Language, Thought and Intelligence 15
Language and Experience 19
A Holistic Approach to Language Development 23
Language and Teaching 25
Conclusion 33

2. **Language Arts Programs in Elementary Schools** 37
Miss Helen Heffernan

Early Language Development 37
Interrelationships Among the Language Arts 39
Language Arts and Other Curricular Areas 44
Planning the School Schedule 50
The Daily Schedule 55
The Weekly Program 56
The Yearly Program 57
Planning for Language Arts Instruction 57
Summary 60

3. **Creative Dramatics** **63**
Dr. H. Beresford Menagh

Introduction 63
Utilitarian Education 64
Nonutilitarian Needs 67
The Nature of Creative Dramatics 70
Requirements of Creative Dramatics 71
The Functions of Creative Dramatics 73
The Processes of Creative Dramatics 79
Mood Development 83
Story Creation 85

4. **A Program for Oral English** **92**
Mr. Robert M. Bloom

Guiding Principles for Building Instructional Programs 93
Development of Speech in the Preprimary Years 94
Goals of Oral Language in the Primary Years 96
Individual Differences Among Children 100
The Objectives of Speech Instruction 103
Advantages of Grouping 107
Education for Leadership in Group Participation 109
Basic Elements in Evaluation of Oral Expression 112
Summary 113

5. **Listening** **117**
Mr. Ralph E. Kellogg

The Knowledge Explosion 117
Listening: A Vital Link to Knowledge 117
Value Formation Through Critical Listening 118
Basic Premises of a Comprehensive Theory 124
Goals of the Listening Instruction Program 129
Role of the Elementary Teacher in Listening Instruction 133
Conclusion 135

6. **Teaching Children to Write** **137**
Dr. Donald R. Ferris

The Nature of Language and Writing 137
Types of Writing 138
Writing as a Process 141

Writing: Function and Purpose 152
Utilitarian Writing 155
Creative or Imaginative Writing 159
Children's Poetry Writing 165
Evaluating Children's Writing 167

7. Teaching and Improving Handwriting in Elementary Schools 170
Dr. Pose Lamb

Typical Handwriting Programs 171
"Why Manuscript Writing" 181
How Do We Begin 184
The Content of Beginning Writing Programs 191
Making the Transition to Cursive Writing 194
The Use of the Typewriter 200
Evaluation of Handwriting 202

8. The Teaching of Spelling: A Linguistic Approach 209
Mrs. Edith Crowell Trager

Relationships of Semantics, Syntax, and Morphology 210
The Consonant Sounds 214
The Vowel Sounds 218
Analyses of the Grapho-Phonemes of English 219
Methods of Teaching Spelling 225
Spelling Methods 230
Standards for Spelling 231
Materials for Spelling Instruction 232

9. Facets of Language-Grammar and Usage 237
Dr. Ruth Hochstetler

Essential Functions of Language 237
Definitions of Grammar 238
Viewpoints Concerning the Teaching of Grammar 240
The Introduction of Transformational Grammar 244
Generative Grammar 246
Teaching Grammar in the Elementary School 246
Criteria for Determining "Good" English 248
Teaching Grammar as a Structural Framework 250
Grammar as an Editorial Tool 255
Improving English Usage in the Elementary School 258
The Parts of Speech 261

Ways of Working With Children 264
Summary 267

10. Foreign Language in the Elementary School 270
Mrs. Elizabeth H. Ratté

A Rationale for FLES 270
Time Required for Mastering a Second Language 271
The Objectives of Foreign Language Instruction 274
Relationships to the Total Curriculum 277
Teaching Techniques and Materials 279
The Role of the Teacher 287
Future Trends 288

11. Evaluation 294
Dr. Mary Montebello

Listening 296
Handwriting 304
Spelling 320
Oral Language 343
Grammar and Usage 358
Summary 359
Index 367

Chapter 1 Joseph L. Frost

Language Development in Children

Language has made it possible for man to attain his superior rank, distinct and apart from all other forms of life. From crude beginnings, language has evolved through rapidly accelerating degrees of refinement to its present state – a highly complex system of symbols and sounds with equally complex devices for transmission from person to person or from place to place. Need and experience have spurred man to develop techniques for communication from original face-to-face confrontation using a few simple sounds, to round-the-world transmission, using any of the dozens of mother languages. From "tom-toms" to "Telstar" the history of communication reveals the ingenuity of man and his burning desire to discover the order and meaning of the universe. The continuous refinement of language forms and communicative devices has provided the tools for man's current assault from outer space, disease, and aging. The secret to survival in an age of nuclear threat lies within the power of language. This, ironically, is the same power through which the threat was created. Thus language can be constructive or destructive, facilitative or threatening.

Language is complex. It involves considerably more than merely speaking and listening. "It includes all forms of human interaction in which a person is made aware of a thought, feeling, or question experienced by another person."[1] Broadly conceived, language is the vehicle for all human communication in its many forms – speaking, writing, printing, expressive behavior – a living, dynamic vehicle. The sounds and

[1]Gardner, Bruce D. *Development in Early Childhood.* New York: Harper and Row, 1964. p. 167.

symbols of language differ widely from country to country as separate peoples have developed patterns which serve their needs most effectively.

The growing child makes the language of family and neighborhood his language. "Differences in accents, usage and structure, colloquialisms of family or regional origin, add spice to language and deepen the appreciation of those who learn to understand and enjoy it."[2] Just how this comes about is quite a story, involving numerous interrelationships between the structure of language and the nature of the child.

Language Development During Infancy

From the moment of birth the child begins to learn from the world around him. For the first few weeks he is a more or less passive recipient of the attention given him by the significant adults in his life. But he quickly learns that he can modify his immediate world and his skill in doing this grows. The primary means for effecting change or activity in the infant's environment is through vocalization, although movement of the extremities may also have some effect. The earliest vocalizations are reflexive and have no pattern of meaning; no particular sound is connected to any one situation.

During the first three or four months adult responses to cooing and crying make it possible for the infant to learn that vocalization has an effect on his immediate comfort. Crying brings relief from pain and hunger; cooing solicits smiles and comforting pats. As a result of continuous reinforcement, the infant begins to associate vocal sounds with the satisfaction of needs. The alert mother is able to determine the significance of early sounds and through her responses plays an important role in the initial language development of the child. In addition to need satisfaction early vocalization appears to give the infant personal pleasure; exercises the maturing speech apparatus, and as Carroll[3] stated, "Certain it is that the infant early develops the capacity of reacting differentially to adult voices." Thus through increasingly meaningful interaction the infant develops simple but effective means of communication.

Early Forms of Communication

The "cooing" of the first few months gradually develops into the "babbling" stage, which continues through most of the first year. During

---

[2]Mackintosh, Helen K. (ed.) *Children and Oral Language.* A joint publication of ACEI, ASCD, IRA, and NCTE. 1964. p. 6.

[3]Carroll, John B. "Language Acquisition, Bilingualism, and Language Change." *Encyclopedia of Educational Research.* New York: The Macmillan Co., 1960. p. 337

the latter part of the babbling stage the child begins to recognize and understand words and phrases. A more flexible and differentiated language system than vocalization alone is emerging. The vocal sounds of cooing and babbling become more meaningful through the use of intonation and inflexion. The child associates rising inflexion and tempo with pleasure or surprise and lower inflexion and tempo with discomfort or disappointment. In addition, expressive behavior – smiling, frowning, speed of movement, and softness or roughness of physical contacts – begins to have more meaning. Opportunity for use of these communicative forms, independently and in combination, is an indispensable prerequisite to later, more articulate use of language. Individual differences in rate and quality of language development are evident during this period. Recently much attention is focused upon the effects of amount and variety of the child's early linguistic experiences.

Near the beginning of the second year of life, genuine talking usually begins. Many eager parents, upon hearing sound duplications which may only remotely resemble "ma-ma" or "da-da," are confident that their child is now talking, but mere repetition of sounds in absence of meaning is only a prelude to genuine speech. It is some time later, when verbal sounds are closely associated with objects, people or activities, that the first true words are spoken. From this point on language is commonly used as an indication of mental development. According to Watts,[4] "it is pretty well agreed that linguistic development is a good index, though, of course, not a complete one, of the general powers of children in their earlier years."

McCarthy[5] and other writers stress that linguistic development during the second year of life is dependent largely upon imitation, which is quite prominent during this period. This is evidenced by the fact that the normal child learns the language of his environment but the congenitally deaf child does not learn to speak at all because he is deprived of opportunity for imitation. It also is general knowledge that the child of English speaking parents learns English to the exclusion of all other languages, the Japanese child learns Japanese, etc., if the parents speak only one language.

Near the end of the second year the child makes rapid vocabulary growth. Single words often represent numerous meanings and may be used in many different contexts. "Drink" may mean water or milk. "Dog" often refers to every walking creature even remotely resembling a dog; "car" means car, truck, bus, or even train. Quite frequently the child, instead of

---

[4]Watts, A. F. *The Language and Mental Development of Children.* New York: D. C. Heath, 1948. p. 34.

[5]McCarthy, D. "Language Development in Children." In L. Carmichael (ed.) *Manual of Child Psychology.* 2nd ed. New York: Wiley, 1954.

using the single sound "dog" or "car" will say "dog-dog" or "car-car." This appears to be a natural tendency. Occasionally a child will become "fixated" at this stage described by Gardner[6] as the "grunt and point" stage. Although mental development or vocal and auditory mechanism *could* be causative factors, most often the reason is simply that the child feels no need for further language sophistication. A crude "grunt" coupled with a pointed finger serves his desires remarkably well. "Language, like other important human skills, is learned. In order for the learning to occur, there must be motivation on the part of the child. The child must somehow discover that he can satisfy his own needs better by talking than by not talking, and by talking well rather than poorly."[7] Between the ages of one and five years mastery of spoken language is normally acquired very rapidly, and ". . . the child whose language development is seriously delayed for any reason labors under an almost unsurmountable handicap in his social and academic relationships."[8] On the basis of numerous investigations it appears extremely important that children acquire skill in linguistic expression at an early age. Parents play a significant role in this development. Watts[9] recorded an illustrative incident ". . . of one small child who was told in a public place to look at the 'bow-wow.'" The child replied, "Don't say 'bow-wow,' mother; people will think that you can't say 'dog.'"

Language Development During the Preschool Period

The preschooler is primarily a self-centered or egocentric person. Language exists for him as a means for getting what he wants. Through meeting and coping with many minor difficulties and through receiving affection and recognition for his early attempts to please, the child begins to recognize the value of interaction with others. Piaget[10] recognizes in addition to egocentric speech a second type which he calls socialized speech. In egocentric speech the child makes no attempt to address himself to a person, does not appear to care if anyone is listening, but talks for himself or anyone who happens to be in his presence. In socialized speech which is usually quite evident at seven to eight years of age the child addresses himself to a particular person, considers his point of view and actually exchanges ideas with him. Considering that each person must perceive, think, and interpret only in terms of his own unique experiences, some degree of self-centered vocalizing is expected for people of all ages.

---

[6]Gardner, op. cit. p. 170.
[7]Gardner, op. cit. p. 170.
[8]McCarthy, op. cit. p. 494.
[9]Watts, op. cit. p. 35.
[10]Piaget, Jean. *The Language and Thought of the Child.* New York: Harcourt, Brace, 1926.

Piaget's findings concerning the functions of language and language as a means of revealing thought have been tested by other investigators with varying amounts of agreement. The differences can be attributed to variability in rate of development which is characteristic for children in any age group, though the sequence of development except under extreme conditions is invariant.

The Nature of Development

We have seen that language development of the child, in its many forms, progresses in an orderly fashion. By the time the child is in kindergarten his vocabulary has usually reached several thousand words, and he clearly demonstrates skill in sentence usage, listening, and other communicative skills. This has come about through trial and error and is dependent largely upon imitation of those around him. First words deal with concrete objects and events but the child's speech is rapidly expanded to include more abstract terms and finally complete sentences. All this has been achieved in absence of any formal lessons in grammar. The wide variation in achievement of a particular language task – learning to talk, to use expressive behavior effectively, etc. – is dependent upon many factors. These factors are internal and external, innate and environmental, but always multiple. Continuous but irregular patterns of development dependent upon multiple factors is characteristic of child growth and development in general. Not only does major achievement of language tasks follow an orderly pattern but as Olson[11] stated,

> Although children growing up in various environments learn to speak many different languages, the time sequence in the acquisition of sound elements is surprisingly constant . . . There is some evidence that gross motor developments precede fine motor coordination in the speech musculature . . . There appears to be some coincidence in linguistic development with phases of motor development . . . There are also anatomical social, and feeding correlates.

At least four major factors are important to growth in language: "(1) mental, (2) physical, (3) social and emotional, and (4) educational."[12] Growth in any of these areas is supplementary to language growth. Total growth of the child generally occurs in a sequential manner with marked variation between individuals and also between separate but related areas of growth. The wise adult does not necessarily buy a size 8 dress for her eight-year-old daughter. She may find that size 6 or size 10 fits better. But adults are not always pillars of wisdom when pacing instruction and learn-

---

[11]Olson, Willard C. *Child Development.* Boston: D. C. Heath, 1959, p. 124.

[12]Hawkes, Glenn R. and Damaris Pease. *Behavior and Development from 5 to 12.* New York: Harper, 1962. p. 225.

ing materials to the educational needs of the child and the idea that children achieving below "average" represent failures in teaching persists to this day. The practices of many schools suggests that it is easier for the child to change his needs than for the school to modify its demands.

The knowledge that growth is modifiable also has powerful implications for the schools. The degree of care and affection given the young child has an impact on the development of a mature personality. Fear and anxiety, rooted in the culture of the home and reinforced by inappropriate school expectations, makes an indelible mark on the personality of the child. An enriched school environment does not erase the effects of a debilitating home environment but enrichment can make a significant difference. The child who arrives at school unhealthy, unhappy, and unready to learn will remain, unhealthy, unhappy, and unready to learn unless the school modifies its expectations and broadens its role in the educative process. Good health – mental, emotional and physical – is prerequisite to school progress. It follows that the school must direct its attention to these needs before teaching-learning proceeds.

Evidence of Language Growth

Language growth in the past has often been determined by investigators in two ways: (1) by the increase in size of vocabulary and (2) by the length of sentences.

There is a wide range of individual differences in vocabulary increase, causing variation in the results of different investigators. Only during the preschool period is it practical to use the complete vocabularies of children in assessment of growth. The wider range of experiences of older children makes necessary the use of sampling.

One widely quoted estimation of vocabulary increase is that of Madorah Smith.[13] Notice (Table 1) that vocabulary increases very slowly during infancy, quite rapidly during the preschool period, and drops off again at about five to six years of age. Using a different set of criteria involving various methods to determine whether a child understood a word, Mary Smith[14] found markedly different results (Table 2). Instead of having a vocabulary of 2,562 words upon entry to first grade (Madorah Smith, 1926) the child may have a vocabulary of 24,000 words (Mary Smith, 1941).

---

[13]Smith, Madorah E. "An Investigation of the Development of the Sentence and the Extent of Vocabulary in Young Children." University Iowa, Stud. Child Welfare, 3:1926, p. 5.

[14]Smith, Mary K. "Measurement of the Size of General English Vocabulary through the Elementary Grades and High School." *Genetic Psychology Monographs. 24*:311-345, 1941.

TABLE 1

Average Size of Vocabularies of 273 Children From 8 Months to 6 Years

Age Group			Vocabulary	
Years Months	Number of Children	Average IQ	Number of Words	Gain
8	13		0	
10	17		1	1
1– 0	52		3	2
1– 3	19		19	16
1– 6	14		22	3
1– 9	14		118	96
2– 0	25		272	154
2– 6	14		446	174
3– 0	20	109	896	450
3– 6	26	106	1,222	326
4– 0	26	109	1,540	318
4– 6	32	109	1,870	330
5– 0	20	108	2,072	202
5– 6	27	110	2,289	217
6– 0	9	108	2,562	273

SOURCE: M. E. Smith, "An Investigation of the Development of the Sentence and Extent of Vocabulary in Young Children," *Univ. of Iowa Stud. Child Welf.*, 1926, 3 (5): 54. Reprinted by permission.

TABLE 2

*The Growth of Vocabulary**

Grade	Basic	Derived	Total
1	16,900	7,100	24,000
2	22,000	12,000	34,000
3	26,000	18,000	44,000
4	26,200	18,800	45,000
5	28,500	22,500	51,000
6	31,500	18,000	49,500

*SOURCE: Mary K. Smith. "Measurement of the Size of General English Vocabulary through the Elementary Grades and High School." *Genetic Psychology Monographs* 24: 311-345, 1941. Reprinted by permission.

The results of a more recent study by Shibles[15] supports the *larger* general size of first grade children's understanding vocabulary. Furthermore, recent follow-up studies, (Templin[16]) using the same methods as early investigations, have shown that children are currently talking in longer sentences and using larger vocabularies. McCarthy[17] believes that this may due to

> . . . the advent of radio and television, fewer foreign born and bilingual children, the rise of nursery schools affording more opportunities for language stimulation outside the home for the formerly underprivileged groups of children, more leisure time for parents to spend with their children, reduced amount of time that children are cared for by nurse-maids of limited verbal ability, better economic conditions allowing parents even in lower income brackets to provide stimulating environments for children to be treated more permissively and to find greater acceptance in the modern home.

Obviously, some degree of artificiality enters into the study of vocabulary because of the degrees of meaning that can be attached to any word. Is the child able to say the word, use it in his speech, read it, define it? How well can he do this? At best, vocabulary estimations are useful as very general estimations for what the child actually knows. The degree of knowing about a word and the related meanings that word holds for a child is very personal, not to be fully understood or completely shared by another.

The average age of the child upon speaking his first sentence is about seventeen and five-tenths months with complete sentences appearing at about four years.[18] McCarthy[19] compiled data from ten investigations of mean length of sentences for one to nine-year-old children. There was quite striking agreement among the investigators, each employing different subjects and methods. McCarthy[20] therefore concluded that mean sentence length is the most . . . "reliable, easily determined, objective, quantitative, and easily understood measure of linguistic maturity." But Watts[21] draws attention to the range and quality of the words which children use. The child who writes or speaks, "He did not know which place he would have

---

[15]Shibles, Burleigh H. "How Many Words Does a First-Grade Child Know?" *Elementary English. 41*: 42-47, January, 1959.

[16]Templin, Mildred. *Certain Language Skills in Children, Their Development and Relationship.* Univ. of Minnesota, Inst. of Child Welfare, Mono. Ser., No. 26, 1957.

[17]McCarthy, Dorothea A. "Research in Language Development: Retrospect and Prospect." *Child Development Monographs. 24*: 13-15, 1959.

[18]Nice, M. M. "Length of Sentences as a Criterion of a Child's Progress in Speech." *Journal of Educational Psychology. 16*: 370-379, 1925.

[19]McCarthy, op. cit. 1954. p. 546-547.

[20]McCarthy, Ibid. p. 551.

[21]Watts, op. cit. p. 31.

to go in the end," has not shown that he possesses a richer or fuller vocabulary by using 13 words than the child who stated, "His ultimate destination was uncertain." It is clear that study of the child's language growth must take into account range and quality in addition to quantity.

The current emphasis on restricting the vocabulary of instructional materials, particularly basal readers, is unrealistic and harmful. Most young children have developed extremely large vocabularies as a result of increased travel, television, and children's books. The basic vocabulary for the beginner in school is that which he has, understands, and uses. Clearly this is a highly individual matter.

Attention to the size of vocabulary and length of sentences as an index of language power has recently been supplemented by attention to structure of language and the familiarity of the child with these structures.

Strickland[22] divided the talk of 575 children into units according to rising and falling intonation, pause, and meaning. A unit of speech ending with a distinct falling intonation was called a phonological unit (indicated by #). Each phonological unit contains one or more meaning or structural units, spoken with varying intonation, and partial pauses (indicated by /). For example:

> I have to be saving my money/you know/ because we're going to be gone// let's see// I guess it is four or five months# I'm saving my money for that and then afterward // I'm keeping it for what I want #.

This study revealed that the length of phonological units used is *not* an indication of language maturity; that some basic patterns appear with great frequency (Table 3), the most used appearing with high frequency at all grade levels; that these structures, learned at an early age, appear to be basic building blocks of children's language.

Difficulties with language appear to involve more than learning hard words and speaking, reading, or writing long sentences. Linguists emphasize the role of vocabulary in later learning of reading and writing, but they also recognize that the learning of oral language *patterns* facilitates the use of printed materials.

Language Development in Nursery School and Kindergarten

For most children school experiences begin upon entry to kindergarten or first grade but many others are fortunate in attending good nursery schools. The nursery school is carefully planned to give the child

---

[22]Strickland, Ruth G. *The Language of Elementary School Children: Its Relationship to the Language of Reading Textbooks and the Quality of Reading of Selected Children.* Bloomington: Indiana University, School of Education. 38: 1962.

TABLE 3

Total Number of Structural Patterns Used and Frequency of Use of Each at Four Grade Levels

Grade	Total number	Frequency of use		
		1 - 4 times	5 - 10 times	More than 10 times
1	658	588	53	47
2	747	652	39	51
4*	722	620	50	52
6	1041	918	69	54

*Based on 75 cases (other grades 100 cases each).

Source: Ruth G. Strickland, *The Language of Elementary School Children*: Its Relationship to the Language of Reading Textbooks and the Quality of Reading of Selected Children. Bloomington: Indiana University, School of Education, 38:16. Reprinted by permission.

many rich, stimulating experiences with materials and other children. These experiences are desirable for *all* children but especially for those from impoverished families. The stimulation provided by peers and understanding teachers, manipulation of many-shaped and many-colored objects, and listening to good children's stories, etc. are essential to language, social, and intellectual development. During recent years, educators and others concerned with children have begun to emphasize, with renewed vigor, the importance of these experiences and are currently active toward making them available. Operation "Headstart" is a direct result of the clearly established need for compensatory preschool enrichment programs for culturally disadvantaged children.

These early nursery school years of the twos, threes, and fours bring rapid growth in language skills. Funds of knowledge and ranges of interests broaden to include real conversation and social interaction, resulting in an ever-widening range of interests and skills. The nursery school child is bright-eyed at the wonders of his world. He explores, he looks, he feels, he hears, he tries it all on for size and, curiously enough, the healthy child takes off and discards the parts that don't fit.

Still wide-eyed with the wonder of it all, the child comes to kindergarten. Here he lives in a world that too often resembles the more formal scene that will come next year upon entry to first grade. The days are too short, the room too small to contain his enthusiasm and exploratory activity. Guidance is no longer dependent upon physical handling. The child responds to verbal suggestions and directions and may offer some of his own. He often substitutes language for force, suggesting to another child, "Let me show you how to do it." On the playground he may resort to name calling rather than hitting and kicking to make his point.

The teacher makes provisions for the social development of children through cooperative group planning, goal setting, working in small and large groups and evaluating behavior and work habits. Planning with the teacher gives opportunity to express ideas, have them tested in practice, and finally revise plans for more effective results.

Parents, siblings, radio and television have all contributed to the background of ideas the child brings to school, but many gaps still exist. He defines words only in terms of their function: "A car is to ride in." "Candy is to eat." He generalizes readily: of the two rabbits in the classroom, one white and one spotted, only the white one had babies so, "All white rabbits are mother rabbits." His speech closely resembles that of the adults in his home; if a child's parent says "We may have precipitation today, so take your raincoat," any discussion of weather in school is likely to bring forth the word, "precipitation," not "rain." "It's a cool day" may call up no image of weather for the slum child who views "cool" as "great," "smooth," or "sharp." The teacher recognizes that growth in language skills is fostered by observing, listening, feeling, tasting, comparing, classifying and generalizing in a social context that values freedom and requires responsibility.

Interrelationships Among Various Aspects of Language Development

The natural sequence of language skills development is listening with some degree of comprehension, speaking with meaning, reading with understanding and finally writing. The interrelated nature of language growth is evident even before the child starts to school. Through interaction with others he has developed speech sounds resembling those that he has heard. The fact that deaf children do not learn to speak during this period is ample evidence that speaking is closely related to listening.

Reading and writing are essential tools for communication in our culture. Some understanding of sharing ideas, feelings and wants, plus the acquisition of certain skills – enunciation and articulation, auditory discrimination, comprehension – is necessary for effective reading. Billy commented to the teacher, "I see a boid in the tree outside the window." The teacher answered, "That isn't a boid, Billy, that's a bird." "Well it looked like a boid to me," said Billy, may reflect a problem of articulation, comprehension, auditory discrimination or a combination of these.

The alert teacher daily observes many minor *effects of* language difficulty but must be very skillful indeed to isolate specific *causes.*

A clearer view of the underlying relationships existing for each of the language arts can be gained by examination of available research findings. Hughes[23] studied 332 fifth grade children and found high relationships among reading, spelling, word meaning, general usage, capitalization, punctuation, sentence sense, and paragraph organization. Hildreth[24] reported several studies that pointed out the interrelationships that exist among oral and written communication, reading, spelling, handwriting. Writing, usually the last of the common communication forms to be developed, is dependent upon oral language and comprehension; it is related to skill in reading and growth in spelling and handwriting. Because of the relatedness that exists among these different phases of language expression, Hildreth believes that more integration should be achieved for language instruction in schools.

The results of investigations on interrelationships among various aspects of language at the first and second grade levels has yielded quite different results. In reply to the question, "Are there developmental interrelationships among the factors of oral language, reading, drawing, writing and spelling?" Martin's[25] evidence indicated that at the first grade level growth in each language variable followed an individual developmental pattern and was unrelated to other variables. There was little indication that the first grader who talked well would succeed in reading or that the poor speaker would have difficulty in it. Some children who were able to write well did poorly in both speaking and reading. Good readers were poor writers! Each child, more or less followed a zigzag pattern of development. Consequently, parallel development at the first grade level may not be expected.

A follow-up of Martin's study using the same children (240) and variables in second grade was done by Winter.[26] Again each child's pattern of language development seemed to be unique. The findings indicated a complete or relative independence among the language variable measured. This implies that many common assumptions about primary age children should be carefully examined, for example, "good readers

---

[23]Hughes, Vergil H. "A Study of the Relationships Among Selected Language Abilities." *Journal of Educational Research. 47*: 97-105, October, 1953.

[24]Hildreth, Gertrude H. "Interrelationships Between Written Expression and the Other Language Arts." In *Interrelationships Among the Language Arts.* Research Bulletin of the National Conference on Research in English. 4-12, 1954.

[25]Martin, Clyde. "Developmental Interrelationships Among Language Variables in Children of the First Grade. *Elementary English, 32*: 167-171, March, 1955.

[26]Winter, Clotilda. "Interrelationships Among Language Variables in Children of the First and Second Grades." *Elementary English. 34*: 108-113, 1956.

are good spellers," and "fluent speakers will be successful in other phases of language development." This study shows the relationship between reading and spelling to be moderate. Both studies (Martin and Winter) imply that learning situations in first and second grades need to be provided in which reading and writing are taught independently as well as in relation to each other.

Much remains to be learned about the extent of interrelations among aspects of language. Loban's[27] longitudinal study has recently yielded important evidence about interrelations for the following factors; oral language with written language; oral language with reading; reading with written language; and health with general language ability. These interrelations extend through the elementary grades and are positive for the intermediate and upper grades.

In successive years third grade pupils who wrote well also ranked high in use of oral language and reading. Children who scored below average of any one of the measures were below average on the other two.

As the children continued into the upper grades a higher relationship was found between writing and reading. By grade six (Table 4),

> The superior group in writing has by far the highest teacher's rating. Even more striking is the fact that every subject ranked superior in writing is *reading above* his chronological age; *every* subject ranked illiterate or primitive in writing is *reading below* his chronological age. (p. 75)

In addition to reading and writing, there was a positive relation between reading and oral language, oral language and listening, and a low positive relation for health and language ability (speaking, writing or reading). "Apathy, lassitude, and low vitality appear to be concomitants of low language ability for some subjects." (p. 75)

These relationships suggest that growth in one area reinforces growth in others. It is logical and necessary, then, that language activities be rich and varied for assuring optimum growth in each. At the same time, accurate assessment of the child's present language status and future needs is highly dependent upon evaluation of other facets of total development; in order to understand the child's pattern of language growth it is necessary first to know about his physical equipment and his social and emotional development. In short, we must know his personality structure.

---

[27]Loban, Walter D. *The Language of Elementary School Children.* Champaign: National Council of Teachers of English, 1963.

TABLE 4*

Interrelations among Reading, Writing, and Oral Language
Grade Six

Written language: classification of subjects	Number in group	Number reading above chronological age	Number reading below chronological age	Average reading achievement above or below expected age norm	Oral language: average teachers' ratings
I Superior group	21	21	0	+3 yr. and 6 mo.	4.08
II Good group	102	83	19	+1 yr. and 6 mo.	3.52
III Inferior group	73	20	53	−0 yr. and 9 mo.	3.01
IV Illiterate group	22	0	22	−2 yr. and 7 mo.	2.61
V Primitive group	4	0	4	−3 yr. and 6 mo.	2.53
TOTAL GROUP	222	124	98	+0 yr. and 5 mo.	3.15

*SOURCE: Walter D. Loban. *The Language of Elementary School Children.* Champaign; National Council of Teachers of English, 1963. p. 74. Reprinted by permission of the National Council of Teachers of English and Walter D. Loban.

Speech itself, highly related to other aspects of language, is also closely related to personal development. "A speech disorder is a disorder of the person as well as a disorder in the reception and transmission of spoken language."[28] Present day language authorities are largely in agreement that personality problems nearly always accompany language disabilities. If we are to understand speech we must understand the person, for the child in need of psychological help usually has symptoms of language difficulty. Most speech disorders such as baby talk and lisping are associated with poor human relations in the home.[29] This, of course, does not refer to children with organic difficulties. Aside from organic causes, language disability appears to be a symptom of emotional disorder.

Maladjusted and backward children are frequently observed to have trouble with speech, and when allowed to continue without correction are commonly regarded by peers, parents, and teachers as "retarded." This form of discrimination is perhaps more subtle in nature than more common

[28]Travis, L. E. (Ed.) *Handbook of Speech Pathology.* New York: Appleton-Century-Crofts, 1957. p. 5.
[29]McCarthy, op. cit. 1959.

forms but the effects on the growing child are equally devastating. Another cause for concern among adults is the late-speaking child. Although all mentally defective children are late in learning to speak, all bright children do not speak early and all late speakers are not mentally retarded.[30] Gifted children *usually,* however, speak early and early speech is a good index of mental ability.

Beck[31] has discovered that children who later have reading disabilities can be identified in the nursery school. Slow readers in fifth grade had shown signs of emotional disturbance as preschoolers at six times the rate for normal readers. Educative procedure for the child with a language disorder ". . . . is to help him organize incoming stimuli so that useful concepts can result."[32] Neither rote production and recognition of words nor the memorization of principles will serve this end. Rather, it is understanding the *meaning* of principles that makes them useful.

It is true that speech mirrors the personality of the child. Image of self and others is closely interwoven with family language patterns and has its roots in early childhood. From early in the child's life the two facets of language which precede reading and writing, namely listening and speaking ". . . are intricately interrelated – neurologically, intellectually and socially . . . continually modified by people and events."[33] Like personality development, social growth is closely interwoven with language power. The quality of the child's social relationships will in large measure determine the level of language power he will attain.

Language, Thought and Intelligence

Because of previous experiences, the child has accumulated certain raw materials – percepts, images, memories, and concepts – that he manipulates during thinking. His *ability* to manipulate these raw materials is called intelligence. Exactly how language fits into this framework is not clear, but language is so closely related to thinking that many psychologists regard them as identical.

> . . . . some members of the behaviorist school of psychology regard thinking as subvocal speech. They have pointed out that,

---

[30]McCarthy, Dorothea. "Language Development." *Child Development Monographs.* 25: 1960.

[31]Beck, Harriet K. "Relationship of Emotional Factors in Early Childhood to Subsequent Growth and to Achievement in Reading." Unpublished Doctoral Dissertation. University of Michigan, 1951.

[32]Wood, Nancy E. "Language Disorders in Children." *Child Development Monographs.* 25: 1960.

[33]Mackintosh, op. cit. p. 4.

> during thinking movements of the throat and tongue are observable, and therefore that thinking may be termed "internal speech." On the other hand, certain experimental evidence contradicts this point of view. Animals cannot speak in the usual sense of the term, but there seems little doubt that they engage in some forms of thinking. An infant understands language before he actually uses it himself. As early as the eighth or ninth month he can understand gestures, look for a dropped object, or reach for an attractive object, before he can talk about them. Furthermore, some thought seems to be based rather directly on kinesthetic, tactual, auditory, and other sensations and images. It seems reasonable, therefore, to consider language and thought as closely related but not identical.[34]

". . . during the later preschool years and in subsequent development throughout childhood, over-all language development is the best single index of intelligence available to psychologists."[35] In addition to measuring other standard items, many tests of intelligence measure vocabulary. It is one of the most valid measures of intelligence.

Russell[36] has developed a schema for thinking (Figure 1) which illustrates the processes which occur from the time a stimulus is received by the child until a conclusion is reached. The four main factors involved are: (1) the materials for thinking – sensations perception, etc., (2) the motives for thinking – feelings, needs, attitudes, etc., (3) the processes in thinking – patterns of activity, such as selecting, eliminating, searching, manipulating and organizing, and (4) the abilities in thinking – habits, techniques and guides which can be acquired and developed.

The raw materials for thinking have been described by Carin and Sund:[37]

> *Sensations* develop an awareness of stimuli without much interpretation. *Percepts* are what is known about an object, a quality, or a relationship as a result of sensations. Percepts are the fabric from which concepts are formed. *Images* are previous percepts. *Concepts* are abstractions which organize objects and events into categories. *Generalizations* or *principles* are concepts involving relationships between two or more abstractions, objects or events.

The steps or sequence of thinking are described by Russell.[38]

> . . . the environment stimulates thinking; the thinking takes its initial direction; there is some search for related materials; these materials are

[34]Russell, David H. *Children's Thinking*. Boston: Ginn, 1956. p. 24, 25.
[35]Gardner, op. cit. p. 182.
[36]Russell, op. cit.
[37]Carin, Arthur and Robert B. Sund. *Teaching Science Through Discovery*. Columbus: Charles E. Merrill, 1964.
[38]Russell, op. cit. p. 28.

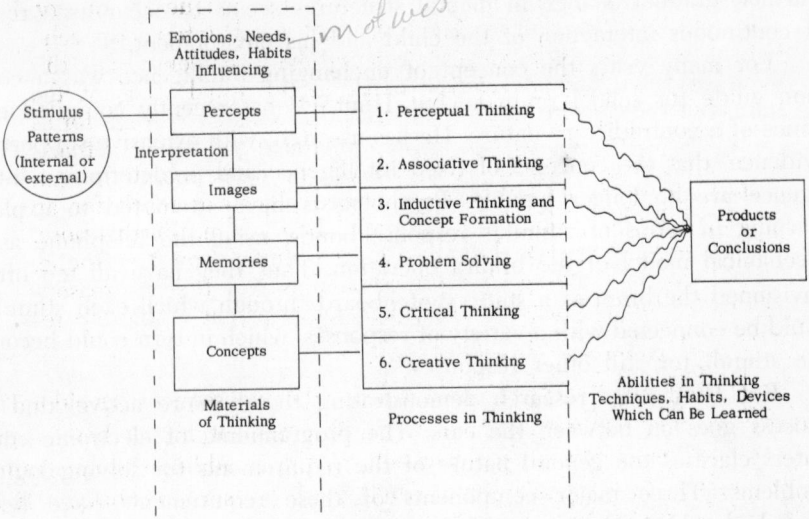

SOURCE: David H. Russell. *Children's Thinking*. Boston: Ginn, 1956. Reprinted through the courtesy of Blaisdell Publishing Company, a division of Ginn and Company.

FIGURE 1.1

Schema for Thinking

organized into tentative patterns or hypotheses; the hypotheses are examined critically; and some tentative conclusion or goal is reached which may eventuate in overt action.

The first three types of thinking are:

> . . . perceptual thinking, associative thinking, and inductive-deductive learning. Problem solving, critical thinking, and creative thinking – the next higher order of thinking which is commonly compared to scientific processes – depend upon the proper formulation of percepts, concepts, and generalizations for their foundation.[39]

The operative efficiency of the child's mental or cognitive structure (schema) appears to be dependent upon opportunity for use.[40] The mental schema becomes more flexible through adjustment to varieties of situations and the child consequently develops a wider range of interests.

---

[39]Carin and Sund. op. cit. p. 40.

[40]Piaget, Jean. *The Origins of Intelligence in Children*. (Margaret Cook, trans.) New York: International Universities Press, 1952. (Originally published 1936).

Further, gradual change in mental structures seems to occur as a result of continuous interaction of the child and his environment.[41]

For many years the concept of unchanging intelligence was a common guide for school practice, but Hunt[42,43] has recently compiled evidence of a contradictory nature. He has asserted, with extensive supportive evidence, that the concepts of fixed intelligence and predetermined intelligence are no longer tenable. Psychologists have attempted to explain learning in terms of stimulus response bonds, using the telephone as a mechanical model of the brain's operation. Thus they have all too often envisioned the brain as a static switchboard through which each stimulus could be connected with a variety of responses, which in turn could become the stimuli for still other responses.

But Hunt cites research demonstrating that a more active kind of process goes on between the ears. The programming of electronic computers clarifies the general nature of the requirements for solving logical problems. Three major components of these requirements have been described: (1) memories, or information, coded and stored; (2) operations of a logical sort which can act upon the memories; and (3) hierarchically arranged programs of these operations for various purposes.

A likely place for equivalents of these components within the brain is the intrinsic portions of the cerebrum which have no direct connections with either incoming fibers from the receptors of experience or outgoing fibers to the muscles and glands. The intrinsic portion of the brain is very small in such animals as the frogs and salamanders used as subjects in some of the early experiments on the embryology of behavior; consequently belief in predetermined development appeared to be consonant with the data on behavioral development. The increasing proportion of the brain constituting the intrinsic portion in higher animals suggests an anatomic basis for the increasing role of infantile experience in development.

Experience may be regarded as programming the intrinsic portions of the cerebrum for learning and problem solving, and the intellectual capacity of a person at any given time may be conceived to be in very considerable part a function of the nature and quality of this experimental programming.[44] Consequently, the I.Q. score may vary as much as 20 to

---

[41]Hunt, J. McV. *Intelligence and Experience.* New York: Ronald, 1961.
[42]Ibid.
[43]Hunt, J. McV. "How Children Develop Intellectually." *Children. 11*: 83-91, May, 1964.
[44]Hunt, op. cit. 1964.

40 points as a result of environmental stimulation or lack of environmental stimulation.[45]

It is not clear whether the child gains language power as a result of high intelligence or gains high intelligence as a result of language power. In either event, the close relationship between language and intelligence suggests that conditions facilitative for the growth of either are essential for the growth of both. Furthermore these conditions are highly dependent upon the degree and quality of the child's daily listening, speaking, manipulating and interacting.

The prevailing controversy as to the relative importance of nature and nurture in the development of children naturally arises here. It is clear that nature and nurture always operate together; they are mutually interdependent; one in absence of the other has no meaning. In fact, without either there would be no life. Nature ordinarily endows the child with a complete set of equipment ensuring the potential for growth, but that potential is achieved only in the course of the child's interaction with his circumstances. The rate and quality of his growth can be accelerated, retarded or even stopped by the conditions of his circumstantial nurture.[46]

Language and Experience

Considerable evidence exists to support the view that socioeconomic status of the family is closely related to the child's linguistic development. McCarthy's[47] review of research related to environment and language shows that children from a restricted environment are retarded in all areas of development but the degree of retardation is greater in language development. They use fewer words, less mature sentences, have greater difficulty in interpreting the language of others, and generally have poorer articulation. The greatest degree of language sophistication is found among children of professional men, with differences increasing as age increases. Several investigators have reported that travel and other events which give opportunities for varied experiences are followed by increase in vocabulary, particularly nouns. It appears reasonable to assume that this increase is accompanied by growth in meaning.

---

[45]Frost, Joe L. and Glenn R. Hawkes. *The Disadvantaged Child.* Boston: Houghton Mifflin, 1966.

[46]Ideas expressed in this section were developed through personal correspondence with J. McVicker Hunt.

[47]McCarthy, op. cit. 1954.

Hildreth[48] reported that "a large proportion of reading disability cases come from homes where language is used for every day, or not particularly intellectual subjects or where a substandard dialect is used: Children that move from one dialect area to another have considerable difficulty adjusting to school. A substantial relationship exists between reading problems and other linguistic deficiencies which appear to be characteristic of children who move from school to school frequently."

Young[49] compared "regular" and "relief" children attending the same school. Regular children surpassed the "relief" children on all aspects of language which were analyzed. "Relief" boys showed greatest retardation. "Regular" girls were the most advanced. As a rule girls surpass boys in language power during the elementary school years. This may be due in part to their more rapid rate of physiological development. Classes for retarded readers usually contain more boys than girls.

Potential intelligence cannot be assessed in terms of linguistic skill, for potentiality can be considerably altered by the experiences of the child. It is unreasonable to assume that merely because a child has been reared in an impoverished home he is restricted by hereditary factors; this conceivably could be true of any child regardless of choice of parentage. Rather it appears that different environments affect language development and the impoverished child lacks opportunities which contribute to development. Bernstein[50] has found that the middle class uses "formal" modes of speech which varies between individuals. This makes possible greater clarification of meaning. The lower class family uses a more "restricted" speech. This places children at a decided disadvantage in the middle-class oriented school which values the verbal linguistic skills and patterns of the middle class. Consequently, children of lower class homes may meet progressive failure in oral communication and in the related areas of listening, reading, and writing. It is clear, then, that restrictions imposed by deprivation of stimulating experiences, especially during infancy and early childhood, commonly delimit the progress of children in school.

Restriction of stimulating experiences during early life can also seriously affect growth in areas other than language. This has been established by numerous studies of both animals and humans.

---

[48]Hildreth, Gertrude. "Linguistic Factors in Early Reading." *The Reading Teacher. 18*: 172-178. December, 1964. p. 174.

[49]Young, F. M. "An Analysis of Certain Variables in a Developmental Study of Language." *Genetic Psychology Monographs. 23*: 3-141. 1941.

[50]Bernstein, Basil. "Language and Social Class." *British Journal of Sociology. 21*: 159-174, 1958.

Studies of animal behavior,[51,52,53] which established conditions closely paralleling the problem of cultural deprivation or sensory restriction of humans, revealed that animals (dogs or chimpanzees) reared in darkness or isolation were greatly restricted in performance of social functions or the solving of problems at maturity.

Although we do not subject children to conditions of deprivation for purposes of experimentation, fate and neglect have provided ample cases for study. In a Teheran orphanage, where children had little opportunity for stimulation, 60 percent could not sit alone at two years of age and 85 percent could not walk alone at four years of age.[54] This illustrates the effect that early experience can have on even the rate of locomotor development and, when compared to other evidence, suggests that retardation in one area of development may be accompanied by retardation in other areas. For example, Goldfarb[55] compared a group of adolescents that had been placed in institutions as infants with a group of adolescents that had been institutionalized much later. The early institutionalized group was much more apathetic and *generally immature* during adolescence.

One of the most dramatic illustrations of the effects of sensory stimulatin or enriched living on intellectual development is a study of Skeels.[56] Thirteen mentally retarded infants were placed in an institution that provided person-to-person contacts; later eleven of these were placed in adoptive homes. A contrast group of twelve children, with higher intelligence initially, remained in a relatively nonstimulating environment over a prolonged period. This contrast group showed progressive mental retardation while the "enriched" group showed progressive mental growth.

A follow-up study after these children had reached adulthood showed that all of the children who had been placed in stimulating environments were self-supporting; none was institutionalized. Eleven of the thirteen married and nine had children. The median grade completed in school was

---

[51]Melzack, Ronald and William R. Thompson. "Effects of Early Experience on Social Behavior." *Canadian Journal of Psychology. 10:* 82-90. 1956.

[52]Riesen, Austin H. "The Development of Visual Perception in Man and Chimpanzee." *Science. 106*: 107-108. 1947.

[53]Thompson, W. R. and W. Heron. "The Effects of Restricting Early Experience on the Problem-Solving Capacity of Dogs." *Canadian Journal Psychology. 8*: 17-31, 1954.

[54]Dennis, W. Causes of Retardation Among Institutional Children: *Journal of Genetic Psychology. 96*: 47-59, 1960.

[55]Goldfarb, W. "The Effects of Early Institutional Care on Adolescent Personality." *Journal of Experimental Education. 12*: 106-129. 1953.

[56]Skeels, Harold M. "Effects of Adoption on Children Fiom Institutions." *Children. 12*: 33-34. January-February, 1965.

twelve. One girl with an initial I.Q. of 35 graduated from high school and completed a semester in college.

Of the twelve who remained in the "nonstimulating" environment, one died after continued residence in a state institution for the mentally retarded; four are still wards of mental institutions. Two of the four females were sterilized. Median school grade completed was three. Cost to the state for this group has been about $100,000.

Studies by Frost[57,58] revealed that welfare recipient children were retarded in intelligence, personality, and academic achievement (reading, language, and arithmetic) at the first grade level, with a pattern of increasing retardation common in the usual elementary school environment. Welfare children in an enriched school environment made slight gains across grade level lines, but failed to reach national norms in any area of development at any grade level. Enrichment of school programs failed to compensate for early restriction of experiences.

Children of migrant laborers are severely limited in language skill. Frost[59] administered the Peabody Vocabulary Test to thirty-two children ranging from six to sixteen years. This ". . . revealed raw scores strikingly similar across chronological age lines. The child of six or seven had essentially the same vocabulary as the youngster of fifteen or sixteen." Although the average I.Q. of these children was 78 with a range of 54 to 100, their behavior often suggested a high degree of skill in areas related to their living patterns.

> Jimmy, with a measured I.Q. of 69, perceived and described possibilities for improving techniques in leather and metal craft before the instructor had completed the initial explanation.
>
> Sue, I.Q. 75, quickly and accurately computed daily and weekly earnings from picking beans without resorting to the use of pencil and paper.
>
> Billy, I.Q. 78, demonstrated proficiency in explaining road map symbols.[60]

Limited cultural experiences, lack of motivation for school achievement, and irregular school attendance contributed to inferior language

---

[57]Frost, Joe L. "School and the Migrant Child." *Childhood Education. 41*: 129-132. November, 1964.

[58]Frost, Joe L. "School Environment and Disadvantaged Children." *Collected Papers* of the Inter-Institutional Seminar in Child Development. The Edison Institute. June, 1965.

[59]Frost, op. cit. 1964, p. 131.

[60]Frost, op. cit. 1964, p. 132.

development and failure in school. It appears that this was not a consequence of heredity but of opportunity.

A Holistic Approach to Language Development

The interrelationships that exist among language, intelligence, thinking and social, physical, and emotional factors imply that the effective language arts program will have as its focus the "whole child." Although this "holistic" concept has maintained theoretical consideration for many years, practical application has lagged. As a consequence, more attention is commonly given to what is "taught" than to how learning occurs. This results in superficial learner commitment and shallow thinking. The child, expected to adjust his needs to the school's goals, modify his goals to grade-level standards, and gear his thinking toward accumulation of facts has limited opportunity for growth in language power.

The process of language development may be described through an illustration (Figure 1.2) which offers a general scheme for a "holistic" outlook on the processes through which the child gains language power. He comes to school with a unique set of learnings and potentialities that have been shaped by nature and nurture. The school environment continues to be influential in further language growth which is shaped largely by the quality of experiences offered by the home prior to school entrance.

The child has certain inborn needs, reinforced by the culture of his home and neighborhood, which seek fulfillment: physiological needs – food, clothing, and health; safety needs – freedom from physical harm and mental stress; affectional needs – loving people around him, and esteem needs – favor and appreciation of his peers. While most children's physiological and safety needs are met by the home, fewer receive the affection and esteem so essential to a high degree of self-fulfillment. Despite contradictory practice, these are essential ingredients for effective school functioning and language development. "Failure of need satisfaction produces narrowness and rigidity of perceptual organization."[61] It follows, then, that the effective educational system will consider these needs ". . . in ways that allow the child to preserve dignity."[62]

Upon arrival at school, the child exhibits language patterns very similar to those used in his home. This has resulted from imitation of models – the adults in his life – and the opportunities he may have had to

---

[61]Combs, Arthur W., "A Perceptual View of the Adequate Personality." In: *Perceiving Behaving, Becoming*. Washington: Association for Supervision and Curriculum Development, 1962. p. 61.

[62]Frost and Hawkes, op. cit.

explore on his own, his freedom to ask questions and get answers which encourage thinking and further questioning, and the variety of manipulative materials available for comparison and discrimination. The variety and quality of reading materials *on the shelf* make little impact on language development. Active use and demonstrated enjoyment of books by significant people in the child's world make a great deal of difference.

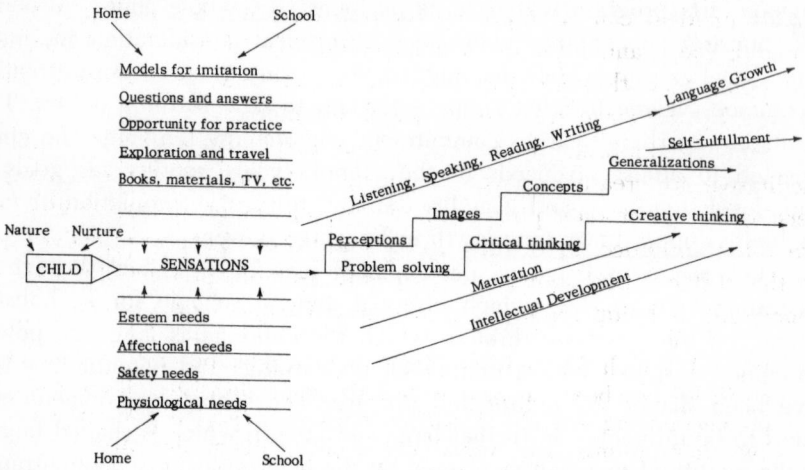

FIGURE 1.2

Schema for Language Development

As the child grows through time he gains skill in language and thinking. As he experiences widely, he engages in more complex thinking. He makes difficult choices which involve more than 2 plus 2 or a distinction between more or less.

He begins to formulate procedures which are widely recognized as scientific problem solving – isolating a problem, gathering information about possible solutions, taking action aimed toward solution, and finally drawing tentative conclusions based upon the evidence available.

Critical thinking emerges as the child becomes aware of, and makes the values and norms of society a part of himself. He judges events and situations in terms of these commonly held values and, hopefully, begins to apply these in varied situations. As he builds backgrounds of meanings, values and norms are called up automatically without undue consideration of consequence or effect. He needs "telling" less often, and weighs information to reach the "best" conclusion.

This growth in thinking is largely dependent upon parallel growth in language. Percepts and concepts must be thrown into fresh combinations to accommodate the child's enlarged world of thinking. This leads to the emergence of the highest form of language and thought activity – creativity.

All children have the potential for creative thinking but conditions of teaching rarely ensure, or even allow, its emergence. The quantity and quality of ideas can be improved through teaching, but pedagogy usually demands facts, and ideas often don't count. The production of new ideas and application through speaking, writing, art, etc. are enhanced or restricted by the structure of the school situation.

Finally, emphasis upon the "whole child" implies that conditions facilitative to creative thinking contribute to self-fulfillment. Adequate persons ". . . not only possess more information or understanding; they are able to produce these when needed and to put them to effective use."[63] In the past creative activity implied only tangible products but this misconception is being replaced by a more dynamic view.

> We still search for and encourage the tangible, but the concept of creativity has been enlarged to include ideas, decisions, relationships, problem solving – results of man's cognitive powers. The product, whatever form it may take would not evolve without the process. The growing realization of the universality of creativity, of man's heretofore unsuspected capacity for creativeness, of the uniqueness of every individual, places the idea of creativity in new perspective . . . Creativity is necessary for a fully adequate personality.[64]

Language and Teaching

At age five or six the child goes to school. The school now shares the home's continuing responsibility for his language development. If the home has done its job well, the school's role is usually uncomplicated. If a course of failure has been established, however, much insight and skill will be needed for alteration. School success hinges upon home success and home support. Consistency of expectations, demands, values, and language patterns between home and school reinforces the behavioral patterns of the child and facilitates school progress. The culturally disadvantaged child often finds that the language patterns of his home are unacceptable by the school and that his usual ways of communicating are ineffective. He finds that books are written about people he has never

---

[63]Combs, op. cit. p. 60.

[64]A.S.C.D. *Perceiving, Behaving, Becoming.* Washington: Association for Supervision and Curriculum Development, 1962. p. 142.

seen using language patterns he has never heard. He therefore has little chance of "catching up" with those who have made this "foreign" language their language since infancy.

The school must not allow the obvious deficiencies of the few to unduly detract its attention from those who seek and require continuous direction toward ever higher levels of language functioning. The gifted, for example, often comprise the most retarded group in a school. Their level of functioning is sufficiently high to get along quite well – even to make the honor rolls – but the depths of their linguistic ability remain untapped. Too little incentive and opportunity for high order thinking exists in their school world of facts and averages. Knowledge of language development and human behavior offers guidelines for teacher action. Among those principles discussed in this chapter that should influence language teaching are:

1. The growing child makes the language of family and neighborhood his language.
2. Linguistic development is dependent largely upon imitation.
3. There are wide individual differences in rate and quality of language development.
4. It is extremely important that children acquire skill in linguistic development at an early age.
5. Good health – mental, emotional, and physical – is prerequisite to success in language.
6. At best, vocabulary estimations are useful as very general estimations for what the child actually knows.
7. Assessment of the child's language growth must take into account range and quality in addition to quantity.
8. The basic vocabulary for the beginner in school is that which he has, understands, and uses.
9. Difficulties with language appear to involve more than learning hard words and speaking, reading, or writing long sentences; meaning units, learned at an early age, appear to be basic building blocks of children's language.
10. Expressive behavior – gestures, drawing, painting, dramatization – are important facets of language which enrich and deepen communicative meanings.
11. Language development is intricately interrelated with mental, social, and personal development.
12. Language and thought are inextricably interrelated.
13. Efficiency of thinking structures is dependent upon use.

14. Attainment of higher levels of thinking requires corresponding growth in language.
15. Language and thinking can be improved through teaching.
16. Language and intellectual growth are highly dependent upon the degree and quality of the child's daily listening, speaking, manipulating, and interacting.
17. Restrictions imposed by deprivation of stimulating experiences, especially during infancy and early childhood, commonly delimit language development.
18. The child has certain inborn needs, reinforced by the culture of home and neighborhood, which seek fulfillment.
19. The process through which language grows is the process that unleashes creativity and promotes growth toward self-fulfillment.
20. The effective language arts program will have as its focus the "whole" child.

The role of the teacher in the language development of the child has long been regarded as one of providing instruction in skills and prescribing assignments in workbooks. As a result, it was hoped, the child would naturally integrate the knowledge thus gained into his language learning structure and growth would logically occur. But language is much more dynamic than this. It is psychological, not logical, and it attains function and power from deep personal meanings gained through living with others, not from external rules and restrictions. As Sylvia Ashton Warner[65] masterfully states,

> What a dangerous activity . . . teaching is. All this plastering on of foreign stuff. Why plaster on at all when there's so much inside already? So much locked in? If only I could get it out and use it as working material. And not draw it out either. If I had a light enough touch it would just come out under its own volcanic power.

Teachers Must Provide Freedom for Exploration

Children are constantly engaged in searching for truth through exploring, manipulating, testing, tasting, feeling – even groping. They learn from mistakes. Even the most creative adults make false starts and test many wrong assumptions for each really productive idea. The fact that children learn to speak about as well as the adults in their lives before encountering the more formal language teaching of the school tells us that this inborn searching and trying on for size has been remarkably

[65]Warner, Sylvia Ashton. *Spinster*. New York: Simon and Schuster, 1958.

effective. Recent studies by Torrance[66] suggest that mental abilities involved in creative thinking and learning are different than those used in learning by authority. In addition, creative thinking and learning depend upon opportunity for active exploration. Fewer than 10 percent of a group of elementary language arts teachers selected a creative thinking category as the most important type of mental operation. Certainly we cannot say that a child is growing toward mental self-fulfillment ". . . if the abilities involved in learning and thinking creatively remain undeveloped or are paralyzed by excessive prohibitions."[67]

Consider a group of first grade children on their first day of using rhythm band instruments.

> On this occasion most teachers are driven to distraction. Wanting to talk about the instruments and how they work, they usually fail to hold the attention of the children. Not so, the teacher of this first grade class. She has learned that the children must first be permitted to encounter their instruments creatively. They want to feel them, smell them, look at them, tap them, and sense them in every way possible. They must find out at once what the instruments will do. After this they are *ready* to learn by authority.[68]

Teachers Must Provide Time for Solitary Thought

In addition to the requirement of exploratory freedom for the release of creativity and the growth of language is the need for solitary thought. Jimmy, two years behind (achievement tests), went to fifth grade. Quiet but not particularly studious, Jimmy had never seemed to fit into the usual scheme of classroom activity. Here, in fifth grade, the teacher introduced group planning. One morning during the regular planning of ongoing activities, Jimmy stated that he needed to use a period of time for *thinking*. The teacher had never heard such a request. What would the principal *think* if he came into the room and found a child *thinking*? (Robert Frost was once dropped from school for such activity!) Jimmy was allowed to have a quiet thinking period regularly that school year. His reflection led to searching through reference materials for information on his previously unrevealed interest – science. He built models; his parents gave him space in the basement for a laboratory; his peers gained a new respect for him. At the end of the school year he scored two to

---

[66]Torrance, E. Paul. *Education and the Creative Potential.* Minneapolis: The University of Minnesota Press, 1963.
[67]Torrance, op. cit. p. 46.
[68]Ibid. p. 48.

four years above his grade level (standardized tests). Three years later, Jimmy continued his search for truth. Oh yes, he regularly makes the honor roll.

Teachers Must Be Good Models

Children learn the language pattern of their geographical region – their community – their family, and these are relatively permanent. But the everyday model set by teachers and other adults can help children correct common errors in language usage. As they hear, see and read good language, changes are made in their own. Some children commonly practice better language than their teachers and demand correctness in both speech and written communication. Bobby, eleven years old, was selected to edit the room newsletter. He carefully reviewed each article and corrected grammatical errors. The material was then typed by the teacher (first year). When completed and handed to the class to take home, Bobby located and drew big circles around twenty-four spelling (typographical) errors. He was so distraught that he refused to have a copy in his possession. For there on page one was the statement – Proofreader, Bobby Jones. Needless to say this was a grievous teaching error.

Teachers Must Provide Many Materials

The provision of basal textbooks is merely a beginning. To accommodate the wide range of abilities within any classroom the teacher makes available numerous books and other printed materials on many levels of difficulty. Many manipulative materials are made available for the child's use. The real object leaves a more vivid mental impression than any amount of reading, hearing about, or looking at pictures. Real objects are also useful for developing vocabulary and concepts of size – more than, less than, fewer, heavier, etc., color, shape-round, square, and texture-smooth, rough, etc. Accurate oral or written description of objects depends upon opportunity to discover their properties just as accurate description of events depends upon direct involvement in them. One second grade teacher had a workbench, complete with vise, hammer, saws, nails, screws, and scrap lumber available for children's use. The ability to use these tools and the possession of words to describe them are not innate – they have to be learned. Many basic concepts which must be developed before more complex learning and thinking is possible are rooted within such simple manipulative activities as these.

Teachers Must Provide Environments Which Foster Security

The absence of emotional security affects language development and learning in general. Lack of security leads to misdirection of drives normally used for desirable learning. The child, of course, continues to learn but these are "failure" learnings, not "success" learnings. His extreme efforts to win approval and security often result in rejection by peers and adults and reinforce the pattern of failure. Thus as the personality is shaped, potentially constructive energy becomes destructive energy. The "creative" writing of Jay reveals the direction of thought and energy commonly resulting from broken homes and lack of parental affection.

THE BEST FRIEND

By Jay Smith

> Once I knew a friend. A kind considerate friend and the best one I had. He was a sixth grader and I was a fifth grader. He was the best friend I had.

And later:

THE SECOND BEST FRIEND

By Jay Smith

> When I was in the fifth grade I had a friend and a kind one too. She encouraged me and I won't forget her . . .

Fortunately, Jay's second best friend was an understanding teacher who was able to "substitute" for parents and help him gain acceptance with the peer group.

Teachers Must Provide for Stimulating Inquiry

Two prevalent practices which stifle inquiry are emphasis on facts and emphasis on competition. Although there are few right answers, only better or worse ones, schools actively seek to instill in children ability to recall quantities of facts upon demand. Studies of the questions teachers ask reveal that over 90 percent require factual answers. This behavior tells the child that what he *thinks* is less important than what other people tell him: that he doesn't have to think to be successful as long as he has a good memory. When asked what she considered the most significant about John Glenn's orbital flight, one wise teacher replied, "The fact that it was associated with a date. Children for decades will have another 1492 to remember."

Teachers should ask questions that require thinking responses and should encourage and respect the questions children ask. Unusual questions and answers lead to deeper thinking. Deeper thinking requires greater communicative ability and greater communicative ability means language growth. All this is learned through inquiry and inquiry cannot function in a restrictive classroom.

Inquiry functions best in a cooperative classroom which values freedom and demands responsibility. It functions least in a highly competitive classroom which values success at the expense of those who fail. Combs[69] derides our false beliefs about competition:

Myth: We live in a competitive society.
Fact: We live in the most cooperative, interdependent society the world has ever known.
Myth: Competition is a powerful motivating force.
Fact: Only those compete who think they have a chance of winning. The rest ignore the competition.
Myth: Competition is a useful device for controlling and improving quality.
Fact: Competition is inefficient and outmoded as a means for quality production.

It comes as quite a surprise, indeed, for Americans who see people in other cultures of the world playing the game of baseball with all the energy and zest of a major league team but refusing to keep score! Some of the children in American classrooms don't keep score but they are the losers and they don't participate in the game. As a result we have more dropouts in school than out-losers, uncommitted to the school's purposes.

Teachers Must Be Diagnosticians

If teachers could accurately diagnose the learning difficulties of children and provide appropriate remediation there would be no "slow" learners. But a high degree of skill is involved in accurately diagnosing the most common learning deficiencies and even greater skill is needed to equate cause and correction. Causes of learning deficiencies are usually multiple and differ from child to child. Often underlying causes are evident only to trained specialists, particularly organic deficiencies. Correction also may require the services of specialists. But within the domain of the classroom many common deficiencies can be discovered and corrected by alert teachers.

---

[69]Combs, Arthur W., "The Myth of Competition." *Childhood Education. 33:* 364-69, February, 1957.

In fourth grade, Sue was unable to read or write beyond a very elementary level. Her paintings however, revealed great insight and appreciation for beauty. An alert teacher discovered through a simple eye test that her vision was faulty (she had missed school when regular eye examinations were given). Seven months later she was reading at grade level with corresponding improvement in writing. Now she could match the beauty of her artistic creations with that of her poetry:

THE FLOWERS

The flowers are the prettiest thing,
I think.
To see in the Spring,
A most beautiful thing.
Their petals quiver when a breeze
passes by,
And birds sing their happy song that
winter has gone by.

In the morning all covered with dew,
The flowers sing a beautiful tune.
Of the sky, and the sea, and of the
beautiful day.

Diagnosis refers not only to deficiencies but also to the regular procedure whereby teachers determine readiness levels for instruction. Instruction should naturally follow diagnosis. Teaching prior to assessment of needs is analogous to the medical doctor proceeding to operate without examining the patient. An individualized classroom program under conditions of *true* nongradedness is most conducive to success in diagnostic teaching.

Teachers Must Themselves Seek Self-Fulfillment

Teachers cannot long conceal their true beliefs from children. They show in day-by-day decisions. Even the infant knows whether adults are doing things *for* him or *to* him and this will have its effects. The teacher's behavior reveals his values and beliefs about training children. If teachers are to maximize the creative potential of children they must be actively seeking growth for self. Creative tendencies of teachers are revealed through the provisions of a classroom atmosphere in which creative language and thought may flourish in children.

Conclusion

The writer began by drawing attention to the importance of language; stated early that language is complex; proceeded to describe interrelated factors; concluded by describing the roles of effective teachers.

The underlying current throughout emphasized the need for a more dynamic view of language development: . . . The degree of knowing about a word and the related meanings that word holds for a child is very personal, not to be fully understood or completely shared by another . . . In order to understand the child's pattern of language growth we must know his personality structure . . . It is understanding the *meaning* of principles that makes them useful . . . The *quality* of the child's social relationships will in large measure determine the level of language power he will attain . . . Language is psychological, not logical, and it attains function and power from deep personal meanings gained through living with others, not from external rules and restrictions.

We are uncertain about what facts will be required of tomorrow's adult, so we are insecure about what to teach today's child. But we can be confident that diversity of skill in language and thought will serve the child well in whatever condition of living he may find himself. Consequently, teachers may well examine their hierarchy of beliefs about teaching – activity or passivity? inquiry or rote? lives or lessons? This writer[70] was speaking to teachers and teachers-to-be when she said:

> The thread which interlaces all of the richness of growth, which becomes one in today and tomorrow, is that of inner personal growth . . . Surely there is time for this kind of looking toward tomorrow. There is always *some* time; never *enough* when life is full. Perhaps when we see tomorrow look at us from little children's eyes we will think, "how carefully we'd teach if we were wise!"

EXTENDING YOUR LEARNING

1. Listen to the speech of two three-year-olds, two six-year-olds. What differences in speech did you notice between the individuals? between the two couples?
2. Observe an elementary class. On the basis of speech try to select a child whom you think may be a slow learner or a fast learner. Select a child who may have emotional problems – fearful, insecure, etc. Note behavior other than speech that influenced your selection. Discuss your observations with the child's teacher. How do your observations differ? Why do they differ?

---

[70]Rexinger, Lena. "How Carefully We'd Teach If We Were Wise." *Childhood Education.* 35:391-393. May, 1959.

3. If possible, make a case study of the language development of one child (you may examine existing case studies). How does the evidence presented compare with ideas previously held?
4. Compare two or more case studies. What are the implications of your findings to language teaching?
5. Observe a class of slow learners. Compare the quantity and quality of language with that of a "typical" class; with a gifted class. Note the incidence of creative activity (including verbal response) in each group. Study the cumulative records – health, tests, teacher observations – of several children.
6. During observations note the extent and kind of intellectual stimulation and the general learning atmosphere (facilitative or restrictive) in each classroom. Does the teacher emphasize creativity or conformity? How does she communicate with the children? What effects do various ways of teacher communication have on the behavior of children? How does the teacher provide for the development of language power? Is this done subtly or overtly?

BIBLIOGRAPHY

Beck, Harriet K. "Relationship of Emotional Factors in Early Childhood to Subsequent Growth and to Achievement in Reading." Unpublished Doctoral Dissertation. University of Michigan, 1951.

Bernstein, Basil. "Language and Social Class." *British Journal of Sociology. 21*:159-174, 1958.

Carroll, John B. "Language Acquisition, Bilingualism, and Language Change." *Encyclopedia of Educational Research.* New York: The Macmillan Co., 1960.

Combs, Arthur W., "A Perceptual View of the Adequate Personality." In: *Perceiving Behaving Becoming.* Washington: Association for Supervision and Curriculum Development, 1962.

Combs, Arthur W., "The Myth of Competition." *Childhood Education.* 33:364-69, February, 1957.

Frost, Joe L. "School and the Migrant Child." *Childhood Education. 41*:129-132. November, 1964.

Frost, Joe L. "School Environment and Disadvantaged Children." *Collected Papers* of the Inter-Institutional Seminar in Child Development. The Edison Institute. June, 1965.

Frost, Joe L. and Glenn R. Hawkes. *The Disadvantaged Child.* Boston: Houghton Mifflin, 1966.

Frost, Joe L. and O. Ray King. "Educating Disadvantaged Children." *Arkansas Education Association Journal.* 37:6, 28. September, 1964.

Gardner, Bruce D. *Development in Early Childhood.* New York: Harper and Row, 1964.

Goldfarb, W. "The Effects of Early Institutional Care on Adolescent Personality." *Journal of Experimental Education. 12*:106-129. 1953.

Hawkes, Glenn R. and Damaris Pease. *Behavior and Development from 5 to 12.* New York: Harper, 1962.

Hildreth, Gertrude. "Interrelationships Between Written Expression and the Other Language Arts." In *Interrelationships Among the Language Arts.* Research Bulletin of the National Conference on Research in English. 4-12, 1954.

Hildreth, Gertrude, *"Linguistic Factors in Early Reading." The Reading Teacher. 18*:172-178. December, 1964.

Hughes, Vergil H. "A Study of the Relationships Among Selected Language Abilities." *Journal of Educational Research. 47*:97-105, October, 1953.

Hunt, J. McV. *Intelligence and Experience.* New York: Ronald, 1961.

Hunt, J. McV. "How Children Develop Intellectually." *Children. 11*:83-91, May, 1964.

McCarthy, Dorothea. "Language Development." *Child Development Monographs 25*: 1960.

McCarthy, Dorothea. "Language Development in Children." In L. Carmichael (ed.) *Manual of Child Psychology.* 2nd ed. New York: Wiley, 1954.

McCarthy, Dorothea. "Research in Language Development: Retrospect and Prospect." *Child Development Monographs. 24,* 1959.

Mackintosh, Helen K. (ed.) *Children and Oral Language.* A joint publication of ACEI, ASCD, IRA, and NCTE. 1964.

Martin, Clyde. "Developmental Interrelationships Among Language Variables in Children of the First Grade." *Elementary English. 32*:167-171, March, 1955.

Melzack, Ronald and William R. Thompson. "Effects of Early Experience on Social Behavior." *Canadian Journal of Psychology. 10*:82-90. 1956.

Nice, M. M. "Length of Sentences as a Criterion of a Child's Progress in Speech." *Journal of Educational Psychology. 16*:370-379, 1925.

Olson, Willard C. *Child Development.* Boston: D. C. Heath, 1959.

Piaget, Jean. *The Language and Thought of the Child.* New York: Harcourt, Brace, 1926.

Piaget, J. *The Origins of Intelligence in Children.* (Margaret Cook, trans.) New York: International Universities Press, 1952. (Originally published 1936)

Rexinger, Lena. "How Carefully We'd Teach if We Were Wise." *Childhood Education. 35*: 391-393. May, 1959.

Shibles, Burleigh H. "How Many Words Does a First-Grade Child Know" *Elementary English. 41*:42-47, January, 1959.

Skeels, Harold M. "Effects of Adoption on Children From Institutions." *Children. 12*:33-34. January-February, 1965.

Smith, M. E. "An Investigation of the Development of the Sentence and the Extent of Vocabulary in Young Children." University of Iowa, Stud. Child Welfare, *3*:1926.

Smith, Mary K. "Measurement of the Size of General English Vocabulary through the Elementary Grades and High School." *Genetic Psychology Monographs. 24*:311-345, 1941.

Strickland, Ruth G. *The Language of Elementary School Children: Its Relationship to the Language of Reading Textbooks and the Quality of Reading of Selected Children.* Bloomington: Indiana University, School of Education. *38*: 1962.

Thompson, W. R. and W. Heron. "The Effects of Restricting Early Experience on the Problem-Solving Capacity of Dogs." *Canadian Journal Psychology. 8*:17-31, 1954.

Torrance, E. Paul. *Education and the Creative Potential.* Minneapolis: The University of Minnesota Press, 1963.

Travis, L. E. (Ed.) *Handbook of Speech Pathology.* New York: Appleton-Century-Crofts, 1957.

Warner, Sylvia Ashton. *Spinster.* New York: Simon and Schuster, 1958.

Watts, A. F. *The Language and Mental Development of Children.* New York: D. C. Heath, 1948.

Winter, Clotilda. "Interrelationships Among Language Variables in Children of the First and Second Grades." *Elementary English. 34*:108-113, 1956.

Wood, Nancy E. "Language Disorders in Children." *Child Development Monographs 25*: 1960.

Young, F. M. "An Analysis of Certain Variables in a Developmental Study of Language." *Genetic Psychology Monographs. 23*:3-141. 1941.

Chapter 2 Helen Heffernan

Language Arts Programs in Elementary Schools

Language is man's most distinctive human characteristic. Susanne K. Langer describes language as "the most momentous and at the same time the most mysterious product of the human mind."[1] She further defines language "as primarily a vocal actualization of the tendency to see reality symbolically."[2]

A large allotment of time in the elementary school program is devoted to the language arts. Proficiency in the various language arts contributes to the development of personality and learning skills in the arts of communication are essential to the child's progress throughout his entire educational program.

Before the child enters school, language behaviors are well established and teachers must adapt instruction to the type of behavior the child brings to the tasks of the school.

Early Language Development

The importance of the early language development of infants and young children is clarified by Susanne Langer when she says:

> . . . there is an *optimum period of learning,* and this is a stage of mental development in which several impulses and interests happen to coincide: the lalling instinct, the imitative impulse, a natural in-

---

[1]Susanne K. Langer, *Philosophy in a New Key,* Cambridge, Massachusetts: Harvard University Press, 1951. p. 103.

[2]*Ibid.,* p. 109.

> terest in distinctive sounds, *and a great sensitivity to "expressiveness" of any sort.*[3]

Langer points out that if language is not developed during infancy and the early years of life (1) by experimentation with "spontaneous phonetic material" and (2) by receiving approval and satisfaction from adults in the environment for producing vocal symbols that represent meaningful words in the language of his culture, language development either fails to take place or is seriously arrested. Constant vocalization, according to Langer is "a passing phase in our instinctive life."[4]

In support of her point of view, Langer cites the cases of lost or deserted children who incited the maternal instinct in animals, were reared by them, and thus were separated from human speech. Among others she cites the case of Kamala, reported originally by Arnold Gesell.[5] Kamala, the "wolf-girl" was found in Midnapur, India, in 1920. After six years in human surroundings, she had learned only forty words and never learned to use sentences of more than two or three words. Significantly, she never spoke unless spoken to. Langer[6] concludes that

> The impulse to chatter had been outgrown without being exploited for the acquisition of language.

Children who come from socially and culturally impoverished environments are frequently two or more years retarded in language development. Such children are immeasurably handicapped in meeting the traditional learning tasks of the school and particularly that important segment of the educational program involving verbal symbolization.

Planned intervention on the part of appropriate societal institutions to improve the home environment and child rearing practices and to provide nursery school or day care centers in which young children can hear and are encouraged to use speech promises some amelioration of this handicap. Participation in a wide variety of rich experiences, unrestricted opportunity to talk and play with other children, the sympathetic attention of understanding adults are promising forms that intervention may take to lessen this cultural handicap which is too frequently interpreted as limited intellectual endowment rather than deprivation of essential conditions for language development.

---

[3]*Ibid.*, p. 123.
[4]*Ibid.*, pp. 121-122.
[5]Arnold Gesell, "The Biography of a Wolf Child," *Harper's Magazine*, January, 1941.
[6]Langer, *op. cit.*, pp. 121-122.

Teachers must never forget what Langer has stated so well

> Language, though normally learned in infancy without any compulsion or formal training, is none the less a product of sheer learning, an art handed down from generation to generation.[7]

No one disputes the necessity for gratifying the dependency needs of the young child. Physical survival depends upon such nurturance. If these needs are not met, the child's development terminates or is arrested at that level. It is equally important for parents to understand that the baby's babbling and the mother's and father's response to his successful effort to imitate words spoken by the parents constitute the foundation of his later success in life. Children whose early language development has had the joyous guidance of parents, who were delighted at their baby's effort, enter school with excellent vocabularies, with most of the patterns of language and with readiness for further language development firmly established. Parents, the child's first teachers, thus play paramount roles in the child's ability to cope with early school demands.

Interrelationships Among the Language Arts

The language arts include listening, speaking, reading and written language comprising handwriting and spelling, all of which involve the use of words. In listening and speaking, ideas are received through words. In reading, writing and spelling ideas are expressed and communicated through words. The ways in which ideas are received and expressed are interrelated. Listening and reading stimulate speaking and writing. Speaking and writing encourage listening and reading. All of the language arts are inextricably interdependent and interrelated.

Listening

Listening is basic to language development. The young child listens to his own babbling and responds joyously as his phonetic experimentation wins smiles of approval from his parents. He listens to the words his parents repeat for him again and again and imitates the use the adult makes of tongue, lips and teeth in producing sounds. His gratification in his success is spontaneous and extravagant.

Young children who have been read to and have followed with an adult the pictures and even the symbols on the printed page soon note any omission designed by the adult to shorten the story-reading period. Children

---

[7]*Ibid.*, p. 108.

who have enjoyed these reading sessions with a loved parent or friend have less difficulty in learning to read than those who have not had such listening experiences. Listening to stories or poems read or told fills an important segment of the educational program in nursery school and kindergarten and should continue through the entire elementary school.

The reading vocabulary of children is much smaller than their understanding vocabulary. Constant visions of literary treats ahead motivate children's efforts to learn when teachers continually enhance their experience with well-interpreted material which the child can understand and enjoy when read to him but which he may be unable to read for himself.

The child must comprehend ideas in the spoken language if he is to recognize them in reading symbols. He can read only what he already knows. A recent government-sponsored motion picture: *Children Without,* produced by the Division of Press, Radio and TV Relations, National Education Association, shows a group of children puzzling over a word. When the difficulty was resolved, one boy said, "Oh, that's how 'sompin' looks in print." No child can read correctly a word he does not understand or which he has not heard spoken correctly.

As the child hears words spoken in context, his stock of word meanings increases. Repeated hearing of an expression that occurs in reading helps the child to read it. The teacher who works on different words the child will later encounter in reading helps him to hear the word correctly and to understand its meaning.

Throughout the child's school experience and in his out-of-school life as a child and as an adult it is important that he be a good listener. Listening implies more than hearing. Listening involves comprehending, interpreting and evaluating. Listening is, of course, a social courtesy to the speaker but its purpose is much broader. Listening critically to what is heard, evaluating the facts, determining the speaker's purpose, and comparing what is said with information from other sources are all a part of intelligent listening. The child can be helped to learn that all communication with other people depends as much on listening as on speaking.

Speaking

One of the basic drives to learning is the desire to share and communicate. Man is gregarious. Since from 75 to 90 per cent of communication is oral, it is of the utmost importance that children have ample opportunity for speaking and considerable instruction in the more formal aspects of speaking such as sharing experiences, story telling, conversing, discussing, making reports, making introductions, interviewing, using the telephone, and participating in meetings. Listening to others and telling about his experiences helps the child develop a conceptual background essential to learning to read. Competence in telling about the episodes in his experiences in correct sequence is one evidence of a child's readiness to read.

Children read with greater ease what they have experienced and talked about. The primary teacher frequently records what the children have said following a study trip to the supermarket, the zoo, the harbor, the dairy farm. Children have no difficulty reading these "experience stories" through which they have lived at firsthand and which contain the actual words with which they have expressed their ideas. Teachers skillful in the experience or language approach to the teaching of reading anticipate words and phrases the children will encounter later in preprimers and primers and thus pave the way to success when children begin reading in a book.[8]

What a child has experienced and enjoys talking about may actually open the door to reading. Ten-year-old Harry, who had experienced much difficulty in learning to read, became the proud possessor of a pair of carrier pigeons. Interest led to Harry's interviewing more mature pigeon fanciers who in turn shared with Harry the books and magazines published for people with this particular hobby. Motivation for reading was established. Harry's need to learn more about pigeons transformed his negative attitude toward reading and produced the eager motivation essential to mastery.

As reading instruction becomes more highly individualized children give oral reports on what they have read, thus revealing to the teacher their level of comprehension as well as their facility in oral language.

Discussion of books, recording brief book reports on the tape recorder or simple pupil-directed dramatization of a story or a dramatic episode from a book several children have read show the close connection between reading and speaking and also foster interest in more extended reading.

Oral reading is important throughout the elementary school because it reveals the individual child's need for teacher help. The child's chances for success in school and in life will be greatly enhanced if he pronounces words clearly and correctly and speaks with good voice quality and normal pitch. Listening to the child read or speak gives the teacher the clues she needs to help him achieve better speech.

---

[8]Dorris May Lee and Roach Van Allen, *Learning to Read Through Experience*, 2nd ed., New York: Appleton-Century-Crofts, 1963.

Reading

Reading, as the skill through which children pursue much of their education, is closely related to all the language arts.

Reading expands the child's vocabulary and gives him new words to enrich his speaking and writing.

Reading provides the child with models of sentence structure and grammatical form which help establish his standards for good language expression in speaking and writing. Oral reading provides him with prac-

Reading can open many doors for children.

tice in using these sentences and grammatical forms correctly so that they become habitual.

Reading enriches the child's reservoir of ideas upon which he can draw for conversation, letters or written reports. Stories may be reorganized into scenes and scripts for puppet shows, informal dramatization or more formal plays.

Literary reading may stimulate in the child an increasingly sensitive perception of his world and thus lead to various forms of creative expression including original written composition.

Written Language

Written language activities are facilitated by the child's fluency in speech. If some person skilled in handwriting will serve as his amanuensis, he can actually compose poems, stories and letters before he can read. Later his reading ability will contribute to his written language ability, but his own original composition uninfluenced by primer models has a quality of uniqueness.

Writing helps to develop the child's ability to recognize and use words and sentences. Writing necessitates close attention to the characteristics of letters and words and thus contributes to learning handwriting and spelling and creates willingness to learn them. Writing reinforces the child's vocabulary and frequently requires additions to his vocabulary in order to express his ideas.

Phonetic skills useful in speaking and reading also are useful to the child in writing a word. The word analysis the child employs in learning to spell also has a transfer value to reading.

Work in vocabulary development, word meanings, word analysis and the use of the dictionary aid the child in reading as well as in expressing himself in written form.

Reports are frequently written on material read. Material composed by children and recorded by them or their teacher often is used as simple reading material in recording progress made in science or social studies.

Language Arts Inseparable

The various language arts are truly inseparable. One component cannot be thought of alone. The *word* is the common denominator in listening, speaking, reading and written language. First the child hears and then begins to understand the speech of others. As these experiences are repeated and extended, he babbles and begins to imitate the sounds he hears. Finally, he differentiates his speech sounds and develops the language of expression. As his comprehension and expresssion develop, he learns the relationship between real experiences and the symbols of oral and written language. Later he encounters systematically arranged letters and words, associates them with experiences, and thus learns to read.

In this developmental continuum, his teacher may encourage him to compose or actually write his own stories[9] *before* he uses a preprimer or primer. The reading of what others have written follows extensive experimentation with his own written language.

In and out of school, the child meets situations requiring the use of the language arts. The more vital and stimulating these situations the more progress he will make toward mastery. We say "toward mastery" advisedly because actual mastery is probably never fully attained by anyone in any language or any component of the language arts. As long as a person lives, he can improve his powers of concentrated listening, the effectiveness and quality of his speech, and his competence in oral and written expression.

The challenge to the elementary school teacher is to provide experiences which will release children to express themselves orally in conversation, discussion, dramatic play and dramatization. Out of the richness and vitality of experience provided by the total program and by conscious direction of attention to the beauty and power of good speech and writing, children can acquire competence in effective communication while developing uniqueness and spontaneity of expression.

Language Arts and Other Curricular Areas

Since language is the means by which ideas are shared, it is basic to all living and learning. It is impossible to conceive of a society in which people work and live together without the facilitating medium of communication. It is equally impossible to think of any activity in the classroom that does not require and also afford opportunity to practice the arts of communication. The language arts have no intrinsic content. Language is used in talking or writing about man's relationship to man, man's relationship to his physical environment and the multitude of systems and institutions—domestic, economic, political, social, educational, religious, vocational, aesthetic – that man has devised to control and promote these relationships.

Language and thinking have a close relationship. In the schools of a democracy, the first concern of the teacher is to help children to learn to think. Teachers guide the learning experiences so children will find

---

[9]Lee and Van Allen, *ibid.*

themselves in problem-centered situations with needs, desires, and questions which stimulate them to think. To solve problems, children must be able to recognize them and to state them clearly; they must be able to gather and summarize pertinent information about their problem, weigh the significance of their facts and draw tentative conclusions. They must be able to test conclusions tentatively accepted and finally act on the basis of their best thinking.

Whether thinking can exist without language is doubtful. Evidence indicates that thinking is done in words. At least it is certain that to share an act of thought it is necessary to clothe the ideas in precise words which convey meaning to the listener. Many variations are told of the story of the little girl who was admonished to think before she spoke. "But," she protested, "how can I tell what I think until I hear what I say?" The idea contained in the story is essentially sound; words do help clarify thought.

Language Arts in the Social Studies

No richer opportunity for language development can be found in the school curriculum than that afforded by a dynamic social studies program.

Many descriptive curriculum units reveal the pathway followed by children exploring a culture, a significant era in history, or the development of an industry.

Courses of study usually recommend *The Westward Movement of the United States* for intensive study in the fifth grade.[10] This is a particularly desirable placement for the great American epic. Boys and girls of ten and eleven crave adventure. They can identify with the simple life of the settlers of Kentucky, the pioneers who opened up the territory west to the Mississippi, and the covered wagon trains crossing the plains to the Pacific. This is their story, their great tradition! They want to get inside the experience and become one with it.

What does such a study do for the development of children in language arts?

Dramatic Play

Oral language development is stimulated by exciting episodes made to order for dramatic play – life at Boonesborough – hunting in nearby woods, bringing water from streams, tending fields outside the fort, washing clothes, caring for infants, cooking, eating, guarding the fort. All of the things the pioneers did can be relived in play. Making candles, spin-

[10]See: Lavonne A. Hanna, Gladys L. Potter and Neva Hagaman, *Unit Teaching in the Elementary School* (Rev. ed.) New York: Holt, Rinehart and Winston, 1963 (pp. 468-499).

ning, going on the long hunt, trapping, Boone's capture by the Shawnees, Indian attack on Boonesborough, Indian life, the Wilderness Road, building a cabin on the Ohio can be exciting episodes in dramatic play. The dramatic incidents are limitless. Day after day the play continues with an accompaniment of the language of the hardy Americans who conquered a continent.

Use of Reference Material

The play is meaningful and fun only if the players have command of accurate facts. What was Boonesborough like? How did the people live? Why did the pioneers move west? Why was Independence an important "jumping off" place? How did the pioneers travel west? What did the pioneers take with them? How were the pioneers organized? How were the wagons organized for the trail? How long did it take to travel along the different routes? What were the hardships encountered? Who were the people the pioneers met in the West? What kind of country did they travel over? What were the main stopping places?

Finding the answers to these questions so the play would be more authentic involved the children in extensive reading of textbooks, library references, charts and graphs. They shared information found in books, they validated questionable information, they increased their vocabulary, they participated in discussion periods to plan and evaluate work to be done or accomplished. In their dramatic play, they wrote letters to folk in Independence. They wrote and told "tall tales." They kept a diary of the trip. They took notes for reports. They recorded locations on maps. They learned folk songs and made up some songs of their own.

Space does not permit recording all the language experiences these children had, much less all the learning experiences. They sewed costumes, made guns, constructed covered wagons, painted, experimented, tried out the industrial arts processes. All these activities went on in the give-and-take of a miniature classroom democracy. Reference materials were rich and numerous. Important as this study was in specific learnings for children, however, its primary justification is the contribution it makes toward establishing a clear understanding of American ideas and ideals and of present day life in America. This understanding is gradually established through constantly contrasting the simplicity of life in pioneer days with the complexity of life in the modern machine age.

Language Arts in Science

In the effective teaching of science, emphasis is on observing, reading, measurement and critical thinking. In science the observer is a "reader" of

Children learn in Science by observing and listening, then asking significant questions.

the things and events of the environment. His reading from books should *follow* and not *precede* experimental verification. The aim of the teacher is to acquaint pupils with the complexities of scientific phenomena. The more the child understands the meaning of these the more easily can he interpret the printed symbols that designate them.

The Los Angeles County Course of Study[11] records a science experience of first grade children triggered by a child's question: "What makes the

[11]A Guide to Curriculum Development and Course of Study for Elementary Schools of Los Angeles County. Los Angeles: Office of the County Superintendent of Schools, 1965, pp. 331-333.

water in our fish bowl green?" The teacher saw in the child's question the opportunity to deepen the group's understanding of interaction and interdependence as she guided them in their search for data to answer the question.

The hypotheses advanced were characteristic of six-year-olds:

> One child thought the fish ate plants and that some of the green from the plants squirted out of the fishes' mouths, causing the water to be green. Another child thought the sun melted the plants, while others thought the green water could have been caused by the fish food, the pebbles, rocks, or a little metal frog in the fish bowl or possibly by something in the air.

Imagine the vitality of this oral language period with the teacher creating a classroom climate where it was safe to advance "guesses" and where the teacher "accepted and attached significance to ideas."

The children interviewed people, looked at books, listened to significant parts read by the teacher. They learned about the "characteristics of fresh water fish, about their habitat, and the fact that algae caused the water to be green. They looked at algae projected by a microprojector." The children discovered that there are many sources of information, pictures, people, books and that wonderful equipment could open new worlds for them.

"But what caused the algae to grow?" was the next question. How could they find out. They could experiment. They decided to:

Clean out the fish bowl
Add only the fish to the clean water
And one thing at a time to the fish bowl
Study the green water and plants
Put fish bowl in different places in room

The amount of planning and discussion that this ambitious project required stretched language capacity to the utmost. Certain children assumed responsibility for tasks related to the project. One girl visited the museum with her parents and saw a display of algae. She painted a picture of the algae which she shared with her classmates.

In the course of their experiences the children arrived at generalizations as follows:

Fish live in water
Water has oxygen in it
Fish get oxygen from water

Plants give off oxygen
Sunlight affects the growth of plants
A great amount of sunlight was involved in making a great amount of algae
Rocks provide a place for fish to hide from the sun
Snails help keep the fish bowl clear

The science understandings were deepened for these young children; they increased their understanding of interaction and interdependence among living and nonliving things. They grew in using methods of observation, inquiry and experimentation. They incorporated new information into their conceptual frameworks. They arrived at sound conclusions based on ability to "read" the phenomena of their environment.

From the point of view of language arts, they discussed a problem of interest to them and planned ways to find out cause and effect for themselves. They acquired new vocabulary. They found it necessary to use some measurements concerning the effect of various lengths of time in the sunlight on the growth of the algae. They found satisfaction in expressing their conclusions in the most precise language they had at their command. Because they were unable to use the skills of reading and writing, they used the scientific methods of observation, inquiry, problem-solving; these are the methods of the scientist although at his level of sophistication he must read what other scientists have discovered and publish his findings.

Language Arts and Mathematics

Mathematics is a special product of man's ingenuity to abstract the property of number from objects and to communicate basic mathematical concepts. Much that has been previously noted about the relation of language arts to science is equally applicable to mathematics.

Today's children are learning to think in terms of basic mathematical concepts through a curriculum which offers continuous opportunities to use concrete models and experiences. Numerals, symbols of operation and relationships, mathematical sentences, graphs, rules have meaning for children when they are learned in a sequence based on gradually broadening and deepening understanding. Children learn by making mathematical discoveries for themselves and developing their own ways of attacking mathematical problems.

Since correctness and precision are characteristics of all effective usage of language, these qualities cannot be applied in higher degree than to the language of mathematics.

Planning the School Schedule

If the time spent in school is to be most productive of learning, the school program must be characterized by careful planning in order to make the most effective use of every day during these important years of a child's school life. The various activities included in the curriculum must be organized and carried out in ways that encourage the highest level of living and learning.

In planning the schedule of activities, a teacher must consider all of the subjects required by law or by the governing authority of the local

The language arts benefit when children are involved in planning the day's activities.

school district. Since communication between and among educators is fostered by powerful professional associations, by the circulation of many professional books and periodicals, and by nationwide use of the same textbooks, however, most educational programs bear a strong resemblance to one another. Restrictions usually refer to subjects to be taught and do not extend to how the teacher will organize for instruction in the classroom. No doubt some teachers feel more comfortable with one type of organization while others seem to believe another is more efficient.

Whatever arrangement of the daily program is made, the language arts will be best served if the elementary school day affords:

1. Time for planning and discussion
2. Time to solve problems
3. Time to acquire knowledge and skills
4. Time to enjoy the aesthetic
5. Time to create
6. Time to play, rest, and secure nutrition

The language arts became an integral part of the entire day regardless of the subject taught or the particular organizational pattern followed.

Time for Planning and Discussion

Children need opportunity to talk over plans for the day, to discuss work that needs to be done and materials needed for doing it, to determine the part each child is to play in planned activities, and to evaluate what has been accomplished in previous work periods.

The teacher uses these periods to keep oral language standards high, to be sure that time is being efficiently used, to develop new interests, to develop new vocabulary and to stimulate higher levels of thinking.

Time to Solve Problems

All life situations are full of questions. Learning to make wise decisions is of supreme value to the individual. Problem-solving is a kind of learning which must begin early in the educative process and continue as a lifelong endeavor. Problem-solving is a daily experience which develops judgment, thoughtfulness and initiative.

A group of eight-year-olds made a study trip to the harbor and saw the fireboat respond to an alarm. When they returned to school many questions were asked about how a fire in the hold of a boat is put out. The problem was clearly stated and written by the teacher on the chalkboard. Several children suggested ways the fire might be put out. These methods were all carefully listed by the teacher for further consideration. Apparently there were differences of opinion, but no evidence was advanced to substantiate any of the children's ideas. The teacher asked: How could we find out? Again a variety of suggestions was offered – another trip to the harbor to interview the captain of the fireboat and a visit to the library to seek information were accepted as feasible suggestions. Then the teacher said that she would perform an experiment which might help them to find the solution. The teacher thus helped the children to find still another way to solve their problems.

A glass beaker became the hold of the boat; an inch length of a burning candle in the bottom of the beaker became the fire in the boat. By pouring a mild acid over baking soda in a retort equipped with rubber cork and tube, the teacher was able to direct a stream of carbon dioxide into the "hold." The experiment was repeated several times by the children with the same result. All the time questioning and thinking went on.

Said one child, "You made a gas in which fire won't burn." Said another, "It takes oxygen for fire to burn. You pushed the oxygen out of the beaker with another gas." For the eight-year-olds this was a sufficient explanation.

The teacher occupies a significant role in problem-solving when guiding and encouraging children to a solution. The opinions offered by the children are all accepted to be tested in various ways – having firsthand experiences, reading authoritative material, interviewing qualified persons, observation, and carrying on experimentation. Children see the importance of clear thinking and clear expression of ideas and are led to extend their knowledge through reading and through discussion with knowledgeable persons.

Time to Acquire Knowledge and Skill

Children learn subject matter in relation to their experiences. Skills must be acquired in reading. oral and written expression including handwriting and spelling. Other skills in the use of numbers, tools, paint, clay, the singing voice must also be acquired.

Because of the wide range of differences in individual capacities, these skills are most efficiently acquired individually or in very small groups where teacher guidance can be largely individual.

Whatever time is provided for skills should be utilized as a teaching period for the teacher as well as a work period for the children. When each child is progressing at his own rate, the teacher has opportunity to give individual guidance. The teacher wishes to develop the child's initia-

An effective teacher takes time to give individual help to children.

tive and so she encourages him to go ahead with his own tasks in his own way but helps him when he needs help. The teacher wants to help the child develop a sense of responsibility and so helps him to accept the obligation of completing his task. The teacher wants to help the child to grow in accuracy and so she encourages him to check his work. Finally, the teacher wants to help each child develop judgment and habits of analytical thinking, and so she helps him to appraise his work, see where he needs to improve and decides whether he is ready for the next step. These activities are at the heart of effective teaching and are best achieved in a face-to-face relationship. The more individual guidance the teacher can provide the more effective will be the results. This is the unanswerable argument for teachable-size classes in the elementary school.

Time to Enjoy the Aesthetic

Children need daily contact with beauty in order to develop the appreciation that comes from frequent and pleasurable experiences. Each day should bring its quota of memorable contacts with art, music, literature and nature. All of these contacts involve the language arts.

The impressions children receive from these experiences stimulate an emotional response which in turn suggests creative expressions. Children will find a variety of individually satisfying ways to express themselves creatively.

Authentic reproductions of paintings, recordings of beautiful poems, stories, music, are available to supplement the teacher's artistic gifts. No environment is so meager that it will not yield rocks, driftwood, flowers or mosses which can be arranged artistically for enjoyment.

Time to Create

If the child's time in school is filled with vital experiences and children are given opportunity for firsthand contact with their environment through study trips, creative expression is most likely to emerge. Learning and creative expression come as children strive to re-create their experiences. Many children will strive to re-create their experiences in patterns of beautiful words; others may choose other media. The teacher sets the stage and protects the child so he can give his own interpretations and express his own unique feelings. A child must feel comfortable in a classroom to be free enough to express his honest self.

Time for Play, Rest and Nutrition

Childhood is the period of significant physical growth. Human happiness and social usefulness depend upon sound bodies. The school must safeguard the child's physical well-being and provide him with a wholesome rhythm of rest and activity.

The school that serves children best permits a maximum of freedom to move about, to use their large muscles, to choose from a variety of strenuous and less strenuous activities.

Children need additional nutrition during the school day for effective school work. You cannot teach hungry children. What this nutrition shall be and when it will be available is a decision which should involve local nutrition experts and the parents of the children. Sound nutritional practices established in childhood, however, are the basis for important lifelong habits.

The Daily Schedule

Providing time each day for the foregoing activities is more important than the number of minutes allocated to a given subject or the sequence in which the experiences are ordered. The best daily schedule is probably one made every day by the teacher and the childrn in terms of the learning needs of the group. In any event, whatever schedule is arranged, the teacher should consider it only as a flexible guide to a well-balanced school day.

A teacher of a second grade class found the following daily schedule useful in providing a balanced program for seven-year-old children.

Daily Program for Second-Year Children

8:30 - 8:45	The children hang up coats, check in library books, may help in getting room ready for the day's work or may play outdoors.
8.45 - 9:45	Planning period. Opportunity to ask questions, to solve individual problems, to determine individual purposes and to focus attention upon new needs as revealed during the play and work periods of the previous day. Work period in social studies and science. Discussion period.
9:45 - 10:00	Midmorning lunch
10:00 - 10:50	Aesthetic experiences
10:50 - 11:00	Recess
11:00 - 11:30	Music — singing songs, playing with rhythm instruments, listening to music, creating music
11:30 - 12:05	Supervised lunch period
12:05 - 12:35	Rest period
12:35 - 1:35	Development of skills in language arts and numbers
1:35 - 2:00	Outdoor play
2:00 - 2:30	Literature
2:30	Dismissal

Although the program seems to show only an hour and a half devoted to the language arts, listening, and speaking, reading and written language permeated all the activities with these young children.

A teacher of a fifth grade finds a comfortable organization in the following schedule.

Daily Program for Fifth Grade Children

9:00	Informal greetings, routine matters, flag salute, current happenings of personal interest which individual children wish to share
9:15	Integrated curriculum unit
10:25	Midmorning lunch
10:40	Health and physical education
11:10	Language arts
12:00	Lunch, rest, playground activities
1:00	Mathematics
1:40	Music
2:00	Rest and recreation
2:10	Reading activities
3:00	Rest and recreation
3:10	Unscheduled time
4:00	Dismissal

This schedule provides for two fifty-minute periods daily devoted to language arts activities per se but again many language arts skills are used in the study of the integrated curriculum unit. Children plan and discuss work, prepare and give individual and committee reports, arrange bulletin boards and the like.

This particular teacher is enthusiastic about the period listed as "unscheduled time." During this period individuals or small groups have an opportunity to pursue their own interests. An abundance of suitable books, pictures, maps, tools and other material must be available for reporting, illustrating and experimenting. The teacher who has a broad background of experience and an inquiring mind will be most successful in guiding the various interests in art, crafts, literature, science, international relations, music, drama, and puppetry that may emerge. Probably his best teaching will be done at such a time when the impetus for learning comes wholly from the children.

The Weekly Program

The teacher must give thought to the scheduling of activities that do not occur daily. These include orchestra and glee club practice, study trips, school newspaper, school council, auditorium periods, gardening activities, safety patrol, library periods, special classes, health examinations. All these can provide valuable learning opportunities if well planned and carried forward at a high level.

Plans for use of facilities or equipment used jointly with other groups will do much to avoid confusion. The full use of the auditorium or multipurpose room, audio-visual equipment and other materials should be carefully scheduled.

Whatever weekly plans are made, the teacher's regular daily schedule is important and must be sufficiently flexible so no activity suffers unduly because of absence of children for other activities. Any plan must be flexible to be useful; variations from the plan are inevitable but the teacher's watchfulness will prevent any significant activity from suffering because of scheduling.

The Yearly Program

The course of study provides the basic yearly program but usually these publications contain more suggestions than any group of children could encompass during a school year. The teacher who knows the particular group of children is the professional person best qualified to study the recommendations in their entirety and select those most suitable for the needs of the group.

Informal testing of children reveals material they may already know and helps the teacher determine the particular learning experiences requiring emphasis. Efforts to diagnose individual pupil's needs early in the school year will justify the expenditure of the teacher's time in revealing the crucial needs upon which the individual's progress depends.

Planning for Language Arts Instruction

At all levels of the elementary school, the teacher must make provision in the daily, weekly and yearly schedule for developmental experiences in all components of the language arts: listening, speaking, reading and written language. School systems frequently provide courses of study, teachers' guides to language arts instruction or textbooks which determine the grade placement of specific learnings.

In general, the following topics are included and have application at all maturity levels:

Listening

Throughout the child's school years, he should be helped to realize the numerous benefits that come to a good listener. He will be able to learn many interesting things, follow directions accurately, avoid many unpleasant situations and have more fun with his friends if he knows what is going on about him.

As he grows older, listening leads to a genuine interchange of ideas in conversation and discussion. Many opportunities arise to test how well children listen by discussions following newscasts or a talk presented on radio or television.

Speaking

Many teachers distinguish between two types of speaking activities: oral language and creative oral expression.

Oral Language

Functional language is used in sharing experiences, conversing, making introductions, conferring and interviewing, using the telephone, and participating in meetings. Oral language is functional when it is used to communicate information and express opinions. The development of effective practical expression is a continuing need through the school. Progress will vary with individual children so grade level placement of specific skills is meaningless. In working with the children, the teacher can develop standards for oral language appropriate to the level of maturity of the particular group.

Creative Oral Expression

Oral expression can be creative as a child is free to express his thoughts and feelings in his unique fashion.

Creative language grows out of a child's reaction to his out-of-school experiences and to planned experiences in school. The teacher provides many opportunities for rich, sensory experiences — seeing, hearing, smelling, tasting, feeling — and for observing changes and distinguishing characteristics. Children are encouraged to express themselves colorfully. Creative oral expression may take the form of sharing experiences, conversation, discussion, dramatic play, dramatization, story telling and reporting. It differs from functional oral language because of the feeling element injected by the speaker. He calls upon his own background of experience to which he has reacted emotionally and expresses himself in patterns of words that share his feelings with the listener. Such spontaneous oral language occurs only in a classroom climate where the child feels safe to be his honest self.

Reading

Learning to read is a major purpose of the primary school child. Reading to learn becomes the purpose of the child in the middle grades. Reading is truly the path to many vicarious experiences. The path can be a rough and thorny one, however, unless the teacher recognizes the readiness, the needs and the capacities of each pupil and adapts instruction and materials to individual needs. Small flexible groups or individualized instruction makes such adaptation feasible. Attempting to teach a large group of children as though they were all alike dooms the teacher to feelings of inadequacy and frustration and his pupils to experiences of failure.

The emphasis should always be on the child rather than on materials to be covered and skills to be learned. It is not important that every child in a grade read the same books or acquire the same skills. What is important is that the child succeed at every step in the process so that every day means growth in power for him regardless of what other children may accomplish.

Written Language

Written language includes functional written expression, creative written expression, handwriting and spelling.

Functional Written Expression

Reporting, class newspaper, reports, letter writing may be classified as forms of functional writing. Their major aim is to present information for a specific purpose. They will be useful at all levels of maturity and will improve as the school provides vital experiences in which they are put to use. As children mature, they learn to keep records of social studies activities, science observations and experiments, meetings of school councils and the like. They learn the art of taking succinct notes for later reference. They learn to outline. Grammar and punctuation become increasingly important to guarantee accuracy and precision. Words continue to be fascinating means of conveying more and more complex ideas.

Creative Written Expression

Schools are striving increasingly to release the creative potential in every form and particularly in written composition. Teachers attempt to maintain a relaxed, flexible supportive classroom atmosphere in which children are encouraged to write. Experiences are provided which offer children something to write about: discussions, conversations, pictures, music, films and filmstrips, study trips connected with social studies or science, listening to stories or poems, sharing original writing with others, producing original plays. Criticism is never negative lest the wells of inspiration be dried up at their source.

Handwriting

No writing is effective unless it conveys ideas to others in a legible form. Individuality in style and form is permissible but not to the point where it interferes with legibility.

Instruction in handwriting usually is given to the entire group of children and followed with individual evaluation and help.

Handwriting is a physical skill that improves with increased muscular and eye-hand coordination and practice. It is a courtesy to write legibly for those who read handwriting, so enough practice must be provided to insure this minimum standard.

In certain cultures, writing is considered a fine art. The royal road to self-realization may be via calligraphy. In our utilitarian culture, the calligrapher is not classified as an artist but many children develop feelings of self-worth because of praise received for the excellence of their handwriting. Most teachers stress correct form, ease of production and legibility of the product as acceptable goals.

Spelling

Writing is not socially acceptable unless words are spelled correctly. In contrast to the casual attitude people take toward handwriting, deviations from standards are not tolerated.

Awareness of the importance of spelling words correctly grows as children use words in writing and never as a result of learning to spell long lists of unrelated words orally or in written form.

Children usually are encouraged to keep a file or notebook of the words they use most frequently for ready reference. Picture dictionaries are useful with young children and small dictionaries with carefully selected lists of words provide early instruction in the employment of this invaluable tool of the scholar.

The ultimate test of a child's competence in spelling is not his daily grade on a list of spelling words but his correct and facile use of a correct spelling vocabulary in all his written expression.

Summary

The language arts are truly inseparable, and while one may receive more emphasis at one point in the school day than another, it must be recognized that one seldom speaks unless someone listens, and that most writing is meant to be read. Facility in one aspect of language suggests a similar level of ability in others – a child seldom reads or writes better than he speaks. Thus, it appears to be a mistake to compartmentalize the facets of the language arts, to ignore the opportunities for developing several skills during one portion of the school day. Flexibility in scheduling allows the teacher and the children an important degree of freedom as they work and learn together. Language, in all its aspects, flourishes in a rich permissive classroom environment and tends to shrivel and diminish under rigid rules and harsh discipline. As teachers work together and as individual teachers plan with groups of children, they will make sure that none of the language skills will be neglected, but they will also be aware of the need for a degree of autonomy, for some "room to breathe," even in today's over-crowded curriculum.

EXTENDING YOUR LEARNING

1. Examine at least three language arts curriculum guides. Be prepared to write an analysis of, or discuss, the following issues:
   a. What is the evidence of articulation from grade to grade? Do goals and objectives appear to be consistent and sequential?
   b. Who wrote the guide? What is the evidence that classroom teachers were, or were not involved in preparing the guide?
   c. The author of this chapter makes a strong plea for an *integrated* or correlated approach to teaching the language arts. Is there evidence of such an "interrelationship" in the guides you've surveyed?
2. Examine two or three language arts textbooks. The following 'guide-points' may help to focus your examination and a written or oral analysis of your findings.
   a. Is the emphasis primarily on *written* language (writing letters, reports, etc.) or is there evidence that the linguists have been heard, and oral language (speaking and listening) is given the emphasis it deserves, considering its utility in out-of-school life.
   b. Are the language arts treated as facets of a unitary developmental process – or as separate entities? What is the justification for the separate subjects approach? the 'integrated' approach?
   c. Is help provided for the teacher who wants to vary his approach, and to adjust his program to better meet the needs of children in his class?
3. Construct dioramas, or prepare diagrams, showing a functional yet creative approach to classroom design. Try this, assuming you are teaching in a self-contained classroom and also assume you have team-teaching responsibilities for teaching writing, spelling, reading and 'language' (grammar and usage).
4. List the materials (projectors, tape recorder, etc.) which you would consider important for a primary classroom; an intermediate classroom.

5. There is no chapter in this text dealing with the implications of a rich and varied literature program for teaching the language arts. How do *you* think an effective literature program would enrich and contribute to the goals of a language arts program, as suggested in this chapter, or in one of the guides surveyed?

BIBLIOGRAPHY

1. Anderson, Paul S., *Language Skills in Elementary Education,* New York: The Macmillan Company, 1964, Chapter 1, pp. 1-44.
2. *Balance in the Curriculum,* 1961 Yearbook, Association for Supervision and Curriculum Development, Washington, D. C.: The National Education Association, 1961.
3. Dawson, Mildred A., Marion Zollinger and Ardell Elwell, *Guiding Language Learning,* New York: Harcourt, Brace and World, 1963, Ch. 2 and 3, pp. 19-56.
4. Fleming, Robert S., *Curriculum for Today's Boys and Girls,* Columbus, Ohio: Charles E. Merrill Books, Inc., 1963. Part 1, pp. 5-88. Chapters 6 and 7, pp. 121-244.
5. Greene, Harry A., and Walter T. Petty, *Developing Language Skills in the Elementary Schools,* Boston: Allyn and Bacon, 1963, Chapters 1, 2, and 3, pp. 3-84.
6. Goodlad, John I, and Robert H. Anderson, *The Nongraded Elementary School,* rev. ed. New York: Harcourt, Brace and World, 1963.
7. *Interrelationships Among the Language Arts,* A Research Bulletin of the National Conference on Research in English, A. Sterl Artley, Chairman, Champaign, Illinois. The National Council of Teachers of English, 1954.
8. Lee, Dorris M., and Roach Van Allen, *Learning to Read Through Experience,* New York: Appleton, Century, Crofts, 1963.
9. Lee, J. Murray, and Dorris May Lee, *The Child and His Curriculum,* 3rd Edition, New York: Appleton-Century-Crofts, 1960, Part I, pp. 3-147 and Chapter 10, pp. 279-370.
10. Peterson, Dorothy G., *The Elementary School Teacher,* New York: Appleton-Century-Crofts, 1964, Chapter 6-10, pp. 195-449.
11. Shane, Harold G., June Grant Mulry, Mary E. Reddin and Margaret C. Gillespie, *Improving Language Arts Instruction in the Elementary School,* Columbus, Ohio: Charles E. Merrill Books, 1962.
12. Trauger, Wilmer K., *Language Arts in Elementary Schools,* New York: McGraw-Hill, Inc., 1963. Part I, pp. 1-24.

Chapter 3 H. Beresford Menagh

Creative Dramatics

Introduction

High on the continental divide in New Mexico, a group of third-grade children at an Indian school were having difficulty reading with understanding the story of "The Three Billy Goats Gruff." The children, ranging in ages from twelve to seventeen, were old for the third grade for they had started school late and now, after a little more than two years' acquaintance with English, were forced with the necessity of speaking, reading, writing, and understanding a foreign tongue. Comprehension was coming slowly: they could read the words but had difficulty in understanding the meaning.

The teacher stopped the reading and began asking questions about hunger – a feeling not unknown to these children – and about the feelings a hungry goat would have while searching for grass. The response was instantaneous. These Navaho children knew all about goats and their search for food because most of them had herded sheep and goats for their parents here on their arid Navaho land. The teacher encouraged the children to show how hungry goats feel when there is no food and how they would feel if they saw green grass on a hillside in the distance. The children got into the spirit of the situation – the solution to the problem was within their capabilities and they proceeded to handle the problem with both understanding and interest. The immediate problem was no longer one of finding how to get three specific goats with odd names to by-pass an unfamiliar creature called a Troll in order to reach a grassy area, but one of how goats in general behave, and most importantly, how they feel. Goats enjoy the sunshine, they said, they like to play and they like to eat. The teacher asked them how they felt when they played in the sunshine; how they felt when the cold rain came; how they felt when the sun came out again. In ones, twos, and as a group, the children imagined the situations and experienced the sensations.

The children were led to imagine the hunger of the goats – not a foreign sensation to them or to their goats. How does a goat feel when he is hungry and what does he do? After they verbalized solutions to this problem, one child volunteered to show what the goat would do. Carefully he looked about the area in the classroom, transformed now by imagination into an arid mesa dotted with scrub piñon pine and juniper. The child saw something that looked like food. He sniffed it: it smelled bad. He handled it: it was rough and full of prickles. He tasted it: it tasted dry and bad. It was just some old, dried-out tumbleweed. He showed his disappointment and his hunger pangs increased. Other children took up the challenge to be hungry goats looking for food. They watched each other carefully, and, with guidance, offered suggestions and criticisms.

Bit by bit the other elements of the story were uncovered. The children experienced the distinct rhythms of the three goats as they crossed the bridge. They viewed the lush grass on the distant hill with delicious anticipation. They faced the Troll. The Troll presented no problem, as Navaho legend abounds with evil or mischievous characters who constantly interfere with someone's progress toward a goal. The children felt the anxiety of overcoming this obstacle, relished the trickery of the first two goats in passing the Troll, and revelled in the strength of the third goat in disposing of the evil character. Various children tried their skill at being piñon pines standing nearby, withstanding a windstorm that had somehow blown up when the Troll made his appearance. Bit by bit the story was acted out using only a table, two chairs and several vivid imaginations until "The Three Billy Goats Gruff" became a complete dramatization with well-defined character, motivated action, dialogue, suspense, climax and resolution. The children then returned to the printed story, read the words with understanding and enjoyment, talked about the story, and wrote about it.[1]

What occurred in this Navaho classroom and has been repeated in many classrooms around America was a venture into improvised theatre or creative dramatics. The children had exercised their imaginations, had created character and action in a group situation using their own personal tools of body and voice, and had come out of the experience not only better equipped in Language Arts but better equipped as human beings.

Utilitarian Education

Becoming fully equipped as human beings and achieving a complete measure of human worth is not easy in a technologically oriented society. There are many tendencies in such a society that militate against it, not

[1]This occurred in the writer's classroom at the United States Indian Service School, Crownpoint, New Mexico, 1952.

the least of which is one toward making education utilitarian, that is, making it serve as training for a job. Almost anyone who is asked why he should get an education will probably reply that an education is necessary for getting a job. A 1965 Harris Survey shows almost three out of four, or 74 per cent of parents believe the primary purpose of going to college is "to get a good job."[2] Newspapers contain items about the problems of young men and women who do not complete high school and consequently fail to obtain employment. Federal, state and local governments exhibit concern about the apparent relationship between unemployment and lack of education. Programs are proposed and instituted in which people are helped not only to complete high school but to obtain a higher education and in some cases even to engage in graduate work. It is taken as almost axiomatic that the more education a person has the greater are his job opportunities. Thus it appears to many that the function of education in our American society is to prepare people for making a living.

Because of this common conception of the function of education, students in colleges and universities can be heard complaining about spending time, even "wasting" time, on a course of study not directly related to their particular job-goals. Students preparing to teach are perhaps less prone than others to complain about such courses because they generally accept the idea that the more they know about themselves, their relationship to others and their relationship to their universe the better they are for teaching growing human beings. But there is hardly a student who has not heard another student complain, "What do I need with botany in mechanical engineering?" or "What do I need with physics when I'm going to be a teacher of American literature?" or "What good is a course in speech for an agronomist?" For these students, the criterion of merit in any educational pursuit seems to be utility.

Contemporary Pressures

Utilitarianism received a strong impetus following the successful launching of Sputnik in 1957. Clamors were heard across America for greater emphasis on mathematics and science in education. One respected scientist became better known in some circles for his views of technological education than for his achievements in physical science. A well-known military officer became a regular writer in newspaper columns about a no-nonsense approach to education. A superintendent of public instruction in one of the large states was elected with a platform that emphasized the

---

[2]Louis Harris, "College Goal Splits Parents, Children." Los Angeles Times, March 18, 1965.

"3-R's" and no "frills." Even Dean Harold Benjamin's charming satire, *The Sabre Tooth Curriculum,* well known to all educators as a call for modernization of educational method and content, became to some a call for utility in education, that is, for specific job training. A dramatic result of this upheaval in educational thought was seen in California where in early 1962 the State Legislature passed the "Fisher Bill" which called for a major revision of credential requirements and empowered the State Board of Education to draw up the regulations necessary to implement the bill. Had the legislative measure been put into effect as originally intended by the State Board, the various arts would have been eliminated as subjects for a teaching credential in California.[3]

Enduring Truths

In spite of the utilitarian tendency in educational thought, that is, the tendency to assume human education has the practical function of preparation for making a living, making a home and raising a family in a technologically oriented society, one ancient, worldwide truth still holds. Any animal makes a living, gives birth to and rears its offspring, obtains shelter, and even explores its universe. It is true that human beings have made some remarkable refinements in these basic pursuits but the unknown man who died in his cave 5,000 years ago after making a living with spear and ax made no less or no greater an impression on human progress than the man who passed away this year after making his living with an electronic computer – or the gray wolf who perished alone in the snows of the Yukon after a successful life with fang and claw. All three received educations that were practical for their societies and all three may have a proportionately narrow or broad understanding of themselves, their relationship to their fellow-creatures and their relationship to their universe. Education for making a living, for making a home and raising a family is a part but only a part of the story – the part which may be called animal, which is carried on in every lair, den, cave and burrow on every hill and in every valley on the face of the earth. Education that is concerned with what a child needs as he grows, that enables the child to continue his growth even after he reaches physical maturity, that helps him achieve an appreciable degree of human worth – this kind of education is the other part of the story. Meeting these needs is a function of education with which every teacher must be concerned.

---

[3]The California situation is summarized in Lee Korf's "Annual Report of Southern California District AETA" (Washington: American Educational Theatre Association, July 24, 1963, Mimeographed).

Nonutilitarian Needs

The needs of a growing human being are many. He has physical needs; he has to do and play. He has mental needs; he must find out what and how and why. His social needs must be met with an understanding of his relation to the group, the community, and the world. His spiritual needs demand development of his personal spirit, his personality and individuality. Finally he has emotional needs; he must learn to release and control his emotions and develop his "feelings." Everyone in education is concerned with these needs. Although some specialists may emphasize one or more of them, none may forget any of them for teachers teach human beings, not animals. A teacher therefore must do more than prepare a person to make a living; he must meet human needs.

Some of the attributes of man that truly set him off from the animal – that give some indication of his worth as a human being – are his imagination, his ability to create, his sense of beauty, his sense of the aesthetic, and his appreciation of form. These are attributes that must be developed if human beings are to achieve some stature, some measure of dignity and of worth. These attributes are expressed in that area of human endeavor generally called the creative arts. Sensitivity to the arts therefore constitutes a uniquely human ability, one which all human beings need to develop.[4]

Reasons for the Arts

There are two major reasons for developing understanding of and sensitivity to the arts. First, the arts are important to human beings because they are ways of arriving at truth. The artist's insight is keener than that of ordinary people; his response to life is more keenly felt and more keenly expressed. This is one of the things, after all, that makes him an artist. He feels or senses the essence or meaning of things whether that meaning be found in a simple emotion stimulated by a silent sunflower whose blossom always seeks the sun, or in a more complex emotion stimulated by compassion for the human predicament of people caught in war. Having gained an insight into a truth lying in an event, situation, or thing, the artist is moved to move others; to transfer the insight he has gained, the truth he has known, to other human beings; to present them with a view of life; to move them to experiencing a truth about themselves, about their relationship to their fellow men, or their relationship to their universe or their deity.

---

[4]Throughout this discussion, "arts" refers to the aesthetic or creative arts rather than what are commonly called the practical arts.

Value of Understanding

As a result of experiencing this revelation of truth, people become better people because they become more understanding people. This is true whether they are moved to pity with Arthur Miller by the effect of false goals on a man or stimulated to laughter with Molière by the foibles of man. It is true whether they are moved by a Renaissance painter to celebrate the magnificence of man or stimulated by a contemporary "pop" artist to sneer at the silliness of man. The arts help people to recognize the intense and continuing value of the human being who can be anything from the exalted figure of the Greek tragedians to the pointless creature of the contemporary absurdists. Because the arts help human beings understand themselves, discover truths about themselves and gain an insight into the nature of their lives, it is important that human beings develop a sensitivity to the arts. Of all the arts, the art of theatre deals exclusively with man and although this art has often been the instrument of the most trivial entertainment, it is nevertheless a universal means of understanding man. The understanding of man is one of the greatest needs facing any child in school, any student in college, or any human being in the world. Truths about the nature of man must be sought and the need to seek and discover these truths must be felt by all children in school. The need exists; it is incumbent on teachers first to develop in children a feeling of the need and then to help them meet the need. Truths about the nature of the human being, his relation to his fellows and to his universe may be discovered through the arts.

Blocks to Communication

The second major reason for developing understanding of and sensitivity to the arts is that the arts are the most universal means of communication among people. There are many things that interfere with communication. Inexactness is probably the most obvious block. Consider the simple concept of "bigness" and compare what the word "big" conveys to the child looking through a window, the biologist looking through a microscope or the astronomer looking through a telescope. Consider the even greater problem in communicating exactly the much more complicated meanings of "love," "hate," or "frustration." It is easily seen why inexactness often results in the confusion or embarrassment of one or all parties involved in the communication.

Another block to communication is ineptness. Many motion pictures, television programs, stage plays, novels, poems, and comic strips have based their laughter-provoking premises on man's clumsiness in attempting to express himself. In a more serious vein, a real problem faces the parent who must discipline his child while somehow still conveying his feeling of love for the child. Consider the predicament of the teacher who must condemn the work of a child while somehow conveying the idea that the child himself is not condemned. The breakdown in communication that occurs at these times due to the ineptness of the transmitter of the communication, the receiver, or both, is a situation familiar to almost everyone.

Misinterpretation of a word or act is another hindrance to communication that nations as well as people go to great lengths to avoid. The ancient joke about the man with a wink in one eye having his malady taken to mean something other than a muscular problem has its counterpart in daily existence. The "Darling!" uttered by a movie star ought not to be misinterpreted as genuine personal endearment. Many an election has been lost by a candidate who misinterpreted opinion polls and many an examination has been failed by a student who misinterpreted instructions.

Finally, and above all, the subjectivity of man constantly hinders communication, that is, man constantly tends to see events in terms of his own experience. The "Oriental mind" was for generations inscrutable to many Occidentals simply because the Occidental placed Oriental thought and behavior in an Occidental frame. "He will react the way I react and behave the way I behave" is an error in assumption made by man throughout his history. Man tends to put things in his own terms. One of the difficult jobs facing a teacher is finding out not just what he must teach but whom he must teach. This is a never-ending quest because the "who" changes with every pupil the teacher has throughout his teaching career. This is one reason that a good teacher can teach the same subject on the same grade level year after year with vigor and excitement: with every class he meets a new challenge to overcome his own subjectivity, to understand new people, to find out who they are, to meet them on their home ground, and to help them move out to uncover new ground. This is what makes teaching young people one of the most demanding, most responsible and most exciting professions in the world. This is what makes teaching an art as well as a science. Unless a teacher can overcome some of his own subjectivity and learn who his pupils are, his communication will be inadequate and he can expect little more than surface learning to occur.

Surmounting Blocks to Communication

It is clear that there are many hindrances to communication and that words alone are frequently an impoverished means of conveying meaning. The artist, on the other hand, can show understanding, meaning, feeling and emotion that cannot be communicated in any other way. The produced play, for instance, through character and action, can form a bridge between the subjectivity of the playwright and that of the viewer; between the subjectivity of the actor or the designer and that of the audience. The costumer or the director may be incapable of communicating in words precisely their feelings, but through the play they communicate their special comment on joy or sorrow, on beauty or sordidness, on hope or despair, without hesitation and without fear of being misunderstood.

In addition to being a bridge between the subjectivity of the artist and that of the audience, the arts are a bridge between one observer's subjectivity and that of another observer. Seated in a theatre, for instance, may be a thousand or more people, all strangers to one another. As the play progresses they laugh in common, are apprehensive in common, share emotions in common and share a common understanding. When the play is over they are no longer strangers. They have been united in a common bond more real and more pervasive than any oath they might take together or any conversation they might hold. Their individual fears, prejudices, loves, hates and many of the other things that create the subjectivity of human beings have been bridged, if only temporarily, by art. That this is so has been demonstrated time and again by strangers in the lobby of a theatre who are willing to exchange smiles or even words after a play but who avoid any such evidence of human recognition and understanding before the play. These bridges between the subjectivity of people are greatly needed and can be built by learning to understand and appreciate the arts.

Those are some of the things that make the arts, and especially the social art of theatre, important to the growing, learning, young person. He can come closer to knowing truth, he can communicate more readily and he can achieve some degree of his potential worth as a human being. If he can do these things he need have no worry about the specific job in which he will make his living. He will have no problem in finding a place in life in which he will be happy, productive and vital. He will make a home and he will make a living. Above all, he will realize some measure of his worth as a human being.

The Nature of Creative Dramatics

Granted the importance of theatre art in meeting needs of growing young people, the question is one of where and how to start. All human beings are potentially creative. Indeed, studies have shown that every child is endowed with those sensibilities that characterize the artist.[5] He has sensitivity, imagination and a willingness, even a desire, to express his feelings and his responses to life openly and imaginatively. All too often his creative urge may be stifled by the requirements of a technological society oriented to utilitarianism. Whenever a child stops being creative, it is held, one can be certain it is because outside influences have inhibited his development.[6] One of the teacher's jobs, to put it simply, is to develop, not inhibit the child's creativity, sensitivity and imagination. The child needs skills, most certainly, but he also needs imagination if he is to use those skills for human ends. He needs to express himself creatively and he needs to improvise imaginatively with those skills and with himself, that is, with his own native tools, his body and his voice.

The process of developing the child's ability to express himself creatively in a group situation, improvising imaginatively with his body and his voice, is known variously as creative dramatics, creative drama, child drama, or playmaking.

The fundamental purpose of creative dramatics, then, is essentially that of education in general: to foster the growth and development of the child. It does this specifically by helping him to develop his individual spirit within the group while at the same time developing cooperation with the group, and by helping him develop self-realization, imagination and creativity. Through creative dramatics the child therefore is enabled to improve social attitudes and relationships, achieve greater confidence and emotional stability, become increasingly aware of his environment, improve vocal and bodily expression, and develop independent thinking and personal creativity.

Requirements of Creative Dramatics

The requirements of creative dramatics are few, consisting only of a group of children with a qualified leader and a space in which to function. There is no need for a script or for the technical aids so frequently associated with theatre production — no scenery, lighting, costumes or make-up. The only physical environment required is a space such as almost any classroom can provide with the tables and chairs pushed back. These tables or desks and chairs may, of course, be used from time to time. There is no audience but that possibly provided by the participants themselves

---

[5]Victor E. D'Amico, *Creative Teaching in Art.* New York: International Textbook Company, 1953.

[6]Viktor Lowenfeld, *Creative and Mental Growth* (New York: The Macmillan Company, 1947), pp. 1-4.

waiting for their turn to create and evaluating the work of their classmates. The absence of an audience indicates one of the differences between creative dramatics and theatrical display. "Theatrical," as Stark Young makes clear in his excellent discussion of the nature of theatre, pertains to the theatre and to performance.[7] Indeed, it is held by some that it is for the sake of an audience that theatre exists.[8] Unlike children's theatre, then, creative dramatics is a participant-centered experience and an audience is to be avoided. Children's theatre, on the other hand, is designed for a child audience and generally uses adult performers. It is a fully sophisticated theatre art utilizing all the techniques of the art to create a finished, polished performance for an audience of children. Although children's theatre is an important part of a child's education, comparable to visiting an art gallery, it lies in an area outside the scope of this chapter.

The requirement of a qualified leader is most important if the dramatic activity of the children is to be truly creative. The fundamentals of creative leadership are those of any good teacher. The creative leader must have imagination: he must be aware, resourceful, able to recognize potentiality in simplicity, and able to awaken the imagination of others. He must have spirit: he must be enthusiastic and able to fire the spirits of others. He must have the quality of greatness: he must be willing to teach by example, to enter into the spirit of the child's activity with genuine enjoyment, and yet be able to guide.[9] Certain attributes of the good teacher can be emphasized as especially important for the creative dramatics leader. In addition to being understanding and creative, the leader must be discriminating and able to help the unselective child to select so that form can be developed from the formless.[10] The role of the leader has been further described as that of one who provides the proper stimulation for creative thinking.[11] Specifically, the leader must have four basic capabilities.

1. He must know how to set the stage, so to speak, for the creative act, that is, he must provide a suitable climate and mood and prepare the child emotionally and intellectually to exercise his imagination in order to create character and motivated action. This frequently includes preparing the parents as well as the children so they will not only be interested but

---

[7]Stark Young, *The Theatre* (New York: Hill and Wang, 1954), p. 49.

[8]Theodore W. Hatlen, *Orientation to the Theatre* (New York: Appleton-Century-Crofts, 1962), p. 269.

[9]Geraldine Brain Siks, *Creative Dramatics* (New York: Harper and Brothers, 1958), pp. 122-130.

[10]Winifred Ward, *Drama with and for Children*. Bulletin 1960, No. 30 (Washington: U. S. Department of Health, Education and Welfare, 1960), p. 20.

[11]Burdette S. Fitzgerald, *World Tales for Creative Dramatics and Storytelling* (Englewood Cliffs, New Jersey: Prentice-Hall, Inc., 1962), p. 1.

will also provide encouragement. The teacher must motivate the child to understand a situation, feeling, or event and, once understanding it, to be enthusiastic about demonstrating it. He might ask the children, for instance, to remember with closed eyes a place they associate with some pleasant event, to recall the various sensual responses associated with the place and event and to relive those responses in their imagination. When the situations are discussed and the children are enthusiastic about demonstrating their feelings, they are then ready to create dramatically.

2. The leader must be equipped to provide the idea or stimulus for dramatic creativity. This may be a situation, event or object uncovered in a "show-and-tell" experience shared by either the child or the teacher; a selection of music or poetry; a true or fictional story; a current or historic event; or an idea uncovered in the preparation for the creative dramatics experience.

3. The leader must provide the opportunity for free response, must encourage that response, and be able to guide it and develop it into form. This requires on the part of the leader not only a strong interest in theatre but a sound understanding of character and action, their interrelationship, and the means of creating them. It follows that the successful leader of creative dramatics must have a sound working knowledge of the art of theatre.

4. The leader must be able to guide the children in evaluation. Through careful questioning, for instance, he must guide the children to distinguish between the believable and the unbelievable in a creation of character or action, to recognize honesty and completeness in expression, and must encourage the children to experiment, to venture, to develop and expand their imaginations, and to improve their skill in the use of their native dramatic tools, their bodies and their voices.

The Functions of Creative Dramatics

Educators generally ascribe two legitimate, basic functions to creative dramatics: that of an art in itself to be taught alongside any other art such as music, and that of a tool or method either for teaching other subject areas or for correcting personal or social aberrations. The first function, that of generally meeting human needs through the art experience, has been discussed above. The function of creative dramatics as a method for treating problems in personal or social adjustment lies in the realm of psychodrama and sociodrama, both highly specialized fields that lie outside the scope of the present discussion. A third function, that of recreation disassociated from education, has been attributed to creative dramatics in the past but has been rightly discredited.[12] Although there may be a few places in the United States where the attitude still prevails that creative dramatics is a useless though harmless way of keeping children occupied during leisure time, such an attitude is fast disappearing. There is, in addition, a growing awareness of the meaning of recreation in modern educational thought, a meaning more closely associated than in the past with the concept of re-creating. It is not unusual today to find close cooperation between workers in recreation programs and those in creative dramatics.

As a teaching tool used in other areas, creative dramatics has been successfully integrated in the elementary school program in many cities not only in language arts but in such areas as nature study, science, and social studies. In all these areas of study, there are five broad, common objectives in using the art:

1. To highlight material studied in a given unit.
2. To intensify the child's experience in the area studied.
3. To stimulate further investigation and study.
4. To develop the ability to integrate subject matter.
5. To increase the desire for learning.

Creative Dramatics and Nature Study

In nature study, for instance, natural phenomena are made a part of the child's experience through dramatization. Events determined by or accompanying the change of seasons thus are made real and meaningful to the child because through his personal creation he makes them part of his personal experience. He may create the story of Mike and Esther, two robins, who have trouble building their nest in the Spring. They search for the right materials, carefully shape the nest in the right kind of tree, and invent a song as they rhythmically flap their wings. Seeds grow, flowers open their petals to the sun, spiders spin their webs, eggs hatch and dangers appear and are overcome in the struggle for life. Finally, clouds blow up, wind bends the trees, leaves fall, seeds are scattered in their own special way, the rain comes down in torrents and the birds give up their home to fly to the South.

Creative Dramatics in Social Studies

Creative dramatics is used successfully in many schools to help the child understand the nature of the events, activities or situations studied

[12]Winifred Ward, *Playmaking with Children* (New York: Appleton-Century-Crofts, Inc., 1957), p. 16.

in a given unit and to understand the feelings, the choices, the lives, and the human predicament of the people involved in historic and current events, in the trades and professions, in government, industry and agriculture, and as an aid to understanding and comparing the various cultures.

Uses of Creative Dramatics in the Language Arts

Creative dramatics is readily used as a tool in conjunction with the language arts for the two arts are closely related. In this connection it has two major values. First, words can be brought to life and their meanings intensified by means of the kinesthetic sense when verbal symbols and mental images are physically portrayed. Thus reading, listening, speaking, and less directly, writing, can be motivated and understanding and appreciation enhanced. The second value, one less obvious but perhaps even more important than the first, involves the nature of language as an art, Creative dramatics can be used to develop an understanding and appreciation of the fundamental qualities of the art of language, written or spoken as poetry or prose. These qualities, common to all the arts under various names, are unity, emphasis, coherence, balance, rhythm, and mood.[13]

1. Unity is adherence to the subject; the relating of all parts to the whole. In any properly constructed paragraph there is a central topic and everything in the paragraph must deal with or contribute to that central topic. In like manner in any dramatic entity there is a central idea or concept and unassociated, irrelevant, or disconnected bits of expression must be avoided. In addition, unity demands the sufficient and proper development of a concept within a unit. Inadequate expression of an emotion or idea in a dramatic entity violates the same principle as inadequate development or support of an idea in a unit of written or spoken composition.

2. Emphasis is the expression of the kernel, the core, the heart and soul of a concept and can be achieved by four general means:

   a. Rearrangement: the positioning in time and space so a specified part is more easily recognizable.
   b. Proportion: the apparent subordination of the less important to the more important.

---

[13]Unity, coherence, emphasis, selectivity, proportion, rearrangement, intensification, and mood are suggested as "principles" underlying all art by Alexander Dean, *Fundamentals of Play Directing* (New York: Holt, Rinehart and Winston, 1941), pp. 5-9.

c. Intensification: the use of contrast, unexpectedness, movement, or vibrancy to achieve a compelling, dynamic, climactic, or "dramatic" effect.

d. Repetition: The recurrence of a line, sound, form, rhythm, movement, color, mood, or other element to make that element insistent or apparent.

3. Coherence is the logical and probable relationship of one part to another part within the whole. In order to maintain coherence, every student of composition avoids such hindrances as misplaced modifiers and dangling participles. A form of coherence in dramatic art known as motivation is highly important. One action must be logically related to another or must evolve from it and an action performed by a character must "grow out of" that character, that is, the action must be motivated by the nature of the character. A more technical application of coherence is the maintaining of logical relationships among sound, sight and sense – what is said and done must suit the meaning of the situation.

4. Balance is an equality in weighting of two or more parts and may be considered as a special kind of proportion. In English composition, parallelism is an example of one use of balance. The dramatic artist is concerned with balance between opposing forces in a conflict, the relationship of one character to another, the relative strengths of the protagonist and the antagonist, the balance of vocal and physical characteristics of the various actors, and the weighting of the visual aspects of a dramatic entity.

5. Rhythm is periodicity or pulsation, the more or less regular recurrence of emphasis. In dramatic art it is sometimes further defined by attributing to it a quality of producing "a conscious or subconscious feeling of organization and progression."[14] Some even suggest that this progression has direction, leading to the final aim of the artist.[15] In music, various types of rhythm are well defined and can be named and specifically described. In poetry, some rhythmic units and devices are well defined and given names such as the iambus, rhyme, and certain kinds of consonance, while other forms of rhythm can be described only generally by such terms as "flippant" or "ponderous." In dramatic art, rhythm occurs in many forms, some exceedingly complex, but unfortunately specific definitions are almost completely lacking. Rhythm is important in dramatic art and in the development of sensitivity and creativity in children, however,

---

[14]H. D. Albright, William P. Halstead and Lee Mitchell, *Principles of Theatre Art* (Cambridge, Massachusetts: Houghton Mifflin Company, 1955), p. 431.

[15]Richard Boleslavsky, *Acting: the First Six Lessons* (New York: Theatre Arts Books, 1949), p. 112.

so its various manifestations and uses in dramatic art are described following.

Rhythm in drama is most easily noted in poetic dialogue where the recurrence of certain accents, sounds and inflections establishes the rhythm of spoken language. The rhythm of such poetry, however, is so arranged that it suits the sense, mood or emotional content of the action. In the following excerpt from a speech by Dromio in *The Comedy of Errors,* Shakespeare created a rhythm that gives a flippant, light, tripping effect by using a great many short vowels, a great many consonants, especially the "stop" consonant sounds of "k," "t," "p," and "b," very few long vowels, and very few of the "glide" consonants such as "l" and "r." In addition, the phrasing is short and abrupt, agreeing with the short and sharply defined thought units.

> The capon burns, the pig falls from the spit;
> The clock hath strucken twelve upon the bell –
> My mistress made it one upon my cheek;
> She is so hot because the meat is cold;
> The meat is cold because you come not home;

The metric pattern that Shakespeare used in this speech is iambic pentameter, the same as that used by Marlowe in the following lines from *Doctor Faustus.* Now, however, the rhythm is ponderous, giving an effect of great sweep and dignity. The words and phrases are longer, there are more long vowels, more use of the gliding consonants of "l" and "r," and longer, larger and more impressive cadences to make the rhythm suit the emotional content and meaning of the action.

> Monarch of hell, under whose black survey
> Great potentates do kneel in awful fear,
> Upon whose altars thousand souls do lie,
> How am I vexèd with these villains' charms!

Poetic Prose

Closely related to poetic dialogue is poetic prose, an outstanding example of which appears in Singe's *Riders to the Sea.* In Maurya's prophetic lament just before the body of her last son is brought in, the individual accents of words and phrases rise to a series of climaxes, each one of which is followed by a three-beat cadence. Not only do the individual beats of syllables work together to form larger or heavier beats, but these small groups work together to form still larger beats of thought or emotion groupings. The tragic rhythm so created, linked to the tragic content of the dialogue and the action, can be detected even in a silent reading of Maurya's speeches but it must be remembered that Singe wrote the play not to be read silently but to be spoken aloud and acted. To the rhythm found in reading the words on the printed page, therefore, must be added the rhythm created by the human voice and that created by bodily movement, all coordinated to create the unified, coherent rhythms of dramatic dialogue.

Rhythm is an essential attribute of dramatic action as well as of dialogue and is achieved through the proper utilization of climaxes in a scene. A scene may begin with relatively low emotional content and gradually increase in intensity to a climax. This climax constitutes a beat or pulsation of dramatic action and these emotional beats are arranged to create a rhythmic pattern suiting the dramatic content of the scene. A play is a series of actions all making up the one, major, unified action. Each minor action has its own beat, that is, its own dramatic climax. An action begins, builds to a climax and is completed, transformed, or stopped by the beginning of a new action. The new action then builds to its climax and gives way to another new action. The line of these pulsations, their relationship to one another, their frequency, intensity, and arrangement create a rhythmic pattern which illuminates the action and gives it movement.

A typical example of this kind of rhythm can be found in a television "Western" play. A poker game is in progress at a table in a saloon. An argument developes between two of the men and builds in intensity. This action is stopped by a third man who demands that the cards be dealt. As the cards are dealt, everyone is suspicious of the dealer and the action of dealing builds to a climax. This action is ended when one man hits the dealer on the head with a bottle whereupon a new action, that of a rough-and-tumble fight, ensues and builds to its climax. This entire scene is ended abruptly with a pistol shot as the United States marshal enters and starts a whole new action.

An alternation in thoughts expressed through both dialogue and movement creates a rhythm which in turn conveys mood and meaning in a dramatic action. The long opening speech of the character, Rose, in Harold Pinter's little play, "The Room," alternates between inconsequential references to household trivia and somewhat fearful references to a dark, basement apartment in what is otherwise a static scene. Yet these changes in thought, illuminated by appropriate changes in the voice and bodily movement of the character, create an erratic but pronounced rhythm that in turn creates an intense and foreboding mood, building suspense almost immediately and creating a sense of tension progression.

Extensive Variety Exists in Rhythm

Other kinds and uses of rhythm found in dramatic art are sometimes simple, sometimes complex, and almost numberless. Musical and dance dramas use the rhythms of music side by side with dramatic rhythms, the one supplementing and clarifying the other. Specific music rhythms can be combined with dramatic action as in *West Side Story* where the syncopated rhythm effects are intrinsic to the meaning of the play. Metrical dialogue is sometimes used for emphasis or to give a mechanical effect as in some expressionistic dramas. The art of drama, being so highly complex, affords a tremendous variety of rhythms but it is also an art that is highly representative of human life and therefore cannot bear rhythms that are made too obvious.

6. Mood is the essence of an object or event in terms of a generalized human feeling. It is a product of both content and form, deriving from the particular ways in which unity, emphasis, coherence, balance, and rhythm are used in the art object, from symbols and from the spectator's approach to the object or event. If a selection of poetry or of music with tripping rhythms and small, bright contrasts is used to simulate the creative activity of a group of children, for instance, one can expect the light, merry mood so created to influence their activity and it is to be expected that the resulting physical movements will be quick and light. The creating of mood is an important process in children's creative dramatics.

The Processes of Creative Dramatics

The processes of creative dramatics, like those of any art, are interwoven and in actual practice can hardly be separated. For obvious reasons, however, they are described separately here and in increasing order of complexity, but it is to be remembered that not all processes will be found in any one creative dramatics experience nor would a series of "lessons" necessarily be built on the ascending order of complexity such as that given below. The experience described at the beginning of this chapter, for instance, though an initial one for the children, involved the enactment of a complete story with concomitant exploration of rudiments of character portrayal, while only a beginning was made in developing some skill with basic sense perception and rhythm appreciation. Specifically, the processes are those found in five kinds of activities or experiences: dramatic play, rhythmic experiences, sense perception, mood development, and story creation.

Dramatic Play

Known to many people as make-believe, dramatic play is an experience common to almost all young children. The child invents an imaginary playmate or imagines himself an astronaut, teacher, rabbit, or railroad engine and creates a suitable environment for the role in which he has cast himself. One six-year-old invented a character he called "George" who lived in the drain of the wash basin and made gurgling sounds as the water went down. For more than a year George was responsible for other sounds about the house and from time to time would come out to play with the child. Then the family moved and when they heard a strange sound in the new house, the parents suggested it was made by George. The child disagreed and in one breath showed that he, like all normal children, recognized the difference between imagination and reality, playing and being, that he could be quite objective about his creations and further, that he could creatively explain the discard of an imaginative object when the natural process of maturation had made that particular creation no longer necessary. The child said simply, "Aw, George isn't real and anyhow, he just lived at the old house." In such dramatic play the child gives expression to a basic creative urge, an urge that is sometimes stifled, unfortunately, by unknowing or unsympathetic adults. By creating a character for himself and inventing situations in which that character can operate, the child learns about his environment and prepares to cope with it. He develops his imagination, gains skill in the use of his body and voice, and improves his ability in problem solving.

Stimuli for Dramatic Play

Motivation for guided dramatic play is found in poetry, music, riddles, stories, class trips, holidays, special events, or just the day-in and day-out routines of school and home life. In turn, properly guided dramatic play motivates attitudes that help get jobs done. It does not substitute phantasy for reality and shield the child from facing and coping with life situations. Instead it helps him prepare for experiences he must meet by developing in him positive, creative attitudes toward those experiences. Thus, for example, he is prepared for making trips, performing social amenities, accepting a new arrival at school or at home, visiting the doctor or dentist, or understanding and observing rules.

Throughout these dramatic play experiences, the involvement of the child's emotion is important. It is not enough for him to assume a character and engage in some action; he must find excitement, perhaps, or suspense, happiness or sadness. Feelings must be involved. Without the involvement of feelings an action by itself is a physical and sometimes an intellectual exercise, valuable enough in itself, but not necessarily creative in terms of dramatic art. If a child says simply, "I'm a bird," and perfunctorily waves his arms up and down, he may reap some physical benefits but hardly any creative ones such as might obtain were he to experience the joy of one of the four-and-twenty blackbirds released from a pie. Action motivated by the feelings of the character differentiates creative dramatic play from other forms of play such as the ordinary singing game. The creative dramatics leader helps the child understand the character, the situation in which the character finds himself and the feelings involved, and encourages him to express through action whatever emotion the situation invokes; in other words the leader helps the child to motivate the action.

Rhythmic Experiences

Of all the underlying attributes of art, rhythm is probably the one most easily recognized by children and is certainly one to which they readily respond. The development of a sense of rhythm is important for the child's understanding and appreciation of and participation in the arts. Creative rhythmic experiences are designed specifically to develop physical, intellectual, and emotional responses to rhythm. In younger children, simpler rhythms are used to develop and coordinate the larger muscles. With older children, more complex rhythms are introduced and greater skill is developed in the control and use of the smaller muscles.

Creative Aspects of Rhythmic Experiences

Like dramatic play, rhythmic experiences are made creative experiences when character and motivation are introduced. There are certain values in simple walking, marching or skipping exercises, generally performed in a circle with a musical accompaniment, but with no motivation other than the request of the teacher. These exercises take on creative values, however, when the children assume the identities of characters motivated by feelings and when their action suits the nature of their characters. Thus the children become members of a United States Olympic team, perhaps, joyfully marching beneath their flag past the reviewing stand on their way to receive a trophy. They might be old men, hot and tired, hobbling along with canes, determined to go the full length of the parade before sitting down and resting. They might be dolphins leaping with excitement as they respond to the applause of children along the shore. Similar dramatic situations involving emotion may be invented for other standard rhythmic exercises: mowing the yard when the grass is easy to cut and when it is tall and tough; throwing snowballs from a snow-fort – and getting hit by a soft, wet one; climbing a steep ladder to rescue a frightened kitten caught high in a tree; swimming away from Captain Hook's ship in cold, rough water to reach the shore where weiners wait to be roasted over a big bonfire.

Older children are challenged by more complex situations. A mechanized factory suggests many starting points for experiences with rhythm that have virtually no limit to their complexity. A trip to a soft-drink bottling plant, a large bakery, or almost any factory will reveal many rhythmic operations of varying complexities which can be personified by the children. Variety and excitement can be introduced when one part misbehaves or when the whole operation speeds up until the machine flies apart or a switch is thrown and the machine grinds slowly to a halt. Sound effects to accompany the various operations can be made with stamping feet, clapping hands, snapping fingers or clucking tongues, or properly selected music can be used to provide background, establish tempo, and create a desired mood. Such experiences require considerable concentration even for adults, and are excellent for developing rhythm appreciation. A wide variety of creative rhythmic experiences are suggested in publications available in most libraries and the leader of creative dramatics should explore the potentials of such experiences.[16]

Sense Perception

Response to environment depends on awareness of that environment and awareness in turn is determined in a large measure by the senses of touch, taste, sight, smell, and hearing. It follows, then, that the development of skill in sense perception and skill in showing response to sense stimuli is an important process in creative dramatics training. The development of sense perception and expression is generally concomitant with the development of other skills in creative dramatics, especially with younger children, and is motivated by the feelings or emotions. It is not difficult, however, to associate the emotions with sense stimuli as many sensations can be roughly classified on the emotional bases of either pleasant or unpleasant. Thus there may be a pleasant smell, a bad taste, an ugly sight, a friendly touch, or a horrible sound.

---

[16]See especially Gladys Andrews, *Creative Rhythmic Movement* (Englewood Cliffs, New Jersey: Prentice-Hall, Inc., 1952).

Sources of Sense Perception Activities

A frequent starting point for work in sense perception is an actual experience of the children which might be provided by a trip to the zoo, for instance, or by a number of objects brought to the classroom by them or the teacher. Adequate preparation is made during such an experience for the subsequent recall of the sensory impressions. When the stimulus is removed, that is, when the trip is over or the objects have been taken away, the children are encouraged to relive the sensory experiences and to react visibly to each remembered impression. Other sources for sensory experiences can be found in poetry, stories, music, objects in the classroom, or the children's own hands, hair, or clothing. Exercises in reacting to sensory stimuli that might be derived from actual life experiences include the following:

Touch: You are eating candy and some sticks to your hands. You are stroking a kitten and come across a burr.

Taste: You are drinking sweet lemonade and start nibbling on a bitter lemon seed.

Sight: You see a beautiful butterfly going from flower to flower and there is a sudden flash of lightning.

Smell: You enter a kitchen where cookies are baking and some milk boils over on the stove.

Hearing: You hear wind in the trees at night and a branch falls to the ground with a crash.

Almost any good text in acting will suggest other exercises to increase sensory awareness and response though such exercises may have to be adapted to suit the needs and experiences of a particular age group.[17]

Mood Development

Closely related to the development of sensory perception and response is the creation of moods. A brightly burning, crackling fire causes certain sensory responses – one sees a number of shades of orange and yellow in various shapes and hears certain explosive sounds in various degrees of loudness – but the sensory responses alone do not adequately convey the

---

[17]See for instance, Samuel Selden, *First Steps in Acting* (New York: Appleton-Century-Crofts, Inc., 1947), pp. 237-58.

essence or meaning of the fire. The essence is obtained by interpreting the information acquired by the senses in terms of feelings. The direction or nature of these feelings will vary depending on other accompanying intellectual or emotional stimuli and on the past experience of the viewer. Thus the same fire might create a warm, friendly, sleepy mood in one person, a merry, lively mood in another, and an apprehensive, even fearful mood in yet another. The overt response of the first person might be to lie down and go to sleep, of the second to jump up and dance, and of the third to cry and run away.

The fact that given stimuli produce varying moods makes a demand on the creative dramatics leader and at the same time provides him with an opportunity. The leader must adequately prepare the children for a creative experience by providing suitable stimuli for a given desired mood. If, for instance, a selection of poetry with a prevailing mood of mystery is used to provide the idea for a creative dramatics experience, it is desirable to establish a sense or feeling of the mysterious to key the children to the mood of the poem. This can be achieved by both sensory and intellectual means. The appearance of the classroom can be changed to make it darker, perhaps, or decorations and exhibits can be introduced. Sound stimuli can be added by means of carefully selected music or appropriate, strange sounds. An appeal to the sense of smell can be made by using one or more unusual perfumes such as are available in a great variety of room deodorants. Even strange flavors can be introduced in the form of mild spices such as thyme, oregano, or rosemary, though younger children are less willing to experiment with unknown tastes than older ones. Whatever sensory appeal is used, the purpose is to stimulate interest and help create the appropriate mood. Anything inappropriate to the central mood and idea of the poem is avoided. Intellectually, the children are prepared by questions designed to stimulate and channel thought and to help them interpret their sensory responses in terms of the appropriate mood.

Ways of Introducing Complex Experiences

Specific exercises in creating mood can be used to introduce more complex experiences in creative dramatics or they can be evolved from simpler experiments or from work with sense perception. Each of the relatively static situations in the list which follows suggests a particular mood and involves a number of creative processes for its realization. To these can be added a great many more situations whose number and variety are limited only by the imagination. As children become experienced in creative dramatics and come to understand the nature of mood, they will have many suggestions of their own for situations that illustrate a specific mood and will delight in creating that mood with the situations they themselves have invented.

1. In a game of hide-and-seek, the person looking for you is just coming up to where you are hiding.
2. The school bus has just left without you.
3. You have just won a race.
4. The candy bar you worked hard to earn has fallen in the mud.
5. A dolphin is doing tricks just for you.

More complex and dynamic mood situations provide the beginnings of story creation. To any of the foregoing situations, for example, might be added a subsequent action that sustains the mood, breaks it, or changes it to another, contrasting mood. With older children, further variety is introduced in these or other situations by experimenting with mood effects on a number of disparate characters. In other complex situations, a musical selection, poem, story, or descriptive paragraph selected for its mood content may require that the children create character and character-motivated action for full realization of the mood. Dramatic play which tends toward establishing a definite mood might well evolve into a complete story with character, action, conflict, and resolution. An example of such play might be "picnic fun" in which the prevailing and sustained mood is one of joy and excitement with a contrast in mood provided at the end. There would be preparation for the picnic, getting to the site, activities at the picnic, and then a rush for shelter because of a sudden rainstorm.

Story Creation

The most obvious and frequent source of stories for creative enactment is the children's own reading, whether it be that prescribed by the course of study in language arts or other subject areas or that come across in collateral materials or simply in free reading. A closely allied and frequently used source is a story read or told, preferably the latter, by the creative dramatics leader. Not all stories, however, are suitable for dramatization. The following criteria are useful as a guide in making a selection.

1. Characters, whether human or not, should be clearly defined, logically motivated, and should be active rather than passive. Younger children are capable of creating characters with relatively simple motivations while more complex characters are challenging to older children. Whether simple or complex the characters, particularly the main ones,

should have interesting though not necessarily pleasing traits, and should be distinct from one another. Generally the nature of the character is determined in a story as in life – by what the character does and why he does it. Other clues are what he says and why he says it; how he responds to others and how they respond to him; and how he behaves in front of others and how he behaves when others are not around.

2. Conflict expressed through action is the key to drama in any story. The main character must want something, must go after it, must face opposition, and must act to overcome that opposition. The action should be organized in a well-defined plot that advances in a relatively straight line from attack, to major climax or crisis, to resolution.[18] If an otherwise good story lacks sufficiently clear organization for a particular age-group, or if one or more subplots obscure the main plot, the story can be adapted and retold. Adequate preparation by the leader is necessary, however, for such retelling.

3. The setting for the action should be interestingly and clearly described. Not only should there be adequate details about the place of the action but such elements as the time of day and the time of year, the weather, and the country should be included. As the action moves from place to place, new settings should be clearly indicated.

4. The language should evoke mental images with strong sensory and emotional appeal. While long descriptive passages should be avoided, descriptive modifiers of substantives and verbs are desirable. Good language is most likely to be found in good literature.

5. The central idea, subject, mood, or theme should suit the age group and the occasion. In dramatic art, the theme is a statement in a sentence of the author's point of view or insight into life as demonstrated by the action in a given work and may be strong in some dramatic stories and weak in others. In a fable by Aesop, the theme is expressed as a moral which the story demonstrates and which is an important element in the story. In some excellent stories that are quite suitable for dramatization, the theme may be weak, unimportant, or even trite. The central idea or subject, sometimes called the literary theme, may sometimes prove a more helpful guide than dramatic theme in selecting a story for creative dramatization.

---

[18]The leader of creative dramatics should become familiar with dramatic structure. See especially Kenneth Thorpe Rowe, *Write That Play* (New York: Funk and Wagnalls Company, 1939).

Extent of Element Representation

Not all of the foregoing elements will be fully developed in all stories suitable for dramatization. Although all elements should be present, their complete development in the printed story is hardly desirable as this would leave little motivation for the children to exercise their own creativity. Before the child can create, however, he must find adequate answers to the questions of who, what, why, where, and when and he must be stimulated to find more answers and to translate those answers into action. A story in which all elements are fully developed might benefit children more as literature on the printed page than as creative dramatics on the classroom floor when few of the purposes of creative dramatics are served.

Stories for dramatizing can be found in narrative poems. Non-narrative poetry demands greater exercise of the imagination in developing plot and lyrical poetry may provide only a mood or feeling as a starting point for story development. News and current and historic events provide action and sometimes character for a story but motivation, feelings, and some sense of intimacy with and understanding of the characters generally has to be developed and a sense of conflict introduced to make the story suspenseful and dramatic.

Music, like lyric poetry, can set a mood as a starting point for story creation. "Programmatic" music is generally more valuable for this purpose than "absolute" music. Some music almost tells a story and some has become traditionally associated with a particular story. The creative dramatics leader guards against any tendency to force children into creating a story that fits preconceived or traditional notions of the program of a particular musical selection. Dukas' "The Sorcerer's Apprentice" does not conjur up in all children a vision of a Walt Disney cartoon character commanding a broom to carry water, although once the children have seen the motion picture *Fantasia* they will likely visualize Mickey Mouse whenever they hear the selection. Some music, like Ravel's "Bolero," sets a very strong mood but with very little and very slow development and may prove discouraging rather than encouraging to the imagination of young children.

Pictures, whether illustrations or individual paintings, are a rich source of story ideas. The pictures should be large enough for all to see clearly and are best if in color. Action pictures with strong mood content provide opportunities for the children to exercise their imaginations as they find answers to Who? What? and Why? Older, more experienced children may find challenges and excitement in developing a story from the stimulation provided by a nonobjective painting but more realistic paintings provide a more productive basis for creative dramatics with young children.

Approaches to Dramatizing Stories

Whether a complete story is told to the children or the children develop their own story from, perhaps, a mood suggested by a fragment of music, the approach to dramatizing the story is essentially the same. Characters must be created – characters who feel and do. A character, even a fully developed one in a story that is told, does not live and breathe until the child creates him with his own imagination, his own feelings, and his own body and voice. The creative dramatics leader therefore leads the child first to understand the character, then to create the feelings of the character, then to act as the character motivated by those feelings. Similarly the story does not come to life dramatically until it is created by the children through their own feelings and actions. In this connection there need be no concern about a possible problem of the child's "being" the character or of his actually living the part. He "tries on" the character through his imagination – experimenting, appraising, rejecting, keeping, evaluating, and trying again. He does not become a tree bending to the wind, a conductor taking tickets, a gnome dancing in the moonlight or any other character or thing; rather he becomes what Martha Graham describes as "the miracle that is a human being, motivated, disciplined, concentrated."[19]

The child, then, does not become anything but rather creates the thoughts, creates the feelings, and creates the actions of the character, making them a part of his own experience. Having created character, with each child trying each character, perhaps, the children then proceed to create the individual segments of action that make up the play. A play is composed of a series of actions each one having its own point or meaning and the leader must have these actions and their meaning clearly in mind before beginning work with the children. The action units or "scenes" are developed one by one and new scenes added as the children find motivation for them, or dropped if there is no need for them. The function of the creative dramatics leader throughout this process is not that of the traditional theatre director but rather that of an inspiring guide who stimulates the children to do their own thinking, their own exploring, their own

---

[19]Martha Graham, "A Modern Dancer's Primer for Action," *Dance: A Basic Educational Technique,* ed., Frederick Rand Rogers (New York: The Macmillan Company, 1941), p. 178.

creating, and their own evaluating as he leads them toward a planned goal.

Uses of Dialogue in Dramatization

Dialogue is introduced when it can be properly motivated by the feelings of the characters. Generally a scene is developed first without dialogue, speech being added when it can be properly motivated by the feelings of the characters and the requirements of the scene. There is good reason for this. When a child reads a story or hears one, he readily translates words into action in his imagination, hence words easily become a substitute for action. When a scene is developed without dialogue, the meaning of the scene therefore has to be made clear by means of action and action alone, which is the very soul of drama. In addition, when the child does not have the crutch of words, particularly someone else's words, to depend upon, he is likely to realize more fully the nature and feelings of his character and likely to develop more fully the portrayal of that character.

After each characterization is attempted, each action performed, each scene played, and the whole play developed, there is a period of evaluation by the children themselves, guided by the leader, to find how something might be better done. Then there is the replaying to put the suggestions to work and to find improvement. This evaluation occurs after rather than during a bit of playing so as not to interrupt the creative process in action. The child creating the smallest Billy Goat Gruff may not be a Rembrandt, a Stravinsky, or an Olivier. He is nonetheless an artist at the moment, unknown and little, using his insight into life, using his imagination, concentrating, creating, communicating, and achieving some measure of his worth as a human being.

EXTENDING YOUR LEARNING

1. Examine and report objectively, on at least one of the various collections of plays for children. Are they childlike? are they interesting to you? (Develop other criteria during your class period.)
2. What is your position with respect to formal drama in the elementary school? Should children memorize parts, create scenery and costumes, etc.? Contrast the following: dramatic play, creative dramatics and formal dramatization. Which in the elementary school should receive major emphasis, or does this vary from level to level?
3. Examine a 'unit' developed for social studies, and list the opportunities within this unit for enrichment through creative dramatics. If no units are available, survey a chapter or group of chapters in a social studies textbook.

4. Select three or four trade (here defined as non-textbook) books written for either primary or intermediate grade children. Which characters might children portray with ease and enjoyment? Which incidents from the books would be interesting to recreate? Select one book which portrays a way of life or a group of characters rather far removed from that which is familiar and commonplace to the children you will probably teach. What might children learn through assuming such an unfamiliar role?
5. In class, in small groups if this would be more comfortable for you, assume the following roles:

   —— a rather embittered, crochety old teacher, about to retire, leaving her elementary classroom for the last time.

   —— a frightened, timid young teacher greeting her first pupils – a shy little boy, a mischievous, busy little girl, a retarded child who will be with you until he can be reassigned, and the rather "spoiled" only child of the wealthiest, most prominent family in the community.

6. Select a poem which has a definite mood. State the mood in terms of human feelings. Then gather objects which enhance or reinforce that mood through appeals to the senses of sight, hearing, smell, taste, and touch. Describe an action with characters and setting which might grow out of the mood.

   Repeat the exercise using as your starting point a selection of music, a painting, a piece of sculpture, a colorful scarf, or other suggestive object.

(Try these – a table makes a perfectly adequate stage for the puppet types suggested – an illusion can be created simply by draping the table with any cloth which is large enough to touch the floor. The puppeteer then crouches behind the table and the illusion is quite effective.)

BIBLIOGRAPHY

1. Albright, H. D., Halstead, William P., and Mitchell, Lee, *Principles of Theatre Art* (Cambridge, Mass.: Houghton Mifflin Company, 1955).
2. Andrews, Gladys, *Creative Rhythmic Movement* (Englewood Cliffs: Prentice-Hall, Inc., 1952).
3. Boleslavsky, Richard, *Acting: The First Six Lessons,* (New York: Theatre Arts Books, 1949).
4. D'Amico, Victor E., *Creative Teaching in Art* (New York: International Textbook Co., 1953).
5. Dean, Alexander, *Fundamentals of Play Directing*; (New York: Holt, Rinehart and Winston, 1941).
6. Fitzgerald, Burdette S., *World Tales for Creative Dramatics and Storytelling* (Englewood Cliffs: Prentice-Hall, Inc., 1962).
7. Graham, Martha, "A Modern Dancer's Primer for Action," *Dance: A Basic Educational Technique,* ed., Frederick Rand Rogers (New York: The Macmillan Co., 1941).

8. Hatlen, Theodore W., *Orientation to the Theatre* (New York: Appleton-Century-Crofts, 1962).
9. Lowenfeld, Viktor, *Creative and Mental Growth* (New York: The Macmillan Company, 1947).
10. Rowe, Kenneth Thorpe, *Write That Play* (New York: Funk and Wagnalls Company, 1939).
11. Selden, Samuel, *First Steps in Acting* (New York: Appleton-Century-Crofts, Inc., 1947).
12. Siks, Geraldine Brain, *Creative Dramatics* (New York: Harper and Brothers, 1958).
13. Ward, Winifred, *Drama with and for Children,* Bulletin 1960, No. 30 (Washington: U. S. Department of Health, Education and Welfare, 1960).
14. Ward, Winifred, *Playmaking with Children* (New York: Appleton-Century-Crofts, Inc., 1957).
15. Young, Stark, *The Theatre,* (New York: Hill and Wang, 1954).

Chapter 4 Robert M. Bloom

A Program for Oral English

Long before the child experiences his first hours in school the pattern of his language growth starts to take shape. His ability to gather meaning and his ability to communicate are closely related and both develop together. His earliest training in speech commences when the names which his elders attach to the common objects of his environment become familiar to him and he begins as part of his basic speech experiments to imitate the sounds they repeat to him. While he is still a toddler, as a matter of fact, he can acquire a really substantial supply of words that are associated with his daily experiences, words that he understands and is able to pronounce fairly intelligibly. He learns to react to simple directives, such as *sit, stand, come, stay, walk, wait,* or *up,* and to make his own characteristic responses to those commands. At this point he begins to substitute verbal replies for nonverbal, oral articulation for gestures or emotional outbursts. His language education, in other words, has begun to "take."

As he continues to mature he is involved in deeper interests and more complex activities which inspire an even wider vocabulary grasp. Every new sensory adventure is likely to be a source of new understandings and might add subsequently to his index of descriptive words. A coaxing curiosity drives him to explore further, to make associations, to enrich his concepts, to ask questions. With careful guidance he can be led to narrate his impressions of what he has seen or heard, and will often do so in creditable fashion. Some of the words may be repeated over and over, some fumbled and mispronounced, some stammered; but the important thing is that in the gush of related ideas there has emerged a genuine pattern – and this word-pattern is a significant landmark in his linguistic achievement.

It is well to remember that by the time the child is ready for pre-primary schooling he has expanded his ability to communicate orally from one-word statements to simple sentences. He has built up an extensive speaking vocabulary which research has indicated may total at least 2,500 words and may perhaps exceed that figure by hundreds more. He can give a running account of what has caused him emotional distress or a detailed description of something he has encountered. It is clear that his education in oral expression is now well advanced.

Language development is not an orderly process that takes place in parallel sequences among children of the same age levels. Like physical growth and intellectual accomplishment it is quite complex in its rate and scale of progress. It depends upon so many factors that it is evident few children can follow a uniform path of mastery. In order to shape her curriculum, the teacher therefore is obliged to capitalize on the attainments of each of her pupils. She must understand the various elements influencing language growth and around them she must cut her pattern.

Guiding Principles for Building Instructional Programs

In the fulfillment of language goals the following principles seem most pertinent and should be considered in setting up a program:

1. *Some growth in language proficiency takes place constantly.* The rate may not be equal among children, but as each acquires a fund of new concepts through experiences of different kinds there is bound to be a vocabulary increase. The same situation occurs in the refinements of speaking. Some children without effort make remarkable gains in pronunciation and expressing ideas; others lag but with help can move ahead to close the gap.

2. *There is a difference in the pattern of maturity.* Progress in development centers first upon the natural endowment of the child and next upon the amount of meaningful experiences which make an impression upon the child. The pupil who is the product of a middle-class home where the parents are intelligent and capable and provide him with a warm and wholesome relationship is most likely to mature at an early age. A child of less fortunate background and experience may take longer in arriving at an acceptable point for formal schooling.

3. *The rate of growth is dependent upon a variety of conditions.* There are different phases of maturity which must be accounted for in the aggregate development of language among children. Any number of

conditions can retard or accelerate the growth of language proficiency. Parents can supply teachers with information for their registration forms which will tell them why one child is withdrawn and inarticulate while another seems independent, outgoing and sophisticated in language ability. The factors which may impede the growth of speech at one time or another during childhood years are too numerous to list in great detail. One example would be a siege of illness during which the child might be bedridden or confined without much companionship. Certainly such a physical defect as a cleft palate or a hare lip unless corrected by surgery may make a child reluctant to call attention to himself by talking. Physical fears, family friction, or feelings of inferiority could deprive a child of normal linguistic development. Other reasons for similar setbacks could include such conditions as periods of unusual insecurity, undernourishment, glandular changes, rapid physical growth, or a temporary deficiency in hearing. Any of these could be an episode which is brief or long-lasting but which might nevertheless be an obstacle in the path of steady progress.

4. *Individual differences offer a challenge to the teacher.* It is essential for teachers to realize that as far as their capabilities and inclinations are concerned children are not shaped in the same mold. Teachers must expect one child to be reserved and often unwilling to communicate while another chatters on tirelessly. Between the two types there may be no distinction in intelligence but in family background, in the kind of upbringing, in interaction among members of the family, in health, sensitivity and breadth of experience there could be a world of difference. The teacher must analyze the influences that have been brought to bear upon the child and take account of them in establishing a program of speech improvement. Both teacher and child stand to gain from such careful analysis.

Development of Speech in the Preprimary Years

For the preprimary pupil the basic means of expression is oral. To a great extent through the apparatus of speech he reveals his thinking processes, his desires, his phantasies; and he discloses as well the depth and breadth of his sensory perceptions – what he has learned by seeing, hearing, feeling, smelling and tasting. In many cases the older members of his family have advanced his readiness for formal training by providing him with calculated opportunities for learning. They have supplied him with the names of many objects in his little universe and have patiently coaxed him to point out the objects and repeat the sounds of their names until he mastered them. They have taught him little songs and poems to widen the scope of his vocabulary and his imagination. They have given him toys to manipulate, simple puzzles, games and coloring books to test his ingenuity and skill at identification.

The problem for the prekindergarten or the kindergarten teacher is to influence the child to reveal the extent of his growth. This can be done through observation – by watching him in his interaction with others, by listening to his conversation, by asking questions, and by analyzing his speech. The latter can often be accomplished with the help of a tape recorder or by listing in a notebook words he uses most frequently. Once the teacher has a clear view of the child's capabilities she can then plan a program tailor-made for progress.

In what ways can the preprimary teacher prepare the child for the more difficult forms of language that are to be taught in the grades? Without a wide assortment of words to make their meanings clear the new ideas and situations which the pupil encounters in school would be baffling and unintelligible. The teaching trend has however already been established for most of her pupils. Parents have already contributed to their power by exposing them to direct experiences from which they derived their concepts. What has been informal teaching must now become formal; what has been casual and occasional must become direct and structured.

The following suggestions can help in organizing a program to broaden the child's horizon still further in the world of conceptual knowledge:

1. *The use of manipulative devices.*

These activities may involve certain large and small toys or blocks of different shapes and sizes which are associated with the child's learning situation. Among other articles would be molding clay or soft plastic which could be kneaded and squeezed into provocative shapes. There is an array of materials like these available for early childhood education. They may motivate the child to build or to balance, to produce forms which stimulate the imagination. Their appearance and colors provide endless opportunities for enriching the vocabulary through discussion and storytelling.

2. *Interchange of ideas.*

In both the prekindergarten (or nursery class as it is sometimes called) and in kindergarten the knowledgeable teacher arranges for a time when the pupils could unburden themselves of any thoughts they have, any information, any items of news which they consider of interest to the group and perhaps worth discussing. This is called "sharing time," and its observance is of paramount importance in the escalation of speech values. No matter how abrupt, disjointed and often irrelevant the flow of discussion seems to be among the children seated around the teacher, what counts is the teacher's strategies in spurring as many pupils as possible to participate and in arousing their zeal for vivid expression.

The ritual of shared experiences, if faithfully repeated, should aim at the following desirable targets:

a. Recognition of courtesy standards: one child speaking at a time without interruptions; an established order of speakers; avoidance of monopolizing the discussion.
b. Ability to regulate the voice – moderating it if too loud, making it more audible if too soft.
c. Acceptance of desirable social attitudes – interest in other children's remarks and willingness to swap ideas without quarreling.
d. Enrichment of vocabulary.
e. Broadening of abstract concepts.
f. Improvement of speaking skills: ability to speak in complete and clear-cut sentences; consciousness of pronunciation and enunciation.

3. *Field trips*

Short, timely walks in the neighborhood of the school or bus rides to places of interest to youngsters can extend the opportunity already given them by their parents to learn something about their environment. These movements outside the school walls are made more meaningful by preliminary discussion to stir the children's curiosity and to focus their attention specifically upon things they are to observe. Immediately after the trip a lively review of what the pupils have seen helps to strengthen their concepts and contributes further to their ability to express themselves.

These practices and others which a teacher is enterprising enough to try are of maximum value in lengthening the strides towards oral proficiency. Their objectives can be reached with imaginative planning and with repeated trials and once they are reached the rewards are quite heartening.

Goals of Oral Language in the Primary Years

The real foundation for language is laid in the early primary grades. In the case of oral English the teacher treats the subject as a concomitant skill to pair with reading or with writing, and all three skills are as a rule assimilated quite rapidly although not always at the same pace. Even though "sentence sense" is fairly well advanced among primary grade children concentration upon the sentence becomes more important since it is emphasized almost from the beginning in reading, while in writing the teacher develops her stories on experience charts in the form of sentences as well. The simple sentence predominates in conversation and will continue to be the most common form. But even in the first grade children have already begun to use in addition the other forms – the compound and the complex. In general, the natural tendency is to speak in longer sentences and to structure the sentences with well-defined elements.

Some children have not as yet reached the point of readiness where they can speak with any amount of ease and clarity. For most of these pupils it is necessary to go beyond the usual procedures. The teacher can try to encourage them to enter into activities which give them the greatest opportunities to improve their oral skills; they should teach these skills directly and they should watch for evidence which shows when the children are more comfortable in exchange of ideas with their classmates.

In their everyday interests children are most concerned with objects and situations which are personal and immediate. These elements therefore are of major importance in preparing oral activities for classwork. If the teacher is alert to provide her pupils with vivid and abundant experiences for further enrichment, their stock of ideas continues to grow, their vocabulary expands, and the children are able to engage in discussions involving ideas that are more abstract and an organization of thought that is more sophisticated.

Progress is seldom achieved and maintained if standards and goals are ignored. Children should be guided into an awareness of the wisdom of rules and objectives for discussion and reports and should be able to evaluate their own progress in terms of these values. In fact, they can be encouraged to devise sets of rules and aims as a part of their class procedure. Once those have been established and accepted the class is more likely to act in conformity with their guidelines.

The following graded list of objectives may be incorporated into a program for oral language on the primary level:

Grade One

Principal Goals

1. Implementation of vocabulary in as many ways as possible to enrich concepts.
2. Emphasis upon the ability to think more clearly and logically.
3. Expansion of children's interests.
4. Improvement of the ability and the desire to share ideas.
5. Increased consciousness of sentence structure.
6. Improvement of speech techniques.

7. Increased awareness of discussion techniques and courtesies.
8. Improvement in the organization of ideas.

ESSENTIAL SKILLS TO EMPHASIZE

1. Speaking in a voice audible to the audience.
2. Selecting topics that are interesting to an audience and timely in their contents.
3. Observing rules of courtesy in discussion and recitation.
4. Using a wide choice of descriptive words.
5. Developing a report or story in a logical sequence.
6. Pronouncing and enunciating words distinctly.

FUNCTIONAL ACTIVITIES

1. Directed discussion derived from various situations, such as:
   a. Ideas gained from experiences in school.
   b. Stories and poems read in class.
   c. School topics, such as science, health, art or mathematics.
   d. Films, filmstrips, tape recordings, phonograph records.
   e. Role-playing with characters demonstrating simple rules of courtesy.
   f. Lessons or episodes in character education.
2. Sharing knowledge in narrative form
   a. Telling stories about experiences which occurred at home or elsewhere.
   b. "Making up" original stories.
   c. Re-creating stories heard or stories read in children's books.
3. Making reports to a group
   a. Giving accounts of simple research on timely topics of interest to the class.
   b. Relating to the class as a whole the results of group activity.
4. Recitation in class
   a. Answering questions in clear-cut sentences.
   b. Manifesting by example the rules of courtesy.
   c. Asking for information.
   d. Asking for permission to leave the room, to take materials, to share other children's materials, etc.

Grade Two

PRINCIPAL GOALS

1. Continuation of the objective pursued in Grade One.
2. Accumulation of an additional fund of vocabulary words.

3. Oral improvement made a daylong activity.
4. Advancement in the organization of more complex thoughts.

ESSENTIAL SKILLS TO EMPHASIZE

1. Review of skills learned in Grade One.
2. Improving pronunciation of more difficult words.
3. Enunciating digraphs, such as *sh, th, wh.*
4. Modulating the voice according to the text and the mood of the talk.
5. Sticking to the point in discussion.
6. Additional rules of courtesy to be observed.
7. Using simple introduction – parent to teacher, parent to friend, etc.
8. Answering the telephone and taking a message.
9. Engaging in more extended conversations.

FUNCTIONAL ACTIVITIES

1. Activities of Grade One continued with further refinements.
2. Role-playing situations.
   a. Telephone conversations with emphasis on courtesy, modulation of voice and choice of words.
   b. Situations involving introductions.
   c. Dramatizations using school topics as centers of planning.
3. Simple book reviews.
4. Storytelling programs for entertainment or for assemblies.

Grade Three

PRINCIPAL GOALS

1. Extension of experiences and concepts.
2. Further enrichment and refinement of vocabulary.
3. Improvement of clarity and fluency in speech.
4. Provision of many situations for the exchange of ideas.
5. Development of courteous and favorable attitudes.
6. Emphasis placed on the importance of self-evaluation.

ESSENTIAL SKILLS TO EMPHASIZE

1. Review of skills previously learned.
2. Enunciating with care the initial and final consonant sounds in words.
3. Giving correct pronunciation of words used in conversation and in formal classwork.
4. Using sentence variation, including more frequent experiments with the compound and complex sentences.

5. Developing familiarity with the paragraph "sense."
6. Explaining ideas and facts in more extended detail.
7. Giving directions that are accurate and clear.
8. Using additional common rules of social courtesy.

FUNCTIONAL ACTIVITIES

1. Continue activities of Grade Two, advancing from simpler to more complicated situations.
2. Discussion of possibilities and planning in class for group enterprises.
3. Practice with role-playing situations in order to achieve more articulation on the part of the pupils involved.
4. Simulated club meetings with different types of introduction included, such as the introduction of officers or speakers.
5. Telephone conversations involving the taking of messages.
6. Dramatization of well-known characters encountered in stories which the pupils have read.

The aims and procedures outlined may be considered as a core of essentials. Further refinements, modifications and extensions are advisable and should reflect the capabilities of the children. A rich assortment of activities could make the primary years memorable for most youngsters. There is however no substitute for a structured program designed to help the child change in his oral behavior. From a creature who is self-centered, hesitant of speech, inexperienced with groups, he can be guided into becoming one who is urbane, articulate, socially responsible and highly effective in the expression of ideas.

Individual Differences Among Children

There are certain frames of reference which the teacher must consider in developing her curriculum whether she is dealing with oral expression or any other topic scheduled for instructional purposes. A most important aspect of education is the provision for individual differences among pupils in a class. A few of these differences are common enough to make it indefensible to overlook or neglect them in the planning of an overall program. A discussion of these distinctions might help to clarify the reasons for their involvement in program-making.

1. *The Intellectual Capacity of Pupils.* The great range of learning ability displayed by the children in a classroom offers a special instructional challenge. The teacher must not only recognize the dissimilarity of

pupils in intellectual power but also should know the techniques which are most important in helping each towards maximum attainment.

It is essential first of all that children proceed at the pace best suited to their abilities. Those who are relatively brighter need the least direction, attain mastery of skills with little drill or repetition, and arrive at abstract relationships with ease. The "slow" child, however, requires careful guidance in proceeding from step to step. His understanding is broadened by means of concepts which are derived through concrete experiences, and the significance of these ideas is fixed in his mind by frequent discussion and explanation. He needs much more practice than the gifted child in building his skills and more time to work out the means of reaching the simplest goals. His vocabulary is likely to be limited and is maintained and increased only with patient treadmill repetition. The gifted pupil, on the other hand, has a flair for values and perceptions which enables him to grasp ideas with speed. It is possible that some bright children may be reserved and hesitant of speech but more of them are quite articulate and bound ahead in their mastery of skills while the dull child trails behind with plodding steps.

2. *Emotional Conditions Affecting Pupils.* Attention must be given also to emotional differences among children in establishing a program for oral training. That language development can be obstructed by emotional instability is a principle underlined by wide-spread investigation. The image of the withdrawn child who isolates himself from his classmates and remains mute and diffident is a common one in educational experience. The aggressive child, the rebellious child, the pupil who is ordinarily quiet and reserved but who occasionally bursts into an explosive temper tantrum – these children are often found to have serious language deficiencies. Sometimes an episode in the life of a child may provide a temporary setback in language growth – perhaps the advent of a new baby who supplants the pupil as the center of attention, anxiety over parental disapproval, or hospitalization of a parent with its accompanying depression of insecurity and fear of possible death. The most any teacher can do when confronted by children burdened with such emotional problems is to provide understanding and extend help in overcoming the language impediments and social inadequacies. This assistance should take a practical form which is to include measures for restoring a sense of security and through this feeling of security renewed self-confidence.

3. *Socioeconomic Status.* One of the foremost factors affecting educational policy is the socioeconomic background of the pupil. The term "middle-class" on the one hand and such expressions as "disadvantaged,"

"underprivileged," or "culturally deprived" are used rather loosely as tags in establishing policies and expectations in educational planning. A whole new literature has developed around the social forces motivating the two groups. Study after study has been made in a search for methods to reduce the gap between them and particularly the apathy, the indifference and the ignorance which all too often characterize the culturally deprived. Informed teachers should be aware of the dislocation and the ferment caused by the steady movement of a vast population from neglected rural or semi-rural areas to the dark and squalid slums of urban centers. They must take into account the frequent shifting from one district to another within the city, from one apartment to another, and from one school to another, with appalling consequences in education. They must recognize the verbal deficiency brought about by the instability of broken home and blighted background. The lack of cultural satisfactions, the poverty of ideas and vocabulary and backwardness in the scale of social maturity are all a part of the same condition.

For those who make up the great middle class there is marked conformity to values which tend to elevate social and educational behavior. In contrast to the more impoverished children, those from affluent homes enjoy a more stable childhood, and in a very high percentage of cases both parents are present to guide them. On the other hand the youngsters from culturally deprived homes exist in families that are quite often fatherless and under conditions that are all but chaotic.

One of the characteristics of the poverty-stricken home, especially one with a large family, is the lack of cohesiveness. At mealtimes and at bedtime this situation is most noticeable. These are usually the occasions for family discussion and interaction between adults and children. But in a great many cases unity is almost unknown as each child comes into the kitchen from play on the street or elsewhere to take what is prepared for him by mother, or else goes to the refrigerator to "fix" himself a meal with whatever is available. Mother is often too busy to sit at the table with the children or even to urge them to sit together. Certainly in this situation there is little conversation between adults and children. At bedtime too there is no attempt at unison; the children often go to bed at their own convenience rather than follow a regular schedule or accept an established time. The reading of stories at bedtime or the pleasure of listening to tales is the exception rather than the rule.

In middle class homes conversation between grownups and children is a natural part of daily living. The adults as a whole are quite articulate and have a tendency to use words so freely that the children learn with little effort. Active teaching continues through the formative years. When the child is very young the adults will urge him to repeat words and correct him if he pronounces any incorrectly or if he is in error when attaching a name to the wrong object. This personal attention continues even when the child is old enough to comprehend the aspects of his environment beyond his immediate surroundings. He is taken to the park, to the zoo, to the beach, and is introduced to different objects there. His parents give him picture books and discuss the contents with him. The child's language is thus increased progressively by the broadening of his horizon and by the interplay of questions and responses relating to all he has seen, heard and done.

In the homes of culturally disadvantaged children the adults use a crude and limited language and the answers to questions are likely to be in monosyllables if they are answered at all. The child is seldom offered the opportunity for enriched experience beyond the confines of his neighborhood. The instability of his family life affects his language growth to such an extent that when there is emotional tension within the family circle the child often attempts to escape the disturbance by closing himself inside a wall of silence, blocking off as much communication as possible.

It is easy to understand why a gap soon opens between the child who is deprived and the one who is privileged. The child who is reared in a solid middle-class home soon begins to use words as precision tools of thought. He learns early in life to express his wants, his emotions and his intentions clearly and effectively. He begins to discriminate in his concepts by comparing, differentiating and abstracting aspects of his environment as well as describing his feelings and his thoughts.

A comparison of the extent of vocabulary between the disadvantaged and the more affluent pupils betrays the result of background conditions. In general, lower class children are deficient in words that deal with abstract ideas – words for class names, categories and subtle comparisons. In their experience with adults they learn language which is terse and often grammatically incorrect. The disadvantaged child, it might be said, begins school poorly prepared for the language tasks of the primary grades and unskilled in handling prolonged speech sequences. These are handicaps which the oral language program must be geared to overcome.

The Objectives of Speech Instruction

To summarize the objectives of speech in the preprimary and primary grades the outline following provides a list of principal expectations demanded of children if they are to assert themselves with outstanding performance.

1. Preprimary Goals
   a. To develop an adequate fund of words
   b. To provide opportunities in discussion to share ideas
   c. To increase skill in expressing ideas in sentence patterns
   d. To foster an awareness of environment
   e. To encourage favorable social attitudes in group situations
   f. To learn stock expressions of courtesy
2. Primary Goals
   a. To enlarge the scope of a speaking vocabulary
   b. To encourage frequent formal discussion
   c. To provide occasions for simple reports and storytelling
   d. To promote progress in using clear-cut sentences
   e. To stimulate organization of thought in logical sequence
   f. To increase sensitivity to environment
   g. To extend concepts and expressions of courtesy
   h. To initiate discrimination of correct usage

Development of Speech in the Elementary Level

In recent years a decided emphasis has been placed on the importance of oral communication. Educators are aware of many new and conflicting factors affecting the course of spoken language today – the impact of television for instance, the pressures of our technological society, an increasing stress upon the desirability of higher education, the steady expansion of employment in the service industries, the attrition of good speech habits in many homes and in the streets. They find the situation so fluid that it demands a constant re-examination of teaching practices, and they know that the school itself to be effective must serve both as a laboratory and a clinic for speech improvement.

In this chapter has been emphasized the idea that systematic instruction in oral language cannot begin too soon. The question is, what measures at each level of schooling will produce the best results? As the pupils advance from the primary to the elementary grades, it is clear that the skills to be taught are so many and so varied that success depends upon an exacting program. Many teachers remember when an occasional on-the-spot training was all that was offered for a program – an incidental lesson in language usage or speech correction after an oral report or a group discussion. It was thought that because this type of lesson served a highly functional purpose it was a most efficient instrument for teaching. Incidental instruction is still a useful device and it still has its place where on-the-spot correction must be made. The tide, however, seems to have turned. Teachers have become more sensitive to the need for extensive oral development. They have come to the conclusion that sporadic drill is not enough; that the principles of speech and of speaking must be taught year after year and thoughout the year as consistently and thoroughly as mathematics.

Such an authority as Angela M. Broening gave her support years ago to a more systematic program when she said, "Speech activities at the present time make a direct attack on the oral language of every pupil in school and include training in the effective use of the voice, gesture, and posture in addition to careful pronunciation and enunciation."[1] Carrie Rasmussen, from a different point of view, remarked that it is "the opportunity and challenge of school to promote on the part of the children both active interest and increasing skill in the use of discussion."[2] Margaret Painter reached the conclusion that "one of the fundamental premises in effective oral training is that the casual or incidental procedure is uncertain and inadequate."[3]

Lauren L. Brink pointed out that there should be not only a consistent building up of basic speaking habits but also generous time allowance granted to the student to find material, to organize, and to practice. He emphasized the importance of careful preparation by the pupil before delivering the talk, through planning, outlining and reviewing the contents in several practice sessions until "the presentation of ideas is smooth and clear."[4] To meet the objectives under this procedure, he says, the teacher's task is twofold: (1) She works with her pupils individually to check on skills and (2) she works with the class as a whole on what has been said.

Oral English Instruction in Other Subjects

If the needs of speech in terms of today's curriculum requirements on the elementary level could be satisfied inside the limits of the language arts period there would be no problem at all, but unfortunately the time allotted for speech work generally is too brief. We can keep in mind

---

[1]Angela Broening and others, *Conducting Experiences in English,* New York: Appleton-Century-Crofts, Inc., 1939, page 325.

[2]Carrie Rasmussen, "The Role of Speech in the Elementary School," *Elementary English,* Jan. 1952, pages 6 - 14.

[3]Margaret Painter, "Oral Emphasis in the English Class," *English Journal,* Sept. 1947, Vol. 36, pages 348-354.

[4]Lauren L. Brink, "Extemporaneous Speaking in the English Class," *English Journal,* Nov. 1947, pages 474-477.

however the fact that oral English is not confined to the language arts alone. Almost every subject is rich in the possibilities for improvement of speaking, and oral activities should be used in conjunction with or as an outgrowth of topical areas within those subjects wherever practicable. A sensible argument has been given that the "terms 'course' and 'period' usually are not associated with speech work nor are any other such terms that devote regular time set aside for 'training.' Rather, speech is involved in areas defined as *experience units* in the self-contained classroom. The urgency of need determines the prominence that speech skills will attain in the daily program."[5]

Experience units provide an answer to the teacher's problem as to how she can fit her oral language into a crowded schedule. They are a logical extension of the "show-and-tell" situations, the "sharing" times and the role-playing, which are devices so common in the primary grades. A vital part of the task is to design those situations which lead children to practice the essential skills with imagination and spirit. For most teachers it takes little ingenuity to conceive of ideal settings. The major subjects in particular arrange themselves without difficulty into topical study units or "centers of interest" (as they are sometimes called) which yield abundant opportunity for development and expression.

Even in the initial phase of these units (the step that is sometimes called the planning session), swift strides can be made towards confidence and fluency. This is the part where the youngsters are called upon to exchange ideas on how and in what form to present the knowledge they would get through their research. During the discussion that is carried on in the classroom the children are rewarded with the satisfaction of seeing actual designs and objectives taking shape. If nothing else, the degree of spontaneity involved often arouses a powerful rivalry among them, drawing them out and making them express themselves. What is most important, however, is that their contributions to the discussion, no matter how insignificant, yield for them a favorable emotional consequence, a feeling of unusual achievement.

The developmental steps of the unit which come next also feature oral activities, but instead of the speaking's being impromptu as it was in the exploratory phase, the oral work is now "prepared." The aim of communication here is to convey in a suitable and logical form the results of the children's findings in research work. The child may be activated into doing his work on his own initiative or under the teacher's direction,

---

[5]Naomi C. Chase, "Speech in the Elementary School," *Elementary English*, March 1953, pages 137-141.

according to his ability. He learns how to limit his topic, then he cultivates his knowledge through the examination of source material in the form of reference books, textbooks, dictionaries, tables, charts, pictures, and other equipment. Having gathered his information he undertakes the problem of organizing it (preferably in outline form), and sharing it first with his teammates and then with the class. In some cases a simple report is all that is necessary. But he may also want to present his knowledge in ways that are even more interesting. He may proffer his information through a chalkboard demonstration, an explanation of an exhibit, or an interview. He may cooperate with others to organize a panel discussion or a group meeting. He may choose to treat his information in some form of dramatization – a narrative, a playlet, a pageant, or the like. No matter what form he selects, however, that type will offer a perfect platform for proficiency in speaking. On her part, the teacher could fit any one of those devices into her current schedule of goals, whether she is stressing enunciation or modulation of voice or building the vocabulary. Then the teaching of oral techniques which she is attempting can go along uninterrupted.

Advantages of Grouping

In the elementary grades and beyond most pupils are ready to undertake the practice of oral skills which grow increasingly more complex. For one thing, the youngsters are likely to experiment with a greater variety of forms; and for another, their contributions become longer and more detailed. As a matter of fact, if the children in an average class were to try performing all in one day, as they often did in the primary grades, one could imagine what would happen to the last few speakers – what a restless and indifferent audience they would meet. But that is not all. As far as the teachers are concerned the worst hazard any one of them may face is a letdown which occurs when several pupils all keyed up to speak are forced to postpone their efforts. Often the mood or spirit which predominated seems ended then and there. When the lesson is resumed the children find it hard to retrieve that "first fine careless rapture." The factors of emotional readiness and the interest curve which are involved are too important to be overlooked.

To avoid disappointment teachers have been using plans which limit the number of speakers each period. A favorite device is to organize committees for special purposes or to divide the class into groups whose talks are based upon similar topics. With this procedure, since the oral work would not be too prolonged, the evils of boredom and interruption can be eliminated and the attitude of the pupils would be more favorable.

Specific Purposes of Grouping

Grouping may serve an infinite number of purposes. In each division activities are often centered around a single problem or theme, and as long as this limitation exists conditions are set up for the pupils to engage in a specialized cooperative venture. The children can interchange the sources of their information or they can develop their ideas together. They can consolidate their efforts in others ways too, such as establishing the goals to be reached or planning the methods of carrying out their assignments. Through all this it is important for teachers to remind themselves that groups must be kept quite fluid. They should last only until their objectives are carried out and then if need be they should be reorganized for further activity or disbanded altogether. When groups are formed again, however, pupils pool their talents and interests with other partners. In this way they learn to accept the challenge and stress of team participation.

To children who are reserved or of timid disposition grouping can be very helpful. It is an almost insurmountable ordeal for some of them to stand up before a large audience, but when they are surrounded by a small number of their classmates they are likely to be more relaxed and have more confidence in their own powers. The effect of physical nearness alone evokes an atmosphere of intimacy which helps them overcome their fears. Pupils like these may not constitute a large element in the average class but they offer an urgent challenge in the learning process, since the conscientious teacher would consider it a failure on her part if she did not bring up a battery of techniques to help the childen. Once she has discovered who they are she can make arrangements to combat their deficiencies with individual instruction or with training in very small groups. Then with patience, resourcefulness and encouragement she can go far towards giving them incentives to conquer their insecurities.

For one thing, she may try a simple arrangement like bunching the children together and working with them in a more secluded part of the classroom. An illusion of privacy may be brought about if necessary by having the rest of the class assigned to work which will divert their attention from the remedial activity at hand. A good idea also is to have some of the children who are advanced in oral accomplishment help occasionally in coaching. Two children who are quite compatible could pair up for more intensive practice and rehearsal. When the actual reports of oral compositions are given the helpers could then sit in as listeners and thereby increase the size of an acceptable audience. In fact, the pupils who receive special training should be accustomed as soon as possible to larger and larger audiences. The ultimate purpose is to integrate them with the class as a whole and thus to avoid any possible distinction which might label them as being inferior in any way.

How would the teacher herself benefit by grouping in oral composition? The dividends for her are rich and gratifying. First of all, the division of a class into groups establishes a logical pattern in which she can teach a well-rounded lesson. With fewer speakers to account for on each occasion she is relieved of anxious clock-watching. She need not hurry the steps in the teaching plan. She will find leisure for a preliminary discussion either to arouse enthusiasm or to "set the stage," as it were. There can be sufficient time allowed for audience participation in the form of pupil evaluation All the speakers can give their talks or make their reports, the listeners can contribute their comments, and there still will be time for the teacher to supplement the children's criticism with her own. In effective teaching none of these elements can be omitted.

The fact that the group is limited gives the teacher another advantage which is of prime importance. It offers her a chance to study the needs of each child more in detail than would otherwise be possible. Her observations can be recorded on a chart or in a notebook or she could capture the pupil's voice and contribution on a tape recorder. When the unit is complete the findings could be studied and could then be incorporated into future plans for individual training.

Education for Leadership in Group Participation

Although the expression of ideas and the sharing of information are purposes of oral language, it must be recognized that communication has another primary role as well. The use of oral expression in the maintenance of social relationships is a function that is interwoven with other services of speech. In fact, the whole adventure into discussion and debate is an effort to apply through group interaction the concepts of personal rights and courtesies. If the ends of democracy in the classroom are to be served, children should be conditioned towards learning those courtesies common to group discussion.

Not only should they be encouraged to master the principles of order in conducting meetings but they should experience something more – they should be guided into displaying initiative through leadership roles within their own groups. Whenever a group or subgroup presents an oral demonstration of some sort it is common to have a pupil chosen to act in a leadership capacity. He may be called chairman, announcer, leader, moderator or "teacher," whichever title is most suitable to the activity. The teacher herself encourages the pupils to take on responsibility for the direction of the group. She advises them on how to conduct themselves, perhaps showing them by example what to do. Then she withdraws into the background as soon as possible, concerning herself mainly with note-taking and supervision, and passes the initiative on to the class.

As far as the children are concerned, this change of position puts a different aspect upon the picture. With the guidance of the group placed in their own hands they themselves become the principal centers of interest. The situation serves as an incentive for courteous attention and lively competition.

In teaching oral expression the functions of the chairman have often been misunderstood. Chairmanship need not be a perfunctory and unchallenging activity. Under proper direction it can be made into something vital, assertive, and stimulating. Most children seem to accept the importance of this office without any persuasion. They see in the chairman's role a chance to gratify their own desires for leadership, and there is a healthy psychology in giving as many as would like an opportunity to show their skill.

If the pupils are willing to undertake the responsibilities of chairmanship, why not place their eagerness on a competitive basis? Why not rate them as critically as are the scheduled speakers in the group? Then at least they will have a basis for measuring their achievement. Chairmanship will no longer be considered a side-product of oral communication. It will rank as a highly important element in itself.

One form of activity in which the chairman may play an especially vital part is the oral report. In this area he learns how essential good introductions are in placing the speakers at their ease and in arousing interest in their topics. He can learn in his remarks to eliminate mechanical repetition and to find with the simplest turn of expression a fresh approach to his introductory statements. Before long pupils can be made aware of the extensive combinations for introduction at their command and will take pride in displaying their creative skills. No matter how trivial it may seem, that little "extra something" which the chairman uses to flavor his comments is a tribute to his teacher's effectiveness.

Many teachers have tried a worthwhile device to help the chairman originate brief remarks. They ask the leader first to distribute small slips of paper on which each speaker will write his name, the title of his report, and perhaps an explanatory comment. The chairman collects the slips and he may shuffle them to prevent anyone's anticipating the order of speakers or he may arrange them according to an order which has been agreed upon in advance. Now before introducing a speaker he has a chance to study the title on the slip and to perpare a comment that will arouse interest in the speaker's topic. With only a little experience he can acquire ingenuity. He can act as an inspiration to the speakers and a model to the listeners. It goes without saying that the benefits of such training are incalculable.

Organization of Pupil Criticism

There is no more valuable learning experience to be gained by any class than in the earnest and careful assessment of a composition. Since evaluation gives life and work its clearest meaning and deepest satisfaction, it is an ideal situation when the audience is sensitive to the merits of each talk and at the same time is able to judge its shortcomings with discriminating intelligence. Every child needs to assess his progress in terms of understanding. But critical appreciation does not come from intuitive judgment only. The youngsters must have some specific standards for guidance "since pupils tend to notice trivial points and often fail to see the more fundamental qualities that make speaking either effective or ineffective."[6]

What are some of the practical aims upon which teachers can depend for standards of evaluation? What steps can be recommended to increase pupil awareness of these aims? How can pupils apply these standards in order to improve their accomplishments?

First, children should have a gradual introduction to criticism. At the beginning of each year as soon as oral work gets under way only one or two points should be emphasized. Questions referring to good introductory and good ending sentences, for instance, might be placed on a chart or on the chalkboard – such questions as *Did the speaker arouse the interest of the audience?* or *Did he have a strong, clear purpose?* The audience could take note of them and use them for guidance in their critical assessments, limiting themselves to those main points alone. As the class gains in mastery, these could be supplemented with others, one or two at a time. Later on, a great deal can be accomplished easily with a separate assignment for each pupil in the group. One student, for example, may volunteer to center his critical discussion after each composition upon the speaker's choice of vocabulary. He can be trained to listen for forceful verbs, colorful adjectives, or especially effective phrases which the speakers used. He can likewise focus attention on limited vocabulary which is usually indicated by stereotyped phrases and repetitive words. Another child may be assigned to criticize techniques used by the speakers to arouse

---

[6]Mildred A. Dawson, Teaching Language in the Grades, New York: World Book Co., 1950, page 179.

interest in their talks and so on. Each of the fundamental points can be reviewed until the children know it perfectly.

As long as they are given the privilege of making remarks about each report, pupils should learn one crucial lesson about criticism, namely that criticism need not be offensive. They can learn to avoid unnecessary bluntness and severity in their critical comments. It can be part of their social training to discover the favorable aspects of each talk as well as the undesirable features and to render as often as possible a balanced value judgment. The child's awareness of this objective may be regarded in fact as a mark of his maturity.

Basic Elements in Evaluation of Oral Expression

To uphold the standards of evaluation for most types of oral expression teachers have depended upon the basic elements listed below. Others may be derived in the course of teaching experience to supplement these until there exists a sound comprehensive catalogue of critical points.

1. Evaluation of the beginning sentences whose function it is to arouse the interest and "set the stage." The introduction must be brief but vigorous enough to maintain a certain excitement or motivating force for the rest of the composition.

2. Emphasis upon the ending sentences as a means of "rounding out" the composition or forming a sort of "picture frame" effect.

3. Evaluation of the structural development – that is, the details of the story fitted into a logical pattern and forming a definite objective.

4. Discussion of sentences used – whether grammatical or rhetorical errors were included.

5. Attention focused upon the use of a colorful vocabulary or distinctive words and phrases which add vigor and originality to the composition.

6. Analysis of details involved – whether there has been the most effective use of description, suspense, or what is known as "climactic ladder-scaling."

7. Discussion of the speaker's vocal mannerisms – his enunciation, pronunciation, use of conversational tone and habits of modulation.

8. Criticism of his physical mannerisms – aimed at elimination of awkwardness or rigidity, and establishing habits that lead to ease and poise in speaking.

9. Consideration of the title – its suitability and its value in promoting attention to the narrative.

10. Evaluation of the interest pattern itself and methods used to maintain the attention of the group throughout the talk.

Summary

Since recent trends indicate the necessity of an intensive program in the teaching of oral communication, teachers should acquaint themselves with the specific problems involved and with the steps which lead to favorable development. The objectives of oral communication should be realized one step at a time, with considerable practice devoted to each technique. Training in the principles of speaking and speech must continue throughout the year and at every opportunity.

Teachers should recognize that oral language is not to be taught within a limited scope but should be tied in with all major subject areas. A most provocative setting for oral expression is the experience unit. It stimulates research work, it encourages a variety of speaking situations, and it provides a natural atmosphere for oral composition.

One advantage of the experience unit is that it promotes the division of a class into small groups for special assignments. This arrangement is a vital factor in several ways. First, it evokes a feeling of informality which makes the lesson in oral English more alluring. Second, it offers more security and helps pupils surmount the fear of speaking before an audience. Third, the small number of children involved in each group gives the teacher a greater chance to individualize her instruction. Finally, it provides an opportunity for more efficient corrective measures.

Grouping in oral English fosters development in areas associated with growth of character and personality as well. Modern techniques of discussion place a spotlight on the role of the chairman or group leader. Where the class is split into small groups the post of chairman is changed quite frequently and each child may have a chance to assert himself with the responsibilities of leadership. Special training in the techniques of chairmanship is therefore quite profitable.

The variety of expression which oral English assumes presents each group with a challenge in the way of organization, in the use of corrective measures. To meet this challenge teachers and pupils alike can establish a permanent set of standards, using each time points of criticism applicable to the project on which they are working. These rules are to be emphasized and discussed until the pupils are sensitive to their requirements, and teaching should be continued until mastery is achieved.

The high road to excellence is reached only through the patient attainment of goals, and skill in oral English also is derived from careful planning, from the steady application of knowledge, and from a program that is bold, consistent and inspiring.

A Route to Explore

A model for an experience unit was one which was "staged" in a sixth grade class to correlate science and oral language. This unit was structured into an extensive learning experience in which the class explored the composition of and the possibilities for survival in outer space – such things as the effect of time, distance, release from gravitational pull, orbital speed, and other data.

Built into the unit was a general objective – an appreciation of the problems involved in man's invasion of outer space during an initial journey to the moon and subsequent return to earth. The more specific goals related to the following: 1) Establishing reasons for outer space conquest – the whys of the unit, 2) Classifying knowledge of outer space and the moon, 3) Defining the relationships between earth and moon, and 4) Conceiving the effect of lunar exploration upon man.

The students brought to the classroom an array of magazine articles and clippings from newspapers which they made available to the entire group for study. The clippings were catalogued and arranged on a bulletin board under separate headings. Pictures and posters of missiles and moon craters were collected and added to the display.

As the study progressed maps and charts of the solar system, both professional and student-made, were posted on appropriate spaces along the wall. Charts with a growing vocabulary list were placed strategically enough to command the attention of the pupils. Before long, a table in the "science corner" was gradually covered with related items – styrofoam mockups of earth and moon, cardboard models of space capsules and three-stage rockets, cutouts of space suits and astronauts, and a diorama of a landing party on the surface of the moon.

The culminating activity, which featured oral English, had the benefit of a powerful motivating force. There was a dramatization in which a script called for three scenes: 1) the countdown and takeoff, 2) the landing on the moon and 3) the return to earth. In preparing for the presentation the committee requested help in lettering transparencies for an overhead projector which they planned to use for an illustrated lecture on physical conditions in outer space and problems which scientists and astronauts must overcome. They also taped a narrative with sound effects to correlate with the takeoff, the journey through space and the eerie arrival on the slope of a lunar crater. They even reproduced the surface of the moon through a pupil-made slide.

When the program was ready the pupils found they had collected a formidable assortment of materials. Each item complemented the others in creating a powerful illusion. The astronauts in their space suits crowded into their paper capsules, the room was plunged into darkness and the capsule shone in the glare of the slide projector. The reels on the tape recorder started spinning and the sound of the countdown lured the audience into complete absorption.

Partly through the accumulated materials and partly through the devices used in the lecture and dramatization and the pupil-directed discussion which followed, a significant lesson took place. In this way it is possible for oral composition to take on a new dimension.

EXTENDING YOUR LEARNING

1. Observe a four-year-old, an eight-year-old, and a ten-year-old. Listen for the *types* of sentences they use, the *length* of sentences, and note the children's ability to vary their speech to fit their audience and the occasion.
2. Keep a list of your own speaking activities for a typical twenty-four hour period. How much time was spent in informal conversation? giving directions? participating in a structured discussion? directing a discussion making a "speech"? In what other types of activities did you engage?
3. Examine several language arts textbooks. How much emphasis is placed upon *oral* language development? What types of activities are suggested?
4. For similar purposes, examine several curriculum guides.
5. It has been said that "children seldom write better than they speak." Survey some of the written work of the eight- and ten-year-old whose speech you carefully observed. Is this claim supported or refuted – at least for these children?

BIBLIOGRAPHY

1. Abercrombie, D., "Conversation and Spoken Prose," *English Language Teacher,* October, 1963, pages 10-16.
2. Bloom, Benjamin S., Davis, Allison, and Hess, Robert, *Compensatory Education for Cultural Deprivation,* New York: Holt, Rinehart and Winston, Inc., 1965.
3. Brink, Lauren L., "Extemporaneous Speaking in the English Class," *English Journal,* November, 1947, pages 474-477.
4. Broening, Angela, and others, *Conducting Experiences in English,* New York: Appleton-Century-Crofts, Inc., 1939.
5. Buck, M., "Helping Children Develop Speaking Abilities," *Education,* April, 1960, page 451.
6. Carpenter, H. M., "Study Skills: Oral Reporting," *Instructor,* May, 1965, pages 13-14.

7. Chase, Naomi N., "Speech in the Elementary School," *Elementary English,* March, 1953, pages 137-141.
8. Dallman, M. E., "Reports Vitalize Social Studies," *Grade Teacher,* February, 1961, p. 44.
9. Davis, D., "Let's Reach for Speech," *Education,* October, 1959, page 745.
10. Dawson, Mildred A., *Teaching Language in the Grades,* New York: World Book Company, 1950.
11. Eastman, M., "Talk Up!" *Grade Teacher,* September, 1961, pages 136-142.
12. Gallegos, B. B., "Toward Better Speech," *Elementary School Journal,* April, 1962, pages 375-379.
13. Hartman, M., "Way to Good Speech for All," *Ohio School Journal,* November, 1963, pages 24-25.
14. Hintze, H. K., "Speech Improvement: An Overview," *Elementary School Journal,* November, 1960, pages 91-96.
15. Hopkins, T. A., "The Spoken Word," *Education,* November, 1963, pages 166-169.
16. Hunter, E., "The Importance of Children's Oral Language," *Grade Teacher,* April, 1964, page 51.
17. Laufer, H., "Show-and-Tell in the Kindergarten," *National Education Association Journal,* October, 1963, page 63.
18. Lavaroni, C., "Mystery Day," *Grade Teacher,* February, 1963, page 22.
19. Maher, A. C., "Look Back: Happy Memories," *Grade Teacher,* February, 1963, page 32.
20. Manolakes, G., "Oral Language and Learning," *Elementary English,* November, 1963, pages 731-734.
21. Sister Mary Florentine, "Speech Habits for Five-Year Olds," *National Catholic Education Association Bulletin,* August, 1963, pages 531-534.
22. Sister Mary Josetta, "Oral Composition: The What, Why and How of It," *National Catholic Education Association Bulletin,* August, 1960, pages 358-360.
23. Sister Mary Nora, "Oral Composition: An Essential Competence in the Language Arts," *National Catholic Education Association Bulletin,* August, 1960, pages 364-366.
24. Millsap, L., "Oral Reporting," *Elementary English,* February, 1965, pages 197-200.
25. Munkres, A., and others, "Helping Children in Oral Communication," *Teachers College,* 1959.
26. Painter, M., "Oral Emphasis in the English Class," *English Journal,* March, 1953, pages 137-141.
27. Ramsey, I. L., "Utilization of Sharing Time Contributions in the Elementary Science Program," *Virginia Journal of Education,* September, 1962, pages 24-25.
28. Rasmussen, Carrie, "The Role of Speech in the Elementary School," *English Journal,* pages 348-354.
29. Scott, Louise B. and Thompson, Jane, *Speech Ways,* St. Louis: Webster Publishing Company, 1955.
30. Van Riper, Charles and Butler, Katherine, *Speech in the Elementary Classroom,* New York: Harper and Brothers, 1955.

Chapter 5 Ralph E. Kellogg

Listening

Children in the elementary schools of today will become the adults of their communities and nations one and two decades in the future. What will their world be like? What knowledges, attitudes, skills and values will they need for their personal welfare and the collective benefit of the society they will help shape and in which they will live? How will they acquire the competencies necessary to prepare themselves for their future roles? These and other similar questions continue to be asked by the lay public and educators alike as they critically analyze the present school program and plan for its improvement. A brief look into the future to discern continuing trends of development is necessary for a perspective of the role of listening instruction in the elementary curricular program.

The Knowledge Explosion

It is obvious to even the uncritical observer that there has been an accelerated rate of technological change in the past decade. Many scholars indicate that this rate of change will increase even more rapidly in the future. A major force in this change is the unprecedented explosion of knowledge. Application of new knowledge causes technological change which, in turn, helps generate additional new knowledge. A prediction that the elementary age child of today will have available in his lifetime at least twice the amount of information compared with that available to his parents is conservative indeed. The explosion of knowledge and rapid technological change will provide oppportunities and problems of greatly increased complexity for the child as he becomes the adult of tomorrow.

Listening: A Vital Link to Knowledge

One future problem will be how all this new knowledge will be learned, communicated, and utilized. In taking advantage of the opportunities and accepting responsibilities for the problems ahead, critical thinking and effective communication of such thinking through all communication media will be necessary. Currently in evidence is the increased utilization of the mass media of television with international television already a technical reality. The linking of persons in their homes to relatives and friends across the nation through direct dial telephone is but a stage of development from which international phone communication by an increasingly large number of persons will be forthcoming. The organization of library sources of knowledge via computer-linked data phone television systems holds promise of nearly instantaneous request and reception of information.

Whatever simple or complex communication systems are devised to transmit information and knowledge, their final link will continue to be the mind of the individual person, child or adult. The vehicle of the mind which the individual will use most in incorporating new information will be language. Language is processed in the mind largely through listening and speaking. The acquisition of knowledge through effective listening will continue to be a high priority need for the citizen of the future.

Value Formation Through Critical Listening

The knowledge explosion, in and of itself, has no positive or negative value. Expansion of knowledge and rapid technological change are presently causing and will continue to cause thoughtful persons to question their effect upon the formation of values in the individual. Will the child – adult of tomorrow – develop his values based upon the individual critical analysis and judgment in the knowledge explosion? Will he recognize such common propaganda tricks of "name calling," "glittering generality," "transfer," "testimonial," "plain folks," "card stacking," and "band wagon" which may be used in attempts to sway his thinking and opinion relative to social, political, and economic issues? Values will be influenced in the mental processing of information transmitted through various communication systems. The final link of any system will continue to be the mind and thought processes of the individual involving the use of language. The need for the adult of tomorrow to be able to assimilate, analyze, synthesize, and evaluate great amounts of information through language and to relate this to a value system will be greater than ever before. An increased quantity and quality of thinking through listening to language cannot be escaped by the elementary child as he progresses through life. The individual and collective cost of evasion will be too great.

Listening; Time Involvement

Another way in which the importance of listening might be considered is in terms of the amount of time spent in listening in comparison with the other language skills. Rankin, in an early study in 1926, found that a selected group of representative United States citizens spent about 45 per cent of their language communication time in listening, 30 per cent in speaking, 16 per cent in reading, and 9 per cent in writing.[1] Wilt found that elementary teachers believed that children were spending a major part of their day reading and that learning to read was the most important skill to be learned. Her timed tabulation of activities of school children in their elementary classrooms revealed quite divergent information however: 57.5 per cent of the classroom activity time was spent in listening.[2]

Casual observation in the elementary classrooms of this nation will reveal that speaking-listening is the major mode of instruction. Mathematically one can see that in the speaking-listening process in classroom instruction a greater amount of time will be spent in listening. If children were organized into teams of two each with one child speaking while the other child listened and vice versa, the percentage in time in speaking and listening each would approximate 50 per cent for each child. When groups of children larger than two are involved in oral language communication, or when the teacher is talking to the total class or subgroups of the class, the percentage of time involved in listening by the individual child necessarily will become greater than time spent in speaking. The importance of listening in terms of quantity of time spent in classrooms and in life generally seems easily apparent. Rankin's and Wilt's investigations are illustrative of other studies which validate this seemingly simple but often unconsidered fact.

Listening Facilitates Social Adaptation

The relationship of listening to social adaptation in our culture is interesting to consider. Early in the history of the United States literacy was consideerd to be very important. Public schools were established to provide opportunities for the development of universal literacy. Literacy was commonly meant to mean competence in reading and writing. Effectiveness in social conversation and public speaking was also recognized as an attribute of the "literate" person. This tradition remains within our culture today. Typically listening skill has not been made explicit as a part of "literacy"; however, its importance is fundamental to the other skills. Barbara states, "In our particular culture, people judge your char-

---

[1]Paul T. Rankin, *The Measurement of the Ability to Understand Spoken Language* (doctoral dissertation; Ann Arbor, Mich.: University of Michigan, 1926). *Dissertation Abstracts,* 12:897, 1952.

[2]Miriam E. Wilt, *A Study of Teacher Awareness of Listening as a Factor in Elementary Education* (doctoral dissertation; State College, Pa.: Penn State College, 1949). Summary: *Journal of Educational Research,* 43:626-36 (April 1950).

acter, your intellectual capacity, your social standing by the way you talk and listen."[3]

Four major reasons for the development of effective listening ability have been cited:

1. The explosion of knowledge requiring the processing of greater amounts of information through listening.
2. The need for critical thinking in the development of values through language listening.
3. The relatively high percentage of time spent in listening as compared with the other intake of thought in language through reading.
4. The facilitation of personal and social adaptation through becoming more "literate" through listening.

Status of Listening Instruction in the Elementary School

Once the importance of effective listening has been accepted the question naturally arises, "What are we doing now?" "What is the current status of listening instruction in the elementary schools?" Anderson states that "except in isolated instances, virtually the only instruction in listening that children and young people receive in the schools is the quite useless admonition of 'pay attention' and to 'listen carefully.' Listening, at all educational levels, has been the forgotten language art for generations."[4] The writer has been recently engaged in one of the twenty-seven research projects funded by the U. S. Office of Education in studying first grade reading and language arts methodologies.[5] Fifty teachers in San Diego County, California, selected because of their teaching competency utilizing the traditional method language arts program and the experience approach language arts program, included little direct instruction in listening skill development. These teachers are judged to be typical of the best elementary teachers across the nation.

A simple test will give face validity evidence of the lack of extensive direct instruction in listening skills. The reader might ask himself or any elementary teacher whom he knows three questions:

1. Did you receive any direct instruction in the improvement of your listening skills while in elementary school or at any level of education?

---

[3]Dominick A. Barbara, *Healthy and Neurotic Aspects of Listening*. Bulletin: Auxiliary Council to the Association for the Advancement of Psychoanalysis (New York), p. 2.

[4]Harold A. Anderson, "Needed Research in Listening," *Elementary English*, 29:215-224 (April 1954).

[5]"A Comparative Study of Two First Grade Language Arts Programs," Research Project Funded by the U. S. Office of Education. Submitted by the San Diego County Department of Education, May 28, 1964.

2. How many elementary teachers do you know or have you heard about who provide systematic instruction for their students in the development of listening ability?
3. What materials of instruction are currently available for use in elementary classrooms to help the teacher provide listening skill instruction?

At a time when critical listening ability is increasing in importance, common practice in elementary schools still includes little conscious systematic or sustained concern for helping children improve their listening.

A Theory of Listening

When someone says, "He listens well!" what is really meant? Clearly an explanation of such a statement would vary from individual to individual depending upon his concept of "listening" and the nature of the listening process. At one level "listening" can be described as the physiological reception of physical pulsation or vibration through the auditory nerve system. Usually such vibrations are transmitted through the air and received initially through the ears. This definition implies no linkage of the vibration with thought processes or meaning and leaves the source of vibration completely open. At this level of "listening" the *acuity* of the ears and related parts of the auditory nerve mechanism of the individual is all that is required. At another level "listening" can be described as the process of receiving the sounds of other human beings' oral language through the auditory nerve system and distinguishing likenesses and differences among the various units of sounds. This narrows the definition to language but still implies no relationships to the process of thinking and interpretation. At this level of "listening" *auditory discrimination* is required of the listener. A third definition of "listening" is that it is the process of hearing, recognizing, and interpreting spoken symbols. This last definition is given by Brown as a definition of "auding."[6] Auding might be conceived as *auditory comprehension* of language signals or symbols. This term has been used to differentiate more precisely the relationship of "listening" to spoken language and its interpretation in the thinking process of the individual. Russell has used a simple formula to show the relationship of these different interpretations and their comparison to a similar sequence of meaning in reading: Seeing; observing; Reading – Hearing; listening;

---

[6]Don Pardee Brown, *Auding as the Primary Language Ability* (doctoral dissertation; Stanford, Cal.: Stanford University, 1954). Abstract: *Dissertation Abstracts*, 14:2281-2282, 1954.

Auding.[7] A more detailed analysis of these relationships is shown in Figure 5.1.

PERCEPTION LEVEL I Hearing Seeing	Scope of Input Total physical world capable of transmission visually or auditorally Requirement of Individual Auditory and Visual acuity Reaction Level of Individual Physical reception, no comprehension or interpretation
PERCEPTION LEVEL II Listening Observing	Scope of Input Total World of Spoken or Written Language Requirement of Individual Auditory and Visual Discrimination Reaction Level of Individual Recognition of likenesses and differences of phonemes and graphemes (sound and visual language units)
PERCEPTION LEVEL III Auditing Reading	Scope of Input Total World of Spoken and Written Language Requirement of Individual Auditory and Visual Comprehension Reaction Level of Individual Comprehension and interpretation of language symbols

FIGURE 5.1

Relationship of Levels of Visual and Auditory Perception in "Reading" and "Listening"

It becomes apparent that the term "listening" is an over-all generic term in general popular usage which has different levels of meaning and interpretation. For purposes of this chapter the reader is asked to retain the term listening to mean all three levels indicated in Figure 1. It should be remembered that focus on improvement of children's listening competence at Level III is the major concern of the language arts program.

[7]David H. Russell and Elizabeth F. Russell. *Listening Aids Through the Grades* (New York: Teachers College, Columbia University, Bureau of Publications), p. 3, 1959.

A further differentiation of levels of listening can be made at perception Level III: Comprehension and interpretation of language symbols. One method by which this can be accomplished is through the use of Bloom's Taxonomy.[8] Six general levels of thought processes are delineated in the taxonomy: Knowledge, Comprehension, Application, Analysis, Synthesis, and Evaluation. Using this model of thought levels, one can readily think of a different purpose or level for listening to a conversation or formal oral presentation relating to each of the given thought levels. A specific example of listening comprehension levels using this model follows.

Assume that the following information was being presented orally. The listener might be required to comprehend at each of the six different levels. A question will be asked after the selection to illustrate each level of comprehension.

Land animals have a harsh living environment such as polar regions, jungles, and deserts. Creatures of the seas have life much easier. Water temperatures in the tropics seldom exceed eighty-five degrees. Waters at the poles usually are not colder than thirty degrees.

Question 1 – Knowledge Level: Recall of Specific Facts Presented

Tropical waters usually do not go above ..... degrees in temperature?

Question 2 – Comprehension Level: Simple interpretation of Facts Presented

The ranges of temperature from tropic to polar waters is approximately ..... degrees?

Question 3 – Application Level: Application of Ideas Presented to a Different Specific Situation

Land animals of the desert region must be more adaptable to temperature extremes than sea animals. Explain.

Question 4 – Analysis Level: Analysis of Relationships of Component Parts of Ideas Presented

The water mass of the world stabilizes temperature extremes of the world's land masses. True or false? Why?

Question 5 – Synthesis Level: Restructuring of Component Parts to Form a Concept or Generalization Not Given in the Presentation.

If you could change the temperature of the land and seas of the earth to be most ideal for all existing life what would you do?

---

[8]Benjamin S. Bloom, ed., *Taxonomy of Educational Objectives,* Handbook I: *Cognitive Domain* (New York: Longmans, Green and Co., 1956).

a. Make no changes.
b. Decrease land temperature range 50 degrees.
c. Increase water temperature range 20 degrees. Why?

Question 6 – Evaluation Level: Judgment of Ideas Presented Against Ideas or Values of the Listener

How would you compare the quality of life on other planets with life on earth knowing the extreme temperature ranges of most other planets?

Basic Premises of a Comprehensive Theory

This model of the cognitive domain ranges far beyond the level of listening comprehension practiced by most persons. The components of the listening theory presented thus far suggest a basic premise of the over-all theory.

Basic Premise A

Listening is a complex process, taking place at many levels ranging from simple reception of vibrations through abstract levels of thinking. In its most meaningful sense, listening must be closley linked with all levels of thought processes.

When one considers the four language skills of listening, speaking, reading, and writing in terms of their development within an individual during his early years and throughout his life the fundamental importance of listening becomes obvious. If one were to consider crying, gooing, cooing, etc., as speaking, it might be technically correct to say that a baby speaks before he listens. But when one thinks of these four skill areas within the framework of the language system of the particular culture, one realizes that the infant listens to the language for a considerable length of time before he speaks the language. A background of much experience in hearing oral symbols and relating them to objects and actions previously experienced is necessary for the child to learn to speak, to read, and to write. The first language symbolization of experience takes place through listening. Understanding this process is central to all other thinking and practice in language arts instruction.

The infant or young child touches, sees, hears, and in most every sensory way possible, experiences his mother. After much repetition of listening to the sound of "mama" as he experiences his mother he gradually begins to understand that the spoken sound of "mama" symbolizes or represents his mother. In this manner he is introduced to the first oral language word of his culture through listening. He reinforces this understanding through speaking by saying "mama." Whatever meaning the word "mama" has when he hears or speaks it will be related directly to the kinds of experiences he has built up in the interaction between him and his mother. From this seemingly simple but very complex intellectual beginning he rapidly builds his own oral language within the scope and limitations of the experiential and linguistic environment of his family and neighborhood. The linguistic environment initially is experienced totally through listening and speaking. Reading and writing will be introduced normally at a later stage of development. Through this process, meaningful experience builds upon prior meaningful experience and is communicated through language symbols building upon language symbols. This process is lifelong and cumulative. A step-by-step progression of this developmental process with concepts central to each step is illustrated in Figures 5.2 through 5.6.

Additional basic premises to the listening theory arise from these ideas:

Basic Premise B

Language is symbolization of experience and has meaning only in relationship to prior experience.

Basic Premise C

Language communication through listening-speaking takes place through a common background of experience which each person using the language brings to the oral sounds of the language.

Basic Premise D

Language meanings may be similar between individuals but in the final analysis are individual in nature because each person is unique, with unique experiences.

Basic Premise E

Experience symbolized in oral language is taken in the mind of the individual through listening, reconstructed by relating the oral symbol to past experience and projected from the mind of the individual in language through speaking or writing.

A developmental hierarchy is typically followed by most children in their natural development of language from early infancy through the elementary school years. This hierarchy is illustrated in Figure 5.7.

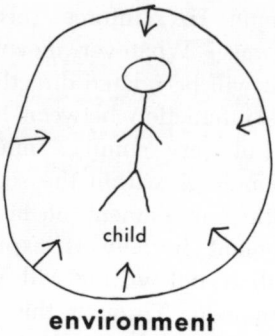

The young child experiences his environment through his various sensory systems.

FIGURE 5.2

Environment Experienced Through Senses

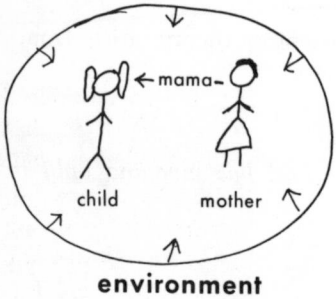

The child hears specific elements of the environment symbolized in language.

FIGURE 5.3

Auditory Symbolic Intake Process

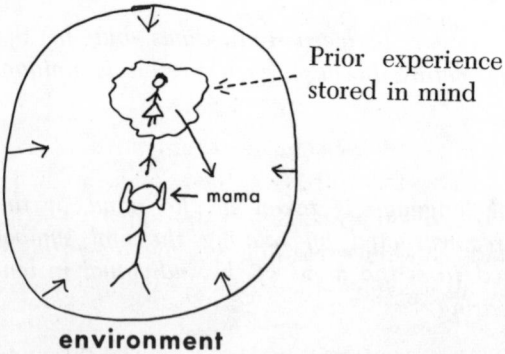

The child takes meaning from his prior experience to the oral language symbols he hears.

FIGURE 5.4

Reconstruction of Experience Process

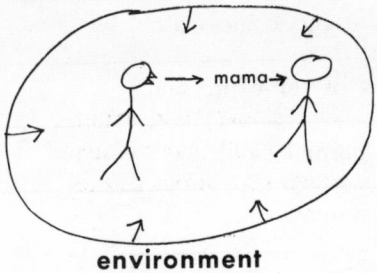

The child speaks about prior experiences using the oral language symbols which he has heard.

FIGURE 5.5

Auditory Symbolic Output Process

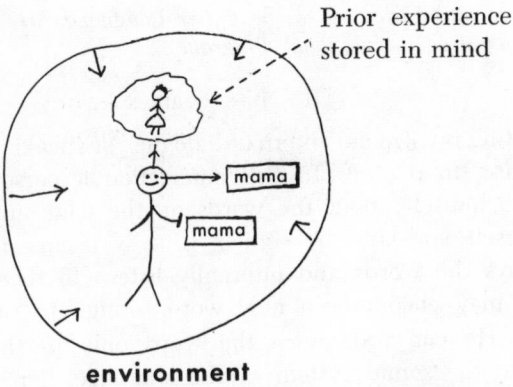

Later the child is introduced to the graphic representation of the sound by seeing someone write it, by someone's showing it to him after it already has been written and by helping him write it for himself.

FIGURE 5.6

Visual Symbolic Intake and Output Process

There is little research evidence to indicate at what stages of development children's reading vocabulary surpasses their oral language usage vocabulary. It has been observed that usually in the upper elementary and junior high years most children's reading vocabulary extends beyond the oral language vocabulary which they use in common social discourse. This phenomenon might cause one to question the fundamental importance of listening as a foundation to the skills of reading and writing in later stages of development. The writer is not aware of any definitive research explaining this phenomenon; however, the following hypothesis

Refinement of language usage comes last.

Writing follows as a means of self-expression.

Reading comes next with the normal child.

Speaking develops early in life.

Listening is the first step toward maturity.

EXPERIENCE is the foundation of all language development.

FIGURE 5.7

The Relationship of Experience and Listening to the Other Language Arts Skills in the Typical Instructional Program

is presented: Reading and writing involve an "internal dialogue" of speaking silently to oneself and listening to oneself. In this connection a person reading silently is speaking to himself about the words on the page and then mentally listens to himself speaking. A similar process occurs in writing, that is, the writer says the words and internally listens to them as he writes. Thus a reader may encounter a new word foreign to his present listening vocabulary. He can pronounce the word only to the extent that he can relate it to the sound system of the language, hence internal listening within the mind becomes involved. The reader may gain an approximate meaning of the word from the context of the sentence and the paragraph in which he finds it. The meaning of the words in the context will have their roots in the prior listening experiences of the reader. Pronouncing a new word is related to sound, therefore is based upon prior listening; understanding a new word in reading rests upon its relationship to other words whose initial meaning first was symbolized through the listening process.

From these ideas two basic premises of the listening theory emerge:

Basic Premise F

Listening is the process which provides the basic foundation upon which all other language skills develop. Comprehension of meaning in Speaking, Reading, and Writing rests upon the base of comprehension in Listening.

Basic Premise G

A person "listens" as he utilizes the other language skills by carrying on an internal mental dialogue as he speaks, reads, and writes.

The theory of listening presented here reflects a range of levels from auditory acuity of sound vibrations through comprehension and interpretation of abstract concepts symbolized in language. The focus of listening instruction beginning in the elementary school and continuing throughout life should be in the direction of improving the meaningful interpretation of higher level concepts symbolized in language.

Goals of the Listening Instruction Program

That listening is a distinctly separate mental process from reading but related to it, has been reasonably well substantiated. Many research studies have investigated the relationship between listening and reading abilities. There is strong but not conclusive evidence that instruction in listening skills will positively influence achievement in reading. The relationship of the design of the listening skills' instructional program to the skills of reading seems to be important to the degree of transfer from listening instruction to reading achievement.

Most persons knowledgeable in the research relating to the skills involved in the language arts and teachers who put language arts instructional programs into effect are aware of the interrelationships of the skills of listening, reading, writing, and speaking. Because of this, a crucial question faces the person developing the design of instructional programs in listening. Should instruction in listening have as its major goal the provision of the foundation support for achievement of more effective reading or should instruction in listening be taught primarily because it is important that all persons learn to listen more effectively regardless of whether or not this affects reading? Generally speaking, it is known that many things can be taught to children in the elementary school which were once thought impossible if appropriate instructional processes are used and enough time is provided. The criterion of efficiency becomes important here: the most learning with the least amount of instructional time. In this framework the teacher should help children improve their listening skills because this is a worthy goal in itself but should always attempt to help children transfer such skills into the reading process whenever possible.

A Synthesis of Listening Skills

A list of the skills of listening, in the final analysis, is a product of an arbitrary decision of the one making the list. Undoubtedly there will be scientific validation of the existence of listening skills in future investigations and research. At present little inquiry along this dimension of listening has been made. Most skills of listening which are given in courses of study, professional journals, and textbooks therefore are the result of best thinking on a logical basis, rather than an empirically determined basis. Perhaps this should not discourage the practicing teacher too much, however, since the same observation would apply to many of the skills of reading which are included in teachers' manuals and student materials which have been and are being used across the nation to teach reading. We do not know everything about how children learn and think, yet we continue to help them to learn and to stimulate them to think.

The lists of listening skills presented here are the writer's synthesis of those indicated in the professional literature. They are drawn largely from the work of Wright[9] and Lundsteen[10]. Illustrative examples or explanations follow the statement of each skill to facilitate greater understanding. The reader is directed to note the relationship of these kills to thinking processes as previously indicated in Bloom's Taxonomy.

Listening to Get Information

Skills requiring attention and following directions

Maintaining attention through a difficult speech

This skill is largely one of mental concentration upon the speaker and what he is trying to say, regardless of the manner of presentation.

Anticipating a speaker's ideas

This skill grows from the maintenance of attention. It involves thinking with the person who is speaking. It may include anticipating the next word, phrase, or thought which the speaker might use or projecting an idea or conclusion far ahead of what the speaker is saying at the moment. Usually the first kind of anticipation is done in small group conversation and the second in listening to longer formal presentations.

---

[9]Evan L. Wright, *The Construction of a Test of Listening Comprehension for the Second, Third, and Fourth Grades* (doctoral dissertation; St. Louis, Mo.: Washington University, 1957). Abstract: *Dissertation Abstracts,* 17:2226-2227, 1957.

[10]Sara W. Lundsteen, *Teaching Abilities in Critical Listening in the Fifth and Sixth Grades* (doctoral dissertation; Berkeley: University of California, 1963).

Following verbal directions given in a sequence

Directions here might range from simple "Do this" and then "Do that" at the preschool or kindergarten level to an involved complex operation in a particular specialty field at the graduate level.

Repeating messages given verbally

Recall of exact detail and sequence after a period of time delay is necessary.

Skills used in detecting speech organization

Discovering the main ideas

Many test items utilized in standardized achievement and intelligence tests which give a short paragraph, and ask the student to select the main idea illustrate this skill.

Determining the plan of organization

The process involved in this skill might be called mental outlining. Discovering the several "main ideas" of a speech and their sequence is required.

Recognizing illustrative examples

Example: Which statements (1, 2, 3, or 4) help prove statement A.

A. An animal is sometimes easy to tell from other animals because one part of its body is very strange or unusual.

1. Some rabbits have tails that look like powder puffs.
2. The dog has hair on his back.
3. The cat has sharp teeth.
4. The tiger has claws.

In a speech, illustrative examples are used to support main ideas.

Critical Listening

Skills requiring analysis and synthesis of information

Relating heard material to own experiences

In this skill the listener thinks about what he knows and its likeness to and difference from his previous experience.

Making use of contextual clues to determine unknown meanings

Example: A. Nancy was playing with a knife.
She wasn't careful, and she lacerated her finger.

1. She bruised her finger.
2. She hurt her finger.
3. She cut her finger.

Discerning between fact and opinion

Example: Are these facts or opinions?

1. Many trees have red leaves in springtime.
2. Birds are happier than animals.
3. St. Louis is the friendliest city in the world.
4. The stars are far away from us.

Recognizing that which is relevant

This skill is similar but more complex than the recognition of illustrative examples. Examples to illustrate a main point or an idea are subordinate to the idea being presented. Relevancy involves degrees of relationship between ideas which may not necessarily be illustrative of each other.

Example: The struggle in Viet Nam is an illustrative example of armed military conflict. The Viet Nam conflict may be relevant to a theoretical discussion of the possible causes of nuclear war but not an illustrative example of it.

Making logical inferences from what is heard

Example: Billy loved to eat. He ate too much every chance he got, especially when sweet things were around. One afternoon, the bakery man gave him a small cherry pie. What do you think Billy did?

1. He sat down and started eating.
2. Billy decided to take the pie home for supper.
3. He ate one bite and threw the rest away.
4. He gobbled up the whole pie.

Keeping an open mind before forming opinions

This skill is more linked to the emotional attitude of the listener than most of the other skills. Mentally it may involve any or all of the other listening skills and withholding the formation of an opinion until those speaking have had opportunity to present all their information.

Skills relating to the analysis and judgment of propaganda

Many of the other skills of listening are involved here. The recognition and identification of certain generalized methods of persuasion used in propaganda should be learned by any competent listener. Some of these included name calling, glittering generalities, transfer, testimonial, card stacking, side tracking, band wagon, bad words, and glad words.

Role of the Elementary Teacher in Listening Instruction

A program in any curricular area should give consideration to several specific components of instruction: time, place, method, content, students, instructional materials including teaching materials or pupil materials, and evaluation. One could analyze the various reading programs today in terms of how each of these components of instruction has been considered in its program design. Currently the writer knows of no listening skills instructional program which has considered all of these components in any systematic fashion for even one entire year of the elementary school. Several researchers have developed a series of lessons usually for a portion of a year at one grade level. Currently there is no commercially available listening skill instructional program which systematically moves from developmental level to developmental level or grade level to grade level. In addition to this lack of assistance for the teacher, teacher training institutions traditionally have included little if any emphasis upon teaching listening skills.

Both of these phenomena are understandable when one realizes that the first research on listening appeared in 1917 and that in 1961 Duker's extensive bibliography on professional articles and studies in listening included only 725 items. In contrast, it has been estimated that 2,700 studies on reading were produced between 1881 and 1945. Until such time as the research into listening has provided a more solid basis of knowledge for pre-service training and the design of instructional programs, there will not be widespread instruction in listening skills. What then is the elementary teacher to do until more favorable conditions exist? Five general suggestions are presented. The teacher might:

1. Engage himself in a long-term project of learning more about effective listening and improving his own listening abilities. Concentration on improving one specific skill at a time, then moving to another skill is recommended. "Are You Listening" by Nicholas and Stevens[11] and "The Art of Listening" by Barbara[12] are excellent general references for the adult who wishes to begin a program of self-improvement. This may seem like a strange first suggestion. It is based upon the following rationale: If the teacher becomes involved in developing his own listening ability, he will begin to understand the many thought processes and techniques which are involved in effective listening and thereby be in a better position to assist children. The self-improvement resulting for the teacher will cause him to

---

[11]Ralph G. Nichols and Leonard A. Stevens, *Are You Listening?* (New York: McGraw-Hill Book Company, Inc., 1957).

[12]Dominick A. Barbara, *The Art of Listening* (Springfield, Ill.: Charles C. Thomas, 1958).

recognize the benefits of improved listening ability and therefore probably become more persistent in helping students he teaches to improve their listening. In the process of becoming a more effective listener, the prospective or practicing teacher will obtain more knowledge of the world around him and become more aware of other individuals within his environment.

2. Apply the concept in Basic Premise F in preparing students for listening, speaking, reading, and writing by providing as much direct experience as possible relating to the concepts which students are expected to learn in any content area. Having students listen or read without adequate related experiential background will only frustrate them and waste instructional time from meaningful learning. In short, the teacher should not expect the listening and reading process to bring about learning unless these processes are cast within the experiences of the learners. Listening and reading can only help the learner enrich, elaborate, extend, summarize, synthesize, analyze, etc., the basic experiences which he brings to the language symbols involved in the listening and-or reading process.

3. Prepare a diagnostic and achievement check sheet of listening skills appropriate to a student grade level. Use it as a basis for instruction in the various skills. Drawing children's attention to the importance of listening, the specific skills involved and providing definite opportunities for their development will give them more help with the evolution of their listening skills than many elementary children will ever receive.

4. Obtain a copy of Russell's "Listening Aids Through the Grades."[13] This paperback publication, listing 190 listening activities for children in the elementary school, gives specific examples of classroom activities which can be utilized to teach listening skills. These might be selecetd on the basis of the organization of listening skills which have been devised in the diagnostic and achievement listening check sheet. Search of other course of study documents in language arts for additional specific suggestions of classroom activities will provide additional assistance.

5. Plan directed lessons in teaching specific listening skills. This is essential to help bring to the students' consciousness what is involved in the skill. Encouragement to practice listening skills whenever there is a speaking situation in all subject areas in the classroom will help reinforce the development of new listening habits. The ultimate goal is for the student to become independently responsible for his continuing improvement in listening wherever he might be.

---

[13]David H. Russell and Elizabeth F. Russell, *Listening Aids Through the Grades* (New York: Teachers College, Columbia University, Bureau of Publications, 1959).

Conclusion

An attempt has been made to point out the importance of effective listening in the world of tomorrow and to indicate the rather bleak reality of the limited listening instruction currently provided in the elementary school. The need for the development of a theory of listening has been cited by writers in the professional literature. A theory has been formulated and presented. The reader should remember that a theory is a hypothesized model of reality. It serves as a way of thinking about something. The theory presented is projected largely on logical bases rather than scientifically validated research, since such research in listening is limited. A list of skills of listening has been presented as a synthesis from the literature on listening not from scientifically validated research. Again research of this specificity is not available. Finally, some first steps have been suggested for the beginning teacher or teacher who is beginning for the first time to delve into the personally and professionally challenging study of the listening process which will enable him to begin giving attention to helping children improve their listening skills.

EXTENDING YOUR LEARNING

1. Illustrate by two specific examples each of the basic premises indicated in the theory of listening presented in this chapter.
2. Develop a diagnostic and achievement listening skill chart and describe procedures by which it might be utilized in a specific grade level.
3. Study a suitable reference on propaganda analysis, listen for and record examples of different propaganda techniques which are heard during the period of one week.
4. With a group of classmates or friends collectively develop or research a series of teaching activities which could be used to help students develop each of the listening skills indicated in the Skills of Listening section of the chapter.

BIBLIOGRAPHY

Anderson, Harold A. "Needed Research in Listening," *Elementary English, 29*:215-224, April, 1954.

Barbara, Dominick A. *The Art of Listening*. Springfield, Illi.: Charles C. Thomas, 1958.

———. *Health and Neurotic Aspects of Listening*. Bulletin, Auxiliary Council to the Association for the Advancement of Psychoanalysis, New York.

Beery, Althea. "Interrelationships Between Listening and the Other Language Arts," *Elementary English, 31*:164-172, March, 1954.

Bloom, Benjamin S. (ed.). *Taxonomy of Educational Objectives*. Handbook I: *Cognitive Domain*. New York: Longmans, Green and Co., 1956.

Brown, Don Pardee. *Auding as the Primary Language Ability.* Doctoral dissertation; Stanford, Cal.: Stanford University, 1954. Abstract: *Dissertation Abstracts, 14*:2281-2282, 1954.

"A Comparative Study of Two First Grade Language Arts Programs," Research Project Funded by the U. S. Office of Education. Submitted by the San Diego County Department of Education, May 28, 1964.

Duker, Sam. "Goals of Teaching Listening Skills in the Elementary School," *Elementary English, 38*:170-174, March, 1961.

———. *Listening Bibliography.* New York: Scarecrow Press, 1964.

Lundsteen, Sara W. *Teaching Abilities in Critical Listening in the Fifth and Sixth Grades.* Doctoral dissertation; Berkeley: University of California, 1963.

Nichols, Ralph G., and Leonard A. Stevens. *Are You Listening?* New York: McGraw-Hill Book Company, Inc., 1957.

Rankin, Paul T. *The Measurement of the Ability to Understand Spoken Language.* Doctoral dissertation; Ann Arbor, Mich.: University of Michigan, 1926. *Dissertation Abstracts, 12*:897, 1952.

Russell, David H., and Elizabeth F. Russell. *Listening Aids Through the Grades.* New York: Teachers College, Columbia University, Bureau of Publications, 1959.

Wilt, Miriam E. *A Study of Teacher Awareness of Listening as a Factor in Elementary Education.* Doctoral dissertation; State College, Pa.: Penn State College, 1949. Summary: *Journal of Educational Research, 43*:626-636, April, 1950.

Witty, Paul A., and Robert A. Sizemore. "Studies in Listening," *Elementary English, 35*:538-552 (December, 1958); *36*:59-70 (January, 1959); *36*:297-301 (May, 1959).

Wright, Evan L. *The Construction of a Test of Listening Comprehension for the Second, Third, and Fourth Grades.* Doctoral dissertation; St. Louis, Mo.: Washington University, 1957. Abstract: *Dissertation Abstracts, 17*:2226-2227, 1957.

Chapter 6 Donald R. Ferris

Teaching Children to Write

Teaching children to write accurately and clearly from their unique view of the world is often exasperatingly difficult. Examining the nature of language – our medium of idea exchange, quite often taken for granted – helps to explain why teaching children to write is difficult and gives some suggestions of how to reduce the difficulties.

The Nature of Language and Writing

Linguists tell us that speech is the real language. By this, they mean that in the history of cultures spoken communication precedes the development of a written language. This is true not only in the history of a culture but it is also true in the developmental history of an individual. The young child's language development follows a general pattern: he learns to listen to language and understand it before he learns to express ideas through spoken language; he expresses ideas in spoken language before he learns the written language of his culture (if his culture has a written language). Children acquire these language skills at different ages but in the same sequence.

Speech serves as the medium of idea exchange among human beings. "Language is a purely human and non-instinctive method of communicating ideas, emotions, and desires by means of a system of voluntarily produced symbols."[1]

Children learn to create patterns of sound symbols which communicate their ideas to others. Sapir's definition of language notes that it is an exclusively human method of communication. The capacity for human language is based upon man's unique brain. The human brain with its

[1]Sapir, Edward, *Language: An Introduction to the Study of Speech.* New York: Harcourt, Brace and World. 1921.

sensitivity to happenings in the surrounding environment enables human beings to communicate their unique perceptions of the environment more or less accurately to each other through the medium of language. The symbols of language are used to represent the reality one perceives. Spoken language is an abstraction of the world of reality. Speech represents reality through sound symbols. Written language, on the other hand, is even further removed from reality. Writing is a symbolization of a symbolization. Written language is a system of scratches and squiggles (graphemes) which stand for the sound elements in human speech. Written language stands for speech which is a rough representation of reality.

In teaching children to learn to write it is essential that the teacher remember the relationship between spoken and written language. Spoken language precedes writing and establishes patterns for it. A child who can create a clear spoken sentence has a skill that is necessary in learning how to write. It might be said that all that remains to be learned are the mechanics and conventions of the language: handwriting, spelling, punctuation, capitalization and conventional forms. This is in no way to minimize the number or difficulty of the skills which remain to be learned. The point is that the child already knows the structure of the language well enough to be able to formulate sentences that are recognizable and understandable to another native speaker. It is also true that the child's written language will usually reflect his habitual level of usage. If the child says "He don't," he will also write it. Any attempts to have the child write at a higher level of usage than he speaks is unrealistic. This does not, however, argue for a postponement of teaching a child to write until he "cleans up his speech." The habit of proofreading what one has written should be taught as soon as the child reaches the stage in his writing where he is accepting some independence – even if it is only checking to see if he has copied something from the chalkboard correctly. This habit of proofreading will not assure that everything the child writes will be cast at an appropriate level of language; however if he reads what he has written it does help him to detect and eliminate garbled sentences. More will be said about techniques for teaching proofreading later in this chapter.

Types of Writing

The terminology related to teaching children to write is confused and confusing. Chiefly, it suffers from being too rigidly dichotomized: there is practical and personal writing; creative and noncreative writing; prose and poetry; utilitarian and imaginative writing; original and stereotyped writing. It is difficult to talk of teaching children using any of these dichotomies. Obviously the categories of prose and poetry overlap with the creative and noncreative categories; it is possible for a piece of utilitarian writing such as a personal letter to be written creatively. Similarly, it is obvious that something written in the form of a poem – let us say in iambic pentameter – may be hackneyed and trite.

The inadequacy of any of the pairs of terms mentioned to describe children's writing accurately lies in their failure to recognize the nature of writing. There are three facts which should be recognized: (1) writing is a *process* which yields a *product;* (2) writing has a *purpose* or a *function* and (3) writing can be evaluated to determine its *quality* – how adequately it fulfills its purpose and to what extent it possesses the literary qualities desired.

Writing as a Process and a Product

Writing as a process involves the application of skills in translating spoken language or thoughts into the conventions of "language written" so that it is intelligible to the reader. (The dyadic nature of the language arts presumes that a writer will have readers just as a speaker will have listeners. Perhaps it ought to be thought as equally strange for a writer to write without a thought for a reader as it is for a man to talk to himself.) Writing one's ideas requires handwriting which is minimally legible, spelling that is at least partially phonetic, a vocabulary adequate to the ideas to be expressed and some skills of organization of the ideas so that they are intelligible to the reader. These skills having been exercised a *product* results, which we may or may not be able to categorize formally as an essay, a short story, a novel, a poem, a friendly letter, a business letter or one of the other kinds of writing which can be classified by form, length, or as fiction or nonfiction.

The Purpose or Function of Writing

The product which results from the writing process will appear in a certain form according to the purpose for which the writing was being done. It is the function of a friendly letter to communicate ideas from one person to another who is beyond the range of voice contact. Before a writer chooses to write a friendly letter, he must have the intent or purpose of communicating with the other person. He probably chooses the form for communicating which is customary and adequate for his purpose. (He may invent a new form which more adequately suits the task he has set for his communication; this might be evaluated as possessing originality. This illustrates the evaluative aspect of writing which is further discussed later.)

Evaluating the Qualities and Adequacy of Writing

Both the process and product of writing can be evaluated. One who would evaluate the process of writing must settle for the subjective introspective evidence of the writer. This makes the evaluation of the mental process of the author less dependable albeit no less interesting. The task of evaluating whether the writer's mental processes were "creative" is difficult to imagine.

The product of the writer is a more tangible thing to evaluate; for example, if the quality of originality in writing is defined as being related to how frequently a particular idea occurs among a number of written products, it is possible to rate writing products as being more or less original.

Even though the qualities of original writing may be listed, the task of evaluating the writing of a particular student is still difficult. Through a survey of several professional publications during the period from 1929 to 1959 Carlson suggests seventeen possible qualities which might be found in original writing and suggests that there probably are many more. The qualities which Carlson found are listed following and will not be discussed in detail. The reader is referred to Carlson's excellent article for a more complete explanation of the qualities.

"(1) novelty or freshness, (2) individuality, (3) a personal quality revealing the self, (4) emotion or feeling, (5) "becomingness," related to identification, (6) imagination, (7) a recombination or restructuring quality, (8) an abstractive element consisting of finding the essence, (9) immediacy, (10) dynamic vitality, (11) curiosity, (12) reservoir of experiential data, (13) perceptive sensitivity, (14) flexibility or versatility, (15) symbolism, (16) coherent unity, and (17) an expressive – communicative element."[2]

An impressive list! Some of the qualities probably are not immediately meaningful and not directly applicable to elementary school children's writing. Carlson simplified her findings on originality for use in a study of original stories of fourth, fifth, and sixth grade children. She defined an original story as "a form of narrative or descriptive composition which is novel, non-imitative, and one which appears with statistical infrequency."[3]

---

[2]Ruth Kearney Carlson, "Seventeen Qualities of Original Writing," *Elementary English*, XXXVIII (December, 1961), 576-579.

[3]Ruth Kearney Carlson, "Recent Research in Originality," *Elementary English, XXXX* (October, 1963), 30-31.

Writing as a Process

Learning to write is a long and complicated process. Because it is a process – which is to say that it moves from step to more complicated step – it builds upon past experiences and learning. It is an emerging ability. The earliest experiences a child has in translating his spoken words into written symbols builds upon his ability to use the patterns of his native language. He can never write anything which he cannot think or speak. The development of thinking, oral language and written language are simultaneous. Just as learning to express thoughts in words is dependent upon listening to the language and learning its patterns, so readiness for learning to write is based upon the development of spoken language to a level necessary to learning to write. The development of oral language has been discussed in Chapter 4 and will not be further discussed here except to point out that readiness for written language is developed through some facility with oral language.

Before a child can write independently he must learn to write the symbols which, when arranged and spaced correctly, create the written equivalent of his spoken language. To put it more conventionally, he must learn handwriting, spelling, punctuation and capitalization. The basic dilemma in teaching children to write with exactness and beauty is that they learn to do this only through opportunities to write without having perfectly formed letters, correctly spelled and capitalized words, and correctly placed punctuation. Handwriting, spelling, capitalization and punctuation, although difficult and complicated to teach, are easier to teach than the selection and arrangement of the words in thought units which are called sentences. As the child's thinking becomes more complex and he develops rich concepts, he learns words which then may become part of his writing vocabulary. Because all of the language arts are interrelated, the source of the child's new written vocabulary is the people with whom he talks and the books that he reads.

The Transition from Oral to Written Communication

The goal of the school in teaching writing is to produce individuals who are independent writers; individuals who can handle the personal and social demands for writing in their lives. More will be said of these specific functions and purposes later. When the child enters school, he will be using oral communication at a more or less adequate level. Some children will be facile in their use of spoken language; others will reflect contact with less stimulating language learning environments. Knowing that readiness for learning to write is based upon a child's development of oral communication skills, the wise teacher will not expect each child to be ready to learn to write at the same time. For the child whose speaking skills are less well developed, the teacher will provide opportunities for listening to stories read or told by him.

Some children will already know that writing is "talk put down on paper." Others will have to learn this. The teacher should create opportunities to write children's sentences on the chalkboard. Through this, children learn not only that spoken language can be translated into written language, but also are introduced to such conventions as capitalizing the first word of a sentence. (The term *sentence* should be used.) They are introduced to the convention that words are made from letters, that writing in our language goes from left to right, and that the end of a sentence is indicated by a "stop sign" or a question mark.

After the children have learned that what they say can be written, the teacher should encourage them to dictate sentences which are then written on the chalkboard or on sheets of paper large enough to be seen by the children involved in the activity. As the teacher does this, the conventions of written communication should be pointed out – the capital letter with which the sentence begins and the terminal punctuation which indicates the end of a thought unit.

An effective and much-used device for recording children's language is the experience chart. An experience chart is written on a large sheet of paper so that it can be seen by all children participating in the activity. The chart is used to record the children's statements about some experience they have had together with the teacher. It might be used to record facts or impressions the children have received from a visit to the firehouse, the bakery, or some other community resource. Writing an experience chart is a good activity to use with a whole class. Although some of the more verbally skilled children will be the ones who clamor to get their sentences written, even the less able child can participate in the writing because he has had the same experience. Through the use of the experience chart the children can discuss alternative ways of expressing their ideas and thereby get some idea of the flexibility of language.

As with any instructional device, the experience chart can be overused. The teacher should use it when the children's interest is high and the purpose for writing is understood by them. When the children have learned enough handwriting, they can copy the teacher's writing. Through this copying they get a feeling of independence in their writing.

Dictating to the teacher followed by copying is the first step in the child's gaining of independence in writing. As his skill in handwriting, spelling, punctuation and capitalization grow, he becomes increasingly independent in his writing. The teacher should encourage each child to become an independent writer as rapidly as he can, but should avoid the risk of the child's perceiving the teacher's refusal to help him with spelling or punctuation as punishment. If the teacher realizes that the child is eager to become independent in his writing, help can be given when it is needed without fear of its retarding the child's growth. In cases where a child is capable of becoming independent but prefers to depend upon the teacher for emotional security, the teacher can encourage the child in such a way that he is rewarded by his accomplishment. If children are given purposeful tasks commensurate with their skills, little difficulty will be encountered in getting them to write.

Developing Skills in the Writing Process

After the child gains some skills in writing and is becoming more and more independent, his continued development requires that he learn increasingly complex skills in spelling, mechanics (punctuation and capitalization) as well as enlarge the size of his vocabulary and his ability to write clear paragraphs which do not contain trite, overused phrases.

Punctuation Skills

Learning to use marks of punctuation often poses a major problem to the pupil and teacher. Perhaps one reason why this is so is that the teacher does not capitalize upon pointing out the similarities between punctuation in written language and the intonation, pauses and other conventions used in communicating meaning in oral communication. The marks of punctuation correspond roughly to signals to the reader which assure that what the writer intended to communicate is communicated. The period indicates the end of a thought. Both the semicolon and the colon, while not full stops, are heavier stops than provided by the comma. The comma in written communication corresponds roughly to pauses in spoken language.

The importance of punctuation to meaning in written communication is obvious in the following sentence: That that is is not that that is not. As the words are read, their meaning is probably not immediately apparent. When a comma is inserted between the first and second "is," the meaning of the sentence (far from a profound observation) is understood. If one were to hear this sentence spoken, the rising inflection on the first *is*, followed by a short pause, less emphasis upon the second *is*, a rising inflection on *not*, carry the major burden of the speaker's thought. This example illustrates the problem the writer faces; he must communicate his meaning with far fewer signals to the reader than are available to a listener. In their study of spoken language the linguists are interested in kinesics (the study of all the nonverbal signals that a speaker gives which helps a listener to understand the message being communicated). Gestures, facial expression, and bodily attitude are examples of kinesics which give signals to the hearer of the intent of the speaker's words. This further illustrates the linguist's statement mentioned earlier that writing is a symbolization of a symbolization. The function of punctuation, then, is the prevention of ambiguity in what the reader perceives as the writer's message.

Teaching of the function of punctuation in written language should not be postponed until the child has become somewhat independent in his writing. From the time he enters school and the teacher begins to read to him, an excellent opportunity exists to teach the function. As the teacher reads, the full stop indicated by a period at the end of the sentence can be indicated. The pause suggested by the comma can be shown. It is not suggested, of course, that the primary function of the teacher's reading to the child is to teach him punctuation. In reading to children "the story's the thing" and the danger of making a pleasurable experience like story-reading a deadly, dull punctuation-learning exercise is to be avoided. The practice of using reading to alert children to the existence of punctuation marks and their function further illustrates the interrelationship of all the language arts.

Rule Versus Style

The extent to which punctuation usage is dictated by strict inflexible rule or by the style, even whim, of the writer is a moot point. Spokesmen for all positions between the two extremes can be found. Perhaps a reasonable compromise between the two positions is suggested in G. V. Carey's delightful little book, *Mind the Stop*. He suggests that punctuation should be "governed two-thirds by rule and one-third by personal taste."[4] Although this position probably does not allow for as much flexibility as demanded by certain present day writers, it probably is about one-third more flexible in its position than that of many teachers. Not to be unfair to the teachers in question, likely it is also true that the two-thirds of the punctuation skills that can be learned by rule are those to be learned in the elementary grades. The one-third personal taste that Carey speaks of in the use of punctuation can probably best be exercised by the individual who is well on the way to developing his own literary style.

What are the punctuation uses that ought to be taught in the elementary school? Professor Furness at the University of Wyoming has suggested what a teacher should know if the pupil is to be helped to overcome the seven most common errors in punctuation.[5]

---

[4]G. V. Carey, *Mind the Stop: A Brief Guide to Punctuation with a Note on Proof Correction.* (Cambridge University Press, 1958), p. 1.

[5]Edna Lue Furness, "Pupils, Pedagogues, and Punctuation," *Elementary English*, March, 1960, pp. 187-89.

Errors	Possible Causes	Suggested Teaching Procedures
1. Omission of period at end of sentence	a. carelessness b. indifference c. poor observation d. haste	1. Have pupil read aloud his sentences and ask him to note that he drops his voice and pauses at the end of the statement. 2. Tell him that this drop pause is a stop and that in writing the period represents this stop.
2. omission of period after abbreviation	a. carelessness b. insufficient practice c. lack of "abbreviation consciousness"	1. Show the difference between a word and an abbreviation. 2. Explain that some words are abbreviated and that others are not.
3. failure to use a colon	a. intellectual immaturity b. lack of sensitivity to emotional overtones of written material	1. Show that the colon is a mark of anticipation, directing attention to what follows. 2. Explain that the colon is a contrast to the semicolon, which is a stop, almost a period.
4. omission of question mark after a question	a. carelessness b. indifference	1. Teach the following concept: Use a question mark when there is a quick rise in voice and then drop back to the basic level.
5. failure to set off a non-restrictive clause by a comma	a. lack of appreciation of a suspension of thought b. lack of observation	1. Show how the relative and its clause can be removed without destroying the sentence. 2. Call attention to the fact that the non-restrictive clause furnishes additional information. 3. Help pupils see a *that* clause as subject or object is an integral part of the sentence and hence is not pointed by a comma. 4. Call attention to the misreading which may occur in a *for* sentence; e.g., The day seemed long (,) for the class was tired.

		5. Use colored chalk to make the commas stand out. 6. Cover the relative and its clause and ask the class to read the sentence.
6. failure to set off a series by commas	a. carelessness b. lack of writing experience c. lack of attention to details d. misunderstanding of the concept of *series*	1. Write on the board the example: *long, hot, sultry afternoons.* 2. Show that *long, hot, sultry afternoons* really stands for *long* and *hot* and *sultry* afternoons. 3. Explain that there are commas between long-hot-sultry because each stands in the same relation to the noun *afternoons.* 4. Write on the board: old rock garden. Explain that *old* modifies *rock garden* rather than *garden.* 5. Explain that in *old, rock garden* the comma throws the emphasis upon *rock.*
7. lack of commas setting off an appositive	a. failure to understand the relation of the insertion to the sentence proper	1. Place on the board several sentences and several appositives. Ask the pupils to choose the proper appositive for each sentence. a. Mary Jones, ——, is an intelligent girl. b. Denver, ——, is in Colorado. a. The Queen City of the Plain b. Miss America of 1965 2. Let the class discover for themselves that the appositive is separated from the rest of the sentence by one comma when the appositive comes last in the sentence.

3. Show that, when the appositive is removed from the sentence, a complete thought remains.
4. Cover up the appositive and ask the class to read the sentence.
5. Show the difference in meaning between
   a. his brother John arrives (implies he has only one brother)
   b. his sister, Dorothy, arrives (implies he has more than one sister)
6. Use colored chalk to make the appositive stand out.

Suggestions for Grade Placement

The suggested teaching procedures listed will not solve all the teacher's problems with teaching punctuation in writing; neither does it suggest the many other uses of punctuation marks in clear, correct writing. The following list suggests the grade placement for the major uses for punctuation marks which children should learn in the elementary school.

Grade one
a. Period at the end of a sentence which tells something
b. Period after numbers in any list

Grade two
a. Items listed for grade one
b. Question mark at the close of a question
c. Comma after salutation of a friendly note or letter
d. Comma after closing of a friendly note or letter
e. Comma between the day of the month and the year
f. Comma between name of city and state

Grade three
a. Items listed for grades one and two
b. Period after abbreviations
c. Period after an initial
d. Use of an apostrophe in common contractions such as isn't, aren't, don't
e. Commas in a list

Grade four

a. All items listed for previous grades
b. Apostrophe to show possession
c. Hyphen separating parts of a word divided at end of a line
d. Period following a command
e. Exclamation point at the end of a word or group of words that makes an exclamation
f. Comma setting off an appositive
g. Colon after the salutation of a business letter
h. Quotation marks before and after a direct quotation
i. Comma between explanatory words and a quotation
j. Period after outline Roman number

Grade five

a. All items listed for previous grades
b. Colon in writing time
c. Comma to indicate changed word order
d. Quotation marks around the title of a booklet, pamphlet, the chapter of a book, and the title of a poem or story
e. Underlining the title of a book

Grade six

a. All items listed for previous grades
b. Comma to set off nouns in direct address
c. Hyphen in compound numbers
d. Colon to set off a list
e. Comma in sentences to aid in making meaning clear[6]

The first item in each list following that for grade one indicates that all items listed for previous grades should be taught. This statement suggests that learning to use punctuation marks in each of the situations listed is not acquired simply by one presentation by the teacher; each punctuation use must be repeated until it is mastered. Although this is not suggested by the list, it is also true that more advanced children should be taught those skills they need when they need them, and that teaching not be postponed because "they aren't supposed to get that until third grade."

Capitalization Skills

Compared to punctuation skills, those relating to the use of capital letters are neither as numerous nor as discretionary. Many elementary school children make the error of using capitals where they are not needed. The problem in teaching the use of capitals is as much teaching when not to use them as it is teaching when to use them. Greene and Petty suggest the following grade placement of capitalization skills:

[6]Harry A. Greene, and Walter T. Petty, *Developing Language Skills in the Elementary Schools.* (Boston: Allyn and Bacon, Inc., 1963), p. 124.

Grade one
a. the first word of a sentence
b. the child's first and last names
c. the name of the teacher, school, town, street
d. the word I

Grade two
a. items listed for grade one
b. the date
c. first and important words of titles of books the children read
d. Proper names used in children's writings
e. titles of compositions
f. names of titles; "Mr.," "Mrs.," "Miss"

Grade three
a. Items listed for grades one and two
b. Proper names: month, day, common holidays
c. First and important words in titles of books, stories, poems
e. First word of salutation of informal note, as "Dear"
f. First word of closing of informal note, as "Yours"

Grade four
a. All that is listed for preceding grades
b. Names of cities and states in general
c. Names of organizations to which children belong, as Boy Scouts, Grade Four, Etc.
d. Mother, Father, when used in place of the name
e. Local geographical names

Grade five
a. All that is outlined for previous grades
b. Names of streets
c. Names of all places and persons, countries, oceans, etc.
d. Capitalization used in outlining
e. Titles when used with names, such as President Lincoln
f. Commercial trade names

Grade six
a. All that is outlined for preceding grades
b. Names of the Deity and the Bible
c. First word of a quoted sentence
d. Proper adjectives, showing race, nationality, etc.
e. Abbreviations of proper nouns and titles[7]

Written Vocabulary Development and Word Selection

As soon as a child begins to read and write he has four definable vocabularies:[8] (1) the recognition vocabulary, (2) the reading vocabulary, (3) the writing vocabulary, and (4) the speaking vocabulary. A study of children's recognition vocabulary by Smith indicates that a first grade

[7]*Ibid., p. 125-26.*
[8]Laird, Charlton, *The Miracle of Language.* (Greenwich: Fawcett Publications, Inc., 1957), pp. 226-27

PEANUTS® **By Charles M. Schulz**

Copyright by United Features Syndicate, Inc.

child's vocabulary may be as large as 24,000 words; since this study was done in 1940 it is highly probable that replications of such a study would show that children's vocabularies have grown through the influence of travel and the mass media.[9]

The recognition vocabulary is the largest of the four, however, and the child does not use all the words in his recognition vocabulary in his writing. The reading vocabulary is likely to be larger than the writing vocabulary and the speaking vocabulary is the smallest of all. Since in the beginning the child is likely to write as he talks, the need for vocabulary development in writing can be seen.

The growth and enrichment of vocabulary, as well as the content and context of his speaking and writing, derives from the child's experiences. The child acquires new vocabulary as the need occurs to communicate his experiences to others. The teacher who is aware of the dynamics of vocabulary development will provide both the new experiences and the opportunity to communicate to others the descriptions of the experiences and the child's reactions to them.

Vocabulary Development Techniques

The following list suggests a number of techniques which may be used by the teacher to develop vocabulary:

1. Informal conversation and discussion, stopping to give attention to words when the situation and the interest make it advisable.

[9]Smith, Mary Katherine, "Measurement of the Size of General English Vocabulary through the Elementary Grades and High School," *Genetic Psychology Monographs* 24:311-45, November, 1941.

2. Reading aloud to children material which they can understand and enjoy and which enriches and supplements their own reading as well as adds to their appreciation of their cultural heritage.
3. Reading textbook material with the children when it is difficult – reading and talking, talking and reading – to make vague and unfamiliar ideas clear ones through association and application to the children's own experience.
4. Taking field trips to gain firsthand experience. Both careful planning and follow-up activities are essential for the complete experience.
5. Using film and other types of auditory and visual aids which fit the study and add to its values.
6. Expressing new meaning graphically through various art mediums.
7. Dramatizing words very simply, as in the old game of charades or through more elaborate play.
8. Encouraging children to keep individual records of new vocabulary.
9. Keeping group records of the new vocabulary found in various experiences.
10. Giving attention to shades of meaning, to colorful words, to action words, to words that are especially vivid and effective.
11. Encouraging children to discover meaning from context and perhaps to check their meaning with the dictionary, at times, to determine their success in deducing meaning.
12. Working various types of exercises which meet the need of the group or individual; there are many kinds:

    a. Working with prefixes and suffixes
    b. Searching for synonyms and antonyms
    c. Checking in a list all words of like derivation
    d. Completing sentences by adding suitable words or word groups
    e. Matching words and definitions
    f. Fitting words into categories; animals, things to eat or drink, words describing people, words dealing with measuring. Keeping lists of these in the classroom to help with writing
    g. Word-meaning tests

    rapid happy slow fast race

13. Carrying on dictionary activities
14. Reading, reading, reading. The more the children read, the more meanings they learn.

    Reading things one is interested in
    Reading easy things for fun

Reading anything and everything that adds to the value of the things one is doing or studying
Reading to build new interests
Reading newspapers, magazines, books, catalogs – anything that adds interest to living[10]

The techniques listed are broadly suggestive of activities which may be used by a skillful teacher; the skillful teacher is still more important than the techniques in teaching children to acquire and use words. The importance of the teacher is well-stated by Applegate:

> "A teacher cannot give children a feeling for words unless she has it herself. But she can get a feeling as her children get it. The door is open to even the most colorless teacher; but to the colorful, not only is the door open, but the windows are up and the sun is shining through. You may be weak in your arithmetic teaching, be a poor writer, and be a worse musician; but, if you can give your children a feeling for words, you have changed their lives and given them genii which will serve them all their days and lead them into new and strange experiences."[11]

Writing: Function and Purpose

Writing is a process which follows the patterns of spoken language, the conventions of spelling, punctuation and capitalization and utilizes forms which are familiar to the reader. The product yielded by the writing process more or less adequately fulfills the function or purpose for which it was created. The degree to which the product is adequate is determined by the clarity of the purpose for which it was created and by the skills possessed by the writer. Both skills and purpose are important to the adequacy of the final product. There must be a purpose for the writer's writing and there must be sufficient skill to achieve the purpose. It is the intent of this section to discuss the possible functions and purposes for the child's writing.

Teachers' and Children's Goals for Writing

In the teacher- and textbook-centered classroom the child's needs for writing are given little attention. The emphasis is placed upon the child's learning the skills necessary to writing with little attention to providing

---

[10]Strickland, Ruth G., *The Language Arts in the Elementary School.* (Boston: D. C. Heath and Company, 1957) pp. 237-38.

[11]Applegate, Mauree, *Helping Children Write.* (Evanston: Row, Peterson and Company, 1954) p. 132.

meaningful opportunities for him to exercise and develop his skills in writing through purposeful writing experiences. The child's purpose in this classroom situation is satisfying the teacher. The teacher sets the tasks and the child is rewarded for following the teacher's directions. In this situation, the child's motivation for writing is extrinsic, that is, the purposes for writing originate with the teacher, not with himself. Intrinsic motivation is more effective in teaching children to write. With intrinsic motivation the teacher is still the director of learning; the classroom environment is structured by him so that many meaningful opportunities for writing are provided for children. Children see writing as fulfilling their personal needs rather than following the teacher's directions. The wise teacher realizes that self-motivated activities in writing are also effective in teaching the skills of writing. When children write real letters that will be mailed to real people, the need to spell correctly, to write neatly and to punctuate correctly is clear. The letter the child has written has purpose and function: the purpose is to communicate ideas to the person to whom he is writing; the letter form serves this function.

Providing Purposes for Writing

As the child gains increasing independence in his written communication, the number of situations in which he can find purposes for writing rapidly increases. While the following list from the Florida curriculum is perhaps most appropriate for the intermediate and upper elementary grades, many of the situations can be adapted to the skills of children in the lower grades.

1. Situations requiring letters
   a. Social notes of thanks, sympathy, invitation, etc.
   b. Business letters, orders for materials, preparations for a trip, or requests for information
   c. Friendly letters to pen pals or foreign friends
   d. Gift tags and greeting cards
2. Situations needing a record
   a. Plans made
   b. Class activities, events, sports, excursions, or science discoveries
   c. Minutes for clubs
   d. Room histories, diaries, or logs
3. Situations requiring filling out forms
   a. Registration slips, examination blanks, applications for admission to Red Cross swimming classes, checks, and receipts
   b. Telegrams or cablegrams

4. Situations requiring
   a. Reports by individuals or groups
   b. Panel discussions
   c. Directions and recipes
   d. Lists of materials – properties needed for a play or similar activity
   e. Dictation or copying of information or directions
   f. Bibliographies
5. Situations needing publicity
   a. Advertisements, notices, or announcements
   b. Articles for school or local newspaper
   c. Headlines for newspaper articles
   d. Legends for bulletin boards and exhibits
   e. Room duties to be posted
6. Situations stimulating
   a. Original arithmetic problems
   b. Riddles, puzzles, jokes
   c. Word pictures of people and places
   d. Editorials, news stories
   e. Stunts, skits, plays
   f. Song dramatizations, original choral readings
   g. Poems, stories, myths, fables[12]

The Importance of Intrinsic Motivation

Before a child begins to write, he must see the writing as being important to him; he must be motivated to write. The chief task of the teacher is to provide the motivation for the child's writing. This is true for the writing which has been called utilitarian or practical writing – the writing of reports, letters and memoranda – as for personal or imaginative writing of diaries, poetry, or creative prose. The division of writing into the categories of utilitarian and imaginative is arbitrary. It is hoped that all writing children do will be personal and imaginative. While a business letter is primarily utilitarian, most people have received a letter written for the purpose of soliciting a subscription to a magazine or even for collecting an overdue bill which, while patently utilitarian, is engaging and "creative" in its appeal. The apparent conflict between imaginative (creative) writing and practical (utilitarian) writing is well resolved by Tidyman and Butterfield:

---

[12]Florida Department of Education, *Experiencing the Language Arts, Bulletin No. 34.* (Tallahassee: State Department of Education, 1948) p. 137.

"Some authorities and teachers regard creative work as the basis of the language program; others regard it as a valuable supplement — another kind of activity. If by creative work is meant expressing one's own thought and feeling, then certainly all work should be creative. If, on the other hand, creative work refers to a kind of expression that is highly imaginative, emphasizing feeling, and emotions, employing many figures of speech and striving for especially vivid words and phrases, then creative work seems to take its place as a distinct activity. Creative work in the latter sense provides an emotional outlet, stimulates the imagination, broadens the vocabulary, and, through efforts at production, lays a basis for the enjoyment of imaginative literature. It has value for children, but a particular value for the child with a gift for literary expression."[13]

Consistent Encouragement of Creative Expression

The position taken in this chapter is that all children's written work should be creative within the limitations imposed by the purpose and the form of the writing. This emphasis upon creative expression is valuable for all children and is particularly valuable for the few children who have literary talent. This position does recognize, however, that some kinds of writing better lend themselves to creative expression. The following examination of the functions and purposes of children's writing therefore has been divided into two sections: utilitarian writing which discusses the primary formal (utilizing a particular form) such as the business letter and other primarily nonimaginative forms and the creative, which discusses the writing of personal, imaginative, self-expressive literary forms, such as poetry.

Utilitarian Writing

The term utilitarian writing in no sense suggests that creative or imaginative writing is not purposeful or useful. Utilitarian writing serves social ends primarily, although not exclusively: a letter to a friend, a business letter, a report to other class members, an article for the classroom newspaper. Because utilitarian writing must clearly communicate the ideas the writer wishes to convey, it offers the teacher opportunities to teach the importance of correct spelling, punctuation and capitalization. In the writing of letters, notes to parents, invitations and the like, the child sees the writing as being purposeful and is motivated to see that the punctuation serves to clarify meaning, the spelling is correct, the handwriting legible

[13]Tidyman, Willard F. and Marguerite Butterfield, *Teaching the Language Arts.* (Second edition; New York: McGraw Hill Book Co., Inc., 1959), pp. 26-27.

and the sentences are complete even if recopying is necessary to assure that his message is understood by the receiver.

Friendly or Social Letters

Many situations requiring the writing of friendly letters or social notes are presented in the typical classroom and many more can be created by the skillful teacher. The following are just a few of the purposeful activities:

Writing get-well notes or informative letters about classroom projects to classmates who are ill.

Invitations to parents to attend open house, plays, work exhibit, culminating activity in a unit of study, lunch, etc.

Notes requesting parent's permission to bring supplies for a science experiment or demonstration.

Notes requesting permission to bring pets to school for the annual "Pet Parade."

Letters to relatives, friends or pen pals. Names and addresses of pen pals in other states and nations can be obtained from the following sources:

The Christian Science Monitor
Boston, Massachusetts

The Junior Red Cross
Washington, D. C.

The International Friendship League
40 Mt. Vernon Street
Boston, Massachusetts
(fifty cents an address)

Parker Pen Company
Janesville, Wisconsin

Foreign Correspondence Bureau
P.O. Box 150
Newton, Kansas

Student Letter Exchange
Waseca, Minnesota
(twenty-five cents an address)

Dyer's Pen-Pal Service Organization
R.F.D. 3
Seguin, Texas

Letters to radio, television or motion picture celebrities and professional athletes expressing appreciation and perhaps requesting photographs.

Thank-you notes for gifts received or favors done.

Writing to Santa Claus.

Letter of congratulation to a friend who has received some honor or won some prize.

Letters to magazines or newspapers expressing an opinion on some topic or thanking the editor for the content.

Almost all of the letters suggested may be written by children in any elementary school grade with varying amounts of help from the teacher. The situations utilized by the teacher will be determined more by the children's interest than perhaps any other factor. Since friendly letters and social notes are essentially intimate and personal communications composed in private, some artificiality is interjected when, in the early grades, friendly letters are composed by the whole class and then copied by each child. Whatever artificiality is interjected in the situation is perhaps justified by the fact that children are introduced to friendly letter writing in a whole class situation and learn from the teacher that it is a satisfying and important activity which more and more assumes its personal and intimate nature when children become increasingly independent through the development of their writing skills. Especially to be stressed by the teacher is the writing of letters and notes of thanks for gifts and services, expressing congratulations, and other social forms which some children may not learn about outside of school.

Given a situation in which the child sees the purpose for writing a friendly letter, the teacher next has to teach the form and content of the letter. The form of the friendly letter is perhaps best introducd through a large classroom chart showing each of the parts labeled: heading, greeting, message, closing, and signature. With this chart on display the teacher can then read a real letter pointing out its parts which correspond to the chart. The chart should be left on display in the classroom until all the children have mastered the form of the friendly letter.

Teaching the content of a friendly letter is more difficult than teaching the form. One way that this might be done is to use the message of the friendly letter mentioned as an example of an interesting letter. After the teacher has read the letter the children discuss the qualities that make it interesting. For contrast, a less interesting letter might be read and the two compared. The letter that the teacher chooses as a model of content for a good friendly letter should contain the following characteristics: (1) it should be informal and conversational in tone, (2) it should relate personal information about the writer and his activities in which the writer feels the reader would be interested, (3) it should help to clarify and communicate the writer's message through correct spelling, punctuation, capitalization and sentence structure, (4) it should invite the writer's response through inquiries about his activities in which the writer is interested.

After the initial teaching (and reteaching to some or all children, if necessary) of the form and content of the friendly letter, the teacher should provide many meaningful situations such as those suggested in which the children may develop their skills in writing many different kinds of friendly letters and social notes.

Business Letters

Teaching children to write business letters has a built-in bonus for the teacher: after they have learned the correct form and appropriate content, the children may write for some of the many free instructional materials available. Writing these letters is purposeful and interesting to the children and the free materials they receive provide the stimulus for further utilitarian writing of reports using the materials. Since writing business letters requesting free materials is one of the best ways to provide meaningful practice, a few sources of the addresses of many industries which provide this service are listed below:

A Wonderful World for Children by Peter Cardozo, published by Bantam Books in 1962 and still available. The price is fifty cents. This is a paperback book containing many sources of free materials for which children can write. There should be at least one copy on every classroom teacher's desk. Bantam Books' address is 271 Madison Avenue, New York 16.

Wonderful World of Science, edited by Shirley Moore and Judith Viorst. Published by Bantam Books (1961) but still available at fifty cents. This paperback contains sources of free or inexpensive science materials which children may order. Since science is of interest to most children, this book may motivate some to write letters for free science materials.

Free and Inexpensive Learning Materials, published by Division of Surveys and Field Services, George Peabody College for Teachers, Nashville, Tennessee, 37203 at $2.00 a copy. This paperbound book of about 275 pages is published biennially and is well-indexed by subjects and topics likely to be studied in schools.

Having first introduced the form and content for the friendly letter, a discussion of the similarities and differences between the friendly letter and the business letter may be led by the teacher. The inside address, the more formal greeting, the terse businesslike tone of the message and the formal closing will probably be the characteristics of the business letter which the children will notice as being different from the friendly letter.

It would be desirable to display a chart in the classroom showing the form of the business letter until it has been thoroughly learned by all children.

In addition to writing for free materials from the sources mentioned, many other situations occur or can be created by the teacher to provide meaningful opportunities for children to write business letters.

> Letters written requesting visits to community resources such as the fire station, post office, airport, beaches, and state parks, television or radio stations, museums, railroad or bus stations, bakery, poultry or fish hatchery, nursery or greenhouse, soft drink bottling plant, dairy, municipal water treatment plant, municipal, state and federal government agencies.
>
> Letters to members of the community who have extensive knowledge of some subject requesting that they speak to the class or give a demonstration.

The key ideas to be remembered in teaching children to write both business and friendly letters are that the purpose for writing should come from a situation which is meaningful and important to the child and that the letters should be prepared according to standards which insure that the letter's message is understood by the recipient. Implicit is the assumption that the letter will actually be mailed. Attention to these details in teaching will help toward the child's acquisition of the important skills and rewards of letter writing.

Creative or Imaginative Writing

The writer's purpose in creative writing is different from that in utilitarian or practical writing. While it is true, particularly in the friendly letter, that utilitarian writing may have some personal creative elements, the purpose for the writing is to communicate a message with little attention to its personal or literary qualities. Utilitarian writing is centered upon the task to be accomplished; creative writing, on the other hand, focuses more upon the individual's unique perception of the world in which he lives and the expression of this perception through the sensitive, original uses of written language. Creative writing seeks more to express the writer's affective or emotional reactions to his experience while utilitarian writing centers more upon the cognitive or intellectual aspects of experience. It should be noted, however, that no consensus exists among the authorities on what constitutes creative writing.

Techniques for Motivating Creative Prose Writing

Assuming that the teacher has created the free, open and supportive classroom atmosphere in which a child's creativity can develop and flourish, techniques for releasing the child's unique personal and original responses through writing must be provided. The techniques in the following list have been used by teachers at all levels in the elementary school. Because of the variation found among children in a typical elementary school grade, the techniques are not arranged according to grade. The teacher is encouraged to experiment with the techniques according to the level of skill and interest of the children in his class. He may wish to modify the techniques to fit the unique characteristics of his class.

1. Make one envelope for each of the five parts of the story:
   a. main character
   b. character trait
   c. scene or setting
   d. the problem
   e what happens

   Have the pupils suggest what will be written on the slips to go into each envelope. The slips in the first envelope will have on them suggestions for the main character in the story the children will write. The slips in the second envelope will have suggestions for the character trait of the main character. For example, the child may draw from the first envelope a slip with "a child of ten" printed on it; this would be the main character for his story. A slip would be drawn from each envelope to get the component parts of his story.
2. The teacher reads the beginning of a story and the children write the ending to the story.
3. Make a "Poetry or Story Box" from a cardboard box and paint it with tempera. Whenever a story or poem is written by a child during his free time, he drops it into the box.
4. Have a "Quiet Hour" every week when everyone, including the teacher, does some sort of creative activity – writes, paints, draws, sews, models.
5. A series of short motion picture films called the "Finish the Story Series" are available for use in teaching creative writing. These films are available for purchase from:

Eastin Pictures Company
707 Putnam Building
Davenport, Iowa

Show the film *The Hunter and the Forest – A Story Without Words* as motivation for writing. This film has the sounds of nature, but includes no speech.

6. The teacher may write on the blackboard several descriptive phrases which concern some experience the children have had. For instance, six or eight phrases such as "rugged lineman," "jump pass" may be written on the board. The children are then asked what subject that reminds them of, and are asked to write a story using those phrases on the board.
7. The whole class makes a beginning for a story and each member of the class writes his or her own ending.
8. Ask the children to write about trips and reactions to trips they have taken. The teacher should ask some motivating questions before the children begin.
9. Listen to classical music and have the children write their reactions to the music.
10. Have the children list topics that have inspired them to write poetry such as:
    a. The First Snow
    b. Some Signs of Spring
    c. Some Smells I Like
11. Show the children a picture, preferably in color, and ask them to close their eyes, imagine they are in the picture, and write the things which they smell, see, and feel while they are in the picture.
12. Have the children write their reactions to situation which the teacher suggests. For example, have them complete the following sentences with their own reactions:
    a. Once I was very frightened when. . .
    b. The most beautiful sight I have seen was. . .
    c. If I had $10,000, I would. . .
13. If the teacher is alert, she can overhear children talking about the things in which they are interested. Then, during the creative writing period, the teacher may suggest topics of interest upon which certain children may write.
14. Suggest that the children write about the things which are on their minds before they go to sleep.
15. Ask the children to write their associations with certain emotionally-colored words such as "cozy." This exercise helps them to recall sense experiences which will help them in other creative writing.
16. As an exercise in recalling sense experiences, suggest that the children make a list of all the things they would see, hear, smell and feel at:
    a. the circus
    b. a baseball game
    c. a hike in the woods
    d. the beach

17. As a first experience in story writing, the teacher writes the beginning sentence of a story on the chalkboard. The class chooses among the sentences suggested by class members and a story is completed. The children might copy the story as a writing exercise.
18. Show the children a picture such as a boat sinking with the survivors in a life raft. After a brief discussion, have the children write a short story telling where the ship was going, how it was sunk, and what happens to the survivors.
19. Read the children a setting to a certain story. Ask them to write a story that might have taken place in that setting. For example, a jungle setting would probably lead to a story about wild animals.
20. Read an adventure story to the children. After having discussed the personalities of the characters, have them pick their favorite character and write a story of an adventure which this character, because of his personality, would probably have.
21. The teacher writes five or six words on the chalkboard. These words would be used to build the plot of the story. For example, log cabin, girl, old man, dog, baby. These words are to be used by the children as the framework for the story with them building the plot.
22. Write six or eight descriptive phrases on the chalkboard. After discussing the associations the children have with these phrases, ask them to write a story using as many of the related, descriptive phrases as they can.
23. Show the class one or more large colored pictures depicting some action. After discussion of the pictures and noting of details, the children are asked to write a paragraph describing what happened either fifteen minutes earlier or fifteen minutes later.
24. The teacher may make a statement of an imaginary situation such as, "What if, when you woke up in the morning, you looked into the mirror and saw it wasn't you?" The children are instructed to write an explanation of the situation.
25. After the completion of a basal reader unit on legends, folklore or tall-tales, these stories are reviewed and the children are told that they may make up a story of their own.
26. The experiences from which children write creatively come through their senses – sight, touch, taste, hearing. To develop a child's sensitivity to sensory experiences the following techniques can be used:
    a. Have the children close their eyes. The teacher passes some object around the room. The children are asked to write *how* it feels rather than *what* it feels like.
    b. Have the children sit with their eyes closed for one minute with the instructions that after that period of time they will write everything they felt, heard and smelled.
27. The teacher tells the story of the god, Neptune. The children write stories about the effect that this god might have on the sea.
28. After reading stories about Paul Bunyan, the children may write stories of other adventures that he might have had.

29. The children and/or the teacher make puppets. Stories or plays about the adventures the puppets might have are written by the children.
30. Have the children write stories about what they would do if they were teacher.
31. Forms which look like Rorschach ink blots may be made by dropping tempera or colored ink into the pre-creased center fold of a sheet of glossy paper. The sheet is then refolded along the center crease making a design as the ink or paint is forced out of the crease onto the paper. Multicolored blots can be made by adding more colors after each preceding color on the sheet is dry. When the ink or paint is dry, the sheets can be pressed flat with a warm iron and mounted with rubber cement on illustration board or other heavy backing. These inkblots can be displayed on a chalkboard tray as motivation for creative writing. Each child will write a different story. (A spray coating of clear plastic from a pressurized can will help to protect the inkblots from soil.)
32. Use the shapes of objects, people or animals discovered in clouds as the subjects for stories.
33. Objects whose source and function are unknown to the children are displayed. The children write stories about the source or function of the objects or about the people who might own or use the objects.
34. Objects such as an old kerosene lantern or other things such as wearing apparel, a book, etc. are displayed. The children write stories in which they assume that they are the object, telling about things they have seen, adventures they have had or people they have known.
35. Have a sealed box or bag containing various objects which the children can shake and feel. The children then write stories about what is in the box or who might have owned the objects.
36. When children get ideas for topics to write about, they write them on cards which are deposited in a box. When children have free time and wish to write, they draw a card from the box to get a topic to write about.
37. The class is divided into groups and each group is given a sack containing various costumes, props, and equipment. The children write a play in which they create characters according to these costumes and props. These plays can then be presented to the class.
38. A picture from a book or newspaper is magnified and copied using an opaque projector. The children write a story about the picture.
39. Use a sequence of three or four pictures as a stimulus for writing a story. To create new pictures, a picture from another unrelated sequence can be substituted for one or more of the pictures.
40. After playing music from *Carnival of the Animals* children can write descriptions of real or imaginary animals suggested to them by the music.
41. Have the children each take two animals and combine their characteristics to make an imaginary animal. Write about the characteristics of the new animal.

42. Have the children write stories about what would have happened to Jack in Jack and the Beanstalk if he hadn't had an ax when the giant was climbing down the beanstalk. Stories can be written about situations in other well-known stories such as Red Riding Hood.
43. After studying units in reading such as fairy tales or adventures the children write stories of the same type.
44. Have children write stories about the adventures of such well-known characters as Tom Sawyer as if they were alive today.
45. Have the children listen to unknown sound recorded on tape. They then write a story or poem about what the sound made them think of.
46. Display a picture about Halloween (or some other holiday), together with some words the children might use in a story about the picture.
47. Mount pictures with rubber cement inside manila folders. On the inside of the folders facing the picture, print, with a felt-tip pen, words which can be used in a story about the picture. These folders can be located in the classroom so that children have access to them for an independent activity. For the older children the pictures should be increasingly ambiguous, that is, they should be differently interpreted by different children.
48. The child is told to imagine that he is a person three inches tall. He is to write about what would happen if a physical law, such as gravity, were suddenly no longer in effect.
49. The child writes about what he would do if he found himself locked in the house alone, without television.
50. Have each child write down ideas for activities to do by himself; with two other people; with four other people.
51. The children are asked to describe something they would like to invent.
52. Each child is asked to selcet some invention and write a humorous or fanciful story about the conditions which led to its invention.
53. The teacher may suggest that the child write an imaginary conversation between the sun and the moon. To give the children some ideas for this, certain facts about the two bodies such as relative size, distance between and the presence of man-made satellites may be mentioned.
54. Play a record to create a mood and background for story writing. Suggested records: The Moldau by Smetana, "On the Trail" from the Grand Canyon Suite by Grofe, Stravinski's Firebird Suite, A Night on Bald Mountain by Mussorgsky.
55. After reading the story of "Pegasus, the Wingéd Horse," ask the children: "What would you do and where would you go if you could have Pegasus for a day?"

The following techniques are suggested by Baker and Rose:

1. Imagine that you are a star creature and make a visit to this world we know. Tell of your surprises.
2. Imagine that you have a space ship that can take you to another planet. Tell of your experiences.

3. Imagine that you have an animal that can talk. Tell of your experiences with this animal.
4. Imagine you have a pair of seven-league boots. Describe a day's adventure in time and space.
5. Imagine that you can put on a special pair of glasses and see a thousand years into the future. Describe a scene that you might witness.
6. Imagine that you are an inch high or three times your size. How would the dimensions of your present world seem to you?
7. Imagine that you can make yourself invisible by using magic fluid or by putting on a special garment. Describe your adventures.[14]

FREDDY **By Rupe**

Children's Poetry Writing

The same classroom atmosphere which the teacher develops to encourage creative response in prose writing will encourage poetry writing. Writing poetry necessitates the use of a different form which better fits the ideas to be expressed and the particular language in which the ideas are to be expressed. Children can be introduced to the form and content of poetry through the teacher's reading poetry to them. The poetry selected should be drawn from experiences which are meaningful to the children. Through the teacher's reading, children gain an appreciation for poetry and upon this appreciation the teacher builds. Poems that children like can be discussed and the poetic uses of imagery discovered. As children's language develops, they will become increasingly able to express their

[14]Baker, G. Derwood, and Elizabeth Rose, *Creative Writing in the Junior High School.* Educational Leadership, May 1957, pp. 478-482.

ideas in imaginative, original and creative words. The developmental sequence in learning to write poetry is similar among all children, but the learning does not take place automatically; the teacher must guide each child's growth.

Guides to Performance Expectancies

While space does not permit a detailed discussion of teaching poetry writing, a helpful guide to subject matter and style expectancy is given by Walter:

1. First and second grades (ages 6 to 8)
   a. Subject matter: immediate experiences
   b. Style
      1) Largely narrative
      2) Little or no rhyme
2. Third and fourth grades (ages 8 to 10)
   a. Subject matter
      1) Immediate experiences
      2) Remembered experiences
   b. Style
      1) Narrative enhanced by picture words
      2) Simple analogies
      3) Little rhyme
      4) Occasional use of couplet and ballad stanza
3. Fifth and sixth grades (ages 10-12)
   a. Subject matter
      1) Immediate experiences
      2) Remembered experiences
      3) Imagined experiences
      4) Ideas about the natural world
   b. Style
      1) Falling off of narrative
      2) Expansion of picture-making quality
      3) Conscious use of analogy and imagery
      4) Use of simple verse forms and some rhyme
      5) Originality of thought and phrasing
      6) Sincerity of feeling but not depth of feeling
4. Junior high school (grades 7, 8, and 9; ages 12 to 16)
   a. Subject matter (change of approach)
      1) Immediate, remembered, and imagined experiences
      2) Emotional experiences; deepening of feeling
      3) Ideas about the natural world
      4) Ideas about the relationship of people
      5) Ideas about self
      6) Beginning of the subjective approach to experience

b. Style
   1) A groping for form and pattern, even in free verse
   2) First use of the vocabulary of emotion
   3) Occasional appearance of the longer poem
   4) The attempt to make a complete statement of the idea[15]

In addition to Walter's excellent book on teaching children to write poetry, there is also an excellent treatment in Arnstein's book.[16]

Hughes Mearns' classic book, *Creative Power* is an excellent resource for the teacher of elementary school creative writing. Chapter XI "Poetry is When You Talk to Yourself," is a delightful reading experience filled with practical suggestions for teaching poetry.[17]

Evaluating Children's Writing

Evaluating children's writing ought to include attention to all those educational values which are pursued in teaching them to write. Among these would certainly be included accuracy in spelling, punctuation, and capitalization and the use of correct forms in writing such as those for the friendly letter and the business letter. Outcomes such as these are relatively easy to assess; these are objectives which deal with correctness and the mechanical aspects of writing. Since these objectives are relatively easy to assess, the teacher is likely to give first attention to them.

One facet of the teacher's role is usually thought of as that of "grader-of-papers." This role persists even in the face of the evidence that children learn the mechanics of writing more readily when they are made responsible for their own proofreading and corrections. In utilitarian writing in particular children should, from the very beginning, be taught to make first drafts, proofread and rewrite in order that the reader is able to understand the ideas the writer is attempting to communicate. Standards and form charts to which the child can refer in the classroom help to encourage independence and correctness. When the child first begins to write, the teacher will of course give more assistance and guidance, but his goal should be to encourage the child to become an increasingly independent writer. This goal is reached most rapidly when the child does not depend upon the teacher to make sure that his writing

---

[15]Walter, Nina Willis, *Let Them Write Poetry;* (New York: Holt, Rinehart and Winston, 1962), pp. 83-84.

[16]Arnstein, Flora J., *Poetry in the Elementary Classroom;* (New York: Appleton-Century-Crofts, 1962).

[17]Mearns, Hughes; *Creative Power: The Education of Youth in the Creative Arts.* (New York: Dover Publications, Inc., 1958), p. 106-115.

is correct. With all good intentions, a teacher may continue to grade or correct a child's papers without realizing that once the child has noted the grade he has received, no further attention is given to improving his writing. He is content to be "a C student."

The outcomes of the child's imaginative writing are less objectively assessed. The content of the writing is more personal and original. The assessment of literary merit and originality requires more subjective judgments. Because this is true, teachers are tempted to follow the pattern of correcting and grading the spelling and mechanics in imaginative writing just as they have in utilitarian writing. Often this results in discouraging the child. When his story is returned by the teacher with errors marked with red pencil he is not encouraged to expose his original ideas to further criticism in the future. He may choose the less threatening alternative of withdrawing into himself.

An alternative approach is one which emphasizes the personal, unique content of imaginative writing rather than correctness on first draft. The teacher should help the child to clarify his ideas and put them into more readable form; ideas which are imaginatively expressed should be pointed out and the child complimented for them. Correctness in writing is not unimportant, it is just less important than the ideas being expressed.

EXTENDING YOUR LEARNING

1. Read more about *kinesics;* prepare a report and demonstration explaining the relation of nonverbal signs to communication.
2. Examine the list on pages 153 and 154. In one column list those writing situations which require utilitarian writing; in another column list those which require imaginative writing. Place a check mark in either column beside those situations which might require both kinds of writing.
3. Find and compare some different definitions of creative writing. With which do you agree? Why?
4. Develop a list of qualities with examples which can be utilized in evaluating children's imaginative writing of prose and poetry. (See Walter, *Let Them Write Poetry,* Chapter 8.)
5. Using some of the techniques for motivating imaginative writing, collect samples of children's writing from several grades and compare them. You may wish to evaluate the samples using the list you developed in suggestion 4.

BIBLIOGRAPHY

Applegate, Mauree. *Helping Children Write.* Evanston: Row, Peterson and Company, 1954. 173 pp.

Arnstein, Flora J. *Poetry in the Elementary Classroom.* New York: Appleton-Century-Crofts, 1962.

Baker, G. Derwood, and Elizabeth Rose. "Creative Writing in the Junior High School," *Educational Leadership,* May, 1957, 478-482.

Burrows, Alvina Treut, Doris C. Jackson, and Dorothy O. Saunders. *They All Want to Write – Written English in the Elementary School.* New York: Holt, Rinehart and Winston, 1964. Third edition. 281 pp.

Carey, G. V. *Mind the Stop: A Brief Guide to Punctuation with a Note on Proof Correction.* Cambridge: University Press, 1958. 130 pp.

Carlson, Ruth Kearney. "Seventeen Qualities of Original Writing," *Elementary English,* XXXVIII (December, 1961), 576-579.

Carlson, Ruth Kearney. "Recent Research in Originality," *Elementary English,* XXXX, (October, 1963), 30-31.

Florida Department of Education. *Experiencing the Language Arts, Bulletin No. 34.* Tallahassee: State Department of Education, 1948.

Furness, Edna Lue. "Pupils, Pedagogues, and Punctuation," *Elementary English,* March, 1960, 187-89.

Greene, Harry A., and Walter T. Petty. *Developing Language Skills in the Elementary Schools.* Boston: Allyn and Bacon, Inc., 1963. 572 pp.

Laird, Charlton. *The Miracle of Language.* Greenwich: Fawcett Publications, Inc., 1957. 255 pp.

Mearns, Hughes. *Creative Power: The Education of Youth in the Creative Arts.* New York: Dover Publications, Inc., 1958. 272 pp.

Sapir, Edward. *Language: An Introduction to the Study of Speech.* New York: Harcourt, Brace and World, 1921.

Smith, Mary Katherine. "Measurement of the Size of General English Vocabulary through the Elementary Grades and High School," *Genetic Psychology Monographs, 24*:311-45, November, 1941.

Strickland, Ruth G. *The Language Arts in the Elementary School.* Boston: D. C. Heath and Company, 1957. 464 pp.

Tidyman, Willard F., and Marguerite Butterfield. *Teaching the Language Arts.* Second edition. New York: McGraw Hill Book Co., Inc., 1959. 403 pp.

Trauger, Wilmer K. *Language Arts in Elementary Schools.* New York: McGraw-Hill Book Company, 1963. 393 pp.

Walter, Nina Willis. *Let Them Write Poetry.* New York: Holt, Rinehart and Winston, 1962. 179 pp.

Chapter 7 Pose Lamb

Teaching and Improving Handwriting in Elementary Schools

We are told that post office employees reject, return to the sender, or assign to the dead letter office thousands of letters every year because names and addresses on the envelopes cannot be read. Pharmacists struggle valiantly to decode physicians' prescriptions correctly. Many college instructors refuse to accept anything but typewritten themes, reports or term papers from students. Today there seems to be little emphasis on "a beautiful hand"; legibility is a goal which is not always achieved, much less attractiveness and neatness. What has caused this apparent deterioration of handwriting in the United States? Is the "second R" being neglected in our schools? More specifically, are our elementary teachers setting a proper example with their own handwriting? Is enough instructional time and energy devoted to this important tool subject?[1,2]

The key word in the last question is *tool.* Handwriting is basically a tool of communication, a means by which we record our ideas for others. Legible handwriting is an essential element in communicating with large numbers of people or someone who is out of sight and voice range. There may soon be a time when typewriters, tape recorders and the telephone may eliminate the need for applying pen or pencil to paper, but we are not now living in such an age.

If legible handwriting is also pleasing to the eyes, this is an added bonus, as is the ability to write rapidly. If one has a great deal to say, there is an obvious advantage to being able to write quickly as well as

[1]J. Kendrick Noble, "Handwriting Programs in Today's Schools," *Elementary English* 40:506-512, 517, May, 1963.

[2]Robert O'Brien, "The Moving Finger Writes – But Who Can Read It," *Saturday Review,* July 18, 1959, p. 8.

legibly. Of the most commonly expressed goals or objectives of handwriting programs – legibility, ease, neatness, and speed – legibility must be termed the most important. Our goal as elementary teachers is to help children acquire a handwriting style which can be read easily without strain, so that the ideas expressed are quite clear to the reader. What is of most importance are the ideas expressed, not the style or speed with which these words are put on paper.

Children must nonetheless be helped first, to learn to write legibly, clearly and neatly, and to work consistently toward better handwriting throughout the elementary school period and beyond. It is an expected courtesy to those with whom one is communicating through writing to eliminate unnecessary flourishes and affectations, to make one letter clearly distinguishable from the next, and to present what is written in a neat and easily interpreted form. To accept a sixth grader's poor handwriting as inevitable, to admit that one's own handwriting is a poor example for pupils to follow seems to be an evasion of responsibility for teaching such an important tool of communication.

One purpose of this chapter is to help clarify the position of handwriting instruction in the elementary school curriculum and to help provide some perspective from which to view handwriting so that its importance is neither underemphasized nor overemphasized. To claim, as some do, that teaching handwriting is unnecessary, that communication will soon be primarily through telephone, telegraph, tape recorder and the typewriter is somewhat analogous to claiming that teaching the basic addition facts is out of date, since pupils will refer to pocket computers for such mundane data in the future. While the telephone and the other means of communication referred to have obviated the need for some laborious writing, there clearly is still a need for teaching and reteaching the skill of communicating through the handwritten word.

Typical Handwriting Programs

What *is* a typical handwriting program in today's elementary schools? How is the sometimes neglected, much-maligned second R taught – if at all? Two studies, with somewhat contradictory findings, will provide some data regarding the present status of handwriting instruction. Petty reports that 30 per cent of all school systems have no handwriting programs at all and 50 per cent of the school systems surveyed do not provide a separate handwriting period.[3] Findings reported in *New Horizons for Research in*

[3]Walter Petty, "Handwriting and Spelling: Their Current Status," *Elementary English* 41: 839-844, December, 1964.

Handwriting[4] are somewhat more reassuring. Herrick reports that 98 per cent of the teachers involved in a national survey and 95 per cent of those in the Wisconsin Survey he directed indicated that they did teach handwriting.

Herrick's findings further suggest that class periods for teaching handwriting are usually fifteen to twenty minutes in length regardless of grade level, but for the first four grades teachers usually planned five periods a week; for grades five through eight, the number of periods per week was reduced to three. In direct contradiction to Petty's statement, Herrick reports:

> Schools favor a separate handwriting class period plus teaching handwriting in some meaningful context in all subject areas. Fifteen percent of the responses indicated handwriting and spelling were taught together regularly.[5]

What factors are emphasized in the handwriting periods? What is the teacher trying to accomplish? In the primary grades, correctness of letter formation, neatness of writing, size and uniformity of letters and spacing of letters and words receive major emphasis. In the fifth and sixth grades, speed receives more emphasis and so does the alignment of words and sentences.[6]

In fourteen per cent of the schools participating in Herrick's handwriting survey only cursive handwriting is taught. In seven per cent of the schools only manuscript writing is taught. In the remaining seventy-nine per cent of the schools, both manuscript and cursive writing are taught. The transition from manuscript to cursive writing is typically made in the second half of Grade Two or the first half of Grade Three.[7]

Grade Level Goals

The surveys reported in the preceding section provide an overview of the content of typical handwriting programs, but it would be helpful to have more specific grade level goals or objectives detailed. The following are composite goals or objectives and represent summaries of material included in several curriculum guides.

---

[4]*New Horizons for Research in Handwriting*, ed. by Virgil Herrick, Madison, Wisconsin: The University of Wisconsin Press, 1963.
[5]*Ibid.*, p. 20.
[6]*Ibid.*, p. 21.
[7]*Ibid.*, pp. 19-20.

Kindergarten and First Grade

1. Children should be familiar with writing as a form of communication. This suggests that the teacher will utilize labels, charts, and stories dictated by children to accompany pictures.

2. Children probably will learn to write their names and usually will master the basic shapes used in manuscript writing. Many will be able to write short notes, stories, invitations, holiday greetings, etc., and most will be able to copy these from the chalkboard.

3. By the last months of first grade most children have mastered the manuscript alphabet, upper and lower case letters. A few will not reach this stage until second grade.

4. Mastery of the ten basic numerals is achieved by most pupils.

Second and Third Grades

1. A majority of children have achieved mastery of the manuscript alphabet to the extent that they can write original stories, reports, etc. By the end of the second grade handwriting has become a truly functional tool for most children.

2. Children are becoming more skillful in spacing words and letters, and alignment of words and letters on a paper does not present the difficulties it once did. As a result papers are neater, more legible, and more attractive.

3. If the transition from manuscript to cursive writing is made in second or third grade, and it usually is, it is made gradually. While certain elements of joining letters, introduction of slant, etc., may be "taught" to an entire class for the purpose of saving time, it is not expected that children will make the transition with uniformity or with equal ease and ability.

4. Although children are making the transition from manuscript to cursive writing, skill in manuscript writing is maintained. Many children will continue to use the latter for independent writing activities because it is faster and easier for them.

5. Children are becoming increasingly aware of the significance of such details as punctuation, margins, paragraphs, etc.

6. Ball-point pens are introduced as writing instruments, usually in third grade.

Fourth, Fifth and Sixth Grades

1. Children are achieving mastery of cursive writing and developing individual writing styles.

2. Manuscript writing is still maintained for labeling, map work, charts, etc. Children are encouraged to retain this skill throughout the elementary school period.

3. Children are acquiring the objectivity necessary for self-evaluation of handwriting. Teachers have encouraged this in the primary grades, of course, but more emphasis is placed upon self-help and individual responsibility for handwriting improvement in the intermediate and upper grades. Proofreading receives a great deal of emphasis.

4. A degree of mastery is achieved in fields related to handwriting such as punctuation, paragraphing, identification and placement of topic sentences, etc.

5. Pens (ball-points) are used with as much ease and fluency as pencils. Fountain pens may also be used.

Commercial Systems

Although there is little evidence that such an adjustment is made in the handwriting programs included in the surveys reported thus far, it appears that there is a genuine need to make more provisions for individual differences in handwriting programs.[8] The left-handed child, the poorly-coordinated child, the child with vision problems generally receive less help than they deserve in learning to write legibly and easily. Undoubtedly some of the reasons for this inattention to individual differences relate to professional disinterest in teaching handwiting. Lack of interest reflects in teaching just as it does in learning. It is submitted that another reason is the general and almost complete reliance upon commercial handwriting systems which may tend to support, tacitly at least, a "lock-step" approach to handwriting instruction.

Herrick writes:

> The greatest single factor in determining the nature of the instructional program in a given school is the commercial system of handwriting instruction being used. This is perhaps more true for handwriting than any other area of the elementary school curriculum.[9]

Petty makes a similar statement, then adds:

> As many as sixteen commercial programs are in use, with another ten commercial systems being used which emphasize other facets of the language arts. These latter ten, therefore, are classified as only

---

[8]*Ibid.*, p. 20.
[9]*Ibid.*, p. 27.

partial handwriting programs. The various handwriting programs show considerable divergence in letter forms sequence in the introduction of letters and recommended teaching practices.[10]

Three of the more popular of these systems will be discussed, primarily to illustrate the variation and the careful attention to articulation and sequential development built into these programs.

Imaginary Line Handwriting, published by the Steck Company in 1956. The author of this series is Rebecca Mae Townsend.

In this series the letters are grouped (for teaching purposes) according to the similarity of strokes used in making them. Difficulty of formation governs the introduction of letters, and capital letters are introduced before lower case letters. Much stress is placed on stopping letters before the base line above is reached. In some handwriting systems, this point is stressed later in the first grade, but in the "Imaginary Line" program it is considered an essential, and is stressed from the beginning. The "imaginary line" concept refers to the relationship between the capital letters and the lower case letters. The child is to "see" a line at the top of the lower case letters and make the capitals, and the tall lower case letters, twice this height. The "t" is one exception, and stops halfway between the first and second imaginary lines. Although the publishers and author recommend delaying the beginning of cursive writing until children have a feeling of satisfaction with manuscript writing, the transition lessons are included in the second grade books. Cursive letters are also introduced in groups, according to the types of strokes involved. The imaginary line is again used to control letter height.

Better Handwriting for Everyone, written and published by Noble and Noble, 1962.

Capital letters and lower case letters are introduced at the same time that children are learning manuscript writing. Emphasis is placed upon teacher demonstration prior to the pupils' writing first on the chalkboard and then in their workbooks or copybooks, the initial experiences in cursive writing (and this transition takes place in the workbooks designed for third grade, not second). The pupils practice the small or lower case letters first in making the transition from manuscript to cursive writing. As the reader surveys the alphabets reproduced following, he will probably want to contrast the "K" lower case and capital, and the "R" lower case and capital, in the Noble and Steck programs:

---

[10]Walter F. Petty, "Handwriting and Spelling: Their Current Status," *Elementary English,* December, 1964, p. 841.

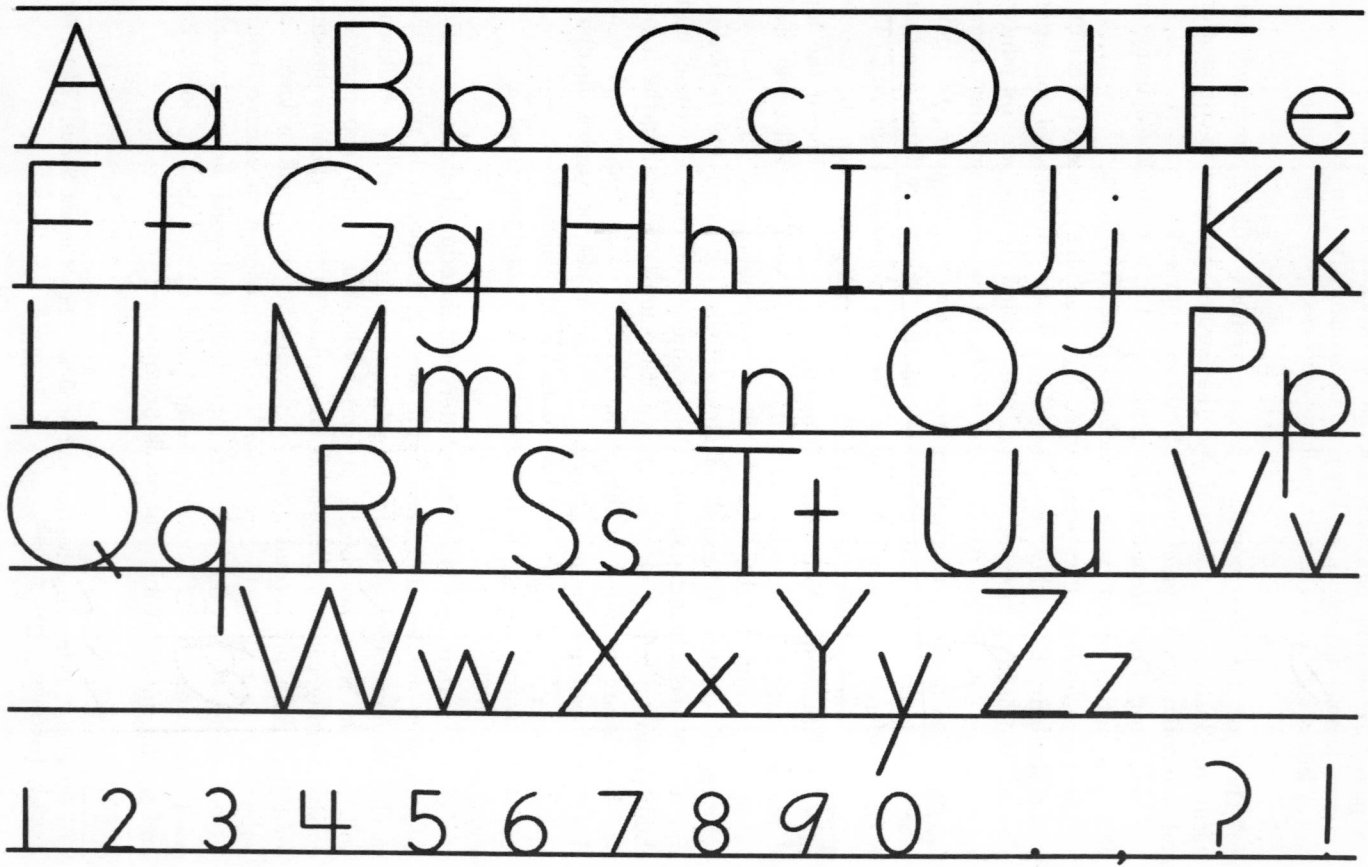
Aa Bb Cc Dd Ee
Ff Gg Hh Ii Jj Kk
Ll Mm Nn Oo Pp
Qq Rr Ss Tt Uu Vv
Ww Xx Yy Zz
1 2 3 4 5 6 7 8 9 0 . , ? !

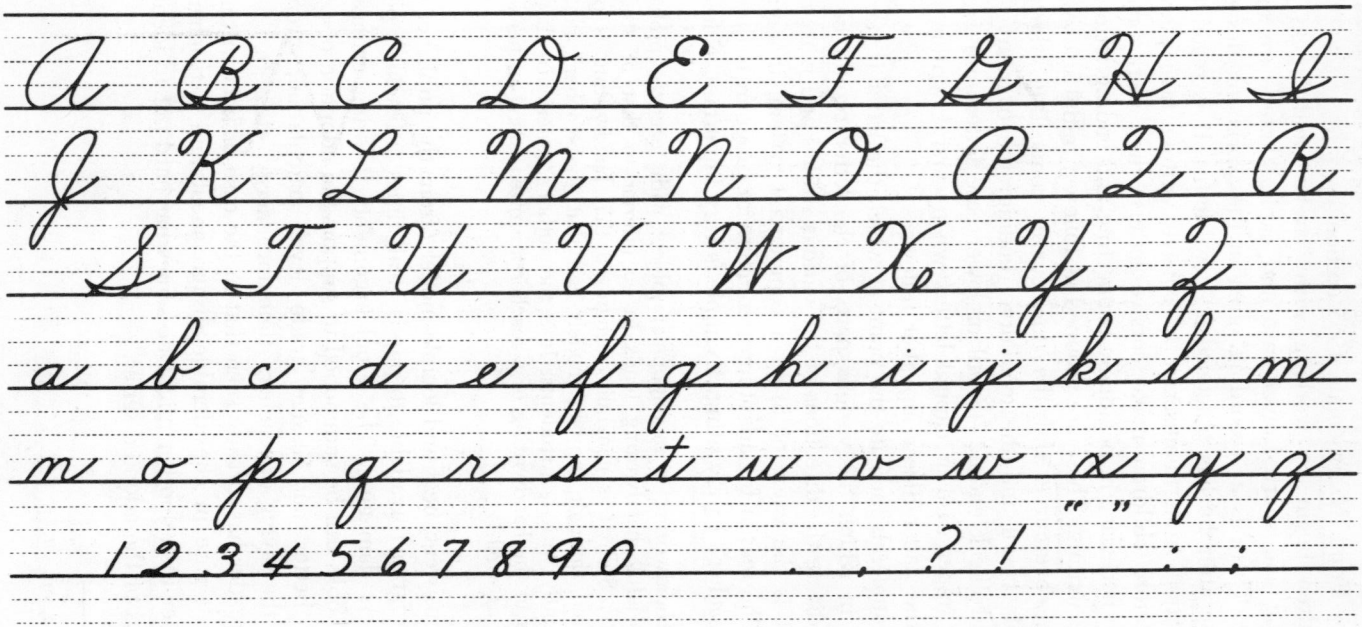
A B C D E F G H I
J K L M N O P Q R
S T U V W X Y Z
a b c d e f g h i j k l m
n o p q r s t u v w x y z
1 2 3 4 5 6 7 8 9 0 . , ? ! " " : ;

Guiding Growth in Handwriting, published by Zaner-Bloser Company, written by Frank N. Freeman, 1965 edition.

Children begin by working with "circles" and "sticks," small and large, long and short. Lower case and capital letters are taught simultaneously. There is a "recording" area in the workbook designed for the child's use after he has practiced a "new" letter. It is recommended that the transition from manuscript to cursive writing take place at Grade Three. Before children make cursive letters, they work on the strokes which are necessary in beginning connecting and ending letters and words in cursive writing. These are grouped as follows: initial strokes; the undercurve, the overcurve and the downcurve; connecting; the undercurve, the double curve and the overcurve; ending; the overcurve, the undercurve, and check endings. Small or lower case letters are presented first and then upper case or capital letters when cursive writing is taught. A copy of the Zaner-Bloser alphabet follows:

The numerals indicate the point at which the letter is started and the sequence in which the various parts of the letter should be made. The arrows indicate the directions of the various strokes and parts of letters.

What is the value of using a commercial system, if any? There are several. One reason for adapting a commercial program is the low quality of most teacher's handwriting. Example is very important. Noble writes:

> Handwriting is an unpopular subject with teachers, probably because adult handwriting tends to be inferior to that of students in quality. Still, it is generally recognized that handwriting is primarily acquired through copying models and that the teacher's models are constantly with her students. It is the author's experience that peculiarities in the handwriting of a teacher are often found in her student's work as well.[11]

With a consistent, neat and legible model (from the publisher of the commercial program) available to pupils at all times, a teacher's poor example may be less damaging. The usual arguments favoring extensive reliance upon textbooks can be summoned to support the adoption of a commercial program: better and easier grade level articulation, preparation by "experts," the saving of teachers' time and energy, etc., etc.

The reader has already seen that in the case of handwriting textbooks the "experts" are in considerable disagreement and a teacher using one series rather than another might be somewhat hard-put to identify specific advantages of the adopted series.

---

[11]Noble, *op. cit.,* p. 511.

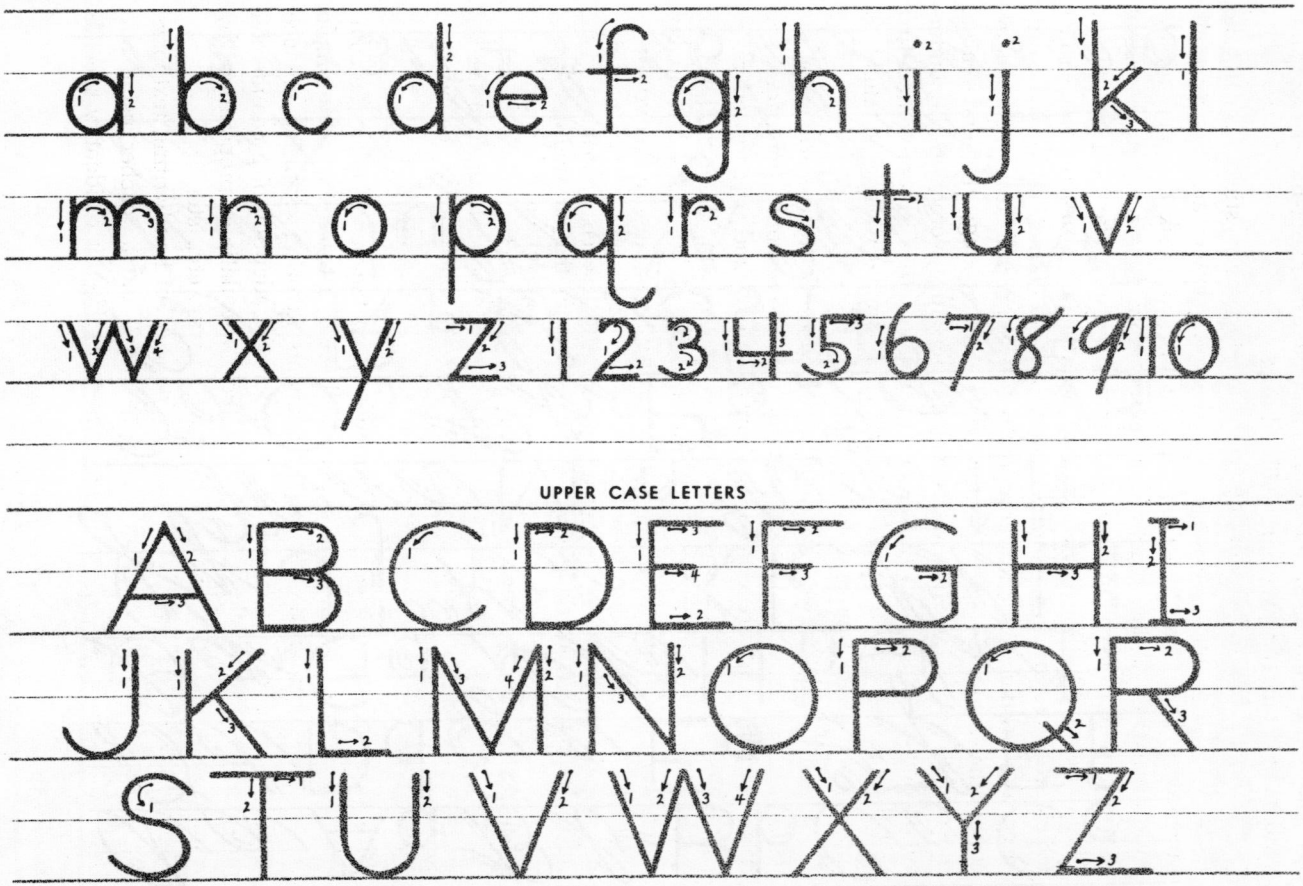
a b c d e f g h i j k l
m n o p q r s t u v
w x y z 1 2 3 4 5 6 7 8 9 10
UPPER CASE LETTERS
A B C D E F G H I
J K L M N O P Q R
S T U V W X Y Z

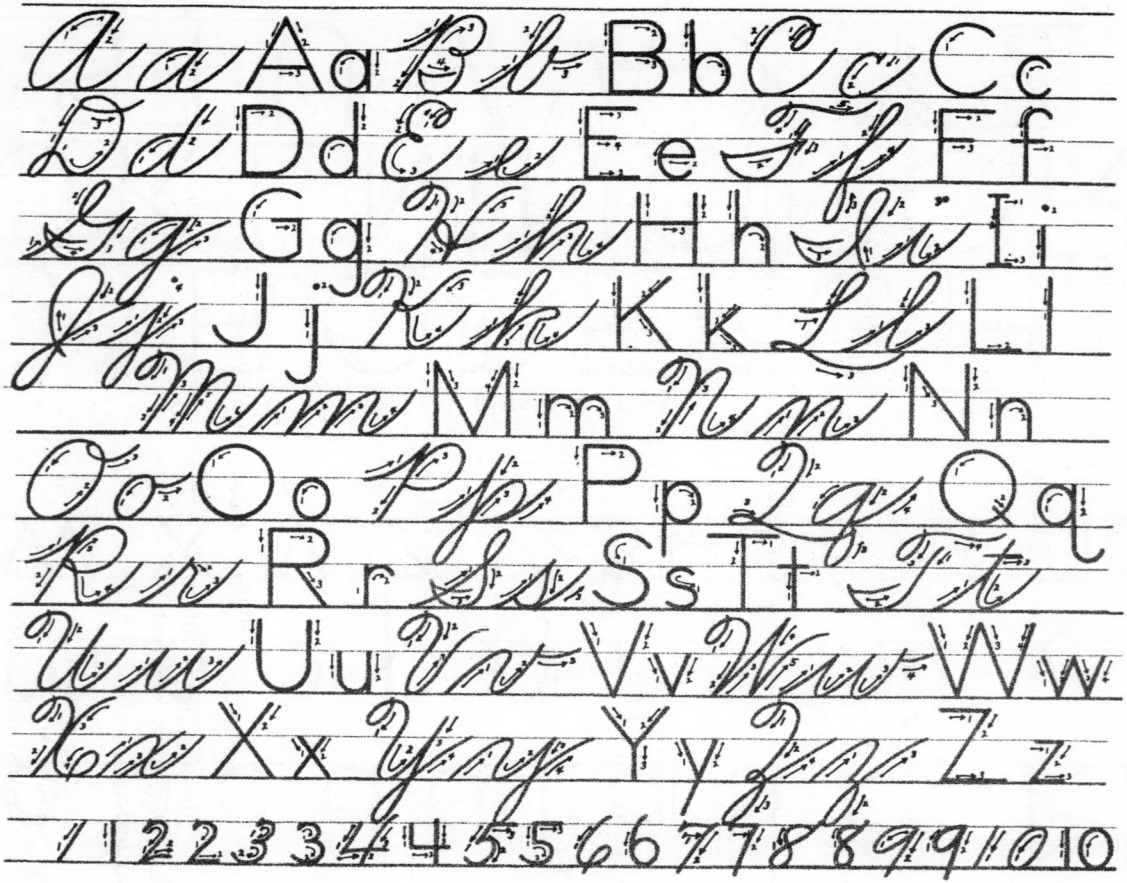
Aa Aa Bb Bb Cc Cc
Dd Dd Ee Ee Ff Ff
Gg Gg Hh Hh Ii
Jj Jj Kk Kk Ll Ll
Mm Mm Nn Nn
Oo Oo Pp Pp Qq Qq
Rr Rr Ss Ss Tt Tt
Uu Uu Vv Vv Ww Ww
Xx Xx Yy Yy Zz Zz
1 1 2 2 3 3 4 4 5 5 6 6 7 7 8 8 9 9 10 10

If a copybook-workbook series is selected the selection should be made by classroom teachers who will have to use the series, with the advice of and in concert with school system administrators.[12] Many publishers employ consultants who will provide in-service help for teachers in the form of workshops and lecture-demonstrations. Referring again to the significance of the teacher's example, such in-service help should be considered a valuable "plus" accompanying the newly adopted handwriting series. Teachers who use an adopted series will try, insofar as it is practical, to use the program in a manner which promotes each child's handwriting growth. This means supplementing lessons taken from the guide or manual with additional practice sessions and omitting some lessons which are unnecessary for reasonably bright, well-coordinated youngsters. It also means that the teacher and the children will be aware of the need for neat, legible handwriting *whenever* communication is the goal, not only during the handwriting period when the example of the copybook is clearly evident. Nor can the teacher excuse his own poor writing on the basis of the good example set by the handwriting series or the alphabet cards accompanying the series.

If handwriting series have caused the programs to become rigid and inflexible, it is not because of anything inherent in the series but because of the way too many teachers have used them. Wisely used a carefully selected handwriting series can be a valuable tool, aiding the teacher in many ways.

In discussing the use of a handwriting series, the terms "cursive" and "manuscript" writing have been employed. These terms may require definition. Manuscript writing is similar to printing; cursive writing involves the connection of letters and frequently some "slant" to the writing. These two styles or methods of writing will be discussed in the following sections.

"Why Manuscript Writing"

"Manuscript" writing, also called print-script and print handwriting, had its genesis in Great Britain in the early part of this century. Enstrom writes:

> Our present primary writing began in London, England in 1913 when a Mr. Edward Johnston gave a talk before a group of London teachers and outlined an 'ideal program in writing'. Mr. Johnston's

[12]For an example of how this process worked in one large school system, see Jessie K. How, "Handwriting is Important: Seattle Prepares a K-12 Program," *Elementary English*, 41: 851-853, 932, December, 1964.

> chief interest was a study of the handwriting of ancient manuscripts and the current use of such writing for formal resolutions, diplomas, etc. Like men who develop a love and enthusiasm for a particular area he waxed eloquent with the desire that men immediately adapt his pet ideas. His fond hope was that his ancient Italic manuscript be taught in the schools of his day. Because of his ability to foresee primary grade difficulties, he recommended that these children begin by learning a simple Roman style and later move to the broad edge pen work he loved so well.[13]

Teachers tried and liked the "simple Roman style;" they liked it so well that the hoped-for move never took place! The name manuscript was given to this simple style – based then, as now, on circles, straight lines and combinations of these shapes – because it was imitative of the style used in ancient manuscripts. In spite of current efforts to change the name (note the title of the article by Enstrom), most primary teachers in the United States refer to this style as manuscript writing and it will be called manuscript writing throughout this chapter.[14]

Johnston's "simple Roman style" came to the United States in the second decade of this century. Classes in the "new method" were taught at Columbia University's Teachers College. Miss Marjorie Wise, from England, taught such a course in 1922, calling the method "print-script." Teachers-educators in this country were almost immediately won over; manuscript writing became as popular in the United States as it had been in Great Britain. Although there are distinct differences in the alphabets devised by various commercial firms, some adaptation of the basic circle-straight line alphabet is used in the great majority of first grade classrooms in the United States today.[15]

Reasons for Use of Manuscript

A careful examination of just one manuscript alphabet will provide several clues as to the reasons for the widespread acceptance of manuscript writing as a tool of communication for young children:

a b c d e f g h i j k l m n o p q r s t u v w x y z
A B C D E F G H I J K L M N O P Q R S T U V W X Y Z

---

[13]E. A. Enstrom, "Print Handwriting Today," *Elementary English,* December, 1964, p. 846.

[14]The writer recalls, with a smile, the confusion of a friend, a newcomer to elementary education, when he was asked to submit a paper on manuscript writing in a language arts methods class. He dutifully prepared a paper dealing with the preparation of authors' manuscripts for publication by book company editors.

[15]Enstrom (op. cit., p. 846) says the teaching of manuscript writing in the primary grades is practically universal in the United States. This supports the data, previously quoted, from Herrick's study.

There are only two basic shapes to master: the circle and the straight line. Every letter *is* one of these two shapes (the lower case o, the lower case l) a *combination* of the shapes (the lower case b and d) or a variation of one or the other shapes (the lower case x or s, for example). The shapes of the letters are not difficult for immature hand and finger muscles to master.

A second reason for using manuscript writing with young children is related to combining the letters of an alphabet into words. Cursive writing, by its very name, suggests the joining of letters in a "running script" or a "course." Words formed of manuscript letters permit a child to pause, to stop, to rest, whether or not a word has been finished. This also contributes to ease and early success in communicating.

A comparison of any of the more widely used manuscript alphabets[16] with the print type used in the reading materials prepared for beginners will illustrate the third and perhaps the most compelling reason for teaching a manuscript alphabet. The letters of most manuscript alphabets and the print used in most primary reading materials (trade banks, basal readers, newspapers and magazines) are so similar to be almost indistinguishable. The upper case or capital M (M), W (W) and the lower case k (k) vary in the different systems, and may differ from the print in books; the a (a) in many textbooks is probably not the manuscript a the children have learned to make. These ordinarily are not difficult adjustments for children to make. Children who learn manuscript writing learn that what they write, just as charts made by the teacher and preprimers can be read. Reading and writing, then, are seen as related processes. Although there certainly is more to writing and reading than translating oral language into and from print, it does seem probable that the beginning reading process is facilitated by the use of a writing system which is not entirely unrelated to reading. Both reading and writing would seem beneficial when children are helped to see the close relationship between the two.[17,18]

---

[16]The student will probably want to compare the beginning writing systems advocated by the commercial firms listed in the bibliography. The publishers' addresses are included, and it has been the writer's experience that these publishers are quite generous in supplying prospective (and in-service) teachers with information about their programs as well as an abundance of sample illustrative material.

[17]E. M. White, *Interrelating Reading and Writing;* in Kindergarten Through Grade Three. Chicago: University of Chicago, Conference on Reading, 25: 123-126, 1963.

[18]Doris May Lee and Robert Van Allen, *Learning to Read Through Experience,* 2nd ed., New York: Appleton-Century-Crofts, 1963.

Why manuscript writing? Most[19] educators and classroom teachers have endorsed and adopted for instructional purposes Edward Johnston's "simple Roman style" for at least three very good reasons:

1. Manuscript writing is easy to learn. Its few basic shapes are usually mastered in a very short time by very young children.

2. The fact that manuscript letters are not joined (until the teacher wishes to join them for purposes of aiding the transition to cursive writing) provides ample opportunity for immature hands and fingers to rest after each letter has been formed rather than waiting until a word has been completed.

3. Manuscript writing resembles the print found on charts and in books much more closely than cursive writing. This probably serves as an aid to learning to read.

One purpose for learning to write is to facilitate the process of communication. Another is to provide an outlet for creativity and self-expression. For young children manuscript writing appears to be a superior tool for achieving each of these long-range goals.

How Do We Begin

Assuming the wisdom of beginning with manuscript writing, the next question seems to be "how?" Several methods have been advocated and each appears to have merit.

Materials for beginning writing. The chalkboard is widely used in the beginning stages, almost universally for demonstration of correct letter formations by the teacher and also for practice by children. The surface is large and the teacher can watch several children at once to check reversals, incorrectly formed letters, etc. Several problems present themselves when the chalkboard is used. Children see poor examples – written by beginners like themselves – not always models worth emulating. When mistakes are made before a group, much tact is required in order to correct a child's errors without embarrassing or unduly discouraging him.

Another problem is fatigue which can result when the child's arm must be raised to form each letter. If the reader has attempted chalkboard writing for any length of time, the fatigue problem has almost certainly

---

[19]In fairness, the reader should be reminded that Herrick, (op. cit., p. 19) found that in 14 per cent of the schools participating in the handwriting survey he directed, manuscript writing was *not* taught. Where a reason was given, it seemed to be this: Why teach a skill children will use for only a year, two years at the most? Cursive writing is a tool with lifelong utility. The acceptance of manuscript writing, although widespread, is not universal.

presented itself. It can be more severe for the hands and arms of immature six-year-olds.

The issue of the correct angle at which the writing paper should be placed is not significant only for the child writing at the chalkboard. The left-handed child is likely to encounter problems similar to those of the left-handed diner placed between two right-handed people at the luncheon or dinner table. Spacing and placement at the chalkboard so each child has all the room he needs and so the left-handed child doesn't interfere with and isn't interfered with by right-handed children is very important.

If the chalkboard is used, lines (often painted on the board in more or less permanent fashion, sometimes in attractive colors) will help the child adjust the size of his letters, the spacing between letters and words and avoid slanting uphill or downhill. If lines aren't painted on the board, the teacher might use a chalkboard liner or a yardstick to provide guidelines which are very helpful to the beginner. It might be added that pointed guidelines on the chalkboard are helpful to the teacher also, and often lines are provided at appropriate heights for children and others are designed for the teacher's use. If the chalkboard is used extensively by the children for drill or practice, the teacher should:

– Attempt to provide guidance rather than criticism, to focus on *correctly* formed letters rather than mistakes, and to make suggestions tactfully and informally. It may be better if other members of the class are busy with other activities rather than at their seats, watching the group working at the chalkboard.

– make sure the group at the board is small enough so that each writer has enough room and so left-handed children are not penalized.

– provide guidelines to help the child gauge the size, shape, spacing and linear evenness of his writing.

– keep practice periods short, to avoid fatigue.

Because most of a child's writing will be done on paper and because holding a pencil is somewhat different from holding chalk, it hardly seems wise to limit even a beginner to writing on a chalkboard. Because the child can write large and can benefit from a teacher's direct supervision at the board (and this is difficult when an entire class of children are using paper and pencil and working individually at desks or tables) it seems that some practice at the chalkboard would be beneficial.

Large (18″ x 24″ or even 24″ x 36″ sheets) of newsprint are also used by many first grade teachers in introducing manuscript writing. Such sheets are either folded to provide guidance for the height and relative size of letters, or lines are drawn as shown in Figure 7.1.

Heavy lines or deep folds (for upper case letters)

light lines or folds, for lower case letters.

FIGURE 7.1

Paper for Beginning Writing

Paper for beginning writers should be large, in keeping with our knowledge about the limited small muscle control of young children. Lines are widely spaced (*at least* ½″ between lines) for first graders, and the spacing may be wider (1″, 1½″) for paper used in the earliest stages. It is to be expected that children will reduce the size of their writing after they progress through the stage in which *drawing* letters is a more accurate description of children's efforts than *writing*.

Large, thick crayons are often used as the first writing instruments. Beginner's pencils, large, thick, and with very soft lead, are tools with which the reader probably is already familiar. For some time teachers (and teacher educators) assumed that long, thick crayons, chalk or pencils were as essential for success in beginning writing as the large paper already discussed. Recent evidence, however, indicates that while extremely short, stubby pencils are not efficient instruments, the beginner's pencils are not as important as we once had thought. Length of the pencil and the point at which the pencil is grasped appear to be significant, but not the thickness of the pencil or crayon.[20]

Ball-point pens perhaps have a place in the writing program of the upper primary grades, but these are seldom used in beginning programs.[21,22]

---

[20]Paul C. Burns, *Improving Handwriting Instruction in Elementary Schools.* Minneapolis, Minn.: Burgess Publishing Co., 1962, p. 54.

[21]Herrick, *op. cit.*, p. 28.

[22]Rosemary Soltis, "Handwriting: The Middle R," *Elementary English.* 40: 605-607, October, 1963.

Introduction of Letters

For some time, educators advocated the introduction of letters on the basis of common elements; all the "circle" letters were worked on together; the letters which were basically "line" letters and those letters which varied or combined these basic shapes were taught last.

A study conducted by the Lewises, reported in 1964, focused on the *difficulty* levels of the various letters, lower case and capital. In other words, they ascertained which of the fifty-two (twenty-six capitals, twenty-six lower case) letters were hardest for the children to learn to make. The following table, reproduced by permission of the writers, summarizes their findings. The most difficult letters are listed first (Numbers 1 to 5 are the hardest, numbers 46 to 52 the easiest).

Order of Difficulty: Manuscript Letters

1	q		14	U		27	K		40	F	
2	g		15	M		28	W		41	P	
3	p		16	s		29	A		42	E	
4	y	(l.c.)*	17	b		30	N		43	X	(u.c.)
5	j		18	e		31	C	(u.c.)**	44	I	
6	m		19	r		32	f		45	v	
7	k		20	z		33	J		46	i	
8	u		21	n		34	W		47	D	
9	a		22	S		35	h		48	H	
10	G		23	Q		36	T		49	O	(u.c.)
11	R		24	B		37	x	(l.c.)	50	L	
12	d		25	t		38	c	(l.c.)	51	o	(l.c.)
13	Y		26	z		39	V		52	1	

*lower case
**upper case

FIGURE 7.2

Table of Difficult Letters

As the reader can see the most difficult letters are those which might be called "descenders" – the q, g, p, y and j – and in the problem of relating the nondescending letters to the guideline the m is the most difficult. The easiest letters are those which are either straight lines or circles, without embellishment.

First grade boys appear to be more prone to errors than girls. As instruction continued throughout the year, girls showed greater progress. Left-handed children were slower beginning to write and continued to make more errors than right-handed children. Chronological age did not seem to make a difference, either in terms of readiness or rate of progress.[23]

Paper Placement

Although a survey of recent literature indicates that there appears to be less stress by teachers upon correct posture, paper placement, and other so-called mechanical aspects of handwriting, Enstrom,[24] among others, has several very specific recommendations about paper placement in particular, and feels that the mechanics have been too long neglected. He summarizes three recommended paper positions for *right*-handed children as follows:

FIG. 7.3

My name
is John

1. square placement, with the writer pulling the downstrokes directly toward him and producing a vertical writing that is similar to that found in reading books.

FIG. 7.4

My name
is John

2. angled placement, with "straight" or vertical writing, parallel to the sides of the paper.

FIG. 7.5

My name
is John

3. angled placement and slanted writing, similar to cursive writing.

The vertical placement (No. 1) is the most common, but arrangements must be made to assure visibility so the child's hand doesn't get in the way of the letter he's making. The angled placement (No. 2) makes the transition to cursive writing more difficult, since the child has been taught not to slant his writing even when the paper is slanted. The major disadvan-

[23]Edward R. Lewis and Helen P. Lewis, "Which Manuscript Letters are Hard for First Graders?" *Elementary English*. 41: 855-858, December, 1964.

[24]E. A. Enstrom, "Paper Placement for Manuscript Writing, *Elementary English*. 40: 518-522, 552, May, 1963.

tage of No. 3 is the dissimilarity of the child's writing to the print he is trying to learn to read in books. Enstrom writes:

> The writer feels that all things considered, the square placement of the paper on the desk along with vertical manuscript is to be preferred at the beginning for right handed writers.[25]

For *left*-handed writers, a clockwise paper placement is suggested, as well as a *sloped* desk. Left-handed children will probably benefit from using a lower desk top than that used by right-handed children.

The incidence of left-handedness appears to be increasing, and the prospective teacher may expect to find not five or ten per cent but perhaps twenty per cent of the children in his classes preferring the left hand to the right. The reason is sociological rather than genetic. It is probable that few contemporary parents and fewer teachers are as rigid about using the right hand as was true in times past. The very term "sinister," with its unpleasant connotations, has its roots in the Latin term for "left"; "dextrous" and "dexterity" to the contrary are relatively complementary terms, deriving from Latin terms for "right."

Left-handed children have had many problems to face as they progressed through school; furniture has been inappropriately designed for them, right-handed teachers have lacked both the knowledge of how to teach them to write legibly, (without hooking and smearing papers or hands) and a sympathetic attitude toward the peculiar problems of a left-handed person in a right-handed world. Fortunately this seems to be changing.[26] Teachers and parents are more permissive about left-handedness than they used to be, but ignorance of the best methods for helping left-handed children persists. The left-handed child must be helped to *see* what he's writing without the awkward "hooking" or the backhand so many develop.

While the reader's attention is still focused upon what might be called the mechanics of handwriting it might be well to discuss the relative stress which a teacher should place upon handwriting *mechanics* in contrast to emphasis upon the *ideas* expressed through handwriting. The controversy proceeds along these lines:

> Legibility is our sole concern; stress on posture, pencil angle, and paper position, can only interfere with the ideas a child has to express.

---

[25]*Ibid.*, p. 522.

[26]Paul S. Anderson, *Language Skills in Elementary Education*. New York: The Macmillan Company, 1964. Ch. 3, "Handwriting," pp. 93-127.

This is the position which has resulted in the demise of the handwriting consultant employed by school systems, and little or no emphasis on handwriting instruction in language arts methods classes for prospective teachers. After reporting the findings of a study which indicated that 30 per cent of the school systems surveyed had no handwriting programs, Walter Petty wrote:

> The absence of handwriting programs in many school systems may result from the lack of attention given handwriting in teacher education programs. Also, of course, the social valuing of other curricular areas over handwriting has had its effect. In a crowded school curriculum something has to go; for a teacher with little ability himself to write well, with handwriting ranking low in popularity with him and with his fellow teachers and with little societal pressure, an easy area to eliminate or denigrate is the handwriting program.[27]

The authors of *Improving Language Arts Instruction in the Elementary Schools* write as follows:

> One of the chief tasks in the cultivation of creative written expression is to protect creativeness from the self-consciousness which some youngsters begin to develop with respect to 'neat' and well spaced handwriting. Boys and girls may become so preoccupied – especially in Grade Two – and above – with the proper appearance of their papers that a lively spirited approach to expressive and vivid writing may evaporate.[28]

Complete acceptance of either extreme position probably would result in a somewhat undesirable handwriting program. Overemphasis on form, correct letter formation and neatness may well result in groups of children who can write neatly and legibly but have little or nothing to say. Too much stress on ideas at the expense of legibility may result in the production of interesting highly creative poems, stories, and reports, which, unfortunately, cannot be read by anyone except the writer. Both extremes should be avoided, and teachers of children who are having their first experiences with handwriting will work to achieve a satisfactory balance between form and content in beginning writing programs.

---

[27]Walter T. Petty, "Handwriting and Spelling: Their Present Status," *Elementary English*. 41: 839-844, December, 1964.

[28]Harold G. Shane, June G. Muley, et. al., *Improving Language Arts Instruction in the Elementary Schools*. Columbus, Ohio: Charles E. Merrill Books, 1962.

The Content of Beginning Writing Programs

The role of dictation deserves brief discussion here, although it is dealt with in more detail in the chapter on Creative Writing. One logical solution to the dilemma presented in the preceding section is to include in the kindergarten and first grade program many experiences in which children dictate their ideas to a teacher, who saves them the labor of recording them. Children's ideas can then "flow" with relative freedom and without the necessity of attending to concerns such as paper placement, letter formation, slant, and other aspects of handwriting which might be termed mechanical. Most of the time, the teacher will probably want to work with small groups of children rather than the whole class, so more of them will have an opportunity to participate and contribute to a particular story, poem, or report, and will not have to wait so long for a turn and a chance to see their ideas recorded on a chart or as an identifying accompaniment for a picture.

What Should Beginners Write?

The problem of content cannot be considered an either-or, black-or white issue. A wise teacher neither begins with meaningless shapes or even letters, the purpose of which eludes the pupil, nor expects the pupil to be able to record ideas simply because he has stated them. Trauger writes:

> Writing is a symbolization of speech and because speech, the primary form of language, is a symbolization of what the speaker had in mind to say, writing becomes a symbolization of a symbolization.
>
> Writing, being a derived form of language, is, therefore, communication twice removed from the original thought. It is not written speech; because of the contrasting natures of speech and writing, it cannot be. Much more happens in oral communication than can be shown with standard symbols on the written or printed page. These differences create problems for pupils; they also complicate the teacher's pedagogy.
>
> Written communication demands skill and pedagogy not required in speech. The child must learn the set of marks (graphemes) which his society uses to represent the elements of language. To make these marks and perform the act of writing he needs a degree of muscular coordination. Then he faces the complexities of spelling and the even greater difficulties of trying to represent, with written punctuation, the pauses, intonations, and kinesics[29] which he uses as eloquent signals

---

[29]The term kinesics is used by linguists to refer to gestures, facial expressions, etc., which deny, refute, or reinforce and support the words of a speaker.

in his speech. Also, there are the conventions of a printed page: spacing, letter and line alignment, and capitals.[30]

Obviously, then, the teacher of beginning manuscript writing must be concerned with something more than the experiential background of his pupils and the level of their spoken language. Just as *content* cannot be considered in isolation, neither can the eye-hand coordination of the child, or his ability to successfully control his small muscles in order to make his hands and fingers do what he wants and intends them to do.

It perhaps should be stated explicitly, although it certainly has already been implied, that each child in a kindergarten or first grade class will exhibit varying combinations of factors indicating readiness for handwriting or lack of it. A few children will remain at the stage at which they will write little more than their names and simple labels for pictures well into the second semester of the first grade. Almost any kindergarten teacher will testify to the fact that few children in kindergarten have the necessary motivation, general linguistic competence, and muscular coordination requisite for simple notes to parents, invitations, and relatively complex stories to accompany paintings, drawings and other art work. To say "*No* handwriting" to a kindergarten teacher is as educationally unsound, and betrays the same lack of understanding of individual differences, as would the edict that *every* child should be able to write at the conclusion of his kindergarten experiences.

The teacher of beginning writers and beginning writing will want to combine introduction of basic letter shapes, instruction in proper paper placement, guidance relative to posture, desk height, distance from the writing surface, etc., without doing violence to the ideas a child wants to express. There is a place in a beginning writing program for lessons in which the ideas are stressed, and for lessons in which the ideas are less important than learning to write certain letters and words correctly, neatly, and easily. In lessons of the first type, help will have to be given individually, there will be some dictation with or without copying from the board, and the teacher may use the literature, program a field trip, or any other especially interesting experience as stimulus. In the second type of lesson, designed to improve children's handwriting competence, the teacher will rely upon the individual child's desire to strengthen his ability to communicate with others and his knowledge of the progress he has made since previous skill, drill or practice lessons to provide the necessary motivation. There is a fiction abroad which suggests that there can be no intrinsic

---

[30]Wilmer K. Trauger, *Language Arts in Elementary Schools.* New York: The McGraw Hill Book Company, 1963, p. 59.

motivation in a practice exercise in which gummed candy bars, or, at the very least, lavish teacher praise, must provide the spark which will cause a child to work upon improving a skill – especially so mundane a skill as handwriting. No teacher who has seen the pride in a child's demeanor as he exhibited to the teacher – or examined privately – an October paper and a much neater, more legible paper written just before Thanksgiving believes that a child gets no pleasure from demonstrated growth in handwriting.

Relationships Between the Creative and the Practical

Another comment is pertinent here; too many professional writers have acted as though there were no articulation between the creative and the practical aspects of the writing program. Teachers know better. The work done on letter formation, spacing, etc., certainly has a beneficial effect upon most children's creative writing, even though the stress in the last type of lesson is on *ideas*, not form, neatness, speed or legibility.

In order to achieve a desirable balance between form and content in beginning writing programs, a teacher will probably make sure that attention to mechanics will not be inhibited by poor lighting, uncomfortable furniture, paper that is too small or has a glossy surface which presents vision problems. These are not central concerns, perhaps, but they must not be ignored.

– use lessons designed to *teach* correct letter formation as well as those designed to promote children's abilities to express themselves creatively. As Enstrom notes:

> Overemphasis on a skill without practical use results in a fine tool of questionable value. Too much emphasis on use without practice (learning) sessions results in a careless, limited product that is hard to defend. . . . The best practice is to teach, then use.[31]

– provide different kinds of help for children with different kinds of problems. Some children will need alphabet cards and copybooks long after others have stopped relying upon such aids. John may need to be reminded to make certain letters in a more acceptable fashion; Amy may need to be told that margins don't matter as much as her ideas.

– recognize that the same standards cannot be applied to each child in the class. Physiological differences, linguistic differences, and intellectual differences have to be considered in the planning and evaluation of handwriting programs just as they must be considered in reading programs

[31]Enstrom, "Print Handwriting Today," *op. cit.*, p. 848.

or any other program for which the elementary school accepts responsibility. Some children will profit from exposure to "formal" handwriting experiences in kindergarten. Other children will benefit more if they are not pushed – if their teacher is wise enough to delay extensive paper and pencil work until the second semester of first grade or even until second grade.

Encouragement of Positive Attitudes

If a teacher is sensitive to children and their varying needs and interests, and if he can achieve a balance in the handwriting program which ensures adequate attention to both *ideas* and the form in which these ideas are expressed, most children will develop positive attitudes toward handwriting and will achieve adequate mastery of this important though sometimes neglected skill.

Making the Transition to Cursive Writing

The majority of elementary school children in the United States learn manuscript writing first, and toward the end of the primary period make the transition to cursive writing. The basis or rationale for manuscript writing has already been detailed, and it has also been suggested that skill and facility in manuscript writing should be maintained and should not be allowed to deteriorate. If manuscript writing has so many advantages and demonstrable utility well beyond the primary grades, why should the transition be made? Is it really necessary that children learn cursive writing at all?

Arguments for Changing to Cursive Writing

Two claims are frequently made for cursive writing. First, cursive writing is supposedly faster, and because a more individual style is encouraged by its use it is reported to be more acceptable than manuscript writing in signatures on checks, legal documents, etc. The research relating to speed and legibility in manuscript and cursive writing is quite contradictory. The detailed summary of extensive handwriting research in the *Encyclopedia of Educational Research*[32] fails to lend support to making the transition to cursive writing on the basis of enhancing speed or encouraging individuality of style. Burns writes:

---

[32]*Encyclopedia of Educational Research,* Edited by Chester W. Harris, 3rd Edition, New York: The MacMillan Company, 1960, "Handwriting," T. Harris, pp. 616-622.

> The question of relative legibility and speed, between manuscript and cursive, has not been conclusively settled. At this time, there is not enough proof available to support the claim of exclusive superiority of either form beyond beginning instruction where manuscript is generally agreed to be better.[33]

Templin surveyed the handwriting of adults who had been taught by three methods – all manuscript, all cursive, and manuscript with a transition to cursive. Her findings indicate that:

1. Males continued to use manuscript writing throughout their adult lives. Thirty-six per cent of the males who had been taught cursive writing from Grade One had learned manuscript writing and perferred to use it socially and professionally.

2. Females used cursive writing to a much greater extent than males. Approximately one-third of the females who had been taught manuscript writing through Grade 6, learned cursive writing and preferred its use because manuscript writing is "too childish" or "not business-like enough."

3. Manuscript writing is generally more legible; "both the male and the female respondents from the all-manuscript population achieved a higher mean legibility than did respondents from either of the other two handwriting populations included in this survey." The most significant finding:

4. ". . . . the transition from the manuscript to the cursive style of handwriting at any age or at any grade level tends to result in less legible adult hand-writing.[34]

Templin's findings suggest that the one overriding reason for changing from manuscript to cursive writing – the only reason which merits very serious consideration – is the greater social acceptance or prestige of cursive writing, so long as manuscript writing is considered "too childish" and "not business-like enough." Most elementary school faculties will probably feel compelled to teach cursive writing. It is not because cursive writing is faster, easier, or more legible, but because of the social stigma which has been attached to manuscript writing which creates the need to teach both manuscript and cursive writing.

Manuscript and Cursive: A Summary of Differences

It may be helpful here to summarize the major differences between manuscript and cursive writing:

---

[33]Burns, *op. cit.*, p. 9.

[34]Elaine Templin, "The Legibility of Adult Manuscript, Cursive, or Manuscript-Cursive Styles," *New Horizons for Research in Handwriting*, Herrick, ed., *op. cit.*, pp. 185-206.

– in manuscript writing, separate letters are combined, but not connected, to make words. In cursive writing, the pencil or pen is not lifted from the page until the word has been completed. In manuscript writing the i and the j are dotted and the t is crossed immediately after the letters are formed. In cursive writing, dotting and crossing do not occur until the entire word has been written.

– for the most part, manuscript writing is vertical, and cursive writing is usually slanted. For right-handed children, the recommended paper placement is straight for manuscript writing and slanted to the left for cursive writing. For the left-handed child, the slant for manuscript writing and cursive writing is adjusted so the writer's hand is never in the way of the letter being made.

– the basic shapes for manuscript writing are ovals or circles and straight line downstrokes. Upstrokes, downstrokes circles and connecting strokes are used in cursive writing.

The difference between manuscript and cursive writing which is probably of most significance to teachers and children is the joining of letters to form words in cursive writing.

Deciding When to Make the Transition

Not all children are ready to make a transition from manuscript to cursive writing at the same time. Flexibility is the key word here. The alert teacher will watch for the following signals:

Is the child slanting or showing a tendency to slant his manuscript writing?

Is the child unconsciously beginning to join manuscript letters?

Can the child *read* cursive writing – on the chalkboard, in the letters he receives, etc.?

Is he interested in learning to write "like grown-ups"?

Has he achieved well in the acquisition skill in manuscript writing?

Is manuscript writing easy for him, and does he write neatly and form letters correctly?

It is important to discuss flexibility and adjustment to individual differences in a text such as this. It has already been noted that a common weakness in most handwriting programs is the failure to make such adjustments; however, is it practical? Is it realistic to advise a prospective or in-service teacher to make the effort and devote the time and energy required to treat children as individuals? Even if this is practical in an area such as reading, can it also be arranged in other subject areas like handwriting?

It should be admitted from the first that grouping for handwriting instruction does take more time and require more planning and effort by a teacher than pacing an entire class of children through each successive page of a handwriting workbook, handbook, copybook, or manual. It is submitted, however, that the results make the expenditure of extra effort and time worthwhile.

It is possible and most practical to present certain basic concepts regarding cursive writing to an entire goup. This is a practical way to present material designed to promote the ability to read cursive writing. Spelling lists, announcements, daily schedules or plans can be written on the board in both manuscript and cursive writing for some time, and similarities and differences pointed out to children – or better still, identified by the children themselves.

A few words – dog, add, cat – with many similarities in the two forms could be given first, since the problems these words introduce are fairly simple for children to present. At first joining should be emphasized without undue concern for slant.

FIGURE 7.6

Method of Teaching Manuscript and Cursive Writing

The chalkboard is a valuable teaching aid for demonstration by the teacher and practice by small groups of children.

Children who master these early introductory concepts easily probably are ready to work on words like "son," in which the s occurs in a new form. Those children who find that their manuscript writing is easier, neater, more legible and who appear to be not quite ready to make the transition should be allowed to continue using manuscript most of the time. This doesn't mean the teacher is discouraging growth or progress or encouraging laziness in his pupils. Rather, encouragement to try a new kind of writing, without undue pressure from the teacher, should aid in developing more favorable attitudes toward handwriting.

Providing Individual Instruction

Grouping has already been suggested as one means of individualizing the handwriting program. Grouping can occur for the purpose of working on specific problems (spacing, alignment, difficult letters) for general practice with more opportunity for a teacher's help and supervision, or children can be grouped for handwriting on the basis of general ability, much as they have traditionally been grouped for reading instruction on the basis of general ability and achievement. Each of these various types of grouping has some merit, and each will almost surely give pupils greater help and instruction than the more traditional whole-class methods usually employed. Each group need not meet with the teacher every day, particularly after the basic manuscript shapes have been mastered and, in the transition period being dealt with here, after children have acquired the most important concepts related to joining letters and slant.

A few children will need much more practice than others; independent work periods can be used for this practice. Children who need extra practice can work at home as well as school, if the teacher will take the necessary time to differentiate homework assignments.

It is probably not necessary to be more specific about making adjustments needed for individual differences. If a teacher is aware of the differences in children in her class, and is really concerned about doing something *about* these differences, a way will be found. A teacher who feels handwriting is an important skill will make a conscientious effort to teach it as effectively as possible.[35,36]

Content in Cursive Writing

The teacher of cursive writing has several advantages over the teacher of manuscript writing. Children's interests are broader, their backgrounds of experiences are wider, and their vocabularies, (speaking, listening and/or understanding, and writing and/or spelling) are considerably larger. The choice of practice material is not nearly as limited as it typically is for beginners.

---

[35]J. Larison, "We Combined Group and Individual Instruction in Handwriting," *Instructor,* 73: 31, January, 1964.

[36]Ernest Horn discusses the need for individualizing handwriting instruction, particularly in remedial programs, in "Questions for Research in Handwriting," *Elementary School Journal.* 62: 305-312, March, 1962.

In the skill sessions leading to proficient cursive writing, it probably is wise to begin with words containing letters which are most similar to the manuscript letters which children already know how to make: lower case, a, e, d, g, h, i, l, m, n, o, p, q, t, u and y; upper case, B, C, K, L, O, P, R and U. Whether upper case or capital letters and lower case letters will be taught together or separately will probably be determined by the handwriting system adopted, but the emphasis should be on meaningful content and, in general, after the introductory phase, words, phrases and sentences will prove more interesting to children than prolonged drill on isolated letters or parts of letters. Spelling lists, group and individual, provide an excellent opportunity for meaningful practice and also afford a time-saving method of working on two important aspects of the language arts simultaneously.

After children have mastered the joining of letters, first those like manuscript letters which are easy to make, then those which are quite different or are difficult to master,[37] slant can be dealt with. The sequence of letters as well as slant can also be taught as suggested by the authors of the commercial system, but the foregoing sequence is commonly used. Slant is a somewhat individual matter, and provided backhand is avoided and the degree of slant in a child's writing is relatively even, the teacher should not attempt to dictate the degree of slant.

Prerequisites to Emphasis on Speed

Speed is one of the last aspects of cursive writing to receive attention. Before devoting instructional time to improving speed, the teacher may want to check for the following:

1. Does the child have mastery over the correct letter formation for the entire cursive alphabet? The relative size of letters often presents a problem, and this problem should be solved before there is any emphasis on speed. Improper formation of a "d" (it should not look like a "c-l") and a "c" (a "c" shouldn't look like an "a," nor an "a" like a "c") should be corrected – these particular mistakes are among the most common.

2. Does the child recognize the need for improving his speed? If the child is continually "caught short" and doesn't finish work which he could reasonably be expected to finish then, together with several other children with a similar problem, he could and should receive the teacher's help. To establish a rigid speed requirement (i.e., 50 words a minute by sixth

---

[37]Burns, (*op. cit.*, p. 24) lists the following as the most difficult cursive letters:
Lower case: a, e, r, t, v, n, o and s – the r and s are quite different in their manuscript and cursive forms.
Capital letters: I.

grade) makes little sense for most children. In fact flexibility in speed – helping children adjust the speed with which they write in terms of the difficulty of the material – would seem to be much more important. We know one speed is inadequate for reading; so is it for handwriting.

3. Can speed be improved without sacrificing legibility and fluency? If not, it should be relegated to its proper position behind these more important goals.

Cursive Writing: A Summary

Because it is a skill which society at present expects children to acquire, cursive writing probably must be taught. Children should not be forced to use cursive writing before they have mastered manuscript writing. Two half-skills are not as useful as one skill thoroughly mastered. Children will vary in their readiness for cursive writing and should be allowed to begin and to progress in acquiring this skill at a rate appropriate for them, not one dictated by the teacher, a curriculum guide or a handwriting system. Manuscript writing will continue to receive some attention, so it will remain functional for children and teachers may want to use it for board work, as well as for charts, maps, and labels. It is quite important that children be able to *read* cursive writing before they learn to write it. The use of manuscript and cursive writing should proceed together and children should be allowed to employ whichever seems more appropriate for them.

The Use of the Typewriter

With the increasing prominence of the typewriter in high schools and colleges as well as in business offices, its use in the elementary classrooms probably should be discussed. Limited research has been conducted on the feasibility of utilizing the typewriter in elementary school classrooms. Such research appears to indicate that children *can* learn to type at the fourth or fifth grade level.[38] With the present emphasis on "pushing down" subject matter and acceptance of the proposition that anything can be respectably taught at any level, we also seem to have a tacit, affirmative answer to the question, *should* elementary children be taught to type?

Questions Pertinent to the Teaching of Typing

The elementary school curriculum is already crowded. Ask any elementary teacher. Should we really attempt to teach typing, in addition to

---

[38]Paul S. Anderson, *Language Skills in Elementary Education, op. cit.*, p. 99.

geometry, economics, cultural anthropology and the six or seven "basic" subjects, to eight, nine, and/or ten-year-olds? The decision to teach typing to intermediate or upper grade youngsters involves finding practical and theoretically sound solutions to a number of problems:

1. Where will typing be taught? The noise of even a few typewriters would seem to prohibit simultaneous instruction in reading, or any other subject, in the typical self-contained elementary classroom. Equipping each classroom with thirty or thirty-five typewriters would probably send taxes still higher. If a special typing room is furnished, would this give still more impetus to departmentalization in elementary schools?

2. To whom should typing be taught? Should all chilldren learn to type? Only the gifted? Those children whose handwriting is almost illegible? Only those children who appear to be college-bound, and who probably won't have an opportunity to take it later in junior high school or high school?

3. Who will teach typing? Can typical elementary classroom teachers teach typing? If not, do we teach typing by tapes, films, television, or should a specialist be hired – a high school typing teacher, perhaps?

4. How much time should be devoted to typing instruction? Should instruction in typing replace, at least in part, instruction in handwriting?

These questions cannot be answered until teachers and administrators have determined the importance of typing for elementary school youngsters. Children enjoy acquiring a new skill like typing. Boys who show little interest in writing neatly and legibly may be more interested in learning to use a machine that writes. Teachers would appreciate reading children's reports and stories which were typed rather than scrawled or scribbled. These appear to be immediate advantages to teaching typing to elementary youngsters; the long range advantage of typing ability in secondary school, college, or business need not be argued. Do we, however, teach something which will have little value, only something a pupil will need to know later?

Arguments Favoring the Inclusion of Typing

Because this necessarily brief section devoted to typing has been somewhat pessimistic, has emphasized problems rather than advantages, it may be well to conclude with a quotation from a writer who takes quite a different position:

> I dare to suggest that 'automated' (chiefly the typewriter at present, though we might well set our sights on a simplified note-taking machine, too,) should be at least as prominent on the educational

scene at all grade levels as are television automated learning devices and the like. All normal children should learn to type early in their school careers and make use of this skill constantly. Perhaps the typewriter and similar devices should largely replace handwriting for everything except brief notes and such things as bank checks. Then children could be taught to handwrite slowly, carefully and legibly, for speed needs would be met mechanically.

The usual objection to typewriters for classrooms, their cost, does not impress me in this day of huge expenditures for educational hardware, much of it of unproved worth. If typewriters are desirable, as I believe they are, efficient ways to procure, use and maintain them can be found. Teachers of the mechanics of written communication who view handwriting in its proper contemporary perspective should be leaders in the move toward automated handwriting. There is much research to do here.

I hasten to add that pencils, and chalk-crayons are by no means obsolescent. Probably they never will be. Perhaps automating handwriting will result in more writing and therefore stimulate the sale of pencils, pens and crayons as much as radio stimulated the sale of phonograph records. Television did not kill radio, and yet airplanes have not reduced the number of automobiles.[39]

We can surely agree that more research of a substantive nature, dealing with the purposes rather than the practicability of typing in the elementary school, is necessary before another curricular area or subject is added to an already crowded curriculum.

Evaluation of Handwriting

Chapter 11 is devoted to a general discussion of evaluation in and of language arts programs. Because the evaluation of handwriting growth in pupils and of handwriting programs in elementary schools presents several somewhat unique problems, however, they will be dealt with here, briefly and specifically.

It might be said that in no other area of language arts instruction are standardized tools for the measurement of growth as readily available and as little used as in handwriting.

Scales for Evaluative Use

Handwriting scales are prepared specimens with which a pupil's handwriting is compared. Samples of good, average, and poor handwriting

---

[39]Julian C. Stanley, "Proposals of Consultants for the Improvement of Research in Handwriting," *New Horizons for Research in Handwriting, op. cit.*, pp. 240-241.

are provided. These vary according to the grade level concerned, and scores are usually interpreted through grade level equivalents. Herrick comments on the use of such scales:

> Only one third of the schools in the nation and in the state of Wisconsin use some scale in evaluating children's handwriting. . . . The use of a scale to evaluate handwriting seems to be tied to the use of a corresponding system.[40]

Since Herrick has already reported that in most schools where handwriting is taught a commercial system is used, he must refer to the type of scale, or the publisher of a scale, not to the prevalence of use.

Handwriting scales have been available to teachers and pupils since 1910, when the Thorndike Scale was developed. "General merit" was the criterion, and the term was intended to include clarity, uniformity of line and artistic quality of the handwriting.[41] The Ayres Scale was developed in 1912 and revised in 1917. This is the familiar "Gettysburg Edition," involving the writing of the first few lines of the Gettysburg Address. In discussing this scale, Andersen comments:

> Ayres contended that since handwriting is produced for others to read and understand what is written, the criterion should be how quickly the specimen can be read.[42]

The Ayres scale is employed in the evaluation programs of several commercial systems.

Freeman's Scale was developed in 1915, and utilized "general excellence" as the criterion. General excellence was held to be a sum of the following:

> letter form
> uniformity of slant
> uniformity of alignment of letters
> quality of line
> spacing between letters and words.[43]

The 1959 revision of this scale also used general excellence as the criterion, without specifying the elements of this quality. Freeman wrote:

---

[40]Herrick, *New Horizons for Research in Handwriting, op. cit.*, p. 27.

[41]E. L. Thorndike, "Handwriting," *Teachers College Record.* 11: 83-175, March, 1910.

[42]Dan W. Andersen, "Handwriting Research: Movement and Quality," *Elementary English.* 42: 45-53, January, 1965.

[43]F. N. Freeman, "An Analytical Scale for Judging Handwriting," *Elementary School Journal.* 15: 432-441, April, 1915.

> Specimens selected should show a balance among all the elements of spacing, alignment, letter formation and uniformity in size and slant.[44]

The West Scale, developed in 1956 and 1957, included the criterion of speed together with the criterion of quality – legibility. His scale was among the first to place an emphasis on speed, and he was among the first to suggest, through his scale, that there is a direct positive relationship between the factors of speed and legibility.[45]

These three scales, the Ayres Scale, the Freeman Scale and the West Scale, are those most commonly employed. All use cursive writing samples almost exclusively and only recently has a scale been developed for evaluating manuscript writing.[46]

Recommended Evaluative Procedures

Scales provide one means by which a pupil's hand-writing can be judged, and like other standardized measurement techniques should be part of a total evaluation program. Standardized scales are probably insufficient in themselves, but together with the following evaluative procedures they provide a teacher or a staff with objective evidence concerning the effectiveness of the handwriting program:

1. Frequently collected samples of pupils' writing should be reviewed and evaluated. It is probably wise for the teacher to collect and save typical samples of reports, stories, etc., as well as for pupils to maintain folders of their written work.

2. Self-evaluation is very important. The children probably are aware of the elements of good handwriting; if they aren't, the teacher can help them develop such awareness. A list of criteria should be referred to as often as necessary. Occasionally the teacher may ask for a rating, a grade, or some other indication that the children can look at his writing with a measure of objectivity.

3. Legible handwriting will be stressed whenever the goal is communication. If the writing is the rough draft of a report, class notes, a memo or reminder and the goal is self expression, not communication, standards may be relaxed a bit. Flexibility is desirable, and the reader needs only check the quality of handwriting in a letter to parents, a shopping list,

---

[44]F. N. Freeman, "A New Handwriting Scale," *Elementary School Journal*, 59: 219, January, 1959.

[45]Paul V. West, "American Handwriting Scale," A. N. Palmer Co., New York, 1957.

[46]Rocky Bezzi, "A Standardized Manuscript Scale for Grades One, Two and Three," *Journal of Educational Research*. 55: 339-340, April, 1962.

and a quiz or midterm to see that an adult's handwriting varies to suit the situation, and it is not realistic to insist upon uniformly high standards for all handwriting pupils.

4. The teacher will work on his own handwriting because he knows the importance of a good example for children. Children will place little importance upon neat, legible writing if the teacher doesn't believe this is essential. In fact, if handwriting programs are to be improved, a starting point is the betterment of teachers' and pupils' attitudes toward handwriting. A recent study suggests that only language ranks lower than handwriting on pupils' lists of subject preferences.[47] The writers suggest that *teacher* attitude is one very significant factor in *pupil* attitudes toward this, as toward other subjects.

5. There is need for faculty study of handwriting programs. Significant and positive results have evolved from such studies of mathematics, science, and reading programs. Similar results may be expected when a group of teachers works together to improve their teaching of this important tool of communication and self-expression.

BIBLIOGRAPHY

Andersen, Dan W. "Handwriting Research: Movement and Quality" *Elementary English,* 42:45-53, January, 1965.

Anderson, Paul S. *Language Skills in Elementary Education,* (Chapter 3, "Handwriting") New York: The Macmillan Co., 1964.

Burns, Paul C. *Improving Handwriting Instruction in Elementary Schools,* Minneapolis: Burgess Publishing Company, 1962.

Encyclopedia of Educational Research, Chester W. Harris, editor. ("Handwriting," by Theodore Harris, pp. 616-622) New York: The Macmillan Co., 1960.

Enstrom, E. A. "Print Handwriting Today" *Elementary English, 41*:846-850, December, 1964.

Freeman, Frank N. "The Transition From Manuscript to Cursive Writing" *Elementary English,* 35:366-372.

Groff, Patrick J. "From Manuscript to Cursive – Why?" *Elementary School Journal,* 61:97-101, November, 1960.

Myers, Emma H. *The Whys and Hows of Teaching Handwriting.* Columbus, Ohio: The Zaner-Bloser Company, 1963.

New Horizons for Research in Handwriting, Virgil E. Herrick, editor. Madison, Wisconsin: The University of Wisconsin Press, 1963.

Noble, J. Kendrick. "Handwriting Programs in Today's Schools" *Elementary English,* 40:506-512, 517, May, 1963.

---

[47]James Inskeep and Monroe Rowland, "An Analysis of School Subject Preferences of Elementary School Children of the Middle Grades: Another Look," *Journal of Educational Research.* 58: 225-228, January, 1965.

Petty, Walter T. "Handwriting and Spelling: Their Current Status" *Elementary English,* 41:839-844, December, 1964.

Shane, Harold G., June G. Mulry, Mary E. Reddin and Margaret C. Gillespie, *Improving Language Arts Instruction in the Elementary Schools,* pp. 176-185, "Developing Handwriting Skills" Columbus, Ohio: Charles E. Merrill Books, 1962.

Trauger, Wilmer K. *Language Arts in Elementary Schools,* (Chapter 4 "Written Communication") New York: McGraw-Hill Book Company, 1963.

Curriculum Guides and Bulletins

These are listed because they are representative and somewhat typical. Curriculum materials centers, which are parts of most education libraries, have copies of many others.

Gary, Indiana. *Handwriting Guide: Kindergarten – Grade 6,* Gary, Indiana: Published by the Gary Indiana Public Schools, 1964.

Long Beach, California, City Schools. *Guide to the Teaching of Handwriting in the Elementary School,* Long Beach, California: Published by the Long Beach City Schools, 1952.

New York (State) Bureau of Elementary Curriculum Development. *Handwriting: See Me Write,* Albany, Division of Elementary Education, New York State Education Department, 1955.

Handwriting Programs – Commercial Systems

These systems are listed not necessarily because they are the best, but because they are so widely used. Other systems, available in curriculum laboratories or materials centers, should be consulted and surveyed also.

Adventures in Handwriting, Grades 1-8, Macmillan Co., 60 Fifth Ave., New York, New York, 10011.

Better Handwriting for Everyone, Grades 1-8, Noble and Noble Publishers, 67 Irving Place, New York, New York, 10003.

Guiding Growth in Handwriting, Grades 1-8, Zaner-Bloser, Publishers, 612 N. Park St., Columbus, Ohio, 43215.

I Learn to Write Series, Grades 1-8, E. C. Seale Co., Publishers, 1053 E. 54th St., Indianapolis, Indiana, 46220.

Imaginary Line Handwriting Series, Grades 1-8, Steck and Company, P. O. Box 16, Austin, Texas, 78761.

Kettle's Penmanship, Grades 1-8, American Book Company, 55 Fifth Ave., New York, New York, 10003.

Learn to Listen, Speak and Write, Grades 1-3, Scott Foresman Company, 433 E. Erie St., Chicago, Illinois, 60611.

(This is one example of a correlated or integrated program; there are, of course, others.)

Films and Filmstrips

(Available for purchase or rent)

Filmstrips:

"Story of Writing," 26 frames, kindergarten through third grade; deals with the history of writing.
Filmstrip of the Months Club, Inc.
355 Lexington Avenue
New York, New York, 10017

"The Story of Writing," 34 frames, grades four through six, junior high school, college; also a history of writing.
Webster Publishing Co.
1154 Reco Ave.
St. Louis 2, Missouri

Films:

"Writing Through the Ages," 76 mm. sound, black and white, 10 minutes, grades four through six. A history of writing as a means of communication.
Encyclopedia Brittanica Films
1150 Wilmette Ave.
Willmette, Illinois

"Between the Lines," 16 mm. sound, black and white, 20 minutes, grades four through six. A history of writing from the invention of the alphabet to the present.
Modern Talking Pictures Service, Inc.
3 E. 45th St.
New York, New York, 10022

EXTENDING YOUR LEARNING

1. Prepare a lesson plan, selecting an activity and adjusting the time limits of the lesson in terms of the age level concerned.
   a. an introductory lesson in manuscript writing for a small group of mature kindergarten children or more typical first graders.
   b. a remedial lesson for a small group of second graders, who are having difficulty differentiating between the "b" and "d," the "r" and "n" and "c-l"and "d."
   c. an introductory lesson for an entire class beginning the transition from manuscript to cursive writing.
2. Select a panel to discuss the relative merits of changing to cursive writing in the second grade and/or waiting until third grade.
3. Develop individually, or in small groups, lists of criteria by which you would judge the legibility and "general excellence" of a child's handwriting (manuscript and cursive). Then collect as many samples of children's handwriting

as possible, and see whether or not your criteria are practical, relatively easy to apply, and actually dfiferentiate.

4. Select one of the following topics for an oral or written report. Such reports should include a bibliography and should present both sides of an issue as well as your own considered opinion.

   a. Should every elementary school child be taught to type?
   b. What should be consideerd in giving a grade in handwriting?
   c. Can handwriting be taught functionally, yet effectively, so the child will learn to write easily but will not develop the unfavorable attitudes toward handwriting that emphasis or drill sometimes promotes?
   d. Why is the teacher's handwriting so important? Is it possible for an adult to improve his handwriting significantly?

5. Following the techniques suggested in the manuals, utilize the material developed by at least one of the commercial systems. In other words "work through" one of the widely adopted handwriting systems listed in this chapter.
6. Using the "quick brown fox" sentence as a sample, write at least four times during the semester or quarter and apply the criteria you have developed. Develop an awareness of your weaknesses, and try to improve your manucript and cursive handwriting during the period you are enrolled in a language arts course and, of course, beyond.

Chapter 8 Edith Crowell Trager

The Teaching of Spelling: A Linguistic Approach

Linguists have found it useful to act as if language were a layer cake: the bottom layer, phonology or sounds; the middle layer, morphology, or words and affixes; the top layer, syntax, and the frosting all around and on top of the layers, semantics.

Of course when you eat the cake or listen to language, you get everything all at once. It is nevertheless still true that for the purposes of analysis the four-way division – into phonemes, morphological units, syntactic structures and meaning – is a useful one.

Our traditional orthography, hereafter referred to as TO, is generally regarded by linguists as an extra-linguistic system, a secondary set of symbols that represents the primary set of phonemes, the smallest units of linguistic structure. This has not prevented some distinguished linguists like Leonard Bloomfield,[1] Charles C. Fries, and Robert A. Hall, Jr.[2] from devoting considerable attention to our spelling system, and pointing out that there is an enormous amount of regularity in it together with the irregularities.

This chapter will be concerned most of all with TO (traditional orthography) and its relation to the phonemes of English. It will also treat

---

[1]Leonard Bloomfield and Clarence L. Barnhart, *Let's Read,* p. 25. "Our system of writing is . . . alphabetic. This is proved by the simple fact that we can write every English word by means of only twenty-six characters, whereas a system of word writing would demand many thousands."

[2]Robert A. Hall, Jr., *Sound and Spelling in English,* (Philadelphia, Chilton Books, 1961), p. 1. "Writing is simply a way of representing speech, and our conventional systems of orthography are always incomplete and inaccurate in their representation of language as it is spoken."

the relevance of this, as seen by a linguist, to teaching American children to read and to spell. First, however, there are things about the grammar of the language and the format of the printed page to be considered.

Relationships of Semantics, Syntax, and Morphology

The study of meaning, classified as *semantics,* has made no systematic contribution to the teaching of reading. The teacher and student both, however, make constant use of their knowledge of the different meanings of words in order to select the appropriate one according to the meanings of the other words and phrases in a sentence. It would be sensible, although it is seldom done consistently in textbooks for beginning readers, to have words with interdependent meanings printed on one or two lines, with a lot of space between the first group of such words and each of the following groups.

It follows that *syntax,* the study of the structure of phrases, clauses, and sentences, usually goes together with the semantics. If you have a noun phrase (say a determiner, followed by two adjectives and a noun) as the subject of a sentence, the rules of English syntax say that if the noun is "house" and the adjectives "adobe" and "enormous," and the determiner an indefinite article, then the noun phrase absolutely must be, in our usual prose style at any rate, "an enormous adobe house." It may not be, for instance, "a adobe enormous house" or any of the other theoretically possible permutations. The tie-in of syntax with semantics involves considerations like these: we can say "an enormous house" and we can say "an enormous molecule" in a sentence like "RNA has an enormous molecule compared to hydrogen." Obviously the referential meanings of "enormous" (the actual range of house-sizes against the range of sizes of molecules) differ by a very large order of magnitude. The linguistic meaning, however, is evidently something like "much larger than other members of a set."

Analysis of Phrase Structure

Syntax furthermore tells us a great deal more about the phrase structure of English, much of what we know intuitively about which words of a sentence belong together. The words in a noun phrase belong together, and so do the words in a verb phrase. Within the verb phrase the auxiliaries and main verb belong together, as do the words in the noun phrase that may follow, if the sentence contains an object or a complement. An adverbial clause like "when the time comes" hangs together, and in a primer for children it would be sensible to keep it all on one line, separated from contiguous words. Figure 8.1, shows the difference between such a book and one which, although for children, uses adult format.

Particular Uses of Phonology

There is at this point a tie-in with *phonology,* not with the vowels and consonants that the linguist calls segmental phonemes, but with the supersegmental phonemes of pitch, stress, and juncture that constitute the intonation patterns of English. While the Smith-Trager analysis cannot be formally taught to children, and can be taught in all its complexity only with difficulty to their teachers, it has implications. It does help the teacher to be aware explicity that the intonation patterns – the first thing each child learns about his language – the syntactic structure, and the semantics of a sentence reinforce each other. They each signal the subdivisions of a sentence. It would be helpful to the beginning reader to have stress marks on the loudest syllables of each phrase, with each phrase separated from the next by white space on the page. Here is a hypothetical example.

John James Jéffrey
Rútherford the Thírd
went dówn to the béach each dáy.
Whenever he wént, he took alóng his hámster.

Justified margins should be regarded as irrelevant, and the only consideration should be the correspondence of linguistic structure to the page format.

Considerations Related to Morphology

This leads us to *morphology,* to the uninflected words which take no grammatical endings, and to the inflected classes of words that do have grammatical suffixes. The uninflected word-classes generally acknowledged at the moment are these: interjection, *oh;* conjunction, *and, if;* determiner, *the, a, some;* intensifier, *very, extremely;* preposition, *with, between* and the sub-class of particles, *up, off* with their additional function of being in two-part verbs like *call up* and *put off;* modal, the nine auxiliaries *can, could, shall, should, will, would, may, might, must* which are followed directly by the basic form of the main verb.

The inflected classes are those ever-changing classes with referential meaning: noun, with possessive and/or plural forms *man, man's,*

Zistel, Era. *Wintertime Cat.* New York: Holt, Rinehart, Winston, 1963	Hazen, Barbara Shook. *Rudolph* The Red-Nosed Reindeer. New York: Golden Press, 1958.
Page 1 Hello. I am a cat. (2 lines on one page separated by white space, photograph of a cat)	Once there was a reindeer named Rudolph, who lived at the North Pole, in Toyland. Rudolph was younger and smaller than the other reindeer there. They all had proud, tall antlers. Rudolph's antlers were only tiny stubs. Worst of all, Rudolph had a nose that was big and bright red. It was so red it glowed in the dark. (6 sentences on one page, colored illustrations)
Page 2 My name is Revey. What's yours? (2 lines on one page separated by white space. Photograph pictures a cat.)	Poor Rudolph! He wanted to be like the other reindeer in Toyland. Oh, to have a small, brown nose, instead of a big, bright red one! The other reindeer made fun of Rudolph and called him names. "Rudolph, the red-nosed reindeer," they teased over and over again until tears glistened on Rudolph's large red nose. (5 sentences on one page, colored illustration)
Page 3 I live in a house in the country. . . (Incomplete sentence but complete thought with photograph of a cat)	Sometimes the other reindeer made a circle around Rudolph and sang: "Red-nose, red-nose, A funny sight! Big as an apple, And twice as bright!" They kicked snowballs with their tiny hoofs and covered Rudolph with a blanket of white fluffy snow. (2 long sentences, illustration)
Page 4 with some other cats. (Completion of sentence from page 3 with photographs of cats)	All the reindeer loved to play games. They played tree tag and snow slide and tumble bones. But Rudolph was never asked to play. He stood behind a pine tree and watched. He was very lonely. (5 sentences with colored illustration)

FIGURE 8.1

men men's; personal pronoun, with subject, object, and two possessive forms, *I, me, my, mine;* verb, with its five forms, *eat, eats, ate, eating, eaten;* adjective and adverb, with their positive, comparative, and superlative forms, *fast, faster, fastest.*

The chief relevance to teaching reading of these morphological facts of life would seem to be that the suffixes should never be separated from their stems by hyphens, and that an uninflected word should never be separated from the inflected word it accompanies, by being on different lines. In other words, "extremely" should never be printed with *extreme-* on one line and *-ly* on the next, nor should a sentence like "These pies must not be eaten" be broken up on the page at any point other than between *pies* and *must.*

Phonology and Its Relation to Reading Instruction

Leaving behind this brief treatment of the relevance of semantics, syntax and morphology to the teaching of reading, let us consider the very great relevance of phonology. The twenty-four consonant phonemes, the thirteen or fourteen vowel phonemes of English, and the spelling patterns used to represent them are of the utmost importance. (The writer says thirteen or fourteen vowel phonemes because for many West Coast speakers, and indeed others, there is no distinction whatever between *cot* and *caught, Lon* and *lawn, odd* and *awed.*)

Fries, in his most recent book,[3] felt it necessary to clarify the usage of the three terms *phonic, phonetic*(s) and *phonemic*(*s*). In this discussion, *phonic* will refer to the familiar methods of teaching children word attack and *phonetics* will mean only the science of speech sounds, with *phonetic* the appropriate adjective. *Phonemics* is the study of *phonemes,* the small number (12 and 65 are the known extremes) of sounds in any one language that makes a difference in meaning. Most of the alphabets used in the world are attempts to represent *phonemic distinctions.* A *minimal pair* of words has words that differ by one phoneme only, e.g. *man/men, man/pan, man/mad.*

In Figure 8.2, the twenty-four consonant phonemes are given. You may have seen them on a chart which used slightly different labels or different symbols, but there is general agreement on the fact there are these twenty-four distinctions for which we can find minimal pairs to prove that they make a difference in meaning.

---

[3]Charles C. Fries, *Linguistics and Reading* (New York, Holt, Rinehart, and Winston, 1964), p. 134.

	LABIALS	DENTALS	PALATALS	VELARS	
STOPS and AFFRICATES	p	t	ch	k	vl. (8)
	b	d	j	g	vd.
FRICATIVES	f	th s	sh	—	vl. (8)
	v	dh z	zh		vd.
NASALS	m	n	—	ng	(3) vd.
RESONANTS	w	r,l	y	h	(5)
	Labio-dental / Bi-labial	Apico-dental / Apico-alveolar		Dorso-velar / Glottal	(24)

FIGURE 8.2

English Consonant Phonemes

The Consonant Sounds

A frequent answer to the question, "How many vowels are there in English?" is "A, e, i, o, u, and sometimes y and w." Subtracting the five letters which unambiguously and always stand for vowel sounds, you have twenty-one that represent consonants. As you know by now, linguists are very stubborn about keeping letters and sounds apart. They also use the technical term *phoneme* for a speech sound in a given language. The statement that linguists, phoneticians, and other people concerned professionally with the phonological aspects of language might all make is this: English has twenty-four consonant phonemes, represented in the spelling system by the twenty-one consonant-letters, alone and in various combinations.

Questions Concerning the Consonant Phonemes

What are these twenty-four consonant phonemes, and how are they described? Whenever we classify a consonant sound, we ask three questions:

1. Where is the sound made?
2. How is the sound made?
3. Are the vocal cords vibrating?

Let us consider each question separately. When we ask where a sound is made, we want to know fairly accurately what the place of articulation is and which of the speech organs are involved. If the lips are involved, we call the sound a *labial*. If we want to be more technical and specify that both lips are involved we say, for instance, that / p, b, m / are bilabial. Say the following words, in order to become aware that you are opening and closing your lips: peppermint, popular, babble, imbibing, mammoth, memory, pygmy, Bemelmans, pablum, mobbing, moppet. Notice also that you are rounding your lips when you say /w/ in these words: willow-ware, wallowing, windshield wiper, wary, weary, whale. The phonemes /f, v/ are also labial sounds, *labiodental* to be exact, because the upper teeth touch the lower lip, as you will notice when you say these words: fife, fluffy, Vivian, revive, involvement, valve-fitter, fever, villify, favorite.

Here we have six sounds, then, which are made with the lips, and we can say that English /p b m w f v/ are all LABIALS.

In order to make almost all the rest of the English consonant sounds, we have to use some part of the tongue, the tip or *apex*, front or *blade*, back or *dorsum*. Some portion of the tongue touches or approaches the *teeth*, the *alveolar ridge* (the gums above the upper teeth), the roof of the mouth or *hard palate*, the soft palate or *velum*.

If the tongue is between the teeth, as is usually the case for both of the sounds spelled TH, we call the resulting sound an *interdental*. First try these words, all of which have the phoneme we write /th/or *θ*/, using the Greek letter *theta*: thin, thick, thwart, thimble, ether, athletic, path, wealth. Now say the following words, all of which have the other interdental sound which we write /dh/ or / ð / with the barred-d borrowed from the Old English alphabet, where it represents the same sound: there, they, thus, then, either, bathe, soothe.

We may use the term DENTAL as a cover term for all the sounds made in the general area of the teeth, the two interdentals /th/ and /dh/, and the six sounds which are more precisely alveolars, made at or near the gum-ridge, /t d n s z l/. Say these words and observe the action of the tip of your tongue against the alveolar ridge: tattle-tale, dedicate, none, Nanny, sassy, zigzag, sissy, sizzle, Zasu, lily, lasso, lining, silly, Lizzie, teller, dollar, Sicily, knitting needle, Linda, lintel.

The eight sounds, then, that we can call DENTALS are /th dh t d s z n l/.

It is hard to generalize about the r-sound in the English-speaking world because it may be an alveolar tap for a Britisher who says "veddy, veddy," a truly retroflexed sound, made with the tongue curled back towards the roof of the mouth of a Midwestern American, or merely a continuation of the preceding vowel for an Easterner.

There are five phonemes, written / ch j sh zh y /, which can be called PALATALS because the front part of the tongue, or blade, touches or approaches the hard palate in the course of the articulation of these sounds. Say the following words and observe that your tongue is near the hard palate, or roof of the mouth, when you make the consonant sounds: judging, Chichester, church, edge, shay, chichi, azure, vision, yea, Jesuit, buying, dying, Zsa Zsa.

Of the twenty-four consonant phonemes of English, there are four which can be called VELARS because they are made in the region of the velum, or soft palate. The sound we write /h/ involves no contact and very little friction, but the other three, written /k, g, ng/ do involve contact of the back part of the tongue, or dorsum, with the soft palate, or velum. Try to observe this as you say the consonants in these words: gag, giggle, khaki, cackle, kick, clock, keg, king, clinging, gang, ganging, groggy, Klieg, cocky, kicking, Gregory, conquer, quick, quahog, quacking, quaking, caking, gargoyle, gangling, Queequeg, crinkle, creaking, Gieseking.

A Summary of Consonant-Sound Articulation

So far we have talked about where along the speech tract the sounds are made – the sound that linguists analyze into the twenty-four consonant phonemes of English. Although many books have been written about the phonetic details of each of the phonemes in many regional and social dialects of English, much of what we, as English teachers, need to know about the place of articulation of the consonant-sounds can be summed up simply. There are four areas of the speech tract which are significant for English, namely labial, dental, palatal, and velar.

6 LABIALS: /p b m w f v / puppy, baby, mummy, wow, five
9 DENTALS: / th dh t d s z n l r / thenceforth, Teddy, sizzle, nearly
5 PALATALS: / ch j sh zh y / josh, church, azure, yea
4 VELARS: /h k g ng / Hague, cake, gong

The Consonant Letters

The common orthographic representations of the twenty-four consonant phonemes of English are listed below. A hyphen preceding a grapheme indicates its occurrence in final position only; hyphens before and after indicate occurrence in medial position only. Parentheses indicate the environment of a grapheme. C represents "consonant" and V, "vowel." Some spellings which are "irregular" are omitted, although they occur in high-frequency words.

CONSONANT GRAPHO-PHONEMICS

/p/	p, pp, -pe
/b/	b, bb, -be
/t/	t, tt, -te, -(e)d
/d/	d, dd, -de, -(e)d
/k/	c(a,o,u,C), k(e,i), -ke, q(u), -cc, -ch, x
/g/	g(a,o,u,C) gu(e,i), gg, -gue, -x-, gh-
/ch/	ch, -tch, -tu-
/j/	j, g(e,i,y), -dge, -ge
/f/	f, ff, -fe, ph, -gh
/v/	v, vv, -ve
/th,dh/	th
/ch/	th, -the
/s/	s, ss, -se, c(e,i,y), -ce, sc-, -(e)s, x
/z/	z, zz, -ze, -se, -(e)s
/sh/	sh, ch, -che, -ti(on), -ssi(on), -ci-, -ce-
/zh/	-ge, -su-, -si-, -zu-, -si(on)
/m/	m, mm, -me, -mb, -mn
/n/	n, nn, -ne, gn, kn-
/ng/	ng, n(k,g,q)
/l/	l, ll, -le
/r/	r, rr, -re, wr-
/w/	w, wh, (q)u
/y/	y, u/ue, ew, iew
/h/	h

The Vowel Sounds

With vowels, there is no stopping the air or putting a speech organ in the way of the airstream to cause friction. There is only changing the shape of the oral cavity by moving the tongue to a position that we call *high* or *mid* or *low* and at the same time, *front* or *central* or *back*. The rounding of the lips also affects the quality of the vowel sound. In English all the front vowels are unrounded, all back vowels rounded.

Their arrangement is given in Figure 8.3.

	SIMPLE		
	Front	Central	Back
High	/ i / pit	—	/ u / put
Mid	/ e / pet	/ ə / putt	—
Low	/ æ / pat	/ a / pot	/ ɔ / paw
	COMPLEX		
High	/ iy / Pete	—	/ uw / boot
Mid	/ ey / pate	—	/ ow / boat / oy / boy
Low	—	/ aw / bout / ay / bite	—

FIGURE 8.3

The common TO representations of the fourteen vowel phonemes are given below.

SIMPLE NUCLEI

/i/	i (C), y(C)
/e/	e(C), ea(C)
/æ/	a(C)
/ə/	u(C), o, ou; unstressed a, e, i, o, u, y
/a/	o(C), a
/u/	oo, u
/ɔ/	aw, au, o(r), al(C), (w)a(r)

COMPLEX NUCLEI

/iy/	e(C)e, ee, ea, e, ei, ie, (VC)y, (VC)ie
/ey/	a(C)e, ay, ai, ey, ei, ei(gh)
/ay/	i(C)e, (C)y, C(ye), C(ie), -igh, -ig(n), i(ld,nd)
/oy/	oy, oi
/aw/	ou, ow
/ow/	o(C)e, oa, o, oe, ow
/uw/	u(C)e, ue, ew, ui, ou, o, oo

NUCLEI BEFORE /r/ IN MONOSYLLABLES

/ir/	ear, eer, ere
/er/	air, are
/ɔr/	or, ore, oar, (w)ar
/ur/	oor, ure
/ar/	ar
/ər/	ur, er, ir, (w)or(C), ear(C)

Lists and charts like those illustrated are, of course, just restatements of information that has long been in the common domain. Figure 4 portrays what have been called grapho-phonemes, that is, the correspondences between the regular spelling patterns, the traditional names for the vowel sounds, and the phonemes, given in Smith-Trager transcription.

Analyses of the Grapho-Phonemes of English

The regular spelling patterns, which many linguists and teachers have long observed, are being systematically investigated by Dr. Paul R. Hanna at Stanford University under the sponsorship of the U. S. Office of Education. The project is called "Phoneme-Grapheme Relationships Basic to Cues for Improvement of Spelling" and is documenting those relationships by computer analysis of the *Thorndike-Lorge Teachers' Word Book* and the *Merriam-Webster Collegiate Dictionary.*

An analysis of the grapho-phonemics of English also underlies Sir James Pitman's initial teaching alphabet, earlier called the Augmented Roman Alphabet. It is now called i/t/a and is beautifully worked out so that it can be used anywhere in the English-speaking world, as no purely phonetic notation could be. Not only is i/t/a independent of dialect variation, it is so designed that a four-year-old can use it with pleasure and profit and make the transition to TO with little trouble.[4] The i/t/a is not only superbly designed, but also successful, as has been demonstrated in hundreds of schools in Great Britain and in ever-growing numbers of schools in this country.

LONG			SHORT	
Symbol				*Symbol*
/ ey /	taped, tape	A	tapped, tap	/ æ /
/ iy /	complete, Bede	E	abetted, bed	/ e /
/ ay /	ripen, ripe	I	ripple, rip	/ i /
/ ow /	moping, mope	O	mopping, mop	/ a, ɔ /
/ uw, yuw /	duly, rule cutest, cute	U	dull, dully cutter, cut	/ ə /
/ ʉw /	fool, kook	OO	full, cook	/ u /
/ oy /	boy, boil	OY	———	
/ aw /	now, noun	OU	———	

FIGURE 8.4

English Vowel Grapho-Phonemes

[4]Sir James Pitman, "The Future of the Teaching of Reading," presented at the Twenty-eighth Educational Conference by the Educational Records Bureau in the City of New York: October 30, 31, and November 1, 1963, pp. 1-5.

'Short'	/ p /	/ t /	/ ch /	/ k /	/ b /	/ d /	/ j /	/ g /	/ m /	/ n /
A	cap	cat	catch	pack	cab	cad	badge	gag	jam	pan
E	pep	pet	fetch	deck	web	wed	wedge	beg	hem	hen
I	rip	pit	pitch	pick	bib	bid	ridge	jig	him	win
O	pop	pot	botch	rock	rob	rod	lodge	log	prow	con
U	cup	but	hutch	luck	rub	dud	budge	jug	hum	fun
OO		foot		book		good				
'Long'										
A	ape	wait ate		cake	babe	maid shade	vague	sage	aim tame	pain lane
E	keep reap	meet heat	screech peach	leek peak	plebe	need bead	siege	league	beam	lean
I	pipe	night kite		like	bribe	ride			time	nine
O	hope soap	tote boat	poach	coke soak	robe	lode road	loge	vogue	home room	stone roan
U		newt mute		cuke	cube	lewd rude	huge	fugue	fume	hewn tune
OO	hoop	hoot	pooch		boob	food	stooge		broom	moon

FIGURE 8.5

Chart of Regular Spellings of Words of One Syllable Ending in a Consonant

'Short'	/ f /	/ th /	/ s /	/ sh /	/ v /	/ dh /	/ z /	/ zh /	/ ng /	/ l /
A	Saff	path	pass	lash			jazz		pang	pal
E	Jeff	Seth	mess	mesh					length	dell
I	tiff	pith	hiss	fish			whizz		wing	will
O	doff	broth	boss	josh					gong long	doll
U	gruff		fuss	lush			buzz		sung	dull
OO	hoof									wool
'Long'										
A	safe waif	faith	case face		save	bathe	phase daze			male sail
E	leaf reef	heath teeth	cease fleece		leave	breathe	please sneeze			seal
I	life		slice		hive	blithe	rise size			file
O	loaf	loath both	coarse dose		loaves rove	clothe	pose doze			coal hole
U			puce use				muse fuze			yule
OO	proof	tooth	loose		groove	soothe	choose ooze			tool

FIGURE 8.6

Chart of Regular English Spellings

'Short'	/ p	t	c	k	b	d	j	g	m	n /
A	ap	at	atch	ack	ab	ad	adge	ag	am	an
E	ep	et	etch	eck	eb	ed	edge	eg	em	en
I	ip	it	itch	ick	ib	id	idge	ig	im	in
O	op	ot	otch	ock	ob	od	odge	og	om	on
U	up	ut	utch	uck	ub	ud	udge	ug	um	un
OO		oot		ook		ood				
'Long'						aid			aim	ain
A	ape	ate		ake	abe	ade	age	ague	ame	ane
E	eep eap	eet eat	eech each	eek eak		eed ead		eague	eam	een ean
I	ipe	ight ite		ike	ibe	ide			ime	ine
O	ope oap	ote oat	oach	oke oak	obe	ode oad	oge	ogue	ome oam	one oan
U		ewt ute		uke	ube	ewd ude	uge	ugue	ume	ewn une
OO	oop	oot	ooch	ook	oob	ood	ooge		oom	oon

FIGURE 8.7

Chart of Regular English Spellings

'Short'	/ f	th	s	sh	v	dh	z	zh	ng	l
A	aff	ath	ass	ash	(ave)		azz		ang	al
E	eff	eth	ess	esh					eng	ell
I	iff	ith	iss	ish	(ive)		izz		ing	ill
O	off	oth	oss	osh					ong	oll
U	uff		uss	ush	(ove)		uzz		ung	ull
OO	oof									
'Long'										
A	aif afe	aith	ase ace		ave	athe		(beige)		
E	eef eaf	eeth eath	eece ease		eave	eathe	eese ease			eel eal
I	ife		ice		ive	ithe	ise ize			ile
O	oaf	ooth oath	ose oarse		ove oaves	othe	ose oze			ole oal
U							use uze			we
OO	oof	ooth	oose		oove	oothe	oose ooze			ool

FIGURE 8.8

Chart of Regular English Spellings

If, however, it is not possible to use i/t/a then the only sensible alternative is to teach the regularities of English spelling. Undoubtedly there are a small number of high-frequency irregularly-spelled words that must be taught as units. Those apart, the vast majority of words in the English lexicon are spelled regularly.

In Figures 8.5 and 8.6 are given charts with each of the six "short-long" pairs of vowel sounds (short A-long A, E, I, O, U, OO) followed by a consonant. Omitted are the four consonants / w y h / and / r / because of their special nature which has been alluded to above. In Figure 8.5, the regular spelling of each of the twelve vowel-sounds (all except / oy / and / aw /) is indicated before the four voiceless and four voiced stops and two of the nasals, / p,t,ch,k /, / b,d,j,g / and / m,n /. It is indicated by giving one of the many regularly-spelled words. In Figure 8.6, the spelling of those same twelve vowel sounds before / l / and the other nasal, the four voiceless and four voiced fricatives, is indicated. That is, the six pairs / æ-ey /, / e-iy /, / i-ay /, / a,ɔ—ow /, / ə -uw, yuw /, and / u-uw / are each represented by a sample word before / f, th, s, sh /, / v, dh, z, zh / and / ng, l /. On both charts, the absence of a sample word indicates the absence of a regular spelling in monosyllables for that V+C sequence. There are in some cases two or even three regular spellings. There are also irregular spellings of many of the V+C sequences. This is far less important than the facts of the regularities of English orthography and the other great regularities, i.e. before the suffixes *-es, -ed, -en, -ing, -y, -ish, -le, -er, -est* a consonant letter is left single to indicate a preceding long vowel and is doubled to indicate a short vowel.

That these basically simple correspondences between sound and symbol are not always taught has been the principal cause of the functional illiteracy from which so many Americans, adults and children, continue to suffer.

Methods of Teaching Spelling[5]

Following the very thorough discussion of the basic linguistic principles involved in spelling the words of the English language, it seems appropriate to devote some attention to problems of teaching these principles of spelling to elementary school pupils. Among the most significant problems which must be solved by elementary teachers are:

---

[5]This chapter supplement was prepared by the editor.

1. How much time should be devoted to spelling instruction?
2. How can an elementary teacher provide for adequate attention to the wide range of individual differences he will encounter in any group of pupils?
3. What method or methods of presentation and study are most effective for children in the elementary school?
4. What materials are most beneficial in a spelling program? How should a workbook or textbook be used, if at all? What types of audio-visual materials are most effective?

Time Allotments for Spelling

The problem of determining the optimum amount of time to devote to spelling instruction is not of recent origin. In 1897 J. M. Rice published an article in the *Forum* dealing with this very issue.[6] Rice reported the results of a study he conducted, which indicated that more time was being devoted to spelling instruction than was justified on the basis of careful examination of pupils' test scores. Children who spent thirty minutes studying spelling appeared to show little superiority over pupils of equal ability who studied fifteen or twenty minutes a day. Petty writes:

Early studies pointed out the faulty reasoning in expecting improved spelling ability to result from increasing the time devoted to spelling instruction, yet time allotments have recently been increased. In most instances not more than seventy-five minutes per week should be devoted to spelling instruction, and there is evidence that even less time accomplishes equal achievement. In most schools, spelling is taught five periods per week, principally because of the ease in the administration of such a program.[7]

Any discussion of time allotments for spelling instruction must concern itself with the *content* of that instructional period. If, in addition to giving attention to spelling, a teacher can also help to guide growth in handwriting and/or enrich children's vocabularies, this is certainly a desirable bonus. It seems obvious that much teaching and learning of spelling proceeds independent of the period of the day identified as "spelling" or "language arts." Spelling instruction is going on when a fifth grader consults a dictionary to learn how a word is spelled and when a second grader experiments with several spellings of a word to *see* which one looks "right" to him. Nonetheless, there appears to be some value to devoting some class time to direct instruction related to the principles discussed in the previous chapter, the

---

[6]J. M. Rice, "The Futility of the Spelling Grind," *The Forum* 23: pp. 169-172, 1897.

[7]Walter T. Petty, "Handwriting and Spelling: Their Current Status," *Elementary English,* 41: 840, December, 1964.

identification and correction of spelling errors and the evaluation of pupils' growth in spelling.

It is appropriate to refer here to the problem of individual differences. Most elementary classes enroll pupils of varying ability and competence in spelling as well as in other subject areas – a range of scores on standardized tests of academic achievement which equals or surpasses the grade level designation (at least three years in third grade, five years in fifth, etc.) is not at all unusual. If fifteen minutes a day, seventy-five minutes a week approaches the maximum time limits which can profitably be spent on spelling instruction, are these limits to be applied to children of varying abilities? Should the same amount of time be planned for the slow, the average, and the bright child?

Because spelling, like the other language arts, is not learned or taught in isolation, the question of how much time to devote to spelling instruction is a difficult one to answer. There is general agreement that incidental instruction, using every opportunity with the group and individual pupils to teach important spelling principles, is essential but by itself inadequate. If time is not scheduled for spelling instruction, this very important skill may be neglected. In deciding how much time to devote to spelling instruction, the teacher must consider the recommendations of state curriculum guides, local courses of study and typical practices in the school in which he teaches. He will also consider the children he is teaching – their strengths, their weaknesses, their attitudes toward spelling and his own ability to make provisions for these differences. An experienced teacher who is skillful in utilizing functional spelling situations – teaching spelling when and as it's needed – may wish to schedule fewer formal spelling periods. It may also be true that time allotments for spelling will vary from week to week. Some lists may be more difficult than others, or other activities may temporarily displace spelling as a subject of emphasis.

For all of the reasons listed, flexibility is essential. Only after a teacher has familiarized himself with the materials provided for spelling instruction, knows the specific state and local requirements, and above all knows the needs and interests of the children in his class can be answered the important but difficult question, how much time should I devote to spelling instruction?

Adjustment to Individual Differences

A teacher can arrange his spelling program to meet the several ability levels represented in his class in several ways:

--- Lists can be selected which are of varying lengths and/or difficulty levels. Brighter children, children with few spelling problems, can be given either more words to learn, words which are more difficult, or both.

—— Once a basic list has been mastered, children can use the time usually spent in studying spelling for some other purpose.

—— Different methods can be used with children of different levels. Slower children may need much more direct teacher guidance than bright children or children who seem to learn to spell easily.

There are several advantages to the first method suggested. Differences in interests as well as differences in abilities can be taken into account when lists are varied. Much has been said about giving the gifted child "busy work" or "more of the same" rather than challenging him at increasingly higher levels. Thus it seems wise to use spelling lists (perhaps taken from several spelling series) of varying difficulty levels and to encourage children to learn to spell words which are foundational to subject areas other than the language arts. The social studies, science, and mathematics are rich sources for words which are of interest and will challenge superior spellers. Simply assigning *more* words does not appear to be as effective a method for challenging gifted children as helping them select words of a somewhat higher difficulty level.

It should be noted that there is little evidence of agreement regarding the difficulty level of words among the several spelling series. A word which appears on the second grade list in one published series may be on the third or even fourth grade list in a different series. Nonetheless a bright child, with a minimum of teacher help, should be able to select or collate a list of words which is both more challenging and more interesting to him than the standard grade level list. Basic or grade level lists may well be organized and patterned in such a way that children will discover and consistently apply the linguistic principles stressed by Professor Trager.

Study Beyond a Basic Spelling List

There are different points of view with reference to children being freed from further study once a "basic" list has been mastered. It is certainly true that a few words comprise the major portion of the words most commonly written.[8] Once a child has mastered a "basic" list, why not free him for other learning tasks? There is certainly some merit to this position, particularly in this era of the "knowledge explosion." However, limiting

[8]Over one-half of our writing consists of a repetition of one hundred basic words; a person who can correctly spell 1,500 words from the Horn basic writing vocabulary can spell 93 per cent of the words he needs for writing.

a child at a particular grade level to learning only the one hundred to five hundred words on a publisher's adapted list hardly seems wise. Our language is a rich one, with from six hundred thousand to eight hundred thousand words – should not an alert, intelligent child have a chance to explore his language to whatever depth he likes? It appears we must refer again to individual differences. If a child has a very strong interest in math, science or history and is quite impatient with the routine of studying spelling words, then meeting minimal grade level requirements in spelling may be adequate. It is surely wrong, however, to set unnatural limits for children who may well develop a real feeling for words – could perhaps develop some unusual abilities as writers – if their interest in language were encouraged. The availability of materials must be considered in discussing this problem. There are elementary schools without dictionaries, without supplementary spelling books and workbooks, indeed, without libraries! If classes are larger, and materials are limited, a teacher can hardly be blamed for feeling satisfied if grade level requirements are met. Other subject areas provide words, and there are surely other textbooks which can serve as supplementary spelling texts – sources for additional words. It is to be hoped that teachers will encourage interest in language and that facet of language we call "spelling" and that bright children won't be permitted to do the same assignment as everyone else and feel they have done enough when this is accomplished.[9]

Procedures With Inefficient Spellers

What about the other extreme – the child who is operating well below the level expected of him in spelling? Teachers have tried some of the following techniques and have found them effective:

- the child chooses a shorter list than the majority of the class, a list he can reasonably be expected to master.
- from a series other than that regularly used, the child selects a different list – he may work on this list during an independent study period, he may ask another child to help him or he may rely upon special "help sessions" with the teacher or his parents.
- a child may join a group of children with similar problems and this group may use different words, different study techniques and methods than other classes.

The techniques used will vary from teacher to teacher and from school to school, but most teachers recognize that growth in the mastery of

[9]Paul S. Anderson, *Language Skills in Elementary Education,* New York: The Macmillan Company, 1964. pp. 185-187.

spelling principles requires some attention to the learner, his needs and interests, his strengths and weaknesses. Diagnosing spelling problems and developing a spelling program which takes into account both the structure of our language and the nature of the learner will result in effective mastery of our spelling system.

Spelling Methods

The two methods most commonly referred to are the "test-study" and the "study-test" method.

For upper grade children who operate at many levels in spelling, it appears to be best to check the pupils' knowledge of a given list prior to asking them to study the list. The "new" list is pronounced, corrected and children see immediately which words they know and which they don't know, which phoneme-grapheme relationships they understand and which they don't understand. They limit their study to mastering the words they don't know. Time thus, is *not* wasted on "studying" words or patterns with which the child is already familiar.

Although there is some evidence to the contrary, the study-test method appears to be best for young children and for intermediate grade children with spelling problems. The child is given the opportunity to look at the new words, to write them, to locate familiar patterns, etc., before he is tested. Young children may be confused and some unfavorable attitudes toward spelling may result if they are asked to write an entire list of completely unfamiliar words.

Writing words is usually recommended as a study technique rather than oral spelling or "writing words in the air." Oral spelling leads to further sound-written symbol (phoneme-grapheme) confusion and it is certainly true that we have little need for spelling when we're speaking. The various spelling series suggest approved methods for studying a word, and most study routines are something like the following:

1. Look at the unfamiliar words, observe their configurations, known patterns, similarities to words already known, etc.
2. Write the unfamiliar words.
3. Check with a correct copy of the word.
4. If the word has been written correctly, use the same technique for the next word.
5. If the word was missed, apply appropriate word analysis techniques – phonetic analysis, structural analysis, etc. – as well as careful observation of the total word as presented.

Several word sources have already been suggested. It has already been recommended that a child be permitted to adjust and select, to make the spelling list fit him, rather than trying to fit a list. If a basic list is to be mastered, it can be shortened, supplemented or altered in terms of group or individual abilities, needs and interests. It has aleady been suggested that lists be presented which will help a child discover many of the regular patterns in our language.

In the primary grades, groups of children may keep a box, alphabetized and indexed, using 3 x 5 index cards to which they add words they are interested in learning to spell. This box also serves as a source for words needed in writing.

Intermediate and upper grade pupils may profit more by keeping individual lists – in a shorthand notebook, perhaps. Such a book should also be alphabetized for easy reference.

Teachers occasionally ask children to draw pictures illustrating these words, to write simple definitions or to use them in sentences. It should be kept in mind that establishing a single definition of a word may not be as beneficial to a child as exploring the many meanings of a word like "run."

Charts listing frequently used words – words related to a unit of work, perhaps, or to a subject of high interest to the children, are helpful in developing an awareness of the importance of spelling and, of course, for reference by children in preparing reports, writing stories and adding to their vocabularies.

Standards for Spelling

Children should accept responsibility for correct spelling whenever communication with someone else or a group is the objective. Proofreading is an important skill. It can be taught and learned. Teachers frequently criticize children for failing to check their work, but teachers have too frequently neglected to prove either the "check points" or the time necessary for proofreading. Even a primary grade teacher should help children determine the qualities essential for an acceptable letter or report (correct spelling is certainly one of the most important of these qualities) and should remind children occasionally that following the established criteria is a primary responsibility of a writer and a debt he owes to those with whom he wants to communicate.

It is also true, however, that the ideas expressed are generally more important than correctly spelled words. At least this is true when the object is self-expression and creativeness. Strict application of spelling rules may inhibit a child's creativity in the initial stages especially. Of course, if the poem is to be a part of a bulletin board display or is to be included in a class notebook or newspaper it will be read carefully, and perfected to the limits of the child's ability. Flexibility in applying standards of acceptable spelling is desirable, and probably *helps* a child's writing more than it *hinders* his spelling.

Materials for Spelling Instruction

Traditionally the hard-backed speller and the spelling workbook have been the most important if not the only spelling tools. These are frequently organized so that there is one activity for each day of the week —a pretest on Monday[10], a phonics exercise on Tuesday, sentences using the words are written Wednesday (or sometimes a second test is administered) another word analysis skill exercise is provided on Thursday, and almost always the final test is given on Friday. A program of this sort requires little planning by the teacher, and meets the needs of perhaps the middle third of the class. Each child is required to learn, or to try to learn the same number of words, using the same methods. For reasons which should be clear to any careful observer of children, such a spelling program is, by itself, inadequate. It is frustrating to the child who has great difficulty with spelling, and boring to the child who spells with ease. Several methods for supplementing this type of program have already been suggested. Individually selected lists, group lists, and adjustments in the one list which a teacher may be expected to use should help to make the spelling program more interesting, more challenging and more effective. Several spelling series now include suggestions to the teacher for varying and supplementing the program.[11]

Dictionaries of several types, at several levels, are an essential part of an effective spelling program. The same dictionary for each pupil can hardly be justified in classrooms where many different reading materials are available at many levels. Publishers have recently made available picture dictionaries, beginning dictionaries, and junior dictionaries, as well as dictionaries designed to help children progress from one dictionary level to the next. If proofreading and checking work prior to handing it in are to be encouraged, dictionaries should be easily available to chil-

---

[10]It is somewhat difficult to see the purpose of the pretest since children proceed through all the other exercises whether all or none of the words were missed.

[11]Mildred Dawson, Marian Zollinger and Ardell Elwell, *Guiding Language Learning*, New York: Harcourt, Brace and World, Inc., 1963, p. 335.

dren.[12] Even a vast number of copies kept in the school library will hardly serve these purposes.

Teacher-made worksheets – crossword puzzles, fill-in-the-blank exercises, etc. – serve a very useful purpose. These can be devised to accompany individual lists or lists chosen by a small group.[13] Pages or exercises from spelling workbooks can be used, and children can locate for themselves the exercises, puzzles, or tests they need if the sheets are filed according to the type of help they can provide – "initial consonants," "syllabication," etc.

One device which has proved extremely useful to teachers who want to individualize their spelling programs is the tape recorder. A teacher can record a particular list, pausing enough between the words pronounced easily to allow the child time for writing the word. Even the correct spelling can be pronounced, or the child can find his own correct copy of the list to see where he has made mistakes. In one classroom, each child has his own tape on which he records his own list for testing purposes. The tapes are, of course, erased and can be used indefinitely.[14]

Charts and lists of words on the chalkboard or bulletin board should also be referred to in any discussion of spelling aids.

Commercially prepared games, "Scrabble," for example, or "Anagrams" may prove interesting to older children. Adaptations of some popular word games also are available for younger children.

Space does not permit a discussion of other aids for teaching and learning spelling – a resourceful teacher will find many ways and devices to enhance and vary what can be but should not be a dull, routine area of the elementary curriculum. Learning to spell can be a key to a useful and interesting facet of our language for teachers and pupils as well.

EXTENDING YOUR LEARNING

1. Of the fourteen vowel sounds, ten have regular spelling patterns. Look at the charts of regularly spelled words and Figure 4. Using the key words, how would you lead students to discover for themselves the regular use of final *-e*, and of single and double consonant letters, to indicate short and long A, E, I, O and U?
2. Take two different desk dictionaries that have dissimilar pronunciation keys. On the chart, record the symbols that each one uses for the fourteen vowel sounds.

---

[12]The entire April, 1964, issue of *Elementary English* is devoted to a discussion of elementary school dictionaries and their use.

[13]Paul S. Anderson, *Language Skills in Elementary Education,* New York: The Macmillan Company, 1964. pp. 185-187.

[14]Dorothy Johnson, "Spelling Self-Taught from Magnetic Tape," *Elementary School Journal.* pp. 78-82.

Chart of English Vowel Grapho-phonemes

Long	*Phonemic Symbol*	*Dictionary 1*	*Dict. 2*	*Short*	*Ph.S.*	*D. 1*	*D. 2*
A	/ey/			A	/æ/		
E	/iy/			E	/e/		
I	/ay/			I	/i/		
O	/ow/			O	/a,ɔ/		
U	/uw,yuw/			U	/ə/		
OO	/uw/			OO	/u/		
OY	/oy/			—			
OU	/aw/			—			

3. Survey two or three dictionaries[15,16] designed for use in the elementary school. Are the systems of diacritical markings used the same or different? How are the following words "phonetically" described in each dictionary?

apple	acre
better	leisure
kitten	mighty
cotton	bloated
cutting	fusion

4. What is a "schwa"? (Consult the same dictionaries used to complete the first exercise.) Why does one dictionary use the schwa in a word like "up" /əp/ while another shows it as follows: *ŭp*? Would you or would you not encourage children to compare and contrast various dictionaries? Would this be enriching or confusing?
5. Consider the influence of dialect upon spelling. Can children correctly spell words containing sounds they neither use nor hear?
   In an area where *witch* and *which* are pronounced identically, you would not try to teach them to pronounce them differently. However, draw up a list of homonyms (like *witch/which,* for areas without /hw/) that the students must learn to *spell* differently.
6. If you are an Easterner who has three different vowel sounds in *merry, marry* and *Mary,* how will you teach the spelling of those three different families of words to Western children for whom they are homonyms, as are *ferry/fairy, very/vary, Harry/hairy* and others?
7. If you are from the large area of the Southeast and Southwest where *pen* rhymes with *pin* and *gem* rhymes with *Jim,* you probably pronounce all words with short I or short E before /n/ and /m/, with the same vowel sound. How would you plan, without the help of a Professor Higgins to change your dialect, to teach Northern or Western children the spelling of such words?

---

[15]G. and C. Merriam Webster, *Websters Elementary Dictionary* (New York: American Book Company, 1961).

[16]Thorndike, Barnhart, Beginning Dictionary, Chicago: Scott, Foresman Company, 1964.

8. If you are from the West Coast and pronounce such words as *cot* and *caught, odd* and *awed* alike, how will you help children from the same area learn the different spellings of the same sound?
9. What might be the cumulative effect of a phonetic alphabet like i/t/a on children's spelling? Several studies have dealt with this very problem; present the findings to your class in the form of an oral report or panel discussion.
10. Survey several spelling series and note any phonetic inconsistencies in the lists – are *come* and *home* presented in the same lesson?
11. Develop a spelling lesson plan, consisting of no more than two typewritten pages based upon the development of one or two of the linguistic principles, discussed in section one of this chapter. List objectives, procedures, materials and evaluative techniques (consult Chapter 11).
12. If you are interested in teaching young children, develop a picture dictionary containing only pictured words with regular and consistent spellings.

BIBLIOGRAPHY

Allen, Harold Boughton (ed.). Readings in *Applied English Linguistics,* second ed. New York: Appleton-Century-Crofts, 1964.

Bloomfield, Leonard. *Language.* New York: Holt, Rinehart and Winston, 1933.

Bloomfield, Leonard and Clarence Barnhart. *Let's Read: A Linguistic Approach.* Detroit: Wayne State University Press, 1961.

Brooks, Nelson. *Language and Language Learning.* Theory and Practice. New York: Harcourt, Brace & World, Inc., 1960, 238 pp.

Fries, Charles G. *Teaching and Learning English as a Foreign Language.* London: Macmillan and Co., Ltd., 1957. 124 pp.

——. *Linguistics and Reading,* New York, Holt, 1964.

Gleason, Henry Allan, Jr. *Workbook in Descriptive Linguistics.* New York: Holt, Rinehart, and Winston, 1955.

——. *An Introduction to Descriptive Linguistics,* rev. ed. New York: Holt, Rinehart and Winston, 1961.

——. *Linguistics and English Grammar.* New York: Holt, Rinehart, and Winston, 1965.

Hall, Robert A., Jr. *Introductory Linguistics.* Philadelphia: Chilton Books, 1965.

——. *Sound and Spelling in English.* Philadelphia: Chilton Books, 1961.

Lefevre, Carl. *Linguistics and The Teaching of Reading.* New York: McGraw-Hill, 1964.

Ohannessian, Sirarpi. *Interim Bibliography on the Teaching of English to Speakers of Other Languages.* Washington, D. C.: Center for Applied Linguistics, 1960. 53 pp.

Sapir, Edward. *Language: An Introduction to the Study of Speech.* New York: Harcourt, Brace and World, 1921.

Stageberg, Norman C. *An Introductory English Grammar.* New York: Holt, Rinehart and Winston, 1965.

Stevick, Earl. *Helping People Learn English.* New York: Abingdon Press, 1957.

Tiedt, Iris M. and Sidney W. Contemporary English in The Elementary School. Englewood Cliffs: Prentice-Hall, 1967.

Trager, Edith C. and Sara Cook Henderson. *Pronunciation Drills for The Learners of English: The P.D.'s.* Washington, D. C.: English Language Services, 800-18th St., N.W., reprinted 1964.

———. "The Systematics of English Spelling." Reprint Series in Language and Linguistics, No. 89. New York: Bobbs Merrill, 1964.

Trager, George Leonard, and Henry Lee Smith, Jr. *An Outline of English Structure.* (Studies in Linguistics, Occasional Papers, No. 3). Reprinted, Washington, D. C.: American Council of Learned Societies, 1957.

Waterman, John Thomas. *Perspectives in Linguistics.* Chicago: University of Chicago Press, 1963.

Chapter 9 Ruth Hochstetler

Facets of Language — Grammar and Usage

Language is magical. Language is miraculous. It is one's use of language through talking — which nearly everyone does, or through reading and writing — which many people do, or through listening — which a few people do — that is the basis of communication. One thinks — he uses language; one explains — he uses language; one persuades — he uses language; one writes — he uses language; one perceives and in his attempt to make sense of his perceptions — he uses language.

Essential Functions of Language

Language is basic to a child's individual development as well as to his role as a participating member of social groups. Children grow in self-knowledge as they learn to use their language with effectiveness. Without understanding between and among people there can be little real empathy and there may be far too few who live harmoniously in a world where harmony is desperately needed.

Language can be and is a tool useful for clear communication based on clear thinking. Language is an important social phenomenon which is culturally derived, i.e., it is involved with information, ideas and values. Paul Roberts has expressed these ideas about the importance of language . . . "it shapes our minds and personalities, ... it gives us power and others powers over us." He further stated that . . . "to understand your language is . . . . to understand yourself, to get a notion of what it means to be a human being."[1]

---

[1]Paul E. Roberts, *English Sentences: Teachers' Manual.* New York, Harcourt, Brace and World, Inc., 1962, p. 6.

Language is defined in a variety of ways. In *Language Explorations for Elementary Grades* from the Nebraska Curriculum Development Center, language is defined as an arbitrary system and as a human activity useful for the communication of thought based on articulated voice symbols.[2]

W. Nelson Francis in *The English Language* stated that language is "a universal form of human behavior" and that all languages have some characteristics in common, namely, that any language is arbitrary; conventional, culturally transmitted, and has a highly complicated multiple structure.[3] Trauger has defined language as "a system embodying certain structural principles."[4]

A definition which has been given by Carl Lefevre is that language is "a commonly understood system or code of vocal systems by which we habitually communicate with one another in terms of our entire culture."[5] In McDavid's article, "The Cultural Matrix of American English," the statement is made that "language . . . is a system of arbitrary vocal signals by which a social group cooperate and interact and transmit their culture."[6] Some of the foregoing statements are comprehensive; however, Mauree Applegate's aptly put phrase "to give children . . . . a more personal vision of the world of words"[7] describes the challenge offered to elementary teachers.

Definitions of Grammar

Since this particular chapter is concerned with grammar, it seems desirable and necessary to define the term. Grammar is in a much-discussed state. There are those who maintain that it is the answer to the lack of skill displayed by those in the American culture so far as writing is concerned; to some, grammar refers to the mechanical skills of expression; to others, grammar is confused with attempts to determine "good" and "bad" usage; to those who think conservatively it is a fixed and unalterable body of knowledge concerning the structure of language.

---

[2]Nebraska Curriculum Development Center, *Language Explorations for Elementary Grades*. Lincoln: University of Nebraska, 1965, p. 4.

[3]W. Nelson Francis, *The English Language: An Introduction*. New York: W. W. Norton and Co., 1965, p. 1.

[4]Wilmer K. Trauger, *Language Arts in Elementary Schools*. New York: McGraw-Hill Book Co., Inc., 1963, p. 135.

[5]Helen Lefevre and Carl Lefevre, *Writing by Patterns*. New York: Alfred A. Knopf, 1965, p. 4.

[6]Raven I. McDavid, Jr., "The Cultural Matrix of American English," *Elementary English* 42: 13-21, January, 1965.

[7]Mauree Applegate, *Easy in English*. Evanston: Row, Peterson and Co., 1960, p. 25.

Pooley has defined grammar as a description of the way we speak and write English.[8] Paul Roberts has stated that grammar is "something that produces the sentence of the language whether the something is a machine or a book, or a human being who speaks the language natively."[9] A technical explanation of grammar written by Noam Chomsky is that "grammar can be thought of as a system of rules that specifies the class of phonetically possible utterances and that assigns a structural description to each well-formed sentence. The description incorporates and expresses just the information about the sentence that is available to the person who understands it." For instance a speaker of English knows that "the tiger looks terrifying" is well-formed but "the tiger looks jumping" or "tiger looks the terrifying" are not well-formed.[10] Whatever the word grammar actually may mean, the concern should be not so much with definition as with the ways in which grammar can be used to help children improve their own oral and written expression. Research supports the conclusion that very little teaching of grammar as it has been done in the past has helped childen speak or write better.

Reasons for Modifying Language Instruction

Changes in the teaching of language have come about through the advance in knowledge about children and how they learn; through the contributions of sociologists, linguists, social psychologists and others interested and concerned with language development; through a knowledge of a wider variety of materials and an understanding of language and its uses. If one is to teach children effectively, he must recognize that language is an essential part of the growth process. There should be emphasis on real experiences which have meaning and purpose for the children in a classroom. Materials and methods should fit each child and his needs and interests. Teachers should have a concern for those whose language is different whether it is a result of a different culture or a result of living in a disadvantaged area. Children need practice but only after there is an understanding of principles. This is not to say that rules should be disregarded. Children need to build their own generalizations from much useful speaking and writing. Above all, a child needs to be highly motivated so that his feelings and attitudes toward language and his own improvement

---

[8]Robert C. Pooley, "What About Grammar?" in MacCampbell, James C., *Readings in the Language Arts in the Elementary School.* Boston: D. C. Heath Co., 1964, p. 21.

[9]Paul C. Roberts, *English Sentences. op. cit.*, p. 17.

[10]Paul C. Roberts, *English Syntax.* New York: Harcourt, Brace and World, 1964, Intro. ix.

are those which push him farther toward the performance of which he is capable.

Viewpoints Concerning the Teaching of Grammar

What grammar should be taught? This is a question which is not easily answered. To approximate an answer one needs time, imagination, knowledge and an understanding of the process of education. These, plus a wise use of words, are a necessity. There are differing views as to the most effective way of teaching grammar. Some authorities have denied that there is as wide a difference among what has been called traditional grammar, functional grammar, structural grammar and transformation-generative grammar as the proponents of each might have us believe.

If the purpose of teaching grammar is to help children develop their language abilities to the utmost of their capabilities, then what kind of grammar will accomplish it? As an elementary teacher one needs to have some knowledge of varying viewpoints so that he can make judgments with some degree of knowing.

Arguments Related to Formal Grammar

Traditional grammar has been maligned and excluded by some and praised by others who appear to be more conservative. In some instances systematic study, formal and non-functional grammar have been regarded as synonymous terms. Traditional grammar has as its objective the achievement of certain grammatical abilities. Considered important are a knowledge of the parts of speech; the ability to define and recognize structural elements of sentences such as subjects, predicates, complements, and modifiers of all types; the ability to choose preferred forms of usage; knowledge of grammatical terms such as case, number, voice, tense, mood, agreement, and comparison; the ability to diagram sentences and to recognize sentence faults which are associated with predication, pronoun reference, parallelism, placement of modifiers and tense sequence. Most research studies prior to 1960 have negated the consistently held belief that an understanding of grammar is related to skill in speech and writing. Grammarians used Latin as their model when they tried to fit English into the pattern of Latin grammar. Many of the rules being taught are those which hold true for Latin grammar but not for the English language, since English has lost most of its inflectional endings.

Because children learn their language through imitation and are able to use structures of the language and to produce these in sentence form without the knowledge of its structure, an analytical approach to understanding seems to meet no need of a child. On the other hand, a well-developed grammar does have value in describing the structural system of the language. If there is understanding of the function of the system and the ability to work within it, there is value because it helps a child to use his language effectively.

Traditional grammar has also been called conventional, formal systematic, prescriptive and normative. Shane and Mulry have listed representative writers who seem to sympathize with a thoroughgoing emphasis on grammar.[11] Such writers as Binney,[12] Jandoli,[13] Miller,[14] and Lessen[15] do not advocate a return to language drills but do favor a better job of teaching grammar. On the other hand Symonds,[16] Frogner,[17] Barghahn,[18] Barnett,[19] Stewart,[20] and Butterfield[21] carried out research which showed little correlation between certain factors in grammar and the ability to write or speak with more facility.

Arguments Supporting Functional Grammar

A second viewpoint of the teaching of grammar is that of using a functional approach. The functional approach becomes more nearly usage than grammar since the very word function implies use. Rather than emphasis on rules and definitions the content of functional grammar is based upon understanding of the structure of the language, on thinking and relating ideas, on the using of a variety of sentence elements in a number of ways and avoiding common mistakes.

---

[11]Harold G. Shane and June G. Mulry, *Improving Language Arts Instruction Through Research*. Washington: N.E.A., A.S.C.D., 1963.

[12]James Binney, "Short Report Concerning Grammar," *Education* 76:472-77, April, 1956.

[13]Russell Jandoli, "What's Happening to English?" *Catholic World* 178:426-31, March, 1954.

[14]C. G. Miller, "Is Correct English Worth the Price?" *Clearing House* 32:135-36, November, 1957.

[15]Sheldon Lessen, "Grammar Has a Place in the Classroom," *English Journal* 43:260-261, May, 1954.

[16]Percival M. Symonds, "Practice vs. Grammar in the Learning of Correct Usage," *Journal of Educational Psychology* 22:81-96, February, 1931.

[17]Ellen Frogner, "Grammar vs. Thought Approach in Teaching Sentence Structure?" *English Journal* 28:518-526, September, 1939.

[18]Kenneth C. Barghahn, *The Effects of Sentence Diagramming on English Usage and Reading Comprehension*. Master's Thesis, The University of Iowa. 1940.

[19]Walter W. Barnett, *A Study of the Effects of Sentence Diagramming on English Correctness and Silent Reading Ability*. Master's Thesis, The University of Iowa, 1942.

[20]James Reece Stewart, *The Effect of Diagramming on Certain Skills in English Composition*. Ph.D. Thesis, the University of Iowa, 1941.

[21]Blair J. Butterfield, *The Effect of Diagramming on Certain Skills in English Composition*. Doctor's Thesis, University of Iowa, 1945.

A child who has the opportunity to present his thoughts clearly, for a purpose real to him, whether in speech or writing, will need to have an understanding of the basic structure of the English sentence. Pooley refers to the functional approach as grammar in a "tool" position. He maintains that grammar is useful only as it is actually used in speaking and writing. Principles underlying such a position are:

1. Most grammar is taught too early. It should be postponed until it is useful to the student.
2. A few concepts should be taught slowly and thoroughly.
3. Emphasis should be placed on those aspects of grammar which help a child improve his sentence structure.
4. Specific situations should be used for the teaching of grammar.[22]

An Approach Through Structural Linguistics

The third approach to the teaching of grammar has been that which owes its impetus to the work of structural linguists. Structural grammar has been introduced in the writings of Fries who emphasized the importance of word order and who later developed "the concept of word classes."[23] Pioneer studies by other linguists such as Whitehall,[24] Smith and Trager,[25] Hill,[26] Lloyd and Warfel[27] and Roberts[28] have added to information about the basic forms and patterns of speech.

Linguistics is concerned with basic components of a language and the patterns in which these components operate. In order to understand structural grammar, one needs to realize that phonemes are the smallest distinctive speech sounds and morphemes are the smallest meaningful unit of sound and the two terms need to be comprehended by teachers of English. To clarify these two terms, one can use the word boy as an example. It contains two phonemes /b/ and /oy/. These two phonemes make up one morpheme. An actual utterance or sentence contains both morphemes and phonemes as well as other linguistic concepts. One needs to understand that classes of words or parts of speech, word arrangement

---

[22]Robert C. Pooley, "What About Grammar," in James C. MacCampbell, *Readings in the Language Arts in the Elementary School.* Boston: D. C. Heath and Co., 1964, p. 212.

[23]Charles C. Fries, *American English Grammar,* in DeBoer, John J., "Grammar in Language Teaching," *Elementary English* 36:413-421, October, 1959.

[24]Harold Whitehall, *Structural Essentials of English* in DeBoer, *op. cit.,* p. 38.

[25]Henry Lee Smith and George L. Trager, *Outline of English Structure Studies in Linguistics: Occasional Papers,* No. 3 in DeBoer, p. 38.

[26]A. A. Hill, Introduction to Linguistic Structures: From *Sound to Sentence in English* in DeBoer, *op. cit.,* p. 38.

[27]Lloyd and H. Warfel, *American English in Its Cultural Setting,* in DeBoer, p. 38.

[28]Paul C. Roberts, *Patterns of English* in DeBoer, *op. cit.,* p. 38.

in sentences, sentence patterns and signals which indicate meaning are further concerns of linguists. Linguistics attempts to describe language by showing how items combine whereas conventional grammar is concerned with classification.[29]

Lefevre has subdivided language as a whole into the following signalling systems: intonation, sentence patterns, structure words and word-form changes. He included levels of pitch, stress or accent, and junctures or pauses as parts of the over-all intonation pattern. There is little agreement on the number of sentence patterns which are commonly found in the language of English speaking people. Lefevre has stated that there are four important sentence patterns but that these can be varied by inversion, by substitution, and by pattern transformation. Function or structure words are the standard, interchangeable parts of sentence patterns. Such words as determiners or noun markers (a, an, the, out, my); intensifiers (very, just, less, more); auxiliaries or verb markers (can, could, might); clause markers (because, if, how, that); phrase markers or prepositions (in, down, toward, with, under); question markers (how, what, where, which, who); and conjunctions or connectors (and, but, for, or, now, yet, so) are known as structure words.

The final signaling system is that of word form changes. This system includes grammatical inflections of the four word classes and derivational prefixes and suffixes. Nouns and verbs are inflected by endings indicating plurals, and the verb forms which are classified as past, past participle, and present participle have the following inflections: the -ed ending for past, the -ed/-en ending for the past participle, and the -ing ending for the present participle. Comparative and superlative adjective and adverb endings are inflectional changes also. A derivational change such as adding -able to peace makes the noun become an adjective. In the same manner, a verb may be changed to an adjective, e.g., -able added to adapt to make adaptable.[30]

Meaning Enhanced By Structure

Finally, structural grammar gets at meaning through structure and emphasizes the need for children to learn to become consciously aware of the sentence patterns which they use so easily in speech. Sentences can be grammatical and nonsensical. As far as word form and order are concerned, the sentence which follows, for example, is grammatically correct.

Tall buildings skip merrily down the street.

---

[29]Trauger, Wilmar K., *Language Arts in Elementary Schools.* New York: McGraw-Hill Book Co., Inc., 1959, p. 149.

[30]Lefevre, *op. cit.,* p. 4.

No one agrees that the sentence is a meaningful or truthful statement. It does, however, follow the rules of English grammar, hence it is grammatical.

Gradually children will learn that the formal patterns can be expanded and changed in an infinite number of ways. Infinite variety means choice and choice enables a person to grow in his own way.

There have been some researchers who have attempted to determine the values inherent in the structural grammar approach. Kraus compared three methods of teaching sentence structure and concluded that all classes made significant gains in reducing errors and detecting weaknesses in sentence structure and that one group achieved greater gain in less time by identifying errors in their own writing and having further instruction as needed.[31]

A review of research in language arts during 1964 reported by Staiger listed 454 studies. This included an increase in the areas of writing, grammar and usage which probably was due to the influence of "Project English."[32]

Structural studies of language emphasize the importance of the formal structure of an English sentence. Some of these are the studies of Hook and Matthews,[33] Fries,[34] Loban,[35] and Glanzer.[36] Squire has reviewed selected research with respect to processes of perception and his comments in the April, 1965, *Elementary English* on form consciousness in the teaching of language are extremely provocative.[37]

The Introduction of Transformational Grammar

Transformational grammar came into being during the 1950's with the work of Zellig Harris of the University of Pennsylvania and Noam Chomsky of the Massachusetts Institute of Technology who developed the theory of transformational analysis. Transformational analysis assumes that there are two basic types of sentences: kernel sentences and transformed sen-

---

[31]Silvy Kraus, "A Comparison of Three Methods of Teaching Sentence Structure," *English Journal* 46:275-285, 311, May, 1957.

[32]Ralph Staiger, "Language Arts Research: 1964," *Elementary English* 42:433-445, April, 1965.

[33]J. N. Hook and E. G. Matthews, *Modern American Grammar and Usage* in Squire, James R., "Form Consciousness, an Important Variable in Teaching Language, Literature, and Composition," *Elementary English* 42:379-390, April, 1965.

[34]C. C. Fries, *American English Grammar,* in Squire, *ibid,* p. 382.

[35]Walter Loban, *Language Ability in the Middle Grades.* Report on Contract Research SAE 7297, in Squire, *op. cit.,* p. 382.

[36]M. Glanzer, "Grammatical Category: *A Rate Learning and Word Association Analysis,* in Squire, *op. cit.,* p. 381.

[37]Squire, *op. cit.,* p. 381-383.

tences. Kernel sentences comprise a relatively small number of basic sentence types which are the core of grammar. Kernel sentences are those which cannot be derived from any sentence or sentence types underlying them. Transformational analysis also demonstrates that immediate constituent analysis applies only to kernel sentences. IC (immediate constituents), a product of American linguistics in the 1930's and 1940's, views sentences as being made up of two-part constructions on a series of levels.[38]

The following sentence is an example of a kernel sentence which can be divided into immediate constituents.

The boys	fly kites.
Noun phrase	Verb phrase
The boys	fly kites.
determiner noun	verb noun

This sentence can be transformed into a passive statement:

Kites are flown by the boys.

An example of a question in active form:

Do the boys fly kites?

An example of a question in passive form:

Are kites flown by the boys?

An example of an emphatic statement:

The boys do fly kites.

An example of a negative statement:

The boys do not fly kites.

An example of a negative question:

Don't the boys fly kites?[39]

Other Applications of Transformational Grammar

Sentences can also be transformed by expansion of the noun phrase or the verb phrase, by the use of coordination as a method of syntax, or by subordination to show relative importance of ideas.

An example of an expanded noun phrase:

The big boys who live on the hill fly kites.

---

[38]Roberts, *English Sentences, Teacher's Manual, op. cit.*, p. 9-10.

[39]Enola Borgh, "The Case for Syntax," *Elementary English* 42:28-34, January, 1965.

An example of an expanded verb phrase:

> The boys fly enormous red kites high in the sky all day.

An example of expansions in both parts of the sentences:

> The big boys who live on the hill fly enormous red kites in the sky all day.

An example of coordination:

> Boys and girls fly kites.
> Boys fly kites and girls make cookies.

An example of subordination:

> Since the boys who lived in the city did not know how to make and fly kites, the boys who lived in the country did fly kites.

Generative Grammar

Generative grammar is a fairly recent development by linguists. Gleason stated that generation is the identification of words as a sentence in English. He defined grammar as a set of ordered rules which characterize the infinite set of grammatical descriptions of its sentences. Generative grammar uses an algebra-like notation, e.g., S NP + VP. It is explicit and scientific but it seems not to be particularly appropriate for instructional purposes in the elementary school.[40]

Types of grammar such as most of those described in the preceding section have at least one thing in common. The aim of studying grammar with any approach is to help children understand language structure so that their speech and writing can be as clear and powerful as possible. Learning isolated rules and definitions has seemed to fall short of this goal; functional grammar often has become accidental rather than planned opportunity; structural linguistics would seem to have exciting possibilities. One drawback is the lack of teachers with enough understanding to actually use this approach. Transformational grammar seems to embody some concepts of the more traditional type but also offers avenues of approach which have not heretofore been tried. Furthermore no approach can be fully subscribed to until a teacher can estimate the needs of a particular group of individual children.

Teaching Grammar in the Elementary School

One of the problems in deciding how and what to teach in the area of grammar is found in the different dialects and different levels of usage

[40]H. A. Gleason, Jr., *Linguistics and English Grammar,* New York: Holt, Rinehart and Winston, 1965, p. 223, 247.

with which children come to school. Since children learn their language through imitation – and since all families do not have the same opportunities and experiences – it stands to reason that children from lower socioeconomic backgrounds, from highly educated parents, those who are a part of a mobile population or who are bilingual, or children with any one of a dozen differences will be vastly unequal in their understanding and use of language. Children from a school district in which parents are fairly young, fairly well educated, and possibly upper middle class will rarely say:

> "There wasn't no paper," or
> "Me and him brung it."

Roberts makes reference to Grammar 1 and Grammar 2. Examples of Grammars 1 and 2 are:

1. Henry brought his mother some flowers.
2. Henry brung his mother some flowers.

The first sentence is used by those who are educated and the second by those people we call uneducated. Who, however, can defend the "better" way of telling what Henry did? There is no difference in the grammaticalness of the two statements. It is not a question of clarity or of a rule about verb endings. The sound of bring is no better than brung – but Grammar 2 is used largely by people who are not well educated and who are not very influential. It is perhaps sufficient to say that a person bent upon entering the business and professional world should have mastered Grammar 1.[41]

Categories of Usage

Pooley has divided usage into other categories. There are six levels of language use described as follows: (1) the illiterate level, (2) the homely level, (3) the informal standard level, (4) the formal standard level, (5) the literary level, and (6) the technical level. These are not mutually exclusive and any single person may use one or more depending upon what is called for in a situation.[42]

Elementary teachers are most concerned with helping children move from the illiterate level to the homely level and having all children use

---

[41]Roberts, *English Sentences, op. cit.*, p. 8.
[42]Robert C. Pooley, "The Levels of Language," *Educational Method* 16:290, March, 1937.

the informal standard level when the occasion demands it. From the illiterate level come such examples as:

1. I seen, done, come
2. growed, clumb
3. drownded, attackted
4. Us boys went
5. She sings beautiful.
6. Two girls was going.
7. We ain't got no milk.

Some authors have suggested that usage should be divided into two categories – standard and substandard speech – with slang as a sort of stepchild in between.

Criteria for Determining "Good" English

Since teachers are concerned with the use of "poor" English, it is essential that they and children alike have some notion of what constitutes "good" English. Teachers need to realize that language is not static; it is constantly changing and what may have been "good" usage a quarter of a century ago hardly fits today's need in language. Teachers must also realize that there are many dialects or variations which do not per se indicate "poor" English just because they are different. Today's teachers also need to recognize that appropriateness of expression is determined by the purpose, the place and the group in which a particular type of language is being used. There are social levels of speech which range from the intimate speech between two people who need few words to the formal literary style which requires an entirely different type of usage. An understanding of "good" English also requires that teachers know something of the historical development of the language.

In other words, an arbitrary set standard for "good" or correct English cannot be acceptable to those concerned with the development of individuals, all of whom have worth.

Memorized Definitions

Applegate has said that an elementary school has no need of definitions learned by heart; it is a place where definitions should be experienced and grown up with. She also intimates that formal grammar is needed but not at the elementary level. Children need to live with correct grammatical forms, which places the responsibility for being a good model on the elementary teacher.[43]

Trauger has delineated the following as objectives in teaching structure and usage:

1. to extend knowledge of language
2. to understand that language is a systematic code
3. to understand the benefits from speaking and writing the code correctly.

This is not to say that all children will speak in exactly the same manner but such objectives as those cited have long-range values. Most children discover that language is exciting and that once achieved the objectives continue paying dividends.[44]

Desirable Directions for Growth

In *Children and the Language Arts* Nemec and Pooley have stated that growth in speech forms and manners, growth in the conventions required in written expression and growth in appropriate word usage should be the major points of emphasis in the elementary school.[45] In other textbooks such as that written by Dawson, Zollinger and Elwell, the major aim in instruction in correct usage and grammar is the development of good language habits.[46]

From the writing of Strickland comes this purpose:

The school's goal is good usage – usage that permits an individual to fuse his activities and interests with others in such a way as to be inconspicuous and with an automatic use of good language habits.[47]

The language program according to Greene and Petty has two major goals 1) development of effective expression in language activities and 2) the development of the related attitudes, abilities, and skills contributing to expressive efficiency. Educators should emphasize a child's clear presentation of thought.[48]

---

[43]Applegate, *op. cit.*, p. 447.

[44]Trauger, *op. cit.*, p. 139-140.

[45]Lois G. Nemec and R. C. Pooley, "Children's Experiences with Usage and Functional Grammar" in Virgil Herrick and Leland Jacobs, *Children and the Language Arts*, Englewood Cliffs, N. J., Prentice-Hall, 1955, p. 289.

[46]Mildred A. Dawson, Marian Zollinger and Ardell Elwell, *Guiding Language Learning*. New York: Harcourt, Brace and World, 1963. p. 377.

[47]Ruth G. Strickland, *The Language Arts in the Elementary School*, Boston: D. C. Heath and Co., 1957, p. 358.

[48]H. A. Greene and Walter Petty, *Developing Language Skills in the Elementary Schools*. Boston: Allyn and Bacon, 1963, p. 155-156.

From such statements as the foregoing, an elementary teacher can recognize his responsibility for understanding the language, its history and its structure and the needs which a child has for easy use of language.

Teaching Grammar as a Structural Framework

In order to understand and make use of the structure of the English language, it is necessary to know what an utterance or a sentence is and what part words play because of their forms.

Structural linguists are not as much concerned with meaning as with the classification of form classes or parts of speech and the order within an utterance which determines their function.

Francis has said that every construction found in a grammatical English sentence belongs to one of the following types: it is a modification (white house); it is a predication (birds have been singing); it is a subordination (along the street); it is a complementation (cutting the grass); or it is a coordination (peace and prosperity). He also maintains that every constituent is either a construction or a single word and that no string of words which does not constitute a construction can be a constituent of a larger construction.[49]

Definitions of a Sentence

The most familiar definition of a sentence is that a sentence is a group of words that express a complete thought. Sledd uses "It is." as an example of words which can be called a sentence but this conclusion is not based on the familiar definition. One could find sentences by the terminal indicated by a different pitch, i.e.,

> Did you go?
> I think he left.

This alone will not, however, identify a sentence. Variance in pitch is sometimes difficult to hear. One can apply another means and that is testing what seems to be a sentence to determine whether there is a complete subject and a complete predicate. There are also "sentence fragments" which are correct English utterances, but these do not meet the requisites. A third condition is to determine whether the sentence contains at least one independent clause.[50]

---

[49]Francis, *op. cit.*, p. 20.
[50]James Sledd, *A Short Introduction to English Grammar*. Chicago: Scott, Foresman and Co., 1959, p. 166.

Sentence Patterns

Common sentence patterns are basic and individuals use them automatically if they learned English as a native speaker.

Lefevre lists the following basic patterns:

Pattern I

N	V	
Your letter		came.

N	V	Ad
Bill	has worked	all day.

N	V	A
The group	arrived	hungry.

Pattern II

N	V	N
I	flew-	the airplane.

According to the author, this is the most common pattern.

Pattern III

N	V	N	N
(call, choose, consider, elect, think)			
Dad	thought	me	a tomboy.
(give, bring, buy, do, cause and others)			
I	bought	myself	some candy.

N	V	N	A
He	painted	the house	gray.

Two contrasting verbs, call and make, are used in all three forms.

He called me a taxi.	N	V	N	N	She made me a cake
He called me a fool.	N	V	N	N	She made me chairman.
He called me stupid.	N	V	N	A	She made me angry.

Pattern IV Using linking verb Lv

N	Lv	N
Mary	will be	a housewife.

N	Lv	A
The candy,	was	sweet.

N	Lv	Ad
Tom	is	in the house.[51]

[51]Lefevre, p. 11-13.

Borgh, in 1963, gave five variations of the simple declarative sentence.

	Subject	Predicate
I	(d) N or Pro	V-int + (adv)

Where d is a determiner
N is a noun
Pro is a pronoun
V-int is an intransitive verb
Adv is an adverb

	The baby		sleeps.
II	(d) N^1 or Pro^1	(Aux) V-t + (d) N^2	(Adv)
	The clown	took the circus	seriously.
III	(d) N^1 or Pro^1	be or Lv	(d) N^1 or Pro^1
	He	was	the speaker.
IV	(d) N or Pro	be or Lv	Adj.
	The night	seemed	dark.
V	(d) N or Pro	be	Adv. (place, time)
	The president	is	here.[52]

Postman indicated basic sentence patterns by using numerals rather than initials. For instance his four sentence patterns are:

1.	1	2	1	Girls like boys.
2.	1	2L	1	Girls are people.
3.	1	2L	3	Girls are loving.
4.	1	2	4	Girls cry easily[53]

The experimental materials from the Nebraska Curriculum Development Center list five basic patterns as the early structuralist approach:

1.	N	V	(a) adverb	
2.	N	V	A	
3.	N	be	N	
4.	N	V	N	
5.	N	V	N	N

---

[52]Enola Borgh, Grammatical *Patterns and Composition*. Oshkosh: Wisconsin Council of Teachers of English. 1963, p. 4-6.

[53]Neil Postman, Harold Morine and Greta Morine, *Discovering Your Language*, New York: Holt, Rinehart and Winston, Inc., 1963. p. 151.

A second stuctural approach extends the basic patterns to ten as offered by Paul Roberts.

1.	N	V (Adv.)		Dolls dance (nicely).
2.	N	V Adj.		The cabin seems damp.
3.	N	V-transitive	N	Bill found a letter.
4.	N	V-become	N	Ann became a bride.
5.	N	V-give	N	The man gave my mother a picture.
6.	N	V-consider	N	He considered her a beauty.
7.	N	V-elect	N	They elected Bill the president.
8.	N	V-be	Adv.	The crowd were outside.
9.	N	V-be	Adj.	The day was hot.
10.	N	V-be	N	They were farmers.[54]

The above examples of basic English sentences are one way of delineating English syntax. Syntax is an important aspect of the study of the English language.

The Parts of Speech

Form classes or parts of speech generally have been classified into four categories by structural linguists. In the English language, there are usually these four: Form Class 1, nouns; Form Class 2, verbs; Form Class 3, adjectives; and Form Class 4, adverbs. Four considerations of words help to determine the characteristics of the form classes: (1) inflectional and derivational endings, (2) word order, (3) structure or function words and (4) stress.

Both nouns and verbs accept the inflectional ending -s but this does not designate a word definitely, i.e., girl, jump. The noun also can be inflected by adding -'s or -s'. So-s, -'s and -s' describe the words we call nouns. Verbs can be classified by the endings -s, -ed and -ing, but derivational affixes also must be considered. Work classifies the same as jump because -s, -ed, and -ing can be added to either. Work will also accept -er, which will, in turn, make workers, worker's and workers'. Suffixes of the noun include many combinations: -eer, -ent, -ian, -ess, -ment, and -ism to

---

[54]Nebraska Curriculum Development Center, *A Curriculum for English: Language Explorations for Elementary Grades.* Lincoln: The University of Nebraska, 1965, pp. 80-81.

mention only a few. Verbs can take both prefix and suffix markers – part can be either a noun or a verb. If the prefix -im is added, however, the word impart is now in the verb form class. Derivational suffixes that mark verbs are -ate, -ize, -fy, -ish, -en. Adjective inflectional suffixes are -er and -est. Examples of derivational endings for adjectives are -y, -able, -ful, -less, -ive, -en, and -ing. An -ly added to a noun marks an adjective whereas -ly added to an adjective marks an adverb. Other derivational suffixes marking adverbs are -wise and -ward (s) and also -a, which is a derivational prefix.

Characteristics of words in the order in which they appear in sentences indicates the parts of speech also. For example the following, "Did you ever see a pen play?" is hardly the same as "No, but I have seen a play pen." "The dog bit the man," is not the same as "The man bit the dog," although the words are exactly the same. A good method of testing word order for classifying parts of speech is to make a test frame. Examine the way in which "girl" patterns in this sentence:

The *girl* can work.

Any word which patterns or fits into the same spot or any word that is the equivalent of girl + x may be said to be a noun. Substitutions can be made. She is a substitute because it does not take the -s ending. Verbs will also follow a pattern. Using the verb jump, a test frame can be made.

The boy *jumps.*

Any word which patterns in the same way or will accept the inflectional endings -s or -ed can be said to be a verb. Words which end in -er and -est or those which accept these endings are adjectives and come before nouns so this is another way of testing for a noun. In the following test frame

The *sweet* girl

words which pattern like sweet are adjectives and indicate the appearance of a noun. Adjectives sometimes follow the predicate verb so if we expand this test frame the same word (an adjective) could be placed in each slot.

The *stronger* boy seems *stronger.*

Adverbs are movable. They are not always found at the end of a sentence. An adverb may be found at the beginning or even in the middle of a sentence – thus:

The boy ran *rapidly.*
Rapidly the boy ran.
The boy *rapidly* ran.

Structure or function words also help determine word classes. *The* is a determiner or structure word or noun maker as in *the* girl. Any word used in the same way is a determiner for a noun. Examples of such words are your, our, my, one, each, no and others. Verbs also have structure words which mark their form class. If the verb ends in -ing, it is usually preceded by am, is, was, are, were, as well as can, may, shall, will, etc. with the base verb.

Characteristics of Qualifiers

Some words are called qualifiers and position after the determiner and before the adjective. Examples of qualifiers are very, somewhat, most, so, too. These qualifiers can also appear with adverbs. Function and structure words are necessary parts of the language for they provide cohesion and lend rhythm to the language. They are called function and structure words since they may afford the structure to build sentences and also the function relating other words to each other. Function word classes include noun determiners, qualifiers, auxiliaries, prepositions, and conjunctions.

Uses of the Stress Method

Stress permits the differentiation of nouns from words which are the same but are used as other parts of speech. For instance the stress pattern / /\ / in a word such as suspect signifies that it is a noun while the stress pattern / \/ / marks the word as a verb. Stress enables one to distinguish between a noun phrase (orderly room, a room that is orderly) and a nominal compound (orderly room, a room for orderlies). The stress pattern for a noun phrase is / \/ /, and the stress pattern for a nominal compound is / /\ /. The stress method may also help differentiate between certain adverbs and prepositions. The word *in* is an example. *The doctor will be in on Wednesday.* is an example of a primary stress on the word in which *in* is an adverbial. The sentence *The doctor was in the* store, is an example of in occurring as a preposition with a weak stress.[55]

Grammar as an Editorial Tool

Most children in the elementary school have an unconscious understanding of what happens to language to cause words to become sentences. What many children learn from an entire elementary school program in language may, however, never come close to a real understanding of sen-

[55]*Ibid.*, p. 62-66.

tence elements or a recognition of the quality of sentences. Children may reach sixth grade level without being able to construct good clear sentences either orally or in writing. What is probably more detrimental to the child's expression is his inability to examine and edit his sentences critically.

A sentence fragment may have meaning when used between two people who know each other intimately but children need to realize that many misunderstandings come about because not enough was said to express a thought completely. The listener becomes confused and must guess at what interpretation to place upon the speaker's or writer's intended meaning. Some children do not seem to realize that there must be two parts or predication as a necessary element in a sentence. Run-on sentences need to be edited also. Children need to be taught that a sentence must make sense. Often a child thinks he knows a subject so well that he fails to use the language skills he has to convey his ideas. He may simply have no sentence sense.

Value of a Permissive, Stimulating Environment

If children live in a warm, accepting school climate and have active, adequate instruction, they will start early to develop the ability to tell experiences, events and facts in structurally complete sentences. Children need much work formulating oral sentences so that they have a background for constructing good written sentences. As language maturity increases, a child grows in his ability to:

1. vary word order
2. sense relationships which eventually become subordinate parts of sentences
3. develop thoughts fully
4. use connectives effectively
5. eliminate run-on sentences

Factors Essential to Complete Understanding

Greene and Petty have selected several factors which need to be present in the speaking and writing of individuals if understanding is to be complete. An individual must be perfectly clear and unconfused himself if his sentences are to possess *clarity*. He can be clear and unconfused only if thinking is based on a wide background of experience and knowledge of what he is talking about. In order to develop clarity, children need to learn that modifiers should be placed next to, or as close as possible to, the words they modify and that pronouns must be positioned so that they indicate their antecedents. Such sentences as "She saw three houses coming down the street." or "Tom decided to put the letter to his mother in the mailbox." indicate the need for more thought about modifiers and pronouns.[56]

Oral and written expression should have *unity*. In other words, each sentence should have unity within itself but it should also have no content that is not related to the principal thought. Each paragraph should be related to the main idea being expressed. Words and phrases in each sentence and the sentences themselves should have the proper sequence so that the idea is expressed logically and clearly.

Children need to learn that rarely does the communication process keep working if there is no interest. Communication breaks down quickly if the speaker is not interested in what he is saying, if the language he uses is unacceptable or if the structure is out of line. Boys and girls need to learn to use colorful and interesting words and a variety of structures to keep up *interest*.

Content may be interesting to the listener or reader but an effective speaker or writer uses illustrations, anecdotes, metaphors and colorful and forceful words to keep interest alive. A good speaker or writer chooses to say things concisely and concretely which also helps to keep an audience from disappearing altogether – at least, mentally.

Organization is another facet of a good presentation. Learning to organize ideas means making use of grammar as an editorial tool. First in importance is learning to stick to the point. Limiting the scope of the topic and relating ideas and thoughts to the topic; presenting material in the most effective sequence; giving attention to the beginning and ending sentences; and learning to outline all contribute to effective organization.

The Fascination of Words

If the teachers are to help children be colorful in their use of words, less boring to their contemporaries and more clearly understandable, then all teachers must help them to experience the fascination of words. A wide vocabulary challenges one's audience and a rich, colorful, concise vocabulary increases one's self-respect and the satisfaction one gets from having said something well. So the final aspect of effective expression is *vocabulary*. It probably is obvious that a wise choice of words for particular occasions and a continuing addition of new words to one's store are both important for helping to keep a vocabulary effective, alive, and growing.

In using grammar as an editorial tool then, children need sentence sense, clarity, unity, interest, organization and an effective vocabulary.

---

[56]Greene and Petty, *op. cit.*, p. 158.

Improving English Usage in the Elementary School

Most authorities agree that usage — the way in which people speak — is of more importance than a formal grammar program for six- to twelve-year-olds; having something to say and being willing to say it is more important than form; and nothing is of more importance than realizing the satisfaction derived from wanting to speak and write and doing it well.

Habits of Usage Tend to Persist

Children bring a wide variety of usage habits to school. A large number of boys and girls enter school with undesirable speech patterns and habits. The problem in usage instruction at the elementary school level is to find ways in which to help children substitute more desirable habits. Not everyone agrees as to the best approach. Some teachers think children will improve more readily by learning grammatical definitions and rules. Others contend that according to the psychological principles of learning children need to have errors corrected and then have much practice. Ear practice is a good way to improve speech habits.

Motivation Is Essential

Habit formation is dependent upon motivation, on having a clear impression repeated over and over with no intervening use of incorrect forms and then putting the correct form into correct use. Language habits can be changed only through drill that is fairly constant. Very few new habitual responses such as "I saw" for "I seen" can be firmly established within a given period of time, even as long as a year in the elementary school. In order to develop a single skill, the following cycle of learning experience was established by Tidyman and Butterfield: 1) discovery of need, 2) recognition of the proper form, 3) practice, and 4) use in context, preferably in original material.[57]

If a child feels that making a real effort is worthwhile, he will attempt to make a basic change in his language patterns. Gross errors are usually a barrier if a person is interested in moving upward from one socioeconomic level to another. School experiences in speaking and writing must be truly important to children if they prompt them to want to change.

---

[57]Willard F. Tidyman, and Marguerite Butterfield, *Teaching the Language Arts*, New York: McGraw-Hill Book Co., Inc., 1959, p. 224.

A Procedure for Attacking Usage Problems

There are a variety of ways to attack a problem in usage. The following sequence of steps is adapted from a similar list by Hatchett and Hughes.

1. Find what your group needs. What abilities, what experiences, what interests, and what weaknesses does the group possess?

   Procedures:

   Note most conspicuous errors.
   Listen to children during all types of oral language activities. Listen for language patterns.
   Listen to children in out-of-school situations, i.e., playground, lunchroom, organization meetings.
   Examine written work for errors that are common.
   Make inventories from either standardized or teacher-made tests to find out what children need.

2. Determine which errors should be attacked.

   Procedures:

   Help children incidentally.
   Make an individual diagnostic rating sheet.

3. Select errors to attack.

   Procedures:

   Check class errors against generally recognized usage errors.
   Make a composite chart showing types of errors and members of the group.

4. Give individual help.

   Procedures:

   Give specific help when needed by an individual.
   Group children by common problems.

5. Help child find his most outstanding errors in his own speech and writing.

   Procedures:

   Use a tape recorder to help him spot speech errors.
   Keep a notebook of his own errors.
   Teach child to proofread for errors.

6. Expand language experiences.

   Procedures:

   Encourage audience situations such as reading, listening to stories, dramatizing, sharing poetry.

Give praise for good use of language.
Read good literature.
Listen to good literature.
Enjoy choral speaking.
Listen to recordings.
Select and view good television shows.
Use reference charts and posters.
Use cartoons to illustrate actions of verbs, power of adjectives and adverbs.
Display children's written work.

7. Help children evaluate.

Procedures:

Set up standards with children.
Take time to evaluate work during and after an activity.
Use an opaque projector to show written work to group.
Use an overhead projector to illustrate errors and corrections.
Copy a part of written work on chalkboard for class to discuss and evaluate.
Give children help where it is needed when they are proofreading.

8. Guide children in practice.

Procedures:

Use skills periods for common errors.
Use oral situations.
Use devices to interest children in usage practice.
Use language games.
Use workbooks as they are needed in small groups or pairs.
Use textbooks as resource books.[58]

A teacher is most successful with usage teaching if the children are highly cooperative. Such cooperation rests upon the interpersonal relationships existing in the classroom. Children respond to corrections made quietly and with regard for their feelings.

In her usual succinct way, Applegate has made an important point regarding wrong speech patterns. She has said that to help children change wrong speech patterns, first of all there must be a "rich wanting" on the part of the child. Using sarcasm and ridicule in correcting children will never promote a "rich wanting" to change. A child must know what sounds right and he must have a great deal of "good" speech practice.[59]

---

[58]Ethel Hatchett and Donald Hughes, *Teaching Language Arts in Elementary School.* New York: The Ronald Press, 1956, p. 147-157.
[59]Applegate, *op. cit.*, p. 154-155.

The Parts of Speech

School grammar classifies words into parts of speech. The system is a fairly uniform one; however, the number of parts varies. Each part of speech is defined sometimes in terms of use and sometimes in terms of meaning. Organization of words into parts of speech is an important part of the system of a language. There are typically eight parts although there may be as many as ten. The eight are: noun, pronoun, adjective, verb, adverb, preposition, conjunction and interjection. Most elementary school textbooks contain definitions of each part of speech and many ways of using it. Most recent textbooks are concerned with a functional approach, that is, children are encouraged to use their language in textbook assignments as well as in their own original speaking and writing. Postman's *Discovering Your Language*[60] is a departure from the more traditional parts of speech. It was originally intended for junior high school use but it appears to have material which could be adapted for upper elementary grades. Paul Robert's *English Sentences, Patterns of English*[61] and a programmed text *English Syntax*[62] are, of course, written for higher levels of education but can be of geat help as background for an elementary teacher. Lefevre's *Writing by Patterns*[63] is a programmed text for adding high school students in improving their writing skills. The materials being written and rewritten by the Nebraska Curriculum Development Center are some of the few which are for use specifically in the elementary school.

An Effort at Functional Classification

Fries objected to the parts of speech of traditional grammar and devised four major form classes and groups of function words. He used arbitrary labels rather than noun, verb, and so on. Four classes are recognized by grammarians and usually with the following names: noun or substantive, verb, adjective, and adverb. Adverbs are difficult to identify so this class of words has been divided into intensifiers, limiters, "sentence introducers" and adverbs. Linguists do agree that there must be some classification of words or other units into parts of speech or some system of classes that can be used functionally. The least promising basis for classification is meaning.[64]

---

[60]Postman, op. cit., p. 51.
[61]Roberts, op. cit., p. 12-15.
[62]Paul Roberts, *English Syntax, Teacher's Edition.* New York: Harcourt, Brace and World, Inc., 1964, p. 11.
[63]Lefevre, op. cit., p. 5-8.
[64]H. A. Gleason, *Linguistics and English Grammar.* New York: Holt, Rinehart and Winston, Inc., 1965. p. 79, 115.

Grade-Placement Practices

Most textbooks in language concentrate on the same types of learning for any one grade level. The following seem to be the points of grammar, usage and other material which are considered important.

First Grade

Eliminate gross errors in usage
(ain't and hain't, brung, growed, knowed)
Recognize a sentence in manuscript
Express ideas so that audience will listen

Second Grade

Eliminate gross errors
(hisself, theirselves, them books, this here)
Put self last
Learn that a sentence tells or asks
Express ideas correctly

Third Grade

Learn and use correct forms
(see, do go, run, come bring, and burst)
has for has got and have for have got
Put self last
Correct use of those and them
Make sentences complete thoughts
See need for statements, questions and commands
Work on run-on sentences and the use of "and" between sentences.
Use correct and original sentences.
Learn function of name, describing and action words

Fourth Grade

Attain mastery of the correct form of common verbs
Learn terms noun and verb
Learn singular possessive noun –'s
Learn subject, predicate and word order
Begin to understand coordination and subordination.

Fifth Grade

Review verbs
(begin, blow, break, fly, give, and so on)
Use a and an correctly
Function of a noun
- common and proper noun
- singular and plural nouns
- singular and plural possessive nouns

Present and past tense of verbs
Function and adjective
Learn subject and predicate

Double negatives
Conjunctions – coordination
Adjectives and adverbs

Sixth Grade

Maintain correct use of forms
Use correct prepositions
(at-to; in-into, among-between)
Compare adverbs and adjectives correctly
Choose correct forms of pronouns
Prepositions and conjunctions – subordination
Agreement of subject and verb
Use grammatical terms functionally
Use a variety of sentence patterns

The following listing of punctuation and capitalization skills are those commonly taught at each grade level:

Grade	Punctuation	Capitalization
First grade	Use period and question for sentence endings	Learn forms of capital and small letters. Capitalize: name of person name of pets first words in sentence street school town
Second grade	Use comma in date Copy letter correctly using commas Put periods after numbers in a list Put commas in alphabetized list of names	Capitalize: Mr. Miss Mrs. Teacher Principal Pets
Third grade	Use period: statement, command, abbreviation, Mr., Mrs., initials Use comma: greeting, closing date, address Use question mark Use apostrophe in singular possessive	Capitalize: Heading on papers First word in sentence First line of verse Word I Proper names Common holidays Buildings In titles: book, report, story, poem, list, outline

Fourth grade	Maintain what has been taught Period: After numbers in a list or outline	Capitalize: All above topics in an outline
Fifth grade	Review end punctuation Review use of comma Use comma: separate parts of a sentence separate words or address from rest of sentence Hyphen at the end of the line Apostrophe in contractions and possessives Quotation marks	Review all uses First word of a quotation Name of an organization
Sixth grade	Review all punctuation Learn: Comma: words in series Exclamation point Comma: compound or complex sentences Quotation marks Hyphen in Compound words (check dictionary)	Review Capitalize: proper adjectives regions of country

Ways of Working With Children

Language experiences are among the most necessary types of experiences for children in today's world. Grammar and usage are two facets of expressional activities that are a daylong concern. The interrelation of all such expressional activities, at least for elementary children, is one of the major goals of a good language arts teacher.

Language Learning Is Related to Opportunity

One must remember that a child's language develops in direct proportion to the opportunities he has for actual use of words and sentences. Children are extremely active linguistically before they ever attend school – and it is an amazing amount of language that many children learn in preschool years. As one thinks of language development, however, one must be aware of the fact that children who live in an environment with adults who speak extremely well will learn "good" grammar and correct usage while just the opposite is true if they live in an environment of low linguistic level. Whatever power a child has in language will be equaled by his power in thinking. Deeper understanding, better organization of ideas, seeking relationships in time or complexity all accompany advances in language ability. As a child develops in language, he also begins to have a means of dealing with his growing self-concept and meeting the demands of his social world.

As a teacher understands children and has insight into the intricacies of the nature of language, so he plans and develops a program which reflects the attitudes, the understandings and the values he holds.

That the four major aspects of language are interrelated, and that growth in one affects growth in the others are supported by much research. Children depend upon their experiences for ideas and opportunity to use words. There is close relationship between growth in language and these same experiences. Growth in language is also related to mental ability, sex, socioeconomic level and sibling status. In addition to these, any language learning situation requires a social situation with purposes and communication needs. Also involved is a variety of related language media and there are always related mechanics, skills and usage agreements and certain conventions – the etiquette of usage.

Arranging a Satisfactory Sequence

Determining what comes next in a program or, in other words, in what sequence these things should be taught, is a serious problem. It is difficult and almost impossible to separate the grammar and usage from many language learning activities. That is as it should be if six-year-olds or nine-year-olds or twelve-year-olds really use the structure, vocabulary, and ideas that are important.

In language arts programs, some findings from child development are used to help in planning the activities. For example, one may

Identify things and activities that children like.
Find out how rapidly they achieve within the program.
Develop some judgment on the maturity level at different grade levels.

A fixed, arbitrary program of specific skills or activities for certain grade levels does not take into account the wide difference in language facility or the fact that children of six or ten need the same things in language. The only difference is in degree of depth.

A child's developmental pattern and his own progress in language can be used for judging his adequacies and inadequacies in language.

Evaluation, then, can become the means of helping children find better and more effective ways to meet their educational needs and their communication needs as well.

Lifelike experiences in language should be offered children through the elementary grades to encourage growth in attitudes, abilities and skills. An example of an attitude is the willingness on the part of the child to participate. Without cooperative attitudes, little can be accomplished. Certain courtesies should be a vital part of language experiences. Children need experiences with selecting and organizing content; they need to acquire a vivid vocabulary and sentence sense. Speech, usage and written mechanics consist of skills which children need in order to communicate effectively.

Levels of Oral Language Experience

In the joint publication, *Children and Oral Language,* examples of oral language experiences at each grade level give an idea of the scope of oral language activities in which children participate.

In kindergarten, a package afforded much conversation and motivation for guessing for five-year-olds. There was a great deal of discussion after it was opened. A first grade dictated original stories into a tape recorder. The stories were later transcribed and made into a book. A group of seven-year-olds decided to dramatize parts of "Charlotte's Web." Learning to speak clearly and loudly enough for an audience helped children as they performed for their peers.

"Sharing time" in a third grade afforded the idea for a weekly plan which varied the items shared – from "Book Reports" on Monday to "Your Choice" on Friday.

A fourth grade interested in a study of sound listed sounds they heard at home; wrote words, phrases or sentences about them; organized a composite list; wrote the information in notebooks; held discussions of the scientific principles involved and used oral language in a functional "method of discovery."

Children in a fifth grade undertook a study of television viewing. This extended to other rooms in the building. They interviewed primary level children and formulated a questionnaire for upper elementary children. They charted summaries and explained the generalizations they had made. This extended to making recommendations for themselves and their schoolmates.

Sixth graders formed committees to select, classify, mount, and file materials from a supervisor's accumulation of current magazines. Children of the sixth grade interviewed teachers and children in all grades to discover what topics would be of value to each room. Some committees set up an expandable file for the use of the whole school. They read, marked, clipped, mounted and filed hundreds of items. Discussion and evaluation of plans went on daily. They eventually explained the project to parents, the school staff and even to prospective teachers.[65]

Summary

A reiteration of the information in this chapter will not guarantee that the reader now knows more about grammar and usage. To know, however, that language is a vital force in a child's life and that teachers have an edge over most other adults in getting to know children from a professional standpoint, in attempting to diagnose strengths and weaknesses in a child's language habits and in influencing their growth for good was the underlying purpose of this chapter.

Before one can teach he must know himself, the children and the content. This is surely true in the areas of grammar and usage. A grammar can stand alone and be useful to those interested in the science of language, but in the elementary school, children need a concerned, sensitive teacher. In what better way can acceptable language habits be understood and practiced by children?

EXTENDING YOUR LEARNING

1. As you think of yourself in the role of a teacher and the importance of being a good model, what specific usage difficulties do you have? How can you eliminate these and change your language habits?
2. As you think about the ways of teaching grammar, how would you defend structural or generative grammar to teachers who prefer the traditional approach?
3. As you think about teaching formal grammar, where in the scheme of a curriculum should it be placed? Why?
4. As you think about your own experiences with grammar, talk with adults not in school, your peers, and children to find out their impressions and memories of grammar. If their ideas about grammar are negative, why do you think they are?
5. As you think about teaching children what choices do you see for the use of programmed texts, or the use of multi-media for instruction in the English language?

---

[65]Helen Mackintosh, (ed.) *Children and Oral Language*. Washington: Joint publication, A.C.E.I., A.S.C.D., I.R.A. and N.C.T.E., 1964, p. 23-25.

6. As you think about trying to improve your children's language habits, what common errors would you start with? Listen to children. Can you find errors that need to be eliminated? How would you eliminate one flagrant error?
7. As you think about "good" and "poor" habits in our use of language, listen to television and radio shows, read comic strips and newspapers and collect the errors of usage for a period of a week.
8. As you think about materials for teaching grammar and usage, examine five different textbooks in elementary school English. Compare the suggestions for teaching lie-lay, we went-gone.

BIBLIOGRAPHY

Books

Anderson, Paul S., *Language Skills in Elementary Education*. New York: The Macmillan Company, 1964. 447 pp. Chapter 9.

Anderson, Verna D., Paul S. Anderson, Francis Ballantine and Virgil M. Howes, *Readings in the Language Arts*. New York: The Macmillan Company, 1964. 503 pp. Chapter 6.

Applegate, Mauree, *Easy in English*. Evanston: Row, Peterson and Company, 1960. 564 pp. Chapters 5, 9, 10, and 11.

Borgh, Enola M., *Grammatical Patterns and Composition*. Oshkosh, Wisconsin: Wisconsin Council of Teachers of English, 1963. 44 pp.

Dawson, Mildred A., Marian Zollinger and Ardell Elwell, *Guiding Language Learning*. New York: Harcourt, Brace and World, Inc. 1963. 430 pp. Chapter 20.

Francis, W. Nelson, *The English Language, An Introduction: Background for Writing*. New York: W. W. Norton and Company, 1965. 273 pp. Chapters 1 and 2.

Gleason, H. A., Jr., *Linguistics and English Grammar*. New York: Holt, Rinehart and Winston, Inc., 1965. 518 pp. Chapters 4, 5, and 10.

Greene, Harry A. and Walter T. Petty, *Developing Language Skills in the Elementary Schools*. Boston: Allyn and Bacon, Inc., 1963. 572 pp. Chapter 12.

Herrick, Virgil E. and Leland B. Jacobs, *Children and the Language Arts*. Englewood Cliffs, New Jersey: Prentice-Hall, Inc., 1955. 524 pp. Chapter 13.

MacCampbell, James C., *Readings in the Language Arts in the Elementary School*. Boston: D. C. Heath and Company, 1964. 470 pp.

Mackintosh, Helen K., *Children and Oral Language*. Joint Publication of Association for Childhood Education International, Association for Supervision and Curriculum Development, International Reading Association and National Council of Teachers of English, 1964. 38 pp.

Nebraska Curriculum Development Center. *A Curriculum for English: Language Explorations for Elementary Grades*. Lincoln: The University of Nebraska, 1965. 151 pp., mimeographed.

Roberts, Paul, *English Sentences*. New York: Harcourt, Brace and World, Inc., 1962. 294 pp. Teachers' manual.

Shane, Harold G. and June Grant Mulry, *Improving Language Arts Instruction*. Association for Supervision and Curriculum Development, Washington: National Education Association, 1963. 153 pp. Chapter 6.

Strickland, Ruth G., *The Language Arts in the Elementary School*. Boston: D. C. Heath and Company, 1957. 464 pp. Chapter 14.

Trauger, Wilmer K., *Language Arts in Elementary Schools*. New York: McGraw-Hill Book Company, 1963. 392 pp. Chapters 7, 8, and 9.

Periodicals

Borgh, Enola M., "The Case for Syntax," *Elementary English* 42:28-34, January, 1965.

Brooks, Charlotte K., "Some Approaches to Teaching English as a Second Language," *Elementary English* 41:728-733, November, 1964.

Brown, Roger and Ursula Bellugi, "Three Processes in the Child's Acquisition of Syntax," *Harvard Educational Review* 34:133-151, Spring, 1964.

DeBoer, John J., "Composition, Handwriting and Spelling," *Review of Educational Research* 31:161-172, April, 1961.

Gleason, H. A., Jr., "What Grammar?" *Harvard Educational Review* 34:267-281, Spring, 1964.

Ives, Sumner, "Some Notes on Syntax and Meaning," *The Reading Teacher* 18:179-183+, December, 1964.

Joos, Martin, "Language and the School Child," *Harvard Educational Review* 34:203-210, Spring, 1964.

McDavid, Raven I., Jr., "The Cultural Matrix of American English," *Elementary English* 42:13-21+, January, 1965.

Marksheffel, Ned D., "Composition, Handwriting and Spelling," *Review of Educational Research* 34:177-186, April, 1964.

Owen, George H., "Linguistics: An Overview," *Elementary English* 39:421-425, May, 1962.

Squire, James R., "The Teaching of Writing and Composition in Today's Schools," *Elementary English* 41:3-14, January, 1964.

Staiger, Ralph C., "Language Arts Research: 1964," *Elementary English* 42:433-445, April, 1965.

Strom, Ingrid M., "Research in Teaching Grammar and Usage," *The Education Digest* 26:50-52, January, 1964.

Chapter 10 Elizabeth H. Ratté

Foreign Language in the Elementary School

Within the past decade a new dimension has been added to the area of language arts in the elementary school. The teaching of foreign languages has been gradually finding a place in the modern curriculum. It is estimated that there are in the United States at present nearly four million language learners in the lower and intermediate grades. Parents, administrators, and teachers have become aware of the need to promote foreign language learning as a tool for communication. Gone are the days when foreign language courses had as their main objective a reading ability, usually intended to satisfy college entrance requirements. Oral communication can no longer be bound by the geographical or intellectual confines of monolingualism.

A Rationale for FLES[1]

The need for an increased number of American citizens qualified to speak one or more foreign languages fluently is evident when we are confronted with the realistic problems of government, business and education in a world without geographical boundaries. A clear and interesting statement of this need is presented in a work paper[2] written at the request of the United States National Commission for UNESCO. In the introduction, the author writes as follows regarding both idealistic and practical reasons for increased study of foreign languages in this country.

---

[1]Foreign Language in Elementary School.

[2]William R. Parker, *The National Interest and Foreign Languages,* 4th ed. (Washington, D. C. Dept. of State, 1962), pp. 1-2.

". . . The common sense of mankind recognizes that inability to communicate readily through the medium of language is a barrier to international understanding – and hence to peace. . . . It is, of course, possible to learn much about cultures through descriptions and analyses of them in English Communication to some degree (occasionally to a high degree) is possible through oral and written translations. What impels men to foreign language study is recognition of the sometimes vexing limitations of such processes. Today, more and more Americans seem to be growing sensitive to these limitations, feeling that a suddenly changing world necessitates more direct communication."

What does this mean in terms of the individual student in our schools? Foreign language learning enables this child who lives in a multilingual world to overcome his monolingual limitations and adjust to his country's new role and his fast changing environment in the contemporary scene. It enlarges his horizon through the introduction of a new medium of communication which is also a new cultural pattern – for language is culture. The director of the language schools of Middlebury College, a recognized leader in this field, sums up the importance of foreign language study in the education of the individual in these words: "(It) provides one of the most basic disciplines for the humanistic ideal. From the very first, the pupil discovers that other peoples, other nations, express themselves differently, but just as effectively. He suddenly comes to the realization that all thought is not cast into English molds. Since words shape thoughts, the pupil comes to the second realization, even more important, that other people think different thoughts. It is a shock to a boy or girl raised in a 100% American environment to discover that another nation may have thoughts which are so different as to be at times contradictory, but they are at the same time just as logical, reasoned, profound, and intellectual as our thoughts. This is a vital step in the real culture of any individual. Slavery to a single vocabulary and syntax is bondage indeed."[3]

Time Required for Mastering a Second Language

Development of the ability to use a second language well takes time. Studies of the nature of language reveal that language is habit. It requires the acquisition of a new set of skills. One of the most important of these skills is automatic and accurate response to the stimulus of spoken language. Like learning to skate or to play a musical instrument, it demands practice before a degree of proficiency can be acquired and

[3]Stephen A. Freeman "Individual Development in the Second Language Experience" – Modern Language Association FL Discussion Pamphlet No. II, p. 4.

continued practice afterwards. The Foreign Institute of the Department of State has established, through experience with adults studying in intensive programs, the average time required for a functional mastery of French, German or Spanish as 600 class hours plus home study ranging from 15 to 24 hours weekly. A child starting a foreign language in the third grade, getting twenty minutes of instruction daily, and continuing through sixth grade, will have about 240 hours of the language. If he continues the program in high school from grades 7 through 12, he will have a total of approximately 1,140 hours of instruction and a good working control of the language. A student beginning the foreign language in ninth grade and continuing through fifteenth will have about 600 hours of instruction.[4] It is probable, however, that he will speak with less fluency and will not feel as much at home in the language as the student who began in third grade and continued through high school.

Early Beginning Capitalizes on Natural Ability

Starting foreign language study in the elementary school not only provides for a span of time that makes a degree of language skill feasible, but also takes advantage of the young child's natural ability to learn language with ease and pleasure. During the preadolescent period, children do not have the self-conscious inhibitions that often make learning the spoken language an unpleasant task at high school age. The young students of elementary school age enjoy imitation and repetition. They memorize easily and enjoy dramatizing. They are naturally curious about people in other countries. They can remember what they have heard and repeat it without seeing the written word. Purely auditory memory becomes difficult for the adolescent and sometimes impossible for the adult. Preadolescent children take pleasure in the type of teaching and language content suitable to the early stages of learning a foreign language. Simple vocabulary and childish concepts, objectionable to the adolescent, are readily accepted in the lower grades. Children like to learn with the aid of action and sensory aids. They enjoy pantomime, songs, dances, and simple rhymes – all activities suitable to elementary school teaching techniques.

The Optimum Age for Beginning Study

Experts in the areas of neurology, psychology, and child development have provided interesting evidence concerning the optimum age to begin the study of a second language, all pointing to the desirability of this

---

[4]Information obtained from "It Takes Time," pp. 29-31. *Modern Foreign Languages and Your Child* (Washington, D. C., U.S.O.E., 1964.)

experience no later than at the age of ten. A conference held in May 1956, by the Modern Language Association of America brought together many outstanding people to discuss this matter, including Dr. Wilder Penfield, director of the Montreal Neurological Institute, and Dr. Frances L. Ilg, director of the Gesell Institute of Child Development. The following statement is part of the report of this conference and expresses the consensus of the experts present: "The optimum age for beginning the continuous learning of a second language seems to fall within the span of ages 4 through 8, with superior performance to be anticipated at ages 8, 9, 10. In this early period the brain seems to have the greatest plasticity and specialized capacity needed for acquiring speech. . . . The specialized capacity includes the ability to mimic accurately the stream of speech (sounds, rhythm, intonation, stress, etc.) and to learn and manipulate language patterns easily."[5]

In a more recent statement Dr. Penfield pursues in greater depth and detail the function of the human brain related to speech. He identifies the cerebral cortex as a thick layer of gray matter covering the outer surface of the brain. Certain parts are used only for sensory and motor purposes. There is a large area which is "uncommitted" at birth, however, and this area is in time used for language and perception. Dr. Penfield writes: "Before the child begins to speak and perceive, the uncommitted cortex is a blank slate on which nothing has been written. In the ensuing years much is written and the writing is never erased. After the age of ten or twelve, the general functional connections have been established and fixed for the speech cortex. . . . The brain of the twelve-year-old is prepared for the rapid expansion of the vocabulary of the mother tongue and of other languages he may have learned in the formative period. If he has heard these other languages, he has developed also a remarkable switch mechanism that enables him to turn from one language to another without confusion, without translation, without a mother-tongue accent . . . (but) the uncommitted cortex must be conditioned for speech in the first decade."[6]

Following the conference in 1956, the Modern Language Association issued its first statement of policy based on evidence from experts in child development and child behavior, and on the study of reports of FLES programs then in existence. This statement of policy endorsed FLES by saying that it deserved the support of administrators and teachers. The statement also called attention to the practical aspects that need careful

---

[5]"Childhood and Second Language Learning," *Foreign Language Bulletin No. 49. (New York: MLA 1961.)*

[6]Wilder Penfield, M.D. "The Uncommitted Cortex – The Child's Changing Brain," *The Atlantic Monthly,* July, 1964.

consideration in initiating such a program. Among these practical considerations were listed well-trained teachers, adequate teaching materials, and provisions for continuity of the program through high school. A second statement followed in 1961 in which the basic principles for setting up a well-planned program were even more clearly and emphatically spelled out. It defined FLES as "an essential part of a long sequence, ten years or more, needed to approach mastery of a second language in school." Such a program, it warned, "should be instituted only if it is an integral and serious part of the school day and if it is an integral and serious part of the total foreign-language program in the school system." In other words, experience had shown that FLES is most effective when it has the full benefit of being an accepted part of the curriculum. In return, the foreign language program can make important contributions to the education of the modern child in a world unrestricted by boundaries that were commonly accepted in the past.

The Objectives of Foreign Language Instruction

The ultimate objectives of a long-sequence foreign language program are twofold: linguistic and cultural. Although the same two objectives exist for the program at elementary school level, the cultural objective is sometimes considered secondary to the attainment of a degree of language skill. In reality, the cultural phase of the program, especially at the beginning stages, forms a part of the linguistic content. It is found in the behavior patterns that are inseparable from authentic language. Among the more evident "patterns" that indicate characteristic attitudes or mannerisms of a people are forms of address, expressions of courtesy and tact, proverbs, exclamations, and the gestures accompanying speech. During the early phases of language learning, the children take part in the cultural patterns as expressed by the language itself rather than hearing or talking about the culture. Oral communication in a foreign language makes a unique cultural contribution not possible in any other area of the curriculum. Further explanation of the nature of this contribution appears in these words in a teacher's guide for FLES: "The active, natural use of a foreign language is participation in a cultural pattern different from one's own. It is also very important that the child learn to imagine himself in the situations illustrating another culture. The cultural understanding contributed by foreign language learnings is gained largely through doing and acting within the other culture, not through hearing about it."

[7]Modern Language Association of America, *Beginning French in Grade Three* Rev. ed., (Darien, Conn.: Teachers Publishing Co., 1959) p. iii.

The Value of Cultural Insights

This does not mean that learning about the people, their country, institutions and cultural achievements is excluded from the program. Learning *about* the people and the country belongs, for the most part, to the more advanced stages of language proficiency when this type of information can be presented in the foreign language orally or by reading. The early stages of learning provide an excellent opportunity for taking the first step toward cultural insight simply by using the language in situations that depict the everyday life of the people. Teaching dialogues in which the children dramatize a situation is one effective procedure. Visual aids are also essential to help the students imagine themselves in a setting that represents the country where the language is spoken. These aids will be of cultural value only if they are authentic illustrations of the country. When this type of learning is meaningful and pleasurable, it is probable that the children's interest in the foreign country and its people will increase. Young students will learn, as well, to accept the strange sounds and patterns of the language as another way of talking and not "odd" or "silly" as older children are apt to do. In these ways, the program will contribute to fulfilling the cultural objectives.

Limitations Likely to Be Encountered

To define realistically the linguistic objective of a FLES program, it is essential to take into account certain limitations which in the past have often been ignored. There is no doubt that there are many advantages to an early start in language learning, but this does not mean that no difficulties will be encountered by these students. It does not mean, either, that second language learning, even at FLES level, is exactly like learning one's mother tongue. First af all, fluency to the point of near bilingualism will take longer than the three or four years of FLES training in a school situation. The limited amount of daily contact with the foreign language in the classroom cannot be compared with the constant contact that the children had with their native language when they learned to speak. Second, there is interference from the habits formed in learning one's mother tongue. In spite of the fact that the young children usually have a much greater facility for the development of audio-lingual skills than their older brothers and sisters, they will still have to acquire a new set of habits in learning a second language. Formation of these habits may be hindered by their experience in learning and speaking the mother tongue. The science of linguistics has revealed, by comparative studies of the foreign language and the student's first language, the points of interference or differences in sounds and structures that will give students trouble. The well-informed teacher must be aware of these areas of difficulty and plan his materials and techniques accordingly. It is not enough merely to present the language to the students. There must be a planned approach that makes them aware of the structure of the language.

Taking the foregoing points into consideration, it is possible to come to a realistic definition of the aims of a FLES program in terms of linguistic proficiency. The first skill that should receive attention is auditory comprehension. It can be expected that the students will be able to understand standard native speech uttered at a normal rate of speed. The other important skill at elementary school level is the ability to speak the language. Here the aims are near-native pronunciation and intonation, and reasonable fluency and accuracy of expression on everyday topics of interest to children of that age level. The amount of language that they will be able to understand and speak is to be measured more in terms of basic speech patterns than vocabulary. Vocabulary is easily increased after the essential speech patterns have been learned. The authors of a recent text on foreign language in the elementary school write concerning linguistic objectives: ". . .we want to give them (our elementary school children) a complete control of the sound system, and we want to teach them to use the second language as normal speech. All phases of foreign language teaching should lead directly or indirectly to the achievement of these goals. We teach the children to express complete ideas using basic speech patterns. Language is cumulative. We . . . must lay a foundation that is just as solid as one started at secondary school, although it is accomplished by a different means."[8] The procedures and techniques that provide this means will be discussed later in the chapter.

Importance of Cumulative Language Learning

If the language learning experience is truly cumulative, it will contribute to the ultimate objectives of the school foreign language program. This means two things in planning the program. Teachers at the elementary school level must be aware of the ultimate objectives and plan accordingly. Those responsible for foreign language teaching in the secondary school must build on and reinforce the skills acquired by the FLES students. The ability to understand the language and to speak it are of prime importance in the elementary school. But the introductory phases of reading and a very limited degree of writing – mostly in the form of

[8]Marguerite Eriksson, Ilse Forest and Ruth Mulhauser, *Foreign Languages in the Elementary School,* (New Jersey: Prentice-Hall, Inc., 1964), p. 10.

copying and dictation — also form a part of the program. These are the skills that the secondary school teacher should continue to develop in the students. Just as this teacher has a responsibility to understand the elementary school program, so the FLES teacher must make her course a solid foundation for the continuing language. Only in this way will each level of instruction work toward the degree of proficiency which is the aim of the long-sequence program, namely, the ability to receive and communicate ideas and information in the foreign language on a mature level.

Relationships to the Total Curriculum

Second-language teaching is still regarded as a newcomer to the elementary school curriculum. Its acceptance as a regular part of the teaching program has often been questioned in light of the fact that it is an extra, an addition to the well-established curriculum. The struggle to find its place and lay a claim to "belonging" is far from over as yet. On the other hand much progress has been made, and well-established FLES programs have pointed out the way to others on uncertain terms with curriculum planners who are reluctant to welcome them. By its very nature, the effective FLES program contributes to the basic principles and procedures of the elementary school program. As shown in the description of its values, linguistical and cultural, it enriches the development of the individual child. It recognizes that children learn by doing. It focuses on the use of the language in simple, everyday situations that are familiar and of interest to young students. It makes the language meaningful by encouraging its use as a means of communication at various times during the school day, in addition to the time devoted to the foreign language lesson. It relates the foreign language experience to other areas of the curriculum.

Functional Aspects Essential to Meaning

It is this functional aspect of language which makes it meaningful to the students and motivates them to learn. To maintain the high degree of interest and motivation usually characteristic of the first year or two of learning, foreign language must assume a new, vital role as soon as possible. To be meaningful to the students it must be related to their immediate environment and it has to be useful in some way. As yet, our society rarely provides occasions for young people of pre-high school age to use foreign language outside the confines of the language class. It is therefore up to those planning the program to provide such occasions. For the elementary school level there are two ways that this can be done. Incidental use of the foreign language during the day is highly recommended, provided the classrom teacher has the linguistic ability. It can also be used in correlation with other areas of the curriculum.

There are numerous possibilities which the alert and industrious teacher can develop. Songs in the new language can be practiced as part of their music lesson. Games which are a part of their foreign language learning can be used in the physical education program. Arithmetic drills can be conducted in the foreign language, a procedure that children usually enjoy. Some children who have difficulty telling time "catch on" easily to the method of telling time used in the foreign language. A careful study of the social studies curriculum at various grade levels can reveal many occasions for related projects involving cultural and linguistic phases of the FLES program. Among the most evident and easily correlated phases of the social studies area are the geography of France and Canada, geographical names of French origin in the United States, French explorers and settlers in America and France – its people and its institutions. In the area of natural science, learning the names of animals and plants in the foreign language is of interest to children. They also like to hear about the contributions of French scientists. These are but a few possibilities that can help to relate the language with other areas of learning.

As soon as the proficiency of the student allows, it would be desirable to have some area or areas of the curriculum taught in the foreign language. This would not only be a strong motivating factor for the improvement of skills in the foreign language, but it would also be a very practical and meaningful way of giving the students the opportunity to continue developing their proficiency. Such an extension of the role of second-language learning may not as yet be feasible in most of our schools. It is hoped that in the future it will enter into the plans of those designing curriculum for tomorrow's schools. On this subject Dr. Emma Birkmaier wrote in a publication of the Association for Supervision and Curriculum Development regarding new curriculum developments: "Much thought is being given to the teaching of other disciplines in the foreign language at the advanced levels in the six and nine-year modern language sequences. Some school systems are teaching world geography and world affairs in Spanish and biology in German. Such projects are usually conducted by a teacher who has a major in another field besides an excellent mastery of the foreign language."[9]

---

[9]Emma M. Birkmaier "Foreign Languages" *Using Current Curriculum-Developments* Chapter 4 (Washington, D. C.: Association for Supervision and Curriculum Development, National Education Association, 1963)

Teaching Techniques and Materials

The foreign language program, like any other area of the curriculum, must be planned according to the basic principles of motivation, habit formation, reward, and success. Consideration must be given to the characteristics of children at these age levels (for FLES usually ages 8 to 12) and recognize their urge to communicate and their need for active participation.

Assumptions Underlying FLES Programs

An effective approach to teaching a second language in the elementary school is based on the following assumptions:[10] 1) that the second language is to be used as normal speech with oral communication as the primary objective; 2) that language learning is primarily a matter of habit formation and the acquisition of a new set of skills; 3) that there will be points of interference or difficulty in learning a second language even for the elementary school children; 4) that language learning is meaningful only when the language is used in familiar, real-life situations within the understanding and interests of the students; 5) that preadolescent children have a remarkable ability to hear and imitate accurately and to memorize; 6) that the elementary school students enjoy activity and learn best by doing.

Essentiality of Auditory Memory and Discrimination

Of prime importance is the development of the skills of auditory discrimination and auditory memory. The development of these skills must not be taken for granted. The teacher must plan the practice and drills needed to enable the students to hear the sounds of the language accurately, otherwise they will not be able to produce them. Auditory memory is usually acquired more easily by the young student than by the high school or college student. He does not feel the urge to analyze the sounds he hears or to identify them by seeing them. Provided the utterance is not too long, is generally understood and meaningful, the FLES student usually is capable of and enjoys auditory memorization of the new language.

Much of this initial stage of learning is based on the observation of how language is learned in general. A child begins to talk after hearing the language spoken around him for a considerable period of time. He

---

[10]Many of these assumptions also form the theory behind the generally accepted new approach to foreign language teaching emphasizing audio-lingual skills at any level.

continues to develop his speech habits surrounded constantly by the sounds of his mother tongue. It is impossible to reproduce these conditions in second language learning in a school situation, but certain procedures can be used in the classroom which will facilitate the use of the second language as normal speech. First of all, the foreign language must be the language of the classroom. On the other hand, the judicious use of the mother tongue by the teacher to explain very briefly the lesson of the day or the dialogue or narrative to be memorized is permissible. In fact, it is preferable to the total exclusion of the mother tongue to the point where misunderstandings and confusion occur because the students do not understand what is to be learned. But, and this is important to note, the use of English must be kept to a minimum and the students should not be allowed to use their mother tongue during the foreign language lesson.

Educational Uses of a Cultural Island

Creating a cultural island in the classroom is also essential to the formation of correct habits and attitudes toward learning the language. At all times the students must realize that they have to try to understand and respond through the use of the new language. To make this cultural island authentic, the model used should be near-native. If the teacher does not have a near-native pronunciation and intonation (which are highly desirable), then the model for hearing and imitating should be provided on discs or tape. The material should be recorded by native voices, preferably boys and girls, as well as both male and female adults. At the beginning stages, it is important to give the students the opportunity to listen to the spoken language with numerous repetitions of the material they are expected to understand, learn and reproduce orally. Much of the language which they hear in the first few months will be passive vocabulary. This passive or "understanding" vocabulary will be much larger than their active vocabulary.

Teaching Foreign Language as Oral Communication

Among the generally accepted techniques for teaching language as oral communication are dialogues, narratives, action series, and short dramatizations. The dialogue is favored as the most natural use of the language because it provides for an exchange of conversation between two or more people. The dialogue also lends itself well to creating lifelike situations within the experience and interests of the students. For young children such topics as "at the dinner table," "buying a pet dog," "going to the circus," and "a day in the country" provide situations in which they can identify themselves in the foreign language as well as in English. Both the narrative and the action series are a form of short monologue in which a student describes or talks about somebody or something. For example, the narrative might be an oral description of one's family or one's house. The action series might consist of telling what one does during the day, the emphasis being on verbs and expressions of time. Dramatizations of familiar children's stories or fairy tales usually appeal to young students in grades 1 to 4. Such dramatizations can combine the use of language with action very effectively in a play-acting situation. They should be short, lively, and carefully chosen or prepared, keeping in mind the language level of the students.

In addition to these contrived situations which create in the classroom a make-believe scene for the use of the language, there are many occasions to talk about real, everyday matters in class. It is important for the teacher to be aware of the background and activities of the children so that he can make appropriate conversation at the right time. For example, birthdays are always a welcome subject for discussion, or the arrival of a baby in the family, or the family vacation, or simply the reason why somebody in the class is absent. This may be called the incidental use of the foreign language, either during the language class or any time during the school day. Other common subjects for this type of everyday conversation would be the weather, the date, the time, and health. The conversation will usually start with a question or remark from the teacher to which one or more students respond. Then the students should be encouraged to ask each other questions, creating a conversation among themselves. At the early stages the teacher may have to direct this exchange by telling the student what to ask or say. For example, the teacher may say: "John, ask Henry if he has a cold" or "Alice, tell Joe that today is your birthday." This type of practice is called directed dialogue.

Guides to Emphasis on Pattern or Structure

The use of pattern or structure drills to teach at FLES level should always be in a meaningful situation, related to a dialogue or narrative learned or to the reality of the classroom. The manipulation of language in drills is desirable only to a limited extent at this level. The drills must be short and take only a few minutes of the class time. Visual aids help to make a drill meaningful and interesting. It is advisable to use only the simplest of drills such as substitution or rejoinders. The two sample drills that follow are based on English structures. The first is an elementary substitution drill. The structure is — It's a .....

It's a dog. (Teacher holds up one picture at a time)
" " (house)
" " (car)
" " (train) etc.

Practice in giving the correct rejoinder might concentrate on this structure:

Is he happy? (Yes, he is.)
" " intelligent? (Yes, he is.)
" " brave? (" " ") etc.
Are they happy? (Yes, they are)
" " hungry? (" " ")
" " tired? (" " ") etc.

The purpose of these drills is to develop accurate, automatic response when using a difficult structure. Usually drills help the student overcome what has already been identified as points of interference or difficulties resulting from differences in structure between the foreign language and the student's mother tongue.

Songs, poems and games in the language provide variety and an element of fun essential to motivating children in elementary school. These are desirable activities and worthwhile teaching techniques as long as the learning of language is the prime objective. Most children like to sing. They learn the words to a song with ease and enjoyment. The meaning of the song must be made clear. Some of the vocabulary may be taught with the aid of pictures or other visual aids. It is not necessary or desirable, however, to try to explain all the vocabulary in a song or in a poem. Music and rhythm facilitate memorization of the words which young children can produce orally with remarkable accuracy. As for games in the foreign language, they serve also as an effective means of motivation and provide a change of pace in classroom activity. A game wisely chosen promotes the use of language closely related to the lesson content. When properly presented and controlled, games can make drill and review a profitable, pleasurable learning experience. Numerous suggestions for language games can be found in teacher guides and books on methodology. (See the Bibliography.)

The importance of well-structured, professionally prepared teaching materials cannot be too strongly emphasized. A successful program depends to a great extent on the curriculum guide and teaching materials put into the hands of the foreign language teachers. Of course skilled teachers are indispensable to a good program, and this will be discussed in more detail later. It is sufficient to point out here that good teaching materials, including a well-written guide with detailed suggestions for teaching procedures, can be invaluable to the inexperienced teacher or to the teacher whose language background is somewhat inadequate.

There is now available a good number of professionally prepared guides and materials for FLES.[11] These should be examined carefully before a choice is made. A special word of advice to those who would like to prepare their own materials – It is best to avoid experimenting or creating materials until those concerned with the program are thoroughly familiar with existing materials and are well informed about the acceptable theories and practices of successful FLES programs. A chapter entitled "How Should Materials Be Prepared?" in a recent book on teaching children foreign language provides a check list for curriculum writers and states that "preparation of instructional materials is a cooperative effort. . . . Working together as a team, many persons should prepare the curriculum and accompanying materials for a FLES program. A native speaker, several classroom teachers, secondary school staff members, and wherever possible, a person with a knowledge of linguistics should cooperate in the development of a curriculum."[12]

Criteria for Judging Instructional Materials

Whether the teaching materials are bought commercially or prepared locally by competent professionals, they must fit the philosophy and needs of the community and the school. FLES programs vary considerably from one district to another in such matters as the grade level where the program starts, provision for continuity, available teachers – classroom or specialists – and, of course, the budget. Differences of this sort are to be expected and, fortunately, there is a variety of materials available. Variety in materials is advisable, however, up to only a certain point. There are basic criteria to determine desirable materials. Experience has indicated the following important considerations: 1) Do the materials provide the means to attain the linguistic and cultural objectives of the program? 2) Is there a carefully planned sequence for instruction through all the grades of the elementary school – and preferably beyond? 3) Does the teacher's guide contain detailed instructions for classroom procedure? 4) Are adequate audio-visual aids provided? 5) Is the language authentic

[11]See *References On Foreign Languages in the Elementary School,* U. S. Office of Education, Washington, D. C., 1963.

[12]Mary Finocchiaro, *Teaching Children Foreign Languages,* (New York: McGraw-Hill, Inc., 1964), pp. 155-157.

and idiomatic? 6) Are the recordings on discs or tapes done by native voices at a natural rate of speech? 7) Have the materials been carefully structured for the progressive development of skills? 8) Is the content within the interests and maturity of the students? Unless most of these criteria can be checked off affirmatively, the materials can be said to be substandard and undesirable.

Materials which contain the elements just mentioned are sometimes referred to as "integrated materials." They provide teacher's guides for each level, reading material or student's book when needed, and all the audio-visual aids. As yet there are only a few courses of this type in existence. (See the Bibliography for a list of integrated materials.) They are prepared by a group of experts which usually includes experienced teachers, outstanding authorities in the field of language learning and linguistics, and native speakers. For the teacher, experienced or inexperienced, highly competent in the language or limited in language proficiency, such materials are the answer to many problems that one very busy teacher cannot possibly solve satisfactorily alone in a short space of time. Among these is the availability of teaching aids correlated with each lesson, providing visuals that are authentic and recordings that are well made. In addition, these materials are usually structured in accordance with the principles of linguistics and planned for the progressive development of language skills.

Uses Made of Audio-Visual Aids

Visual aids are indispensable to the teaching of language by direct oral communication without recourse to translation. In order to minimize identification or meaning by use of the mother tongue, visuals must serve to illustrate and explain the people, things, and concepts expressed by the foreign language. The visual aids in the integrated materials play a vital role in the teaching procedure; for example, the films of the *Parlons Français* program, the filmstrip of the elementary level of *Voix et Images,* and the various components of the *Holt Series* which include illustrated pupils' books, posters and cutout figures and objects. For the teacher who does not use any of these integrated programs but who needs visual aids, there are available commercially prepared sets of language wall charts, flash cards, and filmstrip that can be used as desired – to help teach material in the course of study or to supplement it. Such aids relieve the teacher of the constant search for appropriate objects and pictures often difficult to find. They also have the advantage of a professional visual presentation, containing only what needs to be illustrated in a desirable form, color, and size. Pictures, wall charts, filmstrip and films, if authentic illustrations of the country where the language is spoken, can be used effectively to present elementary culture concepts.

Although the use of a language laboratory is not usual at elementary school level, recorded materials do form an important part of the classroom program. If the teacher's pronunciation and fluency are adequate, his voice may be the model for the children to imitate most of the time. Yet the use of discs or tapes should not be excluded. When all or most of the modelling and oral drill is done by the teacher, he may soon tire. Distortions of the language then can result. A wise teacher, no matter how proficient, will use the content of the lesson professionally recorded by native or near-native voices as a supplement to his "live" lesson. Such recorded materials are indispensable to the teacher who needs a native model for practice in preparing his lesson, and to the teacher who prefers to use native voices as the first model for the children to imitate. In any case, the students should be exposed to a variety of voices using the language – male and female, adults and children. The language should be standard and not typical of any one region.

At the beginning stages of learning the students need to be surrounded by the oral language as much as possible. Tapes and discs can act as an extension of the language lesson at other times during the day in school or in the form of take-home lessons. The teacher who understands the nature of language learning cannot ignore the value of audio aids. The constant practice, which is the only way to form correct language habits and to develop audio-lingual skills, makes demands on the teacher's time and patience beyond what he can afford to give – no matter how willing and skilled he may be. Recorded material is an essential "little teacher's helper" to be used at his discretion. For classwork, recordings on tape are preferable to those on discs. The tape recorder allows easy stopping, starting, and repeating at will. When the students are to listen or listen and repeat by themselves during free time in the school day or at home, discs are the best choice.

Television as an Instructional Aid

A discussion about audio-visual aids would not be complete without reference to teaching by television. This teaching procedure is still a relatively new addition to the school curriculum. In the area of foreign languages, research and experimentation have revealed pertinent facts for those considering television as a means of instruction. Television programs can bring to large numbers of students a master teacher having native or near-native pronunciation, a professionally prepared presentation of the language, and cultural material filmed in the country or countries where the target language is spoken. As a result of research done in three large televised FLES programs,[13] the following evaluation was noted: 1) television instruction without teacher follow-up is ineffective (Modern Language Project, Boston – *Parlons Français,* and Denver-Stanford Project); 2) at least 30 minutes of follow-up per week is needed for desirable results in student achievement (Modern Language Project); 3) enthusiastic and conscientious handling of follow-up by skilled classroom teachers, even though they are limited in language ability, can give satisfactory results (Modern Language Project); 4) the use of specialists is likely to improve student achievement in speaking skills but not necessarily in listening and reading comprehension (University of Illinois Foreign Instruction Project); 5) practice or follow-up sections using recorded materials and carefully worked out procedures in which the classroom directs the practice but does not personally give the model utterances in the foreign language can give adequate results (University of Illinois Foreign Instruction Project); 6) use of tape recorders for listening and recording of the children's voices is a recommended supplement to the televised lessons and teacher follow-up (Denver-Stanford Project); 7) instructional procedures for follow-up (recordings, a second viewing of the television lessons, or entirely teacher-directed activities without special aids) should be chosen according to the teacher's prior training and experience in the foreign language and 8) a second viewing of the televised lesson at home with the parents present has a strong motivating effect (Denver-Stanford Project).

The use of educational television has been an important factor in the expansion of FLES instruction throughout the country. It has been estimated that the *Parlons Français* program alone gives instruction through educational television stations to over 2,000,000 students in various sections of the country. As research and experimentation have shown, however, it is not a cure-all for proposed programs where FLES teachers will not be available. There must be adequate and effective follow-up in the classroom by either specialists or the classroom teacher. In addition, there should be help for the classroom teacher who needs work in methods and the opportunity to better his oral language skills. This help may be

---

[13]Condensed from a paper entitled *Research Results in Three Large Televised FLES Programs,* prepared by Dr. Earle S. Randall, Purdue University, for the International Conference on Modern Foreign Language Teaching, held at Berlin – August 31 - September 5, 1964.

found in special workshops, either in-service or at a nearby institution of higher learning, and in the availability of a foreign language specialist or supervisor employed by the school system.

The Role of the Teacher

The saying that a program is as good as its teacher is a self-evident truth. When speaking about the FLES teacher, this implies two basic qualifications – the ability to be effective in the elementary school classroom and the ability to teach or to present the foreign language to the children. "Presenting" the foreign language may appear to be the same as "teaching" the foreign language, but there is a difference. In the case of the classroom teacher who feels somewhat inadequate in the foreign language, there are ways of presenting the language to the students by the judicious use of integrated materials including films, filmstrip, recordings, and television, as has already been mentioned. The teacher's role is to plan the follow-up using the available aids. His role, in this case, may be more of a selecting and guiding process than actual teaching of the lesson. During the period of shortage of adequately trained teachers, this use of the classroom teacher has at times given desirable results. On the other hand, it must be assumed that the classroom teacher is enthusiastic, willing to take all the means possible to make his role in the FLES program effective, and conscientious in the careful planning of the follow-up class lesson. A teacher who has training adequate to handle the level of FLES assigned to him can be said to truly "teach" the foreign language. Such a teacher is the hope for the continued development of foreign language instruction in the elementary school.

In view of the critical need for FLES teachers, the Modern Language Association presented the following statement: "Ideally, he (the FLES teacher) should be an expert in the foreign language he teaches, with near-native accent and fluency, and also skillful in teaching young children . . . If a teacher's foreign-language accent is not good, he should make every effort to improve it, and meanwhile he should rely on discs or tapes to supply authentic model voices for his pupils. But since language is communication, and a child cannot communicate with a phonograph or a tape recorder, no FLES learning can be wholly successful without the regular presence in the classroom of a live model who is also an expert teacher. The shortage of such doubly skilled teachers is the most serious obstacles to the success of FLES. To relieve this shortage, every institution that trains future elementary-school teachers should offer a major in one or more foreign languages."[14]

The Language Specialist Versus the Classroom Teacher

There is still considerable disagreement about who should teach foreign language in the elementary school – the specialist or the classrom teacher.[15] In reality there is no single solution, at least for the present. The use of specialists is becoming more prevalent, especially in the middle grades (4 to 6), but this is true primarily in the large school systems. Specialist here refers to a teacher who teaches only one area and usually has a major in that area plus training in elementary-school instructional methods and procedures. Specialists in the areas of music, art and physical education are commonly accepted. Perhaps it will be so in foreign languages as well. The role of specialists also varies depending on the school system where they teach. In some cases they do all the teaching of their special area. In others they give demonstration lessons in the classroom, plan and set up the program of instruction. The classroom teacher carries on from there. It is important to visualize the possibilities of handling FLES in the schools in terms of what is happening in other areas. It would be most unrealistic to dictate one way to set up a foreign lauguage program.

Future Trends

Looking to the future, present trends in education would indicate that three types of FLES teachers will be needed in the elementary schools for some time to come. The first category is the regular classroom teacher who chose foreign language as his area of specialization in college. This teacher should have sufficient training to enable him to teach the first year or two of the language program. His college program should have given him adequate facility in the use of the language and a knowledge of methods qualifying him to teach. Provision for this type of training is the responsibility of the institutions of higher learning concerned with the preparation of elementary school teachers. In the case of the prospective FLES teacher, the college program should include time for an area of concentration of at least 24 course hours in foreign language. Proficiency

---

[14]*Foreign Languages in the Elementary School: A Second Statement of Policy* (New York: Modern Language Association, 1961).

[15]For two different opinions see *Foreign Languages in the Elementary School,* M. Eriksson, et al., pp. 98, 99 and *Teaching Children Foreign Languages,* M. Finocchiaro, pp. 11, 12.

must be measured, of course, by testing[16] rather than by the number of credit hours. These teachers should also have the necessary education courses for certification in elementary schools.

The second category is the specialist who teaches only foreign language. The demand for specialists occurs in school systems that favor some type of departmentalization or that place foreign language in the same category as other special subjects like music and art. Their college preparation includes a major in foreign language and sufficient training in education courses to know how to teach effectively at elementary school level. The role of the specialist may extend beyond that of teaching his own classes. He may act as a resource person in the school system to aid the classroom teachers who are teaching some foreign language. The experienced specialist may be called on to supervise and coordinate the whole FLES program.

The third category is the supervisor or coordinator. He must be fluent in the language, well informed about the nature of language learning, methods and materials for teaching foreign language, and have an adequate background in elementary education, preferably certified to teach at that level. His responsibilities extend beyond the classroom or the individual school, although he must be closely in touch with them at all times. One of his main functions is to create and maintain the master plan for FLES in relation to the foreign language program through the high school.

Cooperation of the Entire Staff Is Necessary

Last but not least in the considerations for making foreign language in the elementary school a workable and worthwhile enterprise are the attitudes and relationship of all the school staff members concerned. Unless there is a common philosophy and acceptance of the program that unites their efforts, the chances for a workable situation are not very favorable. Much depends on how the program is initiated and whether all the staff concerned are invited to be members of the team. Even the classroom teacher who does not teach the language, but whose class receives instruction by a specialist, needs to be informed about the nature of language learning and the aims of the program. The regular classroom teacher can do much to create favorable attitudes in his students toward learning a foreign language. He should be urged to remain in the classroom and observe the language class. This teacher may want to make incidental use

[16]*Modern Language Proficiency Tests for Teachers and Advanced Students*, standardized tests recently developed and frequently used for teacher placement and certification. (Modern Language Association – distributed by the Educational Testing Service, Princeton, N. J.)

of the foreign language during the day because of his interest and background in the language. It is up to the coordinator or specialist to encourage and help him to do so. The specialist teacher has an obligation to consult with the regular classroom teacher in order to become well acquainted with the children's background and general scholastic ability. He must also work with the classroom teacher on the best possible ways to correlate the foreign language program with the rest of the curriculum.

When the classroom teachers do much of the foreign language teaching, helped perhaps by specialists, television, or integrated materials, there should be provision for guidance and in-service workshops to improve or maintain their skills. This usually is the responsibility of the coordinator or supervisor who visits the classroom teachers regularly and is aware of their needs. The coordinator or supervisor will also hold frequent meetings with these teachers to discuss techniques, materials, and plans for the integration of FLES with other areas of the school program.

Since foreign language in the elementary school is considered part of a long sequence, the initial planning and continued operation of the program requires the coordinated efforts of administration and teachers at both elementary and secondary school level. This can be accomplished only if there are frequent meetings and mutual consultation of the elementary and high school foreign language staff. The FLES teacher must be aware of the skills expected and the objectives to be attained by the time the students finish the program in the elementary school. The high school teachers must have an understanding of the FLES program, its procedures and aims, and should plan to build their program on the background of the "FLES graduate," using similar techniques to continue development of audio-lingual skills. In other words, it is absolutely essential for all concerned with this long-sequence program to accept the same long-range objectives and to practice similar basic techniques of teaching.

EXTENDING YOUR LEARNING

1. Select a panel to discuss these topics.
   a. the advantages of second language learning at elementary school level.
   b. the place of FLES in the language arts curriculum.
2. Outline a plan for the correlation of French, Spanish or German with other areas of the curriculum in grades 3 to 6.
3. Prepare a written or oral report evaluating a set of FLES teaching materials. Note the basic criteria suggested in this chapter.

4. Conduct a question and answer period with questions prepared in advance by the students. These questions are to be answered by other students during the class period. The following topics are suggested.
   a. the nature of second language learning.
   b. auditory skills.
   c. the formation of language habits.
   d. techniques for teaching oral language.
   e. audio-visual materials.
5. If possible, visit local or nearby FLES classes. Divide into small groups, each group visiting one class. Try to arrange for visits at various grade levels. Give oral reports of the class activity and teaching techniques observed, followed by a general discussion period.

BIBLIOGRAPHY

TEXTS AND BULLETINS

1. Alkonis, Nancy V. and Mary A. Brophy. *A Survey of FLES Practices.* New York: Modern Language Association, 1961.
2. American Association of Teachers of French, *National FLES Committee Reports* 1960-1966. National Information Bureau of the AATF, 972 Fifth Avenue, New York 21, New York.
3. Brooks, Nelson. *Language and Language Learning: Practice and Theory.* 2nd ed. New York. Harcourt, Brace and World, 1964.
4. Dunkel, Harold B. and Roger Pillet. *French in the Elementary School: Five Years Experience.* Chicago: University of Chicago Press, 1962.
5. Eriksson, Marguerite, Ilse Forest and Ruth Mulhauser. *Foreign Languages in the Elementary School.* Englewood Cliffs, N. J.: Prentice-Hall, Inc., 1964.
6. Finocchiaro, Mary. *Teaching Children Foreign Languages.* New York: McGraw-Hill Book Co., 1964.
7. Harvard Educational Review. *Language and Learning.* Cambridge, Mass.: Harvard University Press, 1964.
8. Johnston, Marjorie and Elizabeth Keesee. *Modern Foreign Languages and Your Child.* U. S. Department of Health, Education and Welfare, Washington, D. C., 1964.
9. Keesee, Elizabeth. *Modern Foreign Languages in the Elementary School.* U. S. Department of Health, Education and Welfare, Bulletin No. 29, Washington, D. C., 1960.
   ——— *References on Foreign Languages in the Elementary School.* U. S. Department of Health, Education and Welfare, Circular OE-27008B, Washington, D. C., 1963.
10. Lado, Robert. *Language Teaching: A Scientific Approach.* New York: McGraw-Hill, Inc., 1964.
11. MacRae, Margit W. *Teaching Spanish in the Grades.* Boston: Houghton Mifflin, 1957.
12. Modern Language Association of America. *FL Discussion Pamphlets.*
    ——— *FLES Packet* (collection of articles and statements of policy) New York: Revised 1966.

13. Northeast Conference on the Teaching of Foreign Languages. Reports of the Working Committees 1955-1965. *Foreign Languages in the Elementary School,* Report of Working Committee I, 1964.
14. Parker, William R. *The National Interest and Foreign Languages.* 3rd ed. Washington, D. C.: U. S. Department of State, 1962.
15. Rivers, Wilga M. *The Psychologist and the Foreign Language Teacher.* Chicago: University of Chicago Press, 1964.
16. Stern, H. H. *Foreign Languages in Primary Education: The Teaching of Foreign or Second Languages to Younger Children.* (Report on an Internation Meeting of Experts, April, 1962.) Hamburg, Germany: UNESCO Institute for Education, 1963.

PROFESSIONAL JOURNALS AND MAGAZINES

Articles on foreign language teaching and FLES in particular. A few articles of interest are listed here.

1. *The French Review.* Publication of the American Association of Teachers of French. "A Rationale for FLES," M. Douglas, February 1965.
2. *The German Quarterly.* Publication of the American Association of Teachers of German, "The *Sina Qua Nons* in FLES," G. Scherer, November 1964.
3. *The Grade Teacher.* Darien, Conn: Teachers Publishing Corporation. A French or Spanish play in every issue.
4. *Hispania.* Publication of the American Association of Teachers of Spanish and Portuguese. "Suggested criteria to be used in selecting a course of study for Spanish FLES," A. Brady, March 1962.
5. *The Instructor.* Dansville, N. Y.: F. A. Owen Publishing Co. "FLES Workshop" in each issue.
6. *The Modern Language Journal.* Publication of the National Federation of Modern Language Teachers Association, St. Louis, Mo. "The Effect of Foreign Language Instruction on Basic Learning in Elementary Schools." C. Johnson, F. Ellison and J. Flores, May 1961. "TV FLES Matures in the Detroit Public Schools – A Symposium on Television Teaching," April 1965.
7. *The National Elementary Principal.* Publication of the Department of Elementary School Principals, Washington, D. C. Feature articles on FLES, May 1960.
8. *The NEA Journal.* Publication of the National Education Association, Washington, D. C. "The Teaching of Foreign Languages – A Special Journal Feature" (several articles) December 1961. "Improved Foreign Language Teaching," E. Hocking, January 1965.
9. *The PTA Magazine.* Official magazine of the National Congress of Parents, and Teachers, Chicago, Illinois. "Foreign Accents in the Grades," E. Ratté, September 1963.

INTEGRATED TEACHING MATERIALS

A partial listing of programs for three or four levels of continued instruction, containing audio-visual components and teacher guides or manuals.

1. *Children of the Americas Spanish Series.* San Francisco, Calif.: Harr Wagner Publishing Co. Oral introduction to the series followed by six books

all containing pictures and reading, discs, picture vocabulary cards, teacher's guides.

2. *Elementary French and Spanish Series – Bonjour, Buenos Días,* Boston, Mass.: Allyn and Bacon, Inc. Four student books, the first two with pictures only and the other two with reading material, tapes, teacher's editions of the books with suggestions for teaching procedures.
3. *Introducing French, Introducing Spanish.* New York: Holt, Rinehart and Winston. A series of materials for four levels with student picture books, readers, discs, tapes, posters, cut-out figures and objects, teacher's manuals. The complete Holt series provides a continuation at secondary school level.
4. *Languages Unlimited: French, German, Spanish.* Jamaica, N. Y.: Eye Gate House, Inc. Three levels with color film strip, flash cards, student workbooks, discs, teacher's manuals.
5. *Let's Speak Spanish.* New York: McGraw-Hill Book Co. Four levels of instruction containing student books with pictures for the first two levels and reading for levels three and four, student discs, vocabulary picture cue charts, teacher's guides. (*Let's Speak French* in preparation.)
6. *Parlons Français* and *Una Aventura Española.* Boston, Mass. Heath de Rochemont Corporation. Television-Film series for three or four levels of instruction. The *Parlons Français* films are in color. Student discs, activity books, reader (for *Parlons Français*), teacher practice discs, training films, guides, testing materials.
7. *Voix et Images de France, Cours Elémentaire – Bonjour, Line.* Philadelphia, Pa.: Chilton Books Two parts, *Bonjour, Line I and II,* for three or four levels of instruction. Color filmstrip, tapes, student discs and picture books, reading materials (being developed), teacher text suggesting teaching procedures.

Chapter 11 Mary Montebello

Evaluation

The specific instruments and techniques for measuring and evaluating the results of instruction in the language arts program are discussed in this chapter.

Evaluation is the process of determining the extent to which objectives have been achieved. It includes all of the procedures used by the teacher, children, principal and other school personnel to appraise outcomes of instruction, and it involves such steps as (1) formulating goals as behaviors, (2) securing evidence on the achievement of goals in selected situations, (3) summarizing and recording evidence, (4) interpreting evidence, and (5) using interpretations to improve instruction.

The process of measurement is secondary to that of defining objectives. The ends to be achieved must first be formulated clearly. Measurement procedures then can be sought as tools for appraising the extent to which those ends have been achieved.

One of the most significant lists of general objectives or goals is found in Kearney's report for the Mid-Century Committee on Outcomes in Elementary Education.[1] The report discusses four types of behavioral changes – knowledge and understanding, skill and competence, attitude and interest, and action pattern. Those four areas become guides as schools make specific value decisions about language arts objectives. Evaluation suggestions related to those four areas are found throughout this chapter.

Evaluation techniques include teacher-made paper and pencil tests, standardized tests, questionnaires, directed and informal observations, check lists, inventories, logs, diaries, themes and written work of all kinds, records of discussions and oral reports, diagnostic tests, rating scales, and any other intrument by which teachers can secure evidence of change in behavior. Evaluation can be made by the teacher, by children or themselves, or by children of each other.

Standardized tests and scales in the language arts can be used to assess achievement, status, growth, and quality. Some of these tests are useful

[1]Nolan C. Kearney, *Elementary School Objectives* (Russell Sage Foundation, New York: 1953), p. 35-41.

for detailed diagnosis; however, much of educational and psychological measurement is at a relatively low level of precision. The teacher must recognize this fact, using the best procedures available, but always treating the resulting scores as tentative hypotheses rather than as established conclusions.

The more elegant procedures of formal test and measurement must be supplemented by the cruder procedures of informal observations, anecdotal descriptions, and rating if we are to obtain a description of the individual that is usefully complete and comprehensive in noting changes in behavior. While direct observation is a useful technique, it is difficult to make accurate and objective observations and to observe all children with the same degree of care. Memory is also unreliable and subsequent observations cause the observer to forget previous ones so that growth or change is overlooked. Care needs to be taken that accurate records of observations are made and that all children are observed. Since anecdotal records are time-consuming, some teachers prefer to record their observations on check lists.

Check lists may be constructed from previously established specific goals and can be used either by the teacher or by the children themselves in evaluating progress. Various symbols may be employed to designate (1) strength (+) or weakness (–); (2) satisfactory progress (s) or unsatisfactory progress (u); and (3) degrees of achievement as specific points on a check list are checked such as, Always, Usually, Seldom, Never. Check lists may be used in a number of ways. A few children can be observed in all of the situations on a list. In lieu of this, a teacher may prefer to use one of the lists and record the behavior of the entire class or rotate observations so that during a semester a record will be made of the behavior of each child in each situation. As an aid to recording change in behavior, when a check list is used to observe a child on more than one occasion colors can be used for each observation or the date of the various observations can be noted on the check list. A creative teacher will work out her own codes and plans.

There are times and places for the use of the standardized tests and scales. There are also times and places for the use of the teacher-made test, the check list for teacher guidance, and the cooperative check list prepared by teacher and pupils for the purpose of setting up standards and revealing individual pupil and class growth. No matter the technique employed, whether standardized or informal, the need for interpreting the results from those procedures will never be eliminated. Measurement procedures are only tools. Insight and skill are required in the use and interpretation of such tools.

The following content is discussed in this chapter. Language arts objectives as represented in the value-statements of various school systems are presented. Standardized and informal evaluation techniques as well as remediation possibilities are suggested. In addition, for three reasons meaningful classroom experiences in each language arts area are listed: (a) incidental teaching and learning occur throughout the school day and not solely in the systematically planned instructional program, (b) learning is more efficient when it is meaningful to the child – when he can see the need for a tool of expression as it is used in purposeful experiences, and (c) evaluation is an integral part of all teaching and learning.

Listening

Listening is recognized as an area of major importance in the field of language arts. Since this recognition has been slow in developing and because of the difficulties which have been encountered in specifically identifying the skills essential to good listening, however, the development of measuring instruments to determine the level of listening comprehension as well as measurable factors in the total skill has been delayed. Despite the latent research, the teacher needs to be sensitive and conscientious in providing a developmental and evaluative program in this language art on which all others ar based.

The skills involved in listening have been identified by Taylor in a recent publication.[2] These skills may be useful guides to a school staff as it contemplates listening objectives to be achieved.

1. Directing and maintaining Attention
2. Following Directions
3. Listening to the Sounds of Our Language
4. Using Auditory Analysis
5. Using Mental Reorganization
6. Using Context in Listening
7. Distinguishing Relevant and Irrelevant Information
8. Listening with A Purpose
9. Finding Main Ideas and Important Details
10. Indexing an Aural Message
11. Making Comparisons in an Aural Message
12. Finding Sequence in an Aural Message
13. Making Inferences and Drawing Conclusions
14. Forming Sensory Images from Oral Descriptions

---

[2]Stanford E. Taylor, *What Research Says to the Teacher: Listening*. Department of Classroom Teachers and American Educational Research Association (Washington: National Education Association, 1964), pp. 23-29.

15. Sensing Emotions and Moods Through Words Used and Through Manner of Delivery
16. Critical Listening
17. Appreciative Listening

Listening Objectives

The first step in the process of evaluation is the formation of curricular objectives. General listening expectancies have been well-summarized in the teaching guide that follows.[3] The reacher will note that these objectives can be easily classified under Taylor's seventeen listening skills.

The child:

Signs of readiness for effective listening:

Makes use of past experiences and information in conversation.
Speaks with ease and freedom in simple sentences.
Recalls content, sequence, and import of simple instructions and passages.
Is conscious of similarities and differences in word sounds.
Repeats directions for making something.
Reproduces through dramatics sequential thinking of the kind required for listening comprehension.
Accepts worth of others' remarks, speaks in turn.
Realizes that different people speak in different ways.
Catches added meanings by noting gestures, intonation.
Thinks ahead while listening, anticipates what is coming next.

Listening to get information:

Understands, remembers, and responds to directions of increasing complexity.
Gets answers to his questions from what he hears.
Reproduces accurately messages he is asked to relay.
Acquires facts he needs.
Summarizes an oral report.
Comprehends gist of argument so as to select important facts.
Remembers, takes notes of facts from interviews, discussions.

Listening to exchange ideas and form judgements:

Grasps central idea.
Recognizes subordinate ideas.
Distinguishes relevant and irrelevant materials.
Forms an opinion based on what he has heard.
Discriminates between fact and opinion, fact and fantasy.
Evaluates what is heard in light of evidence presented.
Assesses sources of evidence.
Asks for proof of facts stated.

---

[3]San Diego County Schools, *Oral and Written Language,* San Diego County Schools (San Diego, California: 1957), pp. 15-16.

Knows when and how to agree or disagree.
Recognizes propaganda or prejudice of speaker.
Participates in group discussion.
Contributes to group thinking.
Seeks clarification of vague or ambiguous ideas.
Realizes his own feelings affect his reaction to what he hears.

Listening to enjoy and appreciate:
Becomes aware of beauty in rhythm and sound.
Realizes the power of language.
Appreciates poetry, stories, music, dramatizations.
Realizes how speakers achieve various effects
Selects worthwhile television and radio programs, recordings, and films.
Is aware of some of the techniques used (as in television and radio) to achieve various effects, moods, and so on.
Develops understanding of role and responsibilities of the listener in different situations; face-to-face, telephone, audience-speaker, radio, television, films, recordings.
Develops understanding of the values and limitations of the various media of mass communication.

Meaningful Listening Experiences

The teacher may provide time in her school day for listening activities which foster the systematic growth in the development of this skill. In addition, throughout the school day there are numerous classroom experiences in which listening skills and objectives have opportunities for development and evaluation. The following list is an example of these experiences.

Listening during sharing period to grasp main ideas and important details.
Listening to independent-work assignments in order to follow directions.
Listening to silent-reading directions in order to answer specific questions.
Listening to safety-patrol member in order to know proper conduct at street corners.
Listening to poetry for enjoyment.
Listening to stories for appreciation.
Listening to conversations to distinguish between fact and opinion.
Listening to a social studies report in order to make inferences and draw conclusions.
Listening to music for appreciative listening.
Listening to a newscast for critical listening.
Listening to commercials in order to form sensory images from oral descriptions.
Listening during planning periods in order to contribute to specific purpose.
Listening to reports in order to make comparisons.

Listening to directions and explanations in order to be able to repeat them.
Listening to conversations in order to be able to contribute to the conversations.
Listening to a classmate summarize a news event in order to distinguish between relevant and irrelevant information.
Listening to poetry for appreciation.

Evaluating Listening

Formal Evaluation

At the present time there is only one standardized test for use in elementary schools, that is, the *Listening Comprehension Test of the Sequential Tests of Educational Progress.*[4] This test, available in forms for four levels – grades 4-6, 7-9, 10-12, 13-14 – attempts to measure simple comprehension, interpretation, evaluation, and application. The test is based upon oral presentation by the teacher with the pupil responding with one of four optional answers to each question given after the presentation. The pupil has a copy of the question asked and the four options; hence, certain elements of reading ability are involved.

Informal Evaluation

As was stated earlier, check lists are helpful guides to observation. They are easy to use and specifically descriptive of desirable behavior. Check lists 1 and 2 are illustrative for the appraisal of listening; others are presented in later sections of this chapter. Check list 1 guides the teacher in her informal appraisal of listening attitudes and behaviors. Her own symbols may be determined. Check list 2 is of a more specific nature. It focuses on the specific skills which contribute to the indexing of an aural message. The degree of development would be indicated by one of the code numbers.

Check List 1

Appraisal of Listening Attitudes and Habits

Behaviors and Habits to be Observed	*Names of Children*
1. Does he get ready to listen?	
2. Does he remove distracting objects from his desk top?	

[4]Educational Testing Service, *Sequential Tests of Educational Progress: Listening* (Princeton, New Jersey, 1957).

3. Does he know the purpose for the listening activity?
4. Does he listen attentively throughout?
5. Does he keep his hands and feet still?
6. Does he keep his eyes on the speaker?
7. Does his behavior show that he is interested?
8. Do his contributions show that he grasped the main idea?
9. Do his contributions show that he deduced meanings of unknown words?

CHECK LIST 2

Appraisal of Skills Involved in Indexing an Aural Message

	The child is able to –					
CODE: 1. Always 2. Usually 3. Seldom 4. Never NAMES OF PUPILS	look for main ideas	look for supporting details	separate the relevant from the irrelevant	listen for opinions	listen for inferences	

The ability to follow directions is a specific listening skill necessary for effective learning. Through an informal test, the teacher can appraise that ability as the child reacts to the following situations.

1. Is able to follow directions given in the game "Simon Says."
2. Is able to follow directions on a prepared divided ditto with teacher directing:
   a. Put an "X" in the first square.
   b. Put two "X's" in the second square of the second row.
   c. Cross out the last square.
   d. Put your initials in the upper right-hand corner.

3. Is able to follow more complex directions when being supplied with a variety of colored construction paper which has been cut into various shapes. The teacher may direct:
   a. Put "1" on the piece of paper that is brown and also the shape of a triangle.
   b. Put "2" on the piece of paper that is yellow and also the shape of a circle.
   c. Put "3"on the yellow square.
   d. Put "4" on the red triangle.
4. Is able to repeat directions which have been given:
   a. To a new classmate who needs to know how to get to the principal's office.
   b. To a patrol boy who needs to take a sick classmate home.
   c. To a mother who needs to find Room 16 on the second floor of the school building.
   d. To a new boy who has inquired about fire-drill instructions for their particular classroom.

Only a few suggestions have been given. The teacher, knowing the specific needs of her class, will add accordingly. She will find many suggestions for listening evaluation in the basic reading series used in her classroom. In addition, it would be most profitable to consult *Listening Aids Through the Grades.*[5]

As a part of her total evaluation, the teacher may need to answer certain questions about the child's auditory acuity.

Has his hearing been checked with an audiometer?
Does he have a hearing loss?
Is his voice typically too loud or too soft?
Does he show continual inability to pronounce words distinctly and accurately?
Does he respond hesitantly to phonetic exercises?
Does he continually lean forward when spoken to?
Does he prefer a higher than usual volume when listening to tapes or records?

Listening Remediation Suggestions

As the teacher gathers and analyzes information to determine how well objectives are being achieved, the specific weaknesses which need to be remedied will become evident. Very probably those weaknesses would fall in one or more of Taylor's[6] skill classifications. As the teacher plans for improvement of weaknesses, she will want to consult Taylor's publica-

[5]David H. Russell and Elizabeth F. Russell, *Listening Aids Through The Grades* (New York: Bureau of Publications, Teachers College, Columbia University, 1963).
[6]Taylor, *op. cit.*

tion for he presents activities to guide teachers who are embarked on a program of listening improvement. The activities are presented in the general order in which the skills would be acquired by the pupil. An attempt has been made to provide a number of representative activities appropriate for various listening ability levels. Those activities can be profitably used by the teacher in her remediation program. For example, if appraisal has indicated the class needs further help in finding sequence in an aural message, these are the activities listed to improve that listening skill.

1. Have students listen to a story and then relate the events in the order of their occurrence.
2. Students are to listen to a series of directions before performing any of them. One or more of them may then carry out the tasks, while the others observe and take note of any mistakes in sequence.
3. Read to the students a selection containing a clearcut sequence of events, and ask them to predict what might happen next.
4. Read a short story in which events are scrambled, and ask students to rearrange the events.
5. Students may listen to a lecture which is based largely on a sequence of events. They are to take notes on major and minor happenings. After the lecture, students would read aloud their notes on the sequence of events and discuss whether the sequence was clear and complete.[7]

Self-Evaluation in Listening

Self-evaluation should have an important place in the teaching-learning program.

Pupil Self-Evaluation

Children should have opportunities to evaluate their own growth. In addition, they should have opportunities to participate in setting up self-evaluation check lists with the guidance of their teacher. If a self-evaluation check list has been prepared by the teacher alone, however, class discussion about the meaning of the items would need to precede using the check list. Any questions would need to be clarified.

In Check List 3, each child can check whether he has made much growth, some growth, little growth, or no growth in each item. If the teacher disagrees with the child in his appraisal of his growth, differences should be discussed.

---

[7]*Ibid.*, p. 27.

CHECK LIST 3

Questions About the Way I Listen

	Pupil Evaluation	Teacher Evaluation
1. I have the intention of listening.		
2. I am quiet throughout the activity.		
3. I concentrate throughout.		
4. I wait for the speaker to finish before I speak		
5. I ask questions to clarify something I don't understand.		
6. My questions show that I know what was said.		
7. I distinguish between fact and opinion.		
8. I accept the contributions of others.		
9. I avoid interruptions.		

A – Much growth C – Little growth
B – Some growth D – No growth

TEACHER SELF-EVALUATION

The teacher also must be concerned about self-evaluation. She needs to answer questions about herself and the listening program of her classroom.

Do I develop listening skills through a planned program of listening training?
Do I give the pupils a purpose for listening?
Do I help improve listening attitudes by listening carefully myself?
Do I improve the physical conditions that affect listening?
Does my voice communicate enthusiasm?
Is my voice well-modulated?
Are the listening activities varied?
Do I make certain the pupils are ready to listen?
Do I give attention to unfamiliar vocabulary?
Do I help them recall related experiences which may facilitate their understanding of what they hear?
Do I speak in a well-organized manner?
Am I sensitive to their attention span?
Do I provide the pupils with opportunities to react to what they have heard?

The teacher may wish to ponder the foregoing questions without any qualitative guides, or she may wish to think in terms of these degrees: (1) Exists extensively, (2) Exists to a considerable degree, (3) Exists to a limited degree, (4) Missing and needed.

Handwriting

The skill of handwriting needs to be evaluated throughout the instructional program – by the teacher to check on the effectiveness of pupils' efforts; by pupils to check on the results of their practice; and by both teachers and pupils to determine the corrective measures needed.

Handwriting Objectives

Two commonly accepted broad goals of handwriting are legibility and ease of speed. The specific handwriting objectives of the Columbus Public Schools are an example of guidelines for the elementary grades.[8]

GRADE 1. THE CHILD:

Begins manuscript writing; uses circles and straight lines and, in so doing, emphasizes form.

Observes correct practices in the use of guide lines and the position of the paper and exhibits correct posture.

Writes his name, numbers, and familiar words without a copy.

Recognizes and writes all the letters of the alphabet.

Notes similarities and differences in words and brings into practice eye and hand coordination.

Discusses the value and meaning of periods and capital letters as reading and writing aids.

Recognizes that correct spelling is desirable in all written work.

GRADE 2. THE CHILD:

Recognizes the paragraph as a reading or writing unit.

Checks on written work for misspelled words and corrects them.

Develops his ability to form and space letters, words, and numbers.

Recognizes and learns the names, shapes, sizes, and alphabetical order of letters.

Begins alphabetizing small groups of words and names, making use of a picture dictionary.

---

[8]Columbus Public Schools, *Agreements Booklet*. Grades 1-6, Columbus Public Schools, Columbus, Ohio.

Labels pictures and writes on the chalkboard without using guide lines.
Improves manuscript writing skills through all written expression.

GRADE 3. THE CHILD:

Begins cursive writing and gradually incorporates its use in all subject areas.

Learns correct formation of letters.

Spaces letters, words, and numbers carefully for more attractive, readable writing.

Uses guidelines in writing until no longer necessary.

Retains a practical degree of skill in manuscript writing.

Continues to check all written work and to correct errors.

GRADE 4. THE CHILD:

Continues to improve cursive handwriting skill by writing easily and legibly in all activities.

Continues manuscript writing for special purposes such as maps, labels, and chapter titles.

Develops further understanding of the factors that constitute accepted form for writing, namely margins, spacing, size, slant, and shape of letters.

GRADE 5. THE CHILD:

Strives for legibility, neatness, and comfort in writing.

Makes effective use of manuscript writing for special needs.
Is encouraged to write with a pen.

GRADE 6. THE CHILD:

Acquires speed while maintaining standards of legibility in handwriting.

Maintains manuscript-writing skills for special needs.

Is required to use a pen for some kinds of writing.

Meaningful Handwriting Experiences

In addition to systematic instruction in handwriting, the teacher needs to be concerned with handwriting throughout the school day. Handwriting is a tool of written expression and should be so taught. Learning is achieved most economically when the learner has a need or a reason for learning. The writing of things that are important and meaningful to the child is the best basis for the instruction necessary to develop the skills. The following list exemplifies classroom experiences in which there is a purposeful need for legible communicating with sufficient ease and speed.

Invitations to parents to see unit culminating activities.
Invitations to other classrooms to hear creative stories and poems.
Invitation to school principal to hear a committee report.
Replies to invitations of other classrooms.
Get-well-notes to a teacher or a principal who is ill.
Get-well-notes to classmates who are ill.
Get-well-notes to parents or neighborhood friends who are ill.
Friendly letters to fathers in the service.
Friendly letters to brothers who are in the service.
Classroom news to other classrooms in the school building.
Classroom news for the school paper.
Classroom news-exchange with other classrooms in the school system.
Get-well notes to hospital shut-ins who have few friends or relatives.
Invitations to retired people in the neighborhood to view room exhibits.
Thank-you letters to visiting resource people.
Thank-you letters to the bakery, fire station, or police department after a visit.
Requests to retired people in the neighborhood to come and discuss their favorite hobby with the class.
Copies of creative stories for the school, room, or neighborhood library.
Minutes of class meetings.
Reports of class trips.
Records of class experiments.
Labels of items in unit exhibits.
Summaries of science projects.
Diaries of class activities.
Outlines of important points made by resource people.
Birthday greetings to classmates, friends, and relatives.
Notices of coming events, resource people, special days, special radio programs, special television programs, and special school programs.

Formal Handwriting Evaluation

Two factors constitute the chief approaches to the formal measurement of handwriting. These are (1) quality, or the degree of legibility, and (2) speed, or the quantity of writing produced in a given unit of time. The first of these factors usually is evaluated by means of general merit scales and diagnostic or analytical scales. The second is commonly expressed in terms of the number of letters per minute at which a copy is written.

Evaluating Quality Through General Merit Scales

Knowing what to expect in the way of handwriting achievement from grade to grade is an important factor in the development of the skill. It is for this purpose that scientific measuring scales for handwriting have been prepared. Their use enables a teacher to determine how far the child may be from accepted average attainment for his age level; how intensively he may need to concentrate on this particular skill; and how well he has succeeded in his efforts.

The quality of the pupil's handwriting usually is determined by comparing the specimens to be evaluated with samples of established value on grade level scales. Three scales for evaluating the general quality of cursive writing and three scales for evaluating the general quality of manuscript writing are here described.

The Ayres Scale,[9] the second scale to be developed, was standardized on the basis of legibility alone. This scale, known generally as the Gettysburg Edition because the specimens were based on the first four sentences of Lincoln's Gettysburg Address, has been one of the most widely used handwriting scales.

The American Handwriting Scale, developed by Paul V. West,[10] is one of the most comprehensive of the general merit scales. The scale provides a number of features of which at least two deserve mention: (1) a separate scale is provided for each grade from two to eight; (2) the specimens have been scaled for both quality and rate, taking into account the fact that the better writing is usually done at a more rapid rate and the poorer writing at a slower rate.

The Handwriting Evaluation Scales by F. N. Freeman[11] are similar in many respects to those developed by West. Cursive scales for each grade from three through nine present specimens classified as high, good, medium, fair, and poor. The provision of separate scales for each grade makes possible a somewhat more accurate evaluation of any quality of writing in its relation to the grade in which it is produced than is possible in a single scale.

The Conrad Manuscript Standards is comprised of two separate scales. The scale used in scoring pencil-written forms contains twelve specimens ranging in quality from the scrawl of the beginning first-grade child to excellent manuscript writing at the fourth-grade level. The scale for scoring pen-written forms comprises ten specimens ranging from beginning third-grade work in ink to excellent quality ink work produced by a sixth-grade pupil.[12]

---

[9]Leonard P. Ayres, *A Scale for Measuring the Quality of Handwriting of School Children,* Bulletin No. 113 (New York: Division of Education, Russell Sage Foundation, 1912).

[10]Paul V. West, *The American Handwriting Scale,* (New York: A. N. Palmer Co., 1951).

[11]Frank N. Freeman and the Zaner-Bloser Staff, *Evaluation Scales for Guiding Growth in Handwriting* (Columbus, Ohio: The Zaner-Bloser Company, 1958).

[12]Edith U. Conrad, *Conrad Manuscript Writing Standards* (New York: Bureau of Publications, Teachers College, Columbia University, 1929).

The Freeman Scale contains manuscript scales for grades one and two. The manuscript samples in the scale are classified as high, good, medium, fair, and poor.

The Metropolitan Primary Manuscript Handwriting Scale is available for grades one through three.[13]

To use all of these scales or standards of measurement, the scorer slides each sample along the scale until she finds the quality that closely matches the sample in appearance, quality, or legibility. The quality value of the matching scale sample is then assigned to the pupil's handwriting sample.

These scientifically prepared handwriting measuring scales help the teacher to measure progress in handwriting a little more objectively and accurately than is otherwise possible.

Evaluating Quality Through Diagnostic and Analytical Scales

An example of an analytic and diagnostic scale is the Zaner-Bloser Chart on Handwriting Faults and How to Correct Them.[14] It is an instrument recommended for the location of specific faults in handwriting. The Zaner-Bloser Chart contains the following excellent suggestions on ways to test handwriting copy for such elements as legibility, slant, spacing, alignment, size of letters, and quality of line. This chart is helpful because it enables the teacher as well as the pupil to discover the special handwriting weaknesses that are in need of remedial treatment and gives excellent suggestions for correcting the defects.

How to test legibility:	Make a letter finder by cutting a hole a little larger than the letter in a piece of cardboard. Place the hole of this finder over each letter in turn and mark the letters which are illegible. Have the pupils practice these letters separately, then write the word again and test as before.
How to test slant:	Draw slanting lines through the letters and mark all letters which are off slant. If the slant is too great, the paper is tilted too much. If the writing is too vertical, the paper is too upright and if the slant is backward, the paper is tilted the wrong direction.
How to test for spacing:	Begin each new word in a sentence directly under the ending stroke of the preceding word.

---

[13]Gertrude H. Hildreth, *Metropolitan Primary Manuscript Handwriting* (New York: Harcourt, Brace & World, Inc., 1933).

[14]Frank N. Freeman and the Zaner-Bloser Staff, *Handwritten Faults and How to Correct Them* (Columbus, Ohio: Zaner-Bloser Co., 1958).

How to test alignment: Alignment and size are closely integrated and should be studied together. Use a ruler (a diagnostic ruler is best) and draw a base line touching as many of the letters as possible. Also draw a line along the tops of the small letters. Mark the letters above or below these lines.

How to test size of letters: Draw lines along the tops of the letters. Remember the minimum letters, i, u, v, etc., are ¼ space high; d, t, p, are ½ space; capitals and l, h, k, b, d, are ¾ space high. All the lower loop letters extend ½ space below the line.

How to test for quality of line: Make a letter finder by cutting a hole a little larger than the letter in a piece of cardboard. Place the hole of this finder over each letter in turn and mark the letters which are illegible due to the quality of line. Have pupils practice these letters from their writing books separately until the letters are perfectly legible. Then have them write the whole word again and test as before.

The chart is large and an excellent visual aid for youngsters as they strive to grow in self-evaluation. The nominal price of the chart makes several copies easily available for classroom use.

Children can be guided in the use of these charts for self-diagnosis, especially in the intermediate grades. Before they are turned loose on such a chart, however, some background discussion in the class is needed so that the members of the class will know what they are looking for, i.e., how to analyze their errors. These discussions should point up understandings of what is meant by uniform slant, even spacing, correct proportion, smooth line quality, accurate letter forms, and good alignment.

The habit of evaluation should be developed early and continually in the instructional program. Children should be encouraged to look at their practice efforts critically. They should compare their product with the chart. The teacher should lead them to see where they are making poor strokes or wrong movements. If a child cannot see his errors, the teacher should show him. When his practice shows success in making the correction, she should recognize his accomplishment by a favorable comment, establishing at once her habit of noticing and appreciating improvement and good workmanship.

Measuring Handwriting Speed

Although speed of writing was considered a very important element in handwriting at the turn of the century, this factor has been de-emphasized in school programs in recent years. The ability to write rapidly affords the individual an important advantage in most situations, however, whether in school or outside. In note-taking, in examinations, in letter writing, the pressures of time make the advantage of speed very real.

Standards in speed are set largely on the basis of comparative performance. The various situations in which handwriting is used and the speed demanded in each cannot conveniently be studied. Variations in speed among individuals in different classes or schools have been recorded and a rough average has been estimated. This can be used as a goal for those below the average. "We cannot use the average as a standard for individual children except as a mild incentive for those below that point."[15]

The measurement of rate of writing is accomplished by having pupils write for a specific period selections which they have previously read and memorized. Rate of writing may be expressed in either seconds per letter or in letters per minute, but the letter is the form more commonly used. The rate score is obtained by counting the total number of minutes allowed for the writing. A two-minute copying period has been generally accepted as suitable for the writing of samples, in order to obtain rate scores.

Freeman suggests speed norms in handwriting for Grades II through VIII which are based upon the number of letters written per minute. These figures represent the typical findings of a number of research studies. The Roman numerals indicate the grade; the Arabic numerals give the speed of writing in letters per minute for each garde.[16]

GRADE	II	III	IV	V	VI	VII	VIII
SPEED	30	40	50	60	67	74	80

Although the Ayres Handwriting Scale was standardized solely on the basis of legibility, rate scores can be obtained also. According to the instructions on the scale the teacher is directed to secure the samples of handwriting by writing on the board the first three sentences of Lincoln's Gettysburg Address. The pupils are allowed to read and copy it until they are familiar with it. At the time of the testing they should copy the material in ink on ruled paper, beginning at a given signal and writing for precisely two minutes. The copy with the count of letters is as follows:

> Four 4 score 9 and 12 seven 17 years 22 ago 25 our 28 fathers 35 brought 42 forth 47 upon 51 this 55 continent 64 a 65 new 68 nation 74 conceived 83 in 85 liberty 92 and 95 dedicated 104 to 106 the 109 proposition 120 that 124 all 127 men 130 are 133 created 140

[15]Frank N. Freeman, *What Research Says to the Teacher: Teaching Handwriting* (Washington: Department of Classroom Teachers and American Educational Research Association, National Education Association, 1954), p. 4.

[16]*Ibid.* Also, Theodore L. Harris, "Handwriting," *Encyclopedia of Educational Research,* 1960, p. 620.

equal 145. Now 148 we 150 are 153 engaged 160 in 162 a 163 great 168 civil 173 war 176 testing 183 whether 190 that 194 nation 200 or 202 any 205 nation 211 so 213 conceived 222 and 225 so 227 dedicated 236 can 239 long 243 endure 249. We 251 are 254 met 257 on 259 a 260 great 265 battlefield 276 of 278 that 282 war 285.

While the Gettysburg Address may be suitable for intermediate grades, simple familiar sentences should be used for the primary youngsters. These youngsters may memorize the scale paragraph which appears on the last page of their Recorders. The pupils may open their Recorders to the scale paragraph page so they can remind themselves if they forget. The teacher should instruct them to write at their usual speed and to keep on writing until she says "Stop." When all are ready, the teacher says "Begin." At the end of two minutes, she says "Stop." She then counts the number of letters on each paper, divides by two, and records the score. She must be certain that all followed directions.

The speed of writing is flexible. Without special training, the pressures that come from the requirements of school life or of office work will cause the typical individual to increase his writing speed until it reaches 100 letters per minute.

Informal Handwriting Evaluation

Five informal check lists are presented. They are in keeping with the four broad objective areas set forth in the Kearney report. For an understanding of the first chcek list, Check List 4, comments about "legibility" need to be made.

Legibility is one of the commonly accepted goals of handwriting. Legibility depends, first, on the formation of the individual letters. Effective letter formation depends on how well the child "sees" and "knows" the letter he is trying to make his muscles reproduce. In learning to write, the child is concerned not merely with movement but with the adjustment of movement to the form of the letter which he apprehends through visual perception. Perceiving – seeing – then is an important factor in correct letter formation.

There is also a "knowing" factor to proper letter formation. The child needs to know the specific strokes of a letter and the rhythms involved in its formation. The specific strokes must be discussed with the class. The child should "know" the letter in the sense that he can "talk about" the individuality of this letter, the characteristics of each of its parts. He knows the letter as he is able to "tell about": (a) the kinds of strokes that make up specific letters, and (b) the arrangement of sequence of the strokes within a letter. In essence, he is answering such questions as these: (a) How does the letter begin? How does the letter end? (b) Where does the letter begin? Where does the letter end? He should be able to relate the information in his own words.

By talking about the letters as he thinks through the particular strokes and sequence, he is indicating his knowledge of the letter. His verbalization will contribute to his understanding of what is to be done and achieved in the writing and practice of letters. "Knowing" then as well as "seeing" becomes an important contributor to writing legibly.

As the teacher is presenting a particular group of letters, she shares information with the class. She talks about the strokes, the retraces, etc., as she writes on the chalkboard. At some later time, she may want to call individuals to her desk and ask questions in order to check on knowledge of letter formation. She may ask the child to "show me at the board" as the child answers a specific question.

Check List 4 can be used as the small upper-loop cursive letters are being taught. A checkmark in the "S" column would denote "Satisfactory" knowledge whereas a check mark in the "U" column would denote "Unsatisfactory" knowledge. The last column of the check list could be used to jot down the particular letter or letters in which the child needs help with reference to the particular criteria listed. For example, if the child needed help in knowing about the retrace of cursive "b," the teacher could write "b" in the last column after having checked the "U" column for item three. The particular questions to be posed to the youngsters are suggested in parentheses. While this check list refers to the small upper-loop cursive letters, the teacher may use a very similar check list as she presents other groups of letters to the class.

Check List 4 is an example of a check list that would not need to be used with all the youngsters in a class. When analysis of written work has revealed illegibilities, the teacher may wish to use this check list with only those youngsters whose letters are illegible.

CURSIVE CHECK LIST 4

Knowledge of Letter Formations – Small letter group – – Upper loop letters –	Name _____		
b f l h k	S	U	Specific Help Needed: The letter(s)
1. Does he know where the letter should begin? (Where does the letter begin?)			
2. Does he know where the points and turns occur? (Are there any points or turns? Where?)			

3. Does he know where to retrace?
   (Is there a retrace? Where?)
4. Does he know where the letter ends?
   (Where does the letter end?)
5. Does he know the beginning strokes of the letter? (How does the letter begin? What is the beginning stroke?)
6. Does he know the ending strokes of the letters? (How does the letter end? What is the ending stroke?)
7. Does he know if and where there are pull strokes? (Are there pull strokes? Where?)
8. Does he know if and where there are loops? (Are there loops? Where?)

The teacher needs to make observations not only with reference to verbalization of the letter forms but also with reference to the child's ability to apply what he knows, that is, his actual skillfulness in the writing of the letters. This information can be secured during handwriting period after particular letter groups have been taught, as the teacher circulates around the classroom, or she may wish to analyze the papers collected after the handwriting period. Whereas the information on Check List 4 indicates his knowledge of letter formation, the information on Check List 5 indicates his ability to apply that knowledge.

The teacher may be checking on the letter groupings more than once. It therefore may be helpful when using Check List 5 to use a pencil for the first notings and a green pen for the second observation of the same letter grouping.

CHECK LIST 5

Ability in Letter Formations Name _____
Cursive Letters

	S	U	Comments
SMALL LETTER GROUPS:			
Under turn group: u i w c e			
Hump group: h m n v x y z			
Oval group: a d g q o			
Extended group: t d p			
Upper loop letters: b f l h k			
Lower loop: g j p y z q f			
Retrace group: b o v w r s			
Figures: 1 2 3 4 5 6 7 8 9 10			

CAPITAL LETTER GROUPS:											
Direct oval group:	O	C	E	A	D						
Boat endings:	B	I	G	S	T	F					
Cane group:	H	K	M	N	W	X	U	V	Y	Z	Q
Cap stem group:	T	F	L	K							
Lower loop:	Y	Z	J								
Upper loop:	I	J	G	S	L						
Indirect oval:	P	B	R								

For those youngsters who need help, the teacher may circle the specific letter in question. Specific comments about the help needed may be made in the last column of the check list.

Check List 6 is an informal device for appraising attitudes. Check Lists 7 and 8 are for the appraisal of behaviors, the latter list being specifically oriented to manuscript writing.

Check List 6

Appraisal of Attitudes Contributing to Writing Effectiveness

To what extent has the child developed the following attitudes? Name _____

	To a large extent	To some extent	To a little extent	To no extent
1. Does he appreciate the value of handwriting as a means of expression and not as an end in itself?				
2. Does he regard this skill as important and desirable to learn?				
3. Does he have self-confidence about his handwriting?				
4. Is he interested in improving his handwriting?				
5. Does he have a critical attitude about his letter formations?				
6. Is he willing to look for and discover his own errors?				
7. Does he have a sense of pride regarding his handwriting?				

Check List 7

Appraisal of Handwriting Behaviors

Action Patterns to Be Observed	*Names of Children*
Code: 1. Always 2. Usually 3. Seldom 4. Never	
1. Does he write legibly during handwriting period?	
2. Does he write legibly in all his other written work?	
3. Does he write with a reasonable amount of speed?	
4. Does he show good posture of body?	
5. Does he show correct position of arms and hands?	
6. Does he show correct position of pen and paper?	
7. Does he use a combined movement of arm and fingers?	
8. Does he show proper rhythm regarding strokes and pauses?	

Check List 8

Manuscript Check List

Manuscript Positions to Be Observed	*Names of Children*
Position of Body	
Is the body erect?	
Is the body bent at hips?	
Are both feet on the floor?	
Position of Paper	
Is the paper directly in front of the pupil?	
Is the edge of the paper square with the edge of the desk?	
Are the lines parallel with the edge of the desk?	

Position of Arms

Are both arms on the desk?
Is the right elbow slightly off the edge of the desk for the right-handed child?
Is the left elbow slightly off the edge of the desk of the left-handed child?

Position of Hands

Is the paper held by the left hand if the youngster is right-handed?
Is the paper held by the right hand if the youngster is left-handed?
Is the writing hand round-looking with the palm partially open, facing down?
Does the writing hand rest on the tips of the last two fingers?
Are all three fingers about one inch above the pencil point?
Does the top of the pencil point toward the upper arm and shoulder of the writing hand?

Handwriting Remediation Suggestions

Measuring handwriting by general merit scales and diagnostic charts, evaluating the product closely to find the elements that are detracting from its legibility and pleasing appearance, and remedying those defects are all a part of a well-organized handwriting program. The following list of handwriting irregularities and their underlying causes should aid the teacher in her program of remediation.

Handwriting Irregularities and Their Causes

Slant of Writing	
1. Too much slant	1. Hand, body, pen, or pencil is out of position 2. Paper turned too much 3. Paper slanted too much toward the left
2. Too nearly vertical	1. Paper too straight up and down 2. Incorrect body position.
3. Irregular slant	1. Incorrect body position 2. Hand, arm, pen, or paper out of position 3. The child doesn't sit the same way at all times – there is a shift of body while writing. 4. Movement is not uniform

Forms of Letters	
1. Angular letters	1. Poor visualization of the letters 2. Poor knowledge of formations of the letters 3. Writing is done with jerky motion instead of smooth motion. 4. The child stops at the "turns" and not at the "retraces" of letters
2. Letters too round	1. Writing too fast 2. Writing too slowly 3. Poor visualization of the letters
3. Letters too thin	1. Writing too slowly 2. Incorrect motion or rhythm 3. Too much finger movement 4. Not enough rolling or curving motion on the upstrokes
4. Capital letters weak	1. Not enough arm movement. (There is more arm movement in the capital letters as a general rule than there is in the small letters.) 2. The child needs review of the movements for the letters
5. Small letters weak	1. Poor visualization 2. Poor knowledge of curves, straight parts, and all the different strokes
6. Disconnected letters in words	1. Pen lifts within a word 2. The child thinks in terms of parts of words and not the whole word
Spacing of Letters	
1. Spacing too wide (scattered)	1. Pencil progresses too fast to the right 2. Too much lateral movement
2. Spacing too crowded	1. Doesn't leave the width of a letter between sentences 2. Space between the letters is not about the same as the width of a letter 3. Doesn't regulate space between words by the beginning and ending strokes of the letters in the words
Size	
1. Too small	1. Tight and tense hand position 2. The child needs help with rhythm and movement
2. Too large	1. Poor visualization of correct relationships for different grade levels 2. The child needs motivation 3. The child needs to see visual aids, recorders, charts, etc.

Line Quality	
1. Writing too heavy	1. Index finger pressing too heavily 2. Writing instrument too small in diameter
2. Writing too light	1. Writing instrument held too straight 2. Writing instrument too large in diameter 3. Eyelet of pen turned to side
3. Writing too irregular	1. The child is putting more pressure on some strokes than on others 2. Needs more arm action 3. Needs to hold the pen or pencil lightly
Alignment	
1. Off the line in places	1. Needs to look at the line as he writes
2. Minimum letters vary	1. Needs to rule a few lines as a crutch and practice within the lines 2. Needs visual aids

Self-Evaluation in Handwriting

Teacher Self-Evaluation

Two lists of questions are presented for the teacher's consideration as she self-evaluates her handwriting program. The first list indicates specific questions she may ask about the program in general. The second list suggests questions relative to the developmental handwriting lesson. In answering the questions, the teacher may wish to consider these qualitative degrees: (1) To a large extent, (2) To some extent, (3) To a little extent, (4) To no extent.

The Handwriting Program

Am I aware of the handwriting objectives for my grade level?
Do I provide a developmental handwriting program?
Do I provide a diagnostic and remedial program?
Do I use a standardized chart for diagnosing handwriting faults?
Do I identify problems of slant, uniformity of alignment, letter formation, and spacing for each child?
Do I then proceed to determine causes of the handwriting faults? For example, poor posture, improper paper position, etc.?
In addition to their writing during handwriting period, are samples of children's writing in other curricular areas collected, at intervals, for analysis of difficulties?
Do I encourage the child to grow in self-evaluation by detecting his own illegibilities and poor writing habits?
Do I provide time for group discussion of common class errors?
Is the opaque projector utilized as a means for analyzing writing?

Are drill activities meaningful and never a form of punishment?
Is my handwriting always a good model?

The Handwriting Lesson

Do I demonstrate the letter in large form on the chalkboard?
Do I talk the strokes as I make them?
Do I help them to be concerned with perception? In other words, do I help them to look at the details of a letter?
Do I encourage them to "talk about" the details of the letters?
Do I display alphabet strips so that they have the large-sized impressions of the letters and their details?
Do I encourage them to use their recorders so that they can compare their letters with a close-range model also?
Do I encourage each child to study and analyze which parts of a specific letter he is not making well?
Do I make certain that he understands what needs to be done to correct his illegibilities?
Do I make comments about his improvement and progress so as to increase his interest and motivation?
Do writing periods follow periods of quiet activity rather than periods of strenuous activity?
Are the youngsters physically comfortable?
Do I consult the teacher's manual with its numerous suggestions for the teaching of handwriting?

Pupil Self-Evaluation

Check Lists 9 and 10 are suggestions for pupil self-evaluation. The latter list is based on research which has revealed that a few letter forms are responsible for a large percentage of the illegibilities that occur in handwriting. Youngsters should be told of that research prior to using the list. They may work out the symbols to be used in self-evaluation.

Check List 9

Questions About My Cursive Writing Name _____

1. Are my letter forms consistent?
2. Is my slant consistent?
3. Is there even spacing between my letters?
4. Is there even spacing between my words?
5. Is the size of my letters uniform?
6. Is the alignment of my writing even?
7. Is the line quality acceptable?

CHECK LIST 10

Questions About Illegible Letters	Name _____

1. Is my capital "I" legible?
2. Is my "r" often confused with "i" or "s"?
3. Do I remember to close letters such as "a" and "o"?
4. Do I have a tendency to close loops?
5. Do I have a tendency to make unnecessarily large or long loops?
6. Do I cross the letter "t" carelessly?

Spelling

Among the most important functions served by measurements in spelling are: (a) to show individual differences in spelling ability in the class and hence to enable the teacher to make proper adjustments to these differences; (b) to show which words each child needs to study; (c) to guide learning by depicting its success and failures; (d) to show what progress has been made during a term or year. No one test can serve all these ends; each test must be constructed or administered according to the purpose for which it is to be used.

Spelling Objectives

The most widely accepted objectives for teaching spelling are to help children learn the words they will need to write as adults and the words needed in their present writing, both in and out of school. It is clearly impossible for pupils to learn in school all the words which they may at some time have occasion to write. It is the central words, that is, the words most often needed in writing, that pupils should learn to spell.

Proceeding from the two broad objectives, schools need to make definite decisions on many other specific matters related to the improvement of spelling ability: which words are to be learned at each grade level; what dictionary habits and skills should be developed; what rules and other orthographical generalizations should be learned; what phonic knowledge should be acquired; what emphasis should be placed on proofreading; and how much to rely on incidental learning and how much on direct instruction.

An example of the specifically delineated spelling objectives of one school system follows:

The goal for the end of Grade One is a child who–
Senses a need for learning to spell
Writes his own name without copy
Can name and write individual letters of the alphabet
Can copy accurately words needed in writing
Writes without copy a few frequently used words
Can write a simple sentence with words correctly spelled.

The goal for the end of Grade Two is a child who –
Can spell the basic list of words for the grade
Is learning how to study spelling words independently
Knows and uses accurately the letters of the alphabet
Uses known spelling words correctly in all written work
Refers to lists of supplementary words as needed
Takes pride in his spelling.

The goal for the end of Grade Three is a child who –
Can spell the basic list of words for the grade
Uses an effective method of studying words
Recognizes and uses simple phonetic and structural clues in spelling
Feels responsible for spelling and pronouncing correctly the words he has learned
Can locate words in alphabetical lists
Refers to sources when in need of help in spelling
Proofreads his written work for errors in spelling.[17]

The goal for the end of Grade Four is a child who –
Can spell the basic list of fourth grade words
Arranges the words alphabetically; begins to use the dictionary
Uses what he knows about phonics, structural analysis, and spelling rules to improve his spelling
Is aware of different spellings for vowel sounds
Uses good word-study procedures under supervision
Keeps a list of individual difficulties in spelling
Refers to lists of words used in content subjects
Checks all written work for misspelled words.

The goal for the end of Grade Five is a child who –
Can spell the basic list of words for the fifth grade
Feels added responsibility to spell correctly all the words used in written work
Has increased skill in using spelling aids
Uses the dictionary to find meaning of words or to check spelling
Begins to use the pronunciation key of the dictionary
Applies his knowledge of phonics, structural analysis, and spelling rules in spelling new words

---

[17]Cincinnati Public Schools, *Primary Manual,* revised (Cincinnati: Board of Education, 1963), pp. vi-vii.

Is developing an effective word-study procedure
Lists troublesome words and attempts to master them
Can spell some of the words used most frequently in science, social studies, and arithmetic.

The goal for the end of Grade Six is a child who –
Can spell the basic list of words for the sixth grade
Is alert to the correct spelling of words in all written work
Has developed an effective independent word-study procedure
Uses effective techniques to overcome his specific spelling difficulties
Understands and uses what he knows about root words, derivatives, prefixes, and suffixes to gain skill in spelling
Gains skill in using the dictionary pronounciation key
Is interested in and investigates the origin of words
Spells correctly words used frequently in science, social studies, art, arithmetic, health.[18]

Meaningful Spelling Experiences

Purposeful needs for correct spelling can be found in all of the previously mentioned handwriting experiences. They are not repeated at this time. The reader, however, may wish to refer back to page 305. All of those writing experiences offer meaningful opportunities for teaching and learning related to spelling as well as evaluation of spelling progress.

Evaluating Spelling

There are several types of evaluation which should be made of actual achievement in spelling. These are: (a) Measuring through the spelling section of standardized achievement tests, (b) Measuring as a part of the regular teaching program, (c) Measuring through teacher-made tests from spelling scales, and (d) Measuring through diagnostic tests. Each of these will be discussed fully.

Measuring Through Standardized Achievement Tests

The teacher may measure spelling achievement by testing through the spelling section of standardized achievement tests. Most general achievement tests or language usage tests have sections which attempt to measure spelling ability for particular grade levels. This type of testing has limitations with respect to measuring the effectiveness of the systematic spelling instructional program. These tests, however, are useful as a general survey.

---

[18]Cincinnati Public Schools, *Intermediate Manual,* revised (Cincinnati: Board of Education, 1962), pp. vi-vii.

While the majority of language achievement tests fall short of being really diagnostic, they are valuable screening devices to locate the low-achievement pupils quickly at the beginning of the term and to ascertain the general level of progress for the class as a whole. These survey tests help the teacher to answer these questions: (1) What is this pupil's general achievement level in spelling compared with children of his age and present grade placement? (2) What is this pupil's growth in spelling ability from last year? (3) What type of errors does he make on the test? (4) Which children are seriously in need of remedial work and require further diagnostic study?

It is imperative the teacher remember that this type of testing will not indicate how well the pupil has learned the particular words he studied in his spelling lessons from day to day during the year. The scores made on these tests therefore may not be closely related to the achievement of the specific goals set up for instruction.

Teaching for the test must be avoided, otherwise it will not show how well the child can spell a random selection of words not recently studied. Normative scores made on standardized tests should be interpreted cautiously by the teacher. The norms of standardized tests merely depict the achievement in the school population from which the norms have been developed. It must be remembered that the pupils' scores from which the standards are established are widely distributed above and below the average, and it is therefore to be expected that the scores of a given grade or class also will cover a wide range.

There are single standardized tests of spelling but most of the newer spelling tests are parts of a battery of several achievement tests. The newer tests give the words and sentences in which they are to be dictated. A few tests of the many suitable for teacher use are:

1. The Iowa Language Abilities Tests. These tests are available at two levels. The elementary battery is for Grades 4, 5, and 6 with optional use in Grade 7. The elementary test booklet contains five subtests, one of which is Spelling.[19]

2. Iowa Every-Pupil Tests of Basic Skills: Test C. The elementary booklet is designed for use in Grades 3, 4, and 5. The advanced booklet is designed for use in Grades 6, 7, and 8. Spelling is one of the language arts tested.[20]

---

[19]Harry A. Greene and H. L. Ballenger, *Iowa Language Abilities Tests,* (Yonkers-on-Hudson: World Book Company, 1948).

[20]E. F. Lindquist, general ed., *Iowa Every-Pupil Test of Basic Skills, Test C.* (Iowa City: State University of Iowa, 1940-47.)

3. California Language Test. This test is available at the primary, elementary, and intermediate levels. Grades 1-3, and 4-6. Spelling is one of the language arts tested.[21]

4. Morrison-McCall Spelling Scale. This scale is for use in Grades 2-8. The teacher may use any one of eight lists of fifty words each. The lists are based on the work of Thorndyke and Ayers.[22]

In addition to the tests listed, most of the achievement test batteries contain subtests in spelling. Separate spelling tests are available also from most commercial publishers of standard tests. For a more complete listing and description of these, the reader may wish to consult *Tests In Print.*[23]

Measuring as a Part of the Regular Teaching Program

The foregoing section discussed standardized tests which contain a wide-range sampling of words chosen from general lists. Children must be tested, however, on the specific words in the spelling instructional program. It is necessary to administer tests which cover only the words which a child is to learn, or should have learned, in the regular spelling program. These tests should be given at regular intervals. In the main, this section deals with measuring the outcomes of instruction from the study of particular word-lists in use within a classroom.

An adequate testing program for elementary classroom includes several phases.

1. The general spelling ability of the class should be approximated before teaching. The teacher can discover the approximate spelling ability of the class by giving a preliminary term test on words to be studied during the term. This test should be made up of one to two words from each weekly assignment of the term. The evaluation of the test will give evidence concerning the spelling ability of the class and to some extent of the individuals of the class.

2. The individual study needs and achievement must be determined by a pretest and final test in the weekly program. The pretest on the new words of the week is given so that each child can identify the words he must study. The final test on the new words of the week reveals the learning progress of each individual.

Research indicates that the test-study is the most efficient approach to achieving the objectives of the spelling program. "Some evidence, earlier

---

[21]Ernest W. Tiegs and Willis W. Clark, *California Language Test,* California Test Bureau, 1957.

[22]Cayce Morrison and William A. McCall, *Morrison-McCall Spelling Scale,* Harcourt-Brace & World, Inc., 1923.

[23]Oscar Krisen Buros, editor, *Tests In Print* (Highland Park, New Jersey: The Gryphon Press, 1961).

reported, indicated that tests before study might be somewhat less effective in the lower than in the upper grades, but more recent investigations report them to be superior to study-test procedures even in the lower grades."[24]

Questions are often raised relative to the form of the test. Horn has summarized the evidence on the question of the form in which spelling words should be presented in the following statement:

> Written tests are to be preferred to oral tests. . . . Recall tests are superior to and more difficult than recognition tests. The evidence indicates that the most valid and economical test is the modified sentence-recall form, in which the person giving the test pronounces each word, uses it in an oral sentence, and pronounces it again. The word is then written by the students.[25]

3. Progress on review words also needs to be appraised. The review test determines the degree of mastery and retention of the spelling words of weeks passed.

The review may be a group test. Well-planned reviews are necessary to make the learnings of spelling permanent, but indiscriminate reviews are a waste of time. Some teachers select the hardest words in an assignment and conduct group reviews on these words but neglect to motivate study on other words which, although they may not be misspelled by so many of the group, are difficult for some.

An individual child may have a review test upon his own hard words. Each child should review the demons which testing identifies as persistently difficult for him. As a child expresses himself in writing, he should check his spelling for errors. The words which he misspells frequently, either in tests or in usage, should be written in his own hard-word list so that they can be mastered for a review test.

> "Investigations have shown that children who reviewed words of persistent difficulty by means of the test-study procedure achieved significantly better results than those who followed the study-test procedure. The child who is tested before study on difficult review words may spell 75 per cent of them correctly, but the procedure permits him to concentrate upon the other 25 per cent; the child who studies difficult review words without identifying by testing which words he cannot spell is likely to waste a large portion of time upon words he knows."[26]

---

[24]Ernest Horn, "Spelling," *Encyclopedia of Educational Research,* rev. ed., The Macmillan Company, 1960, p. 1346.

[25]*Ibid.,* p. 1350.

[26]James A. Fitzgerald, *Children and the Language Arts,* edited by Virgil E. Herrick and Leland B. Jacobs (New York: Prentice-Hall Inc., 1955), p. 256.

4. Mastery of "special" words should also be a part of the classroom testing program. As youngsters are involved in units of work, centers of interest, and seasonal highlights, there will be special related words they will wish to master.

5. Progress relative to personal word lists should be ascertained. An individual test should be given to a child who wishes to check the mastery of words he has personally learned to spell because of his demonstrated needs throughout his personal written communications in and out of the classroom.

6. A final test on the term's work, comparable in difficulty to the preliminary-term test, may be administered to determine progress. This test may be administered at the end of a month, semester, or school year.

7. Additional techniques of measurement and evaluation should be utilized.

a. Recognition-type test: Several incorrect forms of a word are presented with one correct form. The student marks the correct form. However, marking the correct form does not mean a student can spell the word correctly. This is also a useful test of visualization.

b. Completion-type test: A sentence is written with a word left out. The student fills in the blank with the correctly spelled word. This is also a test of meaning.

c. Essay-type test: the teacher constructs a simple paragraph or short story which contains many of the words to be taught later to a class. The student writes it as it is dictated. Misspelled words are checked. At a later date when all test words have been taught, the paragraph is again dictated and marked for misspellings.

d. Recognition of errors printed in word lists.

e. Proofreading for errors in context: Some words are spelled incorrectly and pupils are expected to recognize them.

f. Detection of errors in written composition: The pupil is required to detect spelling errors and correct the misspelled words. This technique makes greater demands on the pupil than either "a" or "e."

g. Copying test: A test in straight copying does much to sensitize the pupil to the "hazard" of carelessness.

h. Dictionary tests: Tests in the use of the dictionary are a necessary part of the evaluation program. Anderson has done an excellent job of compiling numerous testing and activity suggestions related to abilities to use the dictionary.[27]

Informal check lists also have a place in the evaluation of the spelling program. Check List 11 refers to spelling knowledges while Check List 12 appraises general spelling abilities. In Check List 13, one spelling ability has been delineated for more specific evaluation. Check List 14 lists perti-

[27]Paul S. Anderson, *Resource Materials for Teachers of Spelling* (Minneapolis: Burgess Publishing Company, 1959), pp. 78-96.

nent questions that need answering concerning the child's attitudes and Check List 15 focuses on behaviors important for spelling effectiveness. With the exception of Check List 13, the teacher will want to work out her own symbols or code.

CHECK LIST 11

Appraisal of Knowledges Contributing to Spelling Effectiveness

Knowledge to be appraised	*Names of Children*
1. Knows the alphabet	
2. Has knowledge of sound-to-letter relationships	
3. Knows an efficient procedure for spelling a word	
4. Knows the meanings of the words he is learning to spell	
5. Has knowledge of spelling rules	
Words ending in silent e usually drop the final e before the addition of suffixes beginning with a vowel, but they keep the final e before the addition of suffixes beginning with a consonant.	
When a word ends in a consonant and y, change the y to i before adding all suffixes except those beginning with i. Do not change y to i in adding suffixes to words ending in a vowel and y, or when adding a suffix beginning with i.	
Words of one syllable or words of more than one syllable accented on the last, ending in a single consonant preceded by a single vowel, double the final consonant when adding a suffix beginning with a vowel.	
The letter q is always followed by u in common English words.	
English words do not end with v.	
Proper nouns and most adjectives formed from proper nouns should always begin with capital letters.	

CHECK LIST 12

Appraisal of Abilities Related to Spelling Effectiveness

The child is able to –	*Names of Children*
1. Pronounce words correctly	
2. Discriminate between sounds	
3. Correctly associate letters with sounds	
4. Correctly associate sounds with letters	
5. Identify incorrect spellings of words in a proofreading test	
6. Tell what he does in studying a word	
7. Write legibly	
8. Alphabetize words	
9. Find the spelling of a word he doesn't know	
10. Use the dictionary	
11. Apply spelling rules in spelling work and tests	
12. Apply spelling rules in daily written work	

CHECK LIST 13

Appraisal of Dictionary Skills

The child is able to –	*How Often*			
	Always	Usually	Seldom	Never
1. Alphabetize				
2. Use guide words				
3. Divide words into syllables				
4. Use the diacritical marks for pronunciation				
5. Evaluate the several meanings for a word to determine which meaning most accurately expresses the thought in consideration				
6. Select a synonym which most exactly fits his requirement for communicating a thought				

Check List 14

Appraisal of Spelling Attitudes

Attitudes to be evaluated	*Names of Children*
1. Is interested in learning to spell correctly	
2. Is self-confident about spelling	
3. Is enthusiastic about broadening his spelling power	
4. Recognizes and appreciates the social importance of spelling	
5. Is concerned about his misspellings and correcting them	
6. Is developing the attitude of independence in word attack	

Check List 15

Action Patterns Important for Spelling Effectiveness

Note: Check each child two or three times during the term to determine if growth has taken place.

Behavior to be observed	*Names of Children*
1. Applies spelling rules in written work	
2. Proofreads his work	
3. Learns to spell misspelled words in his work	
4. Uses an effective method in learning to spell new words	
5. Uses phonetic aids in arriving at the proper pronunciation of unfamiliar words	
6. Pronounces words clearly and accurately	
7. Tries to spell correctly	
8. Shows independence in finding out how to spell words	
9. Uses the dictionary	

10. Writes legibly and with reasonable speed
11. Keeps record of his progress in spelling
12. Uses spelling time wisely

A well-known psychological principle is that the whole child needs to be studied. There may be occasions in spelling evaluation when a teacher may need to secure a comprehensive profile of the child in order to ascertain the causes of his spelling difficulties. The following questions may need answering if any or all of the information is not already available in the youngster's cumulative school record. The questions are suggested in the light of the results of research.

What is his general learning capacity?
Do I have results from a mental test? What are the implications from the result?

"Positive correlations have been reported between intelligence and spelling. Children of low intelligence are very likely to be inferior in spelling ability. On the other hand, high intelligence does not guarantee superior spelling ability."[28]

What is his reading ability?
Do I have the results from silent reading comprehension tests? Do oral reading tests reveal deficiencies in pronunciation or enunciation?

"Deficiencies in reading are serious handicaps in learning to spell."[29]

Does he have visual defects?
Do my observations indicate any visual irregularities? Has he been screened by the school nurse recently?

"Visual perception, visual discrimination, and visual memory have been found to be highly related to spelling ability."[30]

Does he have any speech defects?
Does he correctly pronounce words, syllables, sounds? Has he been screened by the speech therapist recently?

"Shortcomings in speech, such as mispronunciations and articulatory defects, have been found to be related to disabilities in spelling. The removal of these disabilities will be reflected in better spelling."[31]

---

[28]Ernest Horn, "Spelling," *Encyclopedia of Educational Research,* rev. ed., The Macmillan Company, 1960, p. 1348.

[29]Ernest Horn, *What Research Says To The Teacher: Teaching Spelling,* Department of Classroom Teachers and American Educational Research Association (Washington: National Education Association, 1954), p. 12.

[30]*Encyclopedia of Educational Research, ibid.*

[31]*What Research Says To The Teacher: Spelling,* p. 13.

Does he have auditory defects?
Does he hear words accurately? Is he able to repeat pronunciations accurately? Does he often speak too loudly? Does he often ask to have directions repeated? Does he often lean forward when listening?

"Sound perception and discrimination are significantly related to spelling ability."[32]

What is his handwriting profile?
Is he distracted by handwriting deficiencies? Does he write legibly? Does he write with reasonable speed? Does he write with ease? Have I recently evaluated his speed and legibility?

"Poor handwriting is frequently cited among the factors that cause difficulty in spelling."[33]

Is he interested in spelling?
What are his attitudes toward spelling? Does he take pride in spelling words correctly? Is he attentive during the spelling period? Is he self-confident about spelling? Does he have an efficient method for learning to spell words?

"Perhaps no other factors impede learning in spelling as much as does a lack of interest or the presence of undesirable attitude."[34]

Does he have social approval?
Do I realize the potency of the child's need for social approval? Is he accepted by his peers? How does he feel about himself? How does he feel about school?

"One of the strongest social needs during childhood appears to be a desire for social approval. There is substantial evidence that children seek the social approval of their parents, teachers, and peers. There is also the additional finding that children who typically are not able to secure social approval are likely to underrate their effectiveness and worthwhileness."[35]

What is his general health?
Is his general physical health affecting his abilities and educational efforts? Does he get enough food? Does he get enough rest? Does he have the proper seasonal clothing? Has he had a general physical examination recently? Have I secured data from the school

"Illness of various types are part of life in the school years; their effects on behavior should be recognized. . . . To understand and adjust to these various problems, help the children affected, and foster habits favorable to health should be an important part of every teacher's job. Maximal health and vigor should

---

[32]*Encyclopedia of Educational Research, ibid.*
[33]*What Research Says To The Teacher: Spelling,* p. 14.
[34]*Encyclopedia of Educational Research, ibid.,* p. 1347.
[35]George G. Thompson, *Child Psychology* (Boston: Houghton Mifflin Company, 1962), pp. 148-149.

medical or nursing services? Does his cumulative record show that he was absent from school for any extended period of time? If so, what was the reason? Is he absent extensively now? If so, why?

be her goal. Physical well-being and ill-being . . . . affect every individual."[36]

Measuring Through Teacher-Made Tests From Spelling Scales

The specific nature of spelling makes it extremely difficult to guarantee the validity of a standardized spelling test. The words tested must be selected from those presented for instruction. This means, naturally, that the most common and useful measures of spelling are those constructed locally by the classroom teacher or supervisor. *The New Iowa Spelling Scale*[37] gives practical assistance to the elementary school teacher in furnishing useful information for the construction and validation of informal or standardized spelling tests.

Since the values of spelling are almost entirely specific, it is important that the content of a spelling test be sampled from properly validated vocabulary lists comprised of words that are now and will be ultimately of greatest usefulness to the pupil. The Iowa scale provides an extensive and carefully screened list of words which have been found to be used widely in the written communication of children and adults. It provides the teacher with reliable information on the average or typical difficulty of each of these words in each elementary school grade. (The 5,507 words comprising this list were screened from eight different valid vocabulary sources.)

If the directions accompanying the scale are followed, this scale can be used as a source of material for spelling tests that will provide valid and reliable measures of spelling efficiency and the directions are as follows:

> *Selection of Words for Spelling Tests.* While this scale makes no attempt to provide recommended lists of words for learning in specific grades it does make available a highly useful source of words of established social importance and difficulty suitable for testing purposes in specified grades. The typical pre-instruction test in spelling consists of a sample of the words to be studied later by the pupils. The results from such a test, while providing some information concerning the relative ability of individual pupils, also direct attention sharply to the

---

[36]Sidney L. Pressey, Francis P. Robinson, John E. Horrocks, *Psychology in Education* (New York: Harper & Brothers, 1959), p. 27 and p. 30.

[37]Harry A. Greene, *The New Iowa Spelling Scale* (Iowa City: Bureau of Educational Research and Service, State University of Iowa, 1954).

individual words which are the causes of spelling difficulties for these pupils.

Some teachers, in their construction of pre-instruction tests in spelling, may wish to include for testing only words which range around 50 per cent difficulty for a given grade.[38] Others may prefer to use words which represent a wide range of spelling difficulty from very easy to quite difficult. They feel that this type of test is an excellent device for showing growth on the part of pupils from all levels of spelling ability. Regardless of the point of view followed in the construction of the pre-instruction test the data in this scale make the problem quite simple.

By cross-checking the words presented for instruction in the textbook or workbook against the alphabetical list in the scale a list of words of significant social utility and of known difficulty may be obtained. The general validity of such a list of words for preliminary testing purposes is established by the fact that the test would contain only words which the pupils are to have an opportunity to learn to spell following the test. Since the data for the scale were obtained near the opening of the school year, the average spelling accuracy of the words comprising the test may be taken as a general guide for interpreting the class results prior to instruction. Furthermore, if a second test of comparable difficulty is given following instruction, a comparison with the typical expectancy as shown by the scale percentages should offer definite evidence of the class growth in spelling accuracy on these words resulting from instruction or other learning experiences. Naturally the percentages of spelling accuracy shown in the scale would not be usable following instruction except to indicate growth.

As an example of the way in which a valid preliminary or pre-instruction test may be constructed by using this scale, let us assume that a fourth-grade teacher has checked the vocabulary of the local spelling textbook used again the vocabulary of *The New Iowa Spelling Scale*. This chcek has revealed the fact that the following words which are to be taught in this grade appear in the alphabetical list of this scale with the spelling accuracies given immediately following each word: toys (81), boat (77), knife (52), painting (42), baking (43), asks (36), agreed (31), advice (24), describe (6).

In practice, there would almost certainly be many words common to both the spelling text and the scale, and naturally many more than

---

[38]The author of the scale, who corroborated on an evaluation textbook, makes an additional observation relative to the levels of difficulty of the words to be selected for testing. "In general, it is probably safe to say that the words to be included in a test for any grade should be those on which there are from 40 to 70 per cent misspellings. Tests made up of such words will give a reliable measure of spelling ability, since the words will not be so easy that there will be many prefect scores nor so difficult that there will be many low scores." Harry A. Greene, A. N. Jorgensen, and J. R. Gerberich, *Measurement and Evaluation in the Elementary School* (New York: Longmans, Green and Company, 1953), p. 442.

> five or ten words would be included in the spelling test. By using the alphabetical word lists it should be comparatively easy to prepare two or more comparable list dictation tests of from twenty-five to fifty words by including the proper number of words from the various percentage groups to produce equally difficult test lists.[39]

A second useful scale is *The Standard Elementary Spelling Scale*.[40] Here again the words are arranged in alphabetical order with difficulty ratings given for each word for each grade level.

Measuring Through Diagnostic Tests

It is important to discover, as early as possible, pupils who are doing poor work in spelling, to diagnose their difficulties, and to give them help. A teacher recognizes rather easily a pupil with a spelling disability. Recognition is easier, however, than the discovery of the causes underlying the difficulty. Diagnostic tests aid in the discovery of the types and causes of spelling difficulties.

A teacher's first question often is: "When are special difficulties severe enough to warrant particular diagnosis and treatment?" Some authorities state that a retardation of a half-year in Grade 2, of three-fourths of a year in Grade 3, and of one year in grades 4 to 8 warrants special treatment, but this question is best answered in the light of abilities and needs of the pupil concerned.

> In general, "spelling disability" applies to those children who are so incapable of handling the common or special words used by their peers and needed by themselves that they are definitely hindered in the fluent expression of their ideas. "Disability" does not imply that children are incapable of learning to spell as much as that they are far below the norms for their respective grades and ages.[41]

The purpose of spelling diagnosis is threefold:

1. To estimate a pupil's general spelling status and the seriousness of his retardation. This information usually is obtained from his age or grade score on a standardized test of spelling. Those tests were discussed earlier.

2. To discover possible causes of his spelling difficulties. That information is obtained by a study of the types of errors in his written work

---

[39]Harry A. Greene, *The New Iowa Spelling Scale* (Iowa City: Bureau of Educational Research and Service, State University of Iowa, 1954), pp. 11-13.

[40]H. H. Bixler, *The Standard Elementary Spelling Scale* (Atlanta: Turner E. Smith & Co., 1940).

[41]Arthur I. Gates and David H. Russell, *Diagnostic and Remedial Spelling Manual: A Handbook for Teachers* (New York: Bureau of Publications, Teachers College, Columbia University, 1940), pp. 2-3.

and through a series of individual diagnostic tests such as those in the Gates-Russell Diagnostic Series.[42] The teacher who has administered a diagnostic test will have more accurate information as to the causes of the pupil's difficulty. Consequently, she can more accurately give remedial help.

The elements of the Gates-Russell Series are:

1. Spelling Words Orally.
2. Word Pronunciation.
3. Giving Letters for Letter Sounds.
4. Spelling One Syllable.
5. Spelling Two Syllables.
6. Reversals.
7. Learning to Spell Hard Words.
8. Auditory Discrimination.
9. Visual, Auditory, Kinaesthetic, and Combined Study Method.

By utilizing all of the data secured through the foregoing tests, as well as the information in the child's cumulative school record, the teacher will gain a more complete understanding of the pupil and guide him more effectively. "Spelling disability is seldom or never the result of a single casual factor."[43]

Spelling Remediation Suggestions

It is of the utmost importance that pupils whose spelling achievement is low be given help as soon as possible lest they become discouraged by repeated failures, from poor habits of work, and develop undesirable attitudes toward spelling. These pupils should be dealt with with patience and sympathetic understanding. Great harm may be done both to the child's development in spelling and to his personality by holding him to standards of performance which, because of his disabilities, he cannot meet. Some of the disabilities take considerable time to remove. They must be removed, or at least diminished, however, if the pupil is not to be handicapped in learning to spell.

> Except in the case of children who are low in intelligence and those having severe physical handicaps, the factors most frequently associated with low achievement in spelling, are educational: lack of motivation, low reading ability, defective speech, slow or illegible handwriting, and desirable traits of personality. All these shortcomings can be removed or at least alleviated by instruction.[44]

---

[42]Arthur I. Gates and David H. Russell, *Gates-Russell Spelling Diagnostic Tests* (New York: Bureau of Publications, Teachers College, Columbia University, 1937).

[43]Gates and Russell, *Diagnostic and Remedial Spelling Manual*, p. 29.

[44]Ernest Horn, *What Research Says to the Teacher: Teaching Spelling*, Department of Classroom Teachers and American Educational Research Association (Washington: National Education Association, 1954), p. 26.

The following chart should aid the teacher as she makes instructional plans aimed at helping the child improve his spelling abilities. The chart was adapted by Greene and Petty from a current language test manual.[45] The chart provides an excellent summary of the many causes of spelling deficiency as well as remedial suggestions which the classroom teacher can follow profitably.

Diagnostic and Remedial Chart for Spelling

Possible causes of low test scores	Additional evidence of deficiency	Suggested remedial treatment
1. Lack of experience with the testing technique.	1. Low score on test contrasted with high score when words are given on dictation test.	1. Drills on choosing correct spellings from lists of errors of same word; choosing correct forms from long lists, some correct, some incorrect; proofreading on written work.
2. Emphasis on different or wrong vocabulary	2. Low scores on test in contrast with good record for daily work.	2. Check words not taught in your course with lists of known social utility.
3. Failure to develop a critical attitude toward spelling.	3. Indifference to spelling errors in daily written work.	3. Emphasize proofreading of own work. Drill on choosing correctly spelled forms in lists. Check pupil's certainty of his judgment of correctness of spelling.
4. Lack of teaching emphasis on individual's own spelling difficulties.	4. Observation of pupil's misspellings in daily work.	4. Have pupils keep lists of misspellings in daily work as basis for individual study. Focus on pupil's own errors. Try for transfer to all written work.

[45]Harry A. Greene and Walter T. Petty, *Developing Language Skills in the Elementary Schools* (Boston: Allyn and Bacon, Inc., 1964), pp. 546-548.

5. Special learning difficulties: a. Faulty pronunciation by the teacher.	5. a. Observation of speech habits; informal pronunciation tests based on spelling vocabulary.	5. a. Look up word in dictionary. Pronounce it distinctly for pupil. Have him repeat it while looking at word to associate sight and correct sound.
b. Limited power to visualize or "see" word forms.	b. Observation test. Have pupil try to visualize a 3-in. cube painted red. Ask questions: number of faces; number of planes necessary to cut it into 1-in. cubes; number of small cubes; number painted on one side, two sides, three sides, not painted, etc.	b. Emphasize the practice of looking at the word; closing eyes, and attempting to recall the word, as part of every spelling study period.
c. Difficulties in seeing or in hearing.	c. Observation; doctor's or nurse's examination.	c. Refer to nurse or medical service. Move pupil to front of room near window and blackboard. Stand near him in tests and spelling exercises. Make special effort to speak and write clearly.
d. Failure to associate sounds of letters and syllables with spelling of words.	d. Individual interview; analysis of spelling errors in tests and in daily work.	d. Go over words with child while he studies them. Teach him to analyze words himself.
e. Tendency to transpose, add, or omit letters.	e. Analysis of spelling papers; observation of daily work; pronunciation tests.	e. Emphasize visual recall of words. Have pupil practice writing the words, exaggerating the formation of the letters. Underline individual hard spots.

f. Tendency to spell unphonetic words phonetically.	f. Note types of errors made in spelling tests, especially insertion or leaving out letters.	f. Show that all words are not spelled as they sound. Each word must be learned individually. Emphasize steps in learning to spell. See h below.
g. Difficulties in writing; letter formation.	g. Observation of daily written work and spelling papers. Check writing with Ayres or Freeman writing scales.	g. Practice difficult letter formations and combinations. Emphasize need to avoid confusing letter forms, as i, e, r, and t.
h. Failure to master method of learning to spell.	h. Low scores on daily tests; observe the pupil's method of study in spelling; test on steps in learning to spell.	h. Check pupil's method of learning spelling. Teach steps in learning to spell until he uses them. Steps; (1) look at word, (2) listen to teacher pronounce it, (3) pronounce it by syllables then say the letters, (4) use it in a sentence, (5) close eyes and visualize it, (6) write it, (7) close eyes and recall, (8) write word. Repeat steps as necessary.

Gates and Russell also have delineated remedial suggestions in their diagnostic manual. The six classifications of deficiencies and the accompanying remedial suggestions are produced below. In addition, thirty-seven activity suggestions are given in Chapter VI of that publication. Teachers will profit from consulting that chapter.[46]

> 1. General Verbal and Linguistic Retardation: When a pupil is referred for spelling disability, it is sometimes discovered that he is backward in all the language activities. . . . . To meet such a difficulty, the teacher should: (a) Explore possibilities of enrichment in the pupil's environment outside school. (b) Initiate a general program of word

[46]Arthur I. Gates and David H. Russell, *Diagnostic and Remedial Spelling Manual: A Handbook for Teachers,* 1940, pp. 13-17 and pp. 41-50.

study skills which will apply to reading, spelling, and language. More and better reading tends to improve spelling. A program of word-form study which correlates reading and spelling techniques can be most valuable to such a pupil. (c) Provide special opportunities for work with words in the form of letters to the home, considerable oral language, experiences and activities to give a background of ideas such as pictures, movies, or excursions.

2. Pupil Misses Word Entirely: This difficulty is shown when a pupil writes "dark" for "baby" "loke" for "seen," etc. The remedial work should: (a) Check vision and hearing carefully. (b) Check the pupil's school history for the first two or three years. Is there a record of absence, illness, changing schools, etc.? That is, did the pupil ever receive any systematic, continuous instruction in word study? If not, the regular primary reading and language programs may be started. (c) Use remedial devices calling attention to (i) the relationships between letters and sounds and (ii) the form of words.

3. Difficulties in Giving Letter Equivalents of Sounds and Syllables: This is a difficulty in a primary skill which requires, at first, very simple procedures, such as knowing the alphabet and the common sounds of each letter, being able to blend two or three sounds, and being able to recognize common phonograms such as "in," "ol," "st," "de," and the like.

4. Difficulties in Certain Parts of Words: Difficulties in certain parts of words may involve particular letters such as the silent "e" or a number of phonograms such as the "tion" and "sion" forms; or they may lie in certain sections of words generally. In the latter case most errors are likely to be in the center of words and to the right of center. There are usually twice as many errors in the third syllable as in the first, and the letters e, a, i, and u are the most difficult. This difficulty calls for special help in word study, such as taking plenty of time to see the entire word, getting each syllable definitely in mind, and pronouncing each part of the word clearly.

5. Pupil Uses a Letter-by-Letter Method: Pupils using this method have never learned to see word-parts. For example, spelling the word prison p-r-i-s-o-n may be a relatively inactive process compared to saying pri-son. The pupils who can use syllabication, who see pronunciation units in words, who recognize common phonograms or other words within longer words, and who have a rhythm in oral or written spelling, have skilled techniques which the remedial teacher should help the letter-by-letter speller to acquire.

6. Pupil Has an Apparently Restricted Method for Word Study: By watching their classroom practices and by Test 9 of the Diagnostic Series, some pupils are discovered who learn to spell words in only one way. . . . . It is probably an advantage to be able to use a variety of methods in studying words, so if a pupil uses only one type of attack a remedial teacher will; (a) Look for physical defects in

sensory apparatus. (b) Explore the possibility of using more techniques. If a pupil uses only auditory methods, for example, it is well to see if he has the necessary basic information and skills for using visual and kinaesthetic methods. He may lack only a little guidance in these. (c) Use methods of word study adapted to the "special ability" of any pupil if there seem to be definite constitutional difficulties with the others. . . . . .

Additional Spelling Guidelines

1. A plan of continual observation, diagnosis, and remedial guidance should be a part of the total instructional program.

2. It is important that the program in spelling be broadly conceived. The total curriculum is now commonly defined to include all the experiences which children have at school. The curriculum in spelling includes all experiences which facilitate or retard the development of spelling ability. The teacher therefore should be concerned with total curricular experiences as she attempts to evaluate spelling. The evaluation should include the spelling done in all written work as well as the spelling done on a list of words.

3. Each child's spelling status should always be considered in relation to information about his general language abilities.

4. Pupils should be evaluated in terms of individual progress and individual ability and not in terms of class averages.

5. The pupil should know that the words in his speller are words research shows he will need to spell often – words needed now and in the future.

6. The teacher should remember that of the sources of interest and other desirable attitudes which he can control there is probably no other as important as the child's awareness of progress or success.

7. Pupils should be encouraged to keep progress charts of weekly scores made on spelling tests. A simple graph will suffice and pay dividends.

8. In addition, the teacher keeps a progress chart on written activities containing misspellings. For example, how many words per 50 or 100 words written were misspelled? This number can be recorded and a similar check made periodically.

9. Teachers who derive their spelling lists from other units of work, such as those in ahe social studies, should give tests on those lists also.

10. Spelling should never be given as a form of punishment.

11. In the instructional program attention should be given to the correction of the spelling tests.

When corrected by the pupils and the results are properly utilized, the test is the most fruitful single learning activity (per unit of time) that has yet been devised. It helps pupils at all levels of spelling ability. Better spellers will learn all or nearly all the words of a lesson through the corrected test alone, and even the poorer spellers will learn many words. Yet, like all learning activities, its efficiency is greatly reduced if the activity is performed in a perfunctory manner.[47]

Pupils should correct their own tests and record their own scores with only occasional rechecking by the teacher to see that the pupils' checking has been carefully done.[48]

Self-Evaluation in Spelling

Two check lists are presented for pupil self-evaluation. Check List 16 refers to the child's particular spelling method while Check List 17 relates to his spelling behaviors. Following those two check lists, a series of questions for teacher self-evaluation appears.

CHECK LIST 16

Questions About My Spelling Method	*Always*	*Usually*	*Seldom*	*Never*
1. Do I definitely center my attention upon the word?				
2. Do I try to visualize the word, i.e., close my eyes and attempt to recall its appearance?				
3. Do I say the letters of the word softly to myself?				
4. Do I pronounce the word, correctly syllable and try to recall how each syllable appears?				
5. Do I compare the word with the correct written or printed copy?				
6. Do I watch for silent letters, double letters, different vowels having the same sound, and for different combinations of letters?				
7. Do I recall the word repeatedly until I have mastered it?				
8. Do I develop the meaning of the word by using the dictionary?				
9. Do I use the word in sentences?				
10. Do I use the word in written work?				

[47]Ernest Horn, *What Research Says to the Teacher: Teaching Spelling,* p. 18.
[48]Harry A. Greene and Walter T. Petty, *Developing Language Skills in the Elementary Schools,* p. 282.

CHECK LIST 17

Questions About My Spelling Behavior	*Always*	*Usually*	*Seldom*	*Never*
1. Do I try to analyze the word?				
2. Do I consult a source when I'm not sure of the spelling?				
3. Do I take pride in turning in papers with no misspelled words on them?				
4. Do I want to spell and use words correctly?				
5. Do I take time to find synonyms which better express ideas?				
6. Do I keep lists of words that are hard for me and then try to master them?				
7. Do I follow through on the steps necessary for me to master a word?				

Questions to be considered for teacher self-evaluation:

1. Am I concerned with more than one goal in the teaching of spelling?
2. Does my spelling instruction recognize individual differences?
3. Are my spelling lessons spirited and expeditious and not given to dawdling?
4. Do I show interest and enthusiasm in teaching spelling? (Spelling is reported to be one of the subjects which many classroom teachers most dislike to teach.)
5. Are the spelling lessons highly motivated?
6. Do I coordinate instruction in spelling periods with the development of spelling ability in other activities?
7. Do I combine group instruction with individual instruction?
8. Do I teach meanings of words only when it is necessary?
9. Do games and devices supplement rather than supplant teaching instruction?
10. Do I help the pupil discover a definite and efficient method of learning to spell?
11. Do I limit the pupil's study to those words which tests have shown him to be unable to spell?
12. Does the pupil understand the purpose of the pretest?
13. Do I provide opportunities for correction by the student?
14. Do I inform each child of his progress in spelling?
15. Do I help youngsters identify the peculiarities of our language?
16. Do I encourage a spirit of mutual pride and cooperation in spelling achievement?
17. Does the child know that I consider correct spelling important?
18. Do I spell correctly all the words that I write?
19. Do I use the dictionary to check my spelling?

20. Do the pupils have abundant opportunities to write on matters of real concern to them?

Oral Language

Oral language ability is made up of many highly interrelated skills. From the standpoint of its social utility oral language is extremely important. In spite of its social importance, however, evaluative instruments suitable for the reliable appraisal of the products or the oral language skills producing them are extremely limited.

Oral Language Objectives

Clear, complete, effective expression is a widely accepted goal of oral language instruction. The Minneapolis Public Schools have listed comprehensive oral expression goals for the elementary grades. Some of the goals are listed here.[49]

GUIDED CONVERSATION

Specific Goals to be Sought

By the teacher

Encourage, but not force, the shy child to participate.
Help the shy child take turns.
Arrange seating informally (when possible) so that children can speak from sitting position.
Choose suitable topics for conversation, based on pupil's interests and suggestions, or happenings during the day.

By the pupils

Take part in the conversation.	
Wait for their turn.	Early
Listen courteously to others.	Elementary
Keep to the topic.	
Speak in sentences (depending on stage of development).	
Avoid particular errors of usage (pointed out to them).	Later
Ask for help in correcting errors.	Elementary
Choose words carefully to express exact meaning.	

[49]Minneapolis Public Schools, *Communication: A Guide to the Teaching of Speaking and Writing* (Minneapolis, Minnesota: Minneapolis Public Schools, 1953), pp. 18-24.

Informal Discussion

Specific Goals to be Sought

By the teacher

Help pupils sense the need for discussion and choose pertinent problems.
Help pupils face facts and draw valid conclusions.
Help the group as a whole to come to an agreement.

By the pupils

Contribute to group planning.
Answer a particular question.
Make a suggestion.
Help solve a problem – concerned with room, school, or playground – through group discussion.
Look at all sides of a question.
Pay attention to what others have to say.
Suggest possible solution.
Decide what features were good and bad about a particular performance.

Observing the Social Amenities

Specific Goals to be Sought

By the teacher

Build a friendly classroom atmosphere.
Help each child feel accepted by the group.
Eliminate social awkwardness.

By the pupils

Make a new child feel at home.
Don't laugh at others' mistakes. — Early Elementary
Say only kind things about others.
Ask others to join in a game.
Introduce two people to each other.
Express appreciation for a favor.
Answer a summons to the door.
Make a simple apology.
Introduce a speaker to an audience. — Later Elementary

Story-Telling

Specific Goals to be Sought

By the teacher

Help pupils.
Enrich their vocabularies.
Gain freedom and ease of expression.
Feel delight in simple experiences.
Acquire a love for a good story.

By the pupils
Retell accurately a story that has been told to them or read to them.
Make up an interesting story just for fun.

Meaningful Oral Language Experiences

Opportunities for meaningful oral language experiences occur abundantly throughout the school day. Only a few are listed here.

Telling a story about an experience on the way to school
Telling about an experience during Christmas vacation
Sharing a family trip experience
Reporting interview results related to a unit of work
Describing steps in a science experiment
Contributing to unit discussion plans
Conversing in committee meetings
Greeting newcomers to the classroom
Greeting parents and student teachers
Introducing parents to teachers
Introducing student teacher to some of the students
Explaining an arithmetic problem and answer
Contributing to setting up room standards
Relating the results of student council meeting
Participating in class group evaluation of behaviors during work period

Formal Oral Language Evaluation

At the present time there are no acceptable standardized instruments similar to the merit scales for written composition for use in evaluating the quality of oral expression. Reasonably accurate analytical appraisal of pupil accomplishment is, however, securable in some oral areas. The particular instrument will be discussed shortly.

Informal Evaluation of Oral Language

Because of the paucity of standardized instruments for the measurement of effective oral expression, teachers must use informal devices for appraisal. A large part of oral language activity and evaluation will be closely integrated with other content subjects. Pupils will need to speak effectively in social studies reporting, in summarizing science experiments, and the like. Check List 18 can be used for many situations. It may be employed for pupil self-evaluation, for teacher evaluation of the pupil, or for teacher-pupil evaluation.

CHECK LIST 18

How Did I Speak?	Pupil Evaluation	Teacher Evaluation
1. Did I get and hold the attention of my listeners?		
2. Did I have a good opening sentence?		
3. Did I speak clearly and not too rapidly?		
4. Was I relaxed and at ease?		
5. Did I pronounce and enunciate correctly?		
6. Was I careful in the selection of words?		
7. Did I make myself understood as well as heard?		
8. Did I look directly at the group?		
9. Was I enthusiastic?		
10. Were my thoughts well-organized?		
11. Did I summarize information so that listeners could easily recall main points?		

A – Much growth
B – Some growth
C – Little growth
D – No growth

Analytical and remedial suggestions as well as teacher self-evaluation questions will be deferred until there has been some discussion of written-language expression.

Written Language Objectives

The Kearney Report has set forth these composition objectives for composition. In the interest of space, knowledge and action pattern objectives are not listed.[50]

Skill and Competence

Primary Period – Composition

He is acquiring a "sentence sense." He uses capitals to begin sentences and for proper names, uses a period at the end of sentences, and groups together two or more sentences that follow each other easily.

He is able to compose and write simple letters independently with at least a realization that there should be a heading, salutation, message, complimentary close, and signature. He should be able to copy forms for writing friendly notes, letters of thanks, letters of request,

[50]Nolan C. Kearney, *Elementary School Objectives* (New York: Russell Sage Foundation, 1953), pp. 106-108, 110.

and letters of invitation. He should be able to write notes to parents about school events.

He should be able to write a one-paragraph story, using some descriptive words about people. He should be able to write his street address (city, state, and country) and the date.

Intermediate Period — Composition

Within the limits of his stage of development, he can express himself in writing. He follows an orderly arrangement of ideas; develops well-organized paragraphs centered around a topic; uses correct grammar, capitalization, punctuation, sentence structure, and spelling and chooses words within the range of his experience. He uses a separate paragraph for each direct quotation.

He begins to avoid run-on or stringy sentences. He can write correctly 9 out of 10 simple 5-to 10-word sentences. His verbs and subjects agree in number in 9 out of 10 of his written sentences. He tries to distinguish between adjectives and adverbs. He attempts to form good opening and closing sentences, and can use an occasional compound or complex sentence.

He uses periods at the end of sentences and after abbreviations, uses question marks and exclamation marks, and begins to use commas where needed. He knows how to read commas and apostrophes. In order to get the meaning, he notes transition words and phrases (yet, but, and, however, on the other hand).

He avoids using general words when specific words are better. He tries to keep pronoun and verb in a proper relationship. He uses capital letters for names, initials, book titles.

Attitude and Interest

Primary Period

The child likes to write short friendly notes, to read for recreation or information, to talk and listen to others respectfully and thoughtfully, to recite poems, and to retell favorite stories. He is interested in the sounds of words in word-families, in rhymes, in secret languages and codes. He characterizes his efforts in absolute terms of good and bad. He begins to develop attitudes toward radio and television programs.

Intermediate Period

He is developing an interest in evaluating his communication skills in an effort to overcome his errors and tends to be critical of his own performance in reading, writing, speaking. He enjoys a wide variety of reading materials, and relates his reading to this past experience. He reads and listens critically and expresses opinions frankly. He enjoys listening as well as talking, and takes pleasure in gratifying intellectual curiosity. He regards reading as an important source of information; he enjoys newspapers and magazines as well as books. He reads to further his hobby interests, and enjoys using reference books and newspapers. He enjoys communicating in groups and using group skills. He gets pleasure from composing stories, writing letters, making up rhymes and expressive phrases and sentences. He enjoys literature but is not hesitant in making choices between types.

Meaningful Written Language Experiences

Those experiences listed in the handwriting section of this chapter all represent meaningful experiences for the development of written language skills. They will not be repeated at this time; however, the reader may wish to refer to page 304.

Formal Written Language Evaluation

The possibilities for the objective and reliable evaluation of pupil achievement and growth are much greater in the case of written expression than in oral expression.

The Willing Scale for Measuring Written Composition is made up of eight scaled specimens of composition written on the subject, "An Exciting Experience." In this scale, two special features are introduced. The relation of form errors to the general quality of the written work is included in the scoring. In addition, a list of stimulating topics is suggested as the basis for encouraging written expression. The use of the standardized list of topics and the control of the conditions under which the writing takes place add to the reliability with which the written products can be evaluated.[51]

For each written product two separate scores are available, a "story value" and a "form value." Rating for "story value" follows the usual process of comparing the pupil's product with the scale specimens and assigning it the scale value of the specimen it most closely resembles. Following the assignment of the "story value" to a product, all errors in grammar, punctuation, capitalization, and spelling are marked and counted. This total number is multiplied by 100 and the result is then divided by the number of words written by the pupil. The resulting index is the "form value" score. Value scores begin at the fourth grade level.

The Hudelson English Composition Scale consists of sixteen scaled samples of written expression. All except the two top value specimens

[51]M. H. Willing, *The Willing Scale for Measuring Written Composition,* (Cincinnati, Ohio: Educators' Tests & Services Associates).

were written by school children. Midyear norms are provided for all elementary school grades above grade four. One unique feature of this scale is the provision of three sets of sample composition of known merit as assigned by experts for use in training teachers inexperienced in the use of the instrument.[52]

The STEP Essay Tests are devised for ability levels which begin at the fourth grade. The pupils are directed to write essays on particular topics in a thirty-minute writing period. The pupil's paper is then matched with evaluated comparison essays on the same topic and assigned one of seven ratings. Each rating is weighted for quality of thought and content, for style, and for mechanics of writing.[53]

The evaluation of letter writing as effective language expression consists largely in the appraisal of the quality of the product itself in terms of content, form, and mechanics. Class discussions, models, and dictated letters are learning and appraisal techniques. When more objective measures of letter-writing abilities and products are desired, however, a copying test such as that comprising Part 8 of the Iowa Primary Language Test can be used. This test measures the child's ability to insert the correct punctuation marks, greeting, and signature in a printed letter form. The test is scored on the following ten points, allowing one point for each correct response: comma after city, year given correctly in date, Dear written correctly in salutation, comma after name in salutation, period after first sentence, capital M in Miss, period after last sentence, comma after sincerely, whole name written correctly, name placed at right of paper and below closing. The test is standardized for use in second and third grades.[54]

While composition scales of the types described may not be accepted with enthusiasm by some teachers, the scales do help focus on qualities which can be appraised.

In the actual use of these scales in the classroom, the pupil's written product is compared with each of the scaled specimens until a scaled sample is found that on the basis of the reader's best judgement reveals approximately the same elements of quality as the pupil's product. The scale value of the comparable scale specimen is then assigned to the pupil's sample.

---

[52]Earl Hudelson, *Hudelson English Composition Scale* (Yonkers-on-Hudson: World Book Company).

[53]Educational Testing Service, *Sequential Tests of Educational Progress: Handbook for Essay Tests* (Princeton, New Jersey: Educational Testing Service, 1957).

[54]Lou A. Shepard and Harry A. Greene, *Iowa Primary Language Test* (Iowa City: Bureau of Educational Research and Service, State University of Iowa, 1936).

Evaluating the quality of written products by using composition scales is of course limited by: (1) the reader's subjective ratings and (2) the usually brief and inadequate samplings of written products on which the ratings are based. There can, however, be compensations. By constantly stressing the elements of quality in written expression and by collecting extensive samples of the written products of his pupils at the beginning and conclusion of instruction, the teacher can evaluate class and individual improvements and at the same time determine whether or not his pupils are expressing themselves as well as they should at their present grade and maturity level.

If the teacher avoids the error of thinking of the appraisals as having the accuracy of objective test scores, these measures of general merit of written expression can be extremely valuable aids to the teacher.

Informal Evaluation of Written Language

The involvement of youngsters in cooperatively developing criteria is a useful informal evaluation procedure. Children learn as they contribute to standards. Their cooperative decisions then serve as guidelines for their written endeavors. As a result of class discussion, one fifth grade class prepared the following list of questions which then served as guidelines for their creative writing. A teacher can stimulate her class to undertake a similar effort.

Questions to Ask About My Creative Writing

Do I try to write creatively?
Does the story have a good beginning?
Is the story interesting?
Does the story end with a surprise or a satisfactory outcome?
Are the details organized?
Are the words and phrases colorful?
Is the title suitable?
Have I taken care of periods, commas, capitals, etc.?

Written language experiences, both in school and outside of school, include numerous occasions for the writing of friendly and business letters. Check List 19 is adapted from standards listed in *Building Better English, Grade 5*. In the list of individual differences, the list may very well be usuable in grade four.

CHECK LIST 19[55]

Appraising the Quality of My Business Letter

How Good Is My Business Letter?	Pupil Evaluation	Teacher Evaluation
1. Is my whole letter brief, courteous, and easy to read?		
2. Is the spelling correct?		
3. Did I write the heading correctly at the upper right side of my paper?		
4. Did I block the inside address even with the left margin?		
5. Did I write the name of the person or firm correctly?		
6. Did I give the street address and the name of the town and the state?		
7. Did I use a greeting suitable for a business letter, such as "Dear Sir:" "Dear Madam:" "Gentlemen:" or "Dear Mr. Blye:"?		
8. Did I make my meaning clear in the body of the letter in good paragraph form?		
9. Did I indent the first word and write the body of the letter in good paragraph form?		
10. Did I use a suitable closing, such as "Yours truly," or "Sincerely yours"?		
11. Did I sign the letter correctly?		
12. Did I use paper suitable for a business letter?		

(The pupils should be able to answer "yes" to each of the twelve questions above.)

Analytical and Remedial Suggestions for Oral and Written Language

When the currently available language tests are examined in the light of modern criteria for diagnostic measurement the majority of such instruments appear to fall short of being really diagnostic. Certain of these tests, however, do provide an analytical program in language of rather adequate breadth in grade and content coverage.

An analytical appraisal of pupil accomplishment in Grades 1, 2, and 3 in eight different oral and written skill and product areas of

[55]Adapted from *Building Better English, Grade 5* (Evanston, Ill.: Row, Peterson and Company, 1947), p. 93.

language is provided by the Iowa Primary Language Test.[56] The eight tests may be administered by the second semester of the first grade. No reading is required and the pupil reactions are simple and objective. Of particular value to classroom teachers is The Examiner's Manual which presents an inventory of the language skills ordinarily emphasized in these grades. The language areas sampled by the test are listed here.

1. Filling in forms
2. Conversation
3. Oral composition
4. Telephone conversation
5. Correct usage
6. Recorded composition
7. Miscellaneous social usage
   - A. Description
   - B. Introductions
   - C. Announcement, message, invitation
   - D. Directions for finding a place
   - E. Forms of courtesy
8. Letter writing

The elementary battery of the Iowa Language Abilities Tests contains five subtests on spelling, word meanings, language usage, capitalization, and punctuation.[57] That battery is for use in Grades 4, 5, and 6 with optional use in Grade 7.

The language test booklet of the current Iowa Every-Pupil Tests of Basic Skills possesses considerable analytical power.[58] The skill coverage of this booklet closely parallels that of the Iowa Language Abilities Tests. The elementary booklet is designed for use in Grades 3, 4, and 5 while the advanced booklet is for Grades 5 to 9.

The Manual for Interpreting the Iowa Language Abilities Tests[59] presents remedial suggestions in four language areas. This suggestion can be profitably used by elementary teachers as they become aware of the language needs of their particular classrooms and plan a remedial program.

---

[56]Lou A. Shepard and Harry A. Greene, *Iowa Primary Language Test* (Iowa City: Bureau of Educational Research and Service, State University of Iowa, 1936).

[57]Harry A. Greene and H. L. Ballenger, *Iowa Language Abilities Tests* (Yonkers-on-Hudson: World Book Company, 1948).

[58]E. F. Lindquist, general ed., *Iowa Every-Pupil Tests of Basic Skills, Test C* (Geneva, Illinois: Houghton-Mifflin Company).

[59]Reproduced here with the permission of the publishers, World Book Company, Yonkers-on-Hudson, New York.

Language Usage

Possible causes of low test scores	Additional evidence of deficiency	Suggested remedial treatment
1. Failure to comprehend testing technique.	1. Misunderstanding of method of recording responses to items.	1. Prepare and use drill exercises similar to those used in test. Work with pupil until he understands technique.
2. Poor control over special language usages	2. Observation and check on daily habits or oral and written expression.	2. Check pupil's test paper to identify types of usages missed. Check with text and course of study for grade emphasis. Emphasize individual drill on specific errors. Contrast correct forms with those to be avoided. Supplement with oral drill.
3. Poor language background.	3. Careless, inaccurate usage in oral and written expression.	3. Corrective instruction is the only remedy here. Select a limited number of usages and proceed as in No. 2 above.
4. Foreign language in the home.	4. Observed foriegn accents. Evidence of two languages in the home.	4. Use direct corrective instruction here. Follow suggestions in No. 2 above.
5. Poor general reading comprehension.	5. Erratic response to test items; poor reading ability in other subjects.	5. Drill on sentence and total meaning comprehension as required for general improvement in reading.
6. Low mental ability.	6. Difficulty in following directions; erratic response to difficulty with common usage; low MA and IQ shown by reliable mental test.	6. Follow general procedure as outlined in Nos. 2 and 3 above. Have pupil prepare and memorize a key sentence for troublesome usages.

7. Careless language habits.	7. Erratic responses to test items; carelessness in informal expression.	7. Develop self-critical attitude toward usage errors. Bring pressure to bear favoring correct usages. Stress proofreading in all written work.
8. Confusion caused by emphasis on formal rather than functional usages	8. Inaccurate responses to items emphasized mainly through rules.	8. Emphasize individual drills; stress definite habits of correct response to important usages.

Sentence Sense

Possible causes of low test scores	Additional evidence of deficiency	Suggested remedial treatment
1. Limited meaning vocabulary.	1. Low scores on vocabulary tests; observation of pupil's use of words in oral and written work.	1. Drill on meaning vocabulary. Develop different meanings of common words. Stress using words in sentences demonstrating differences in meanings.
2. Poor reading comprehension.	2. Low scores of information and on reading comprehension tests.	2. Drill on word meanings, sentences and paragraph meanings, and comprehension of total meaning of content suitable for the grade.
3. Inability to recognize subjects and predicates of sentences, and to sense what is missing in a fragment.	3. Note pupil's habits in speech and writing; individual work with pupils on analysis of sentences and fragments.	3. Drill on choosing complete subjects and predicates from pupil's own writing. Use matching exercises made up of complete subjects in one column and complete predicates in parallel column.

4. Failure to think of sentence as complete unit of expression.	4. Note pupil's spoken and written work for sentence errors.	4. Stress use of complete sentences in daily oral and written work. Point out that there are times when fragments may be used but that they must be recognized as such. Drill on completion of exercises in which subjects or predicates are missing. Drill on exercises calling for identification of fragments and sentences.
5. Use of "run-on" sentences; loose and	5. Analysis of pupil's expression for use of loose and's and "run-on's."	5. Explain and illustrate various types of incorrect sentences. Stress individual practice in writing good sentences. Drill on identifying poor sentence structure and in recasting poor sentences.

Capitalization

Possible causes of low test scores	Additional evidence of deficiency	Suggested remedial treatment
1. Lack of knowledge of capitalization situations.	1. Analysis of pupil's test paper and other written work to determine types of errors made.	1. Check specific capitalization skills missed by pupil on test paper with textbook and local course of study. Stress proofreading drills on skills in which pupil is weak.

2. Limited knowledge of exceptions and irregularities in capitalization.	2. Analysis of test paper and daily written work; note tendency to over-capitalize.	2. Give direct drill on capitalization skills taught in this grade. Point out exceptions and irregularities in the use of capitals.
3. Tendency to over-capitalize.	3. High correction for over-capitalization in test.	3. Inspect test paper and written work for excessive use of capitals. Use dictation and proofreading designed to emphasize correct use of capitals.
4. Lack of self-critical attitude toward capitalization. Poor proofreading ability.	4. Erratic and careless work in daily written expression in other subjects; limited ability to note errors in own or other written copy.	4. Emphasize need for self-critical attitude toward pupil's own written work. Drill on proofreading exercises designed to emphasize use of capitals.
5. Poorly developed sentence sense.	5. Low scores on sentence sense tests.	5. Use suggestions in remedial chart for sentence sense.
6. Carelessness in writing.	6. Analysis of handwriting characteristics in daily work.	6. Drill on distinctive characteristics of capital letters and small letters which analysis shows cause trouble.

Punctuation

Possible causes of low test scores	Additional evidence of deficiency	Suggested remedial treatment
1. Lack of knowledge of specific punctuation skills.	1. Check test papers to determine types of skills missed; observation of daily written work.	1. Check punctuation items missed on test with textbook and course of study. Use proofreading drills on skills missed by pupil. Stress drills on correct punctuation, avoiding over-punctuation, and self-editing of own copy.

2. Tendency to over-punctuate.	2. Analysis test and daily work for evidence of over-punctuation, especially commas.	2. Use dictation and proofreading drills for the elimination of improper or excessive punctuation.
3. Lack of self-critical attitude toward own written work.	3. Careless punctuation in daily work; fails to note errors in own or other written copy.	3. Emphasize self-criticism of own daily written work. Use proofreading exercises to emphasize correct use of punctuation marks.
4. Poor general comprehension in reading.	4. Low scores on comprehension tests; poor reading in other subjects.	4. Drill on word meaning, sentence comprehension, and comprehension of total meaning in varied subject-matter fields.
5. Poor vision or hearing.	5. Observation of pupil at work; nurse's or doctor's examination.	5. Refer pupil to doctor for medical attention. Move pupil to front of room. Encourage pupil to make special effort to write carefully and to make punctuation marks distinctly.
6. Poorly developed sentence sense.	6. Observation of pupil's daily usage.	6. Explain types of sentences and the relation of sentence structure to punctuation. Stress practice in writing sentences and punctuating them correctly. Use dictation and proofreading exercises calling for punctuation
7. Carelessness in matters of form in written expression.	7. Observation and analysis of characteristics of handwriting and punctuation.	7. Stress essentials of good form in written work. Insist that pupils edit and proofread all written work.

Teacher Self-Evaluation

There are some questions a teacher may wish to consider about her oral language program.

Do I give the youngsters many experiences to talk about?
Do I take them on field trips, show them films and film-strips, bring in resource people?
Do I provide time for youngsters to talk about their experiences?
Do I use the tape recorder as an aid to the improvement of oral language?
Do I set good example by sharing experiences with the youngsters?
Do I set good example in the manner of my presentations?
Do I expand my own vocabulary and share new words with the class?
Do I introduce them to such word-building trade books as *A Gaggle of Geese, The Abecedarian Book, Wally the Wordworm,* and the like? [60,61,62]
Do I read to them often?
Do I listen to them and show interest when they are speaking?

As a teacher ponders the written lanuguage program in her classroom she should be able to answer the following questions in the affirmative.

Do I believe that children can write?
Do I give them many experiences to write about?
Do I involve them in projects, experiments, units of work, centers of interest?
Do I provide the time for them to write about experiences?
Do I make them aware of the many events in their daily lives that are stimulants to creative expressions?
Do I write creatively and share the written product with them?
Do I provide time for them to share their products with others?
Do I make a place for their written products on the library shelves?
Do I accept all creative efforts?

Grammar and Usage

Scientific attempts to prove the usefulness of a knowledge of grammar have failed. Grammar must live in all experiences where youngsters are expressing themselves. Usage, rather than grammar, should be taught.

---

[60]Eve Merriam and Paul Galdone, *A Gaggle of Geese* (New York: Alfred A. Knopf, 1960).
[61]Charles W. Ferguson, *The Abecedarian Book* (Boston: Little, Brown, and Company, 1964).
[62]Clifton Fadiman, *Wally the Wordworm* (New York: The Macmillan Company, 1964).

Usage, rather than grammar, should be evaluated. The approach must be functional.

A functional program consists of pupils' meeting and mastering the essential language habits in situations that are as lifelike as possible. Pupils develop habits as those are needed in meaningful classroom situations. All of the previous lists of meaningful classroom experiences, as well as other experiences too numerous to list here, become occasions in which grammar may function. In all of those situations youngsters are building toward an understanding of, not a memorization of, subject-verb relationships. Clear, complete, effective expression is stressed and evaluated at all times.

That less space is devoted to grammar does not mean that grammar is of less importance. Rather, it is of utmost importance. Functional usage has the potential to occur in every experience throughout the school day.

Today's language textbooks for the elementary school provide numerous suggestions for the identification and correction of deficiencies in functional usage. From those textbooks and the accompanying teachers' manuals, there are numerous worthwhile suggestions for the interested teacher. Those suggestions give helpful assistance in the construction of any needed tests.

Summary

Functions of Evaluation

Evaluation serves five major instructional functions: (1) to determine the extent to which children are making progress toward goals; (2) to provide evidence to children, parents, and teachers concerning such progress; (3) to discover basic causes behind any deficiencies; (4) to determine individual reteaching needs; and (5) to determine teaching effectiveness. In carrying out the first and second functions, the teacher should be concerned with measuring both short-term and long-term gains. The teacher is also concerned with the diagnosis of individual needs as a basis for remedial instruction, the diagnosis of class needs as a basis for the reteaching of certain topics, the measurement of individual growth as a basis for grading and reporting, and any resultant implications regarding the teacher's methods of instruction.

Criteria for Evaluation

The functions of evaluation cannot be achieved by an uncoordinated program. In order to serve all functions, an evaluation program should meet the following criteria:

1. It should be based on a realistic statement of educational objectives. Educational values need to be determined and understood. Goals need to be interpreted.

2. The behavior changes sought in pupils need to be expressed, that is, goals need to be expressed in behavioral terms.

3. Situations in which children's behavior can be studied need to be established.

4. Evidence on the extent to which changes in behavior have been achieved need to be secured.

5. A variety of instruments and techniques to gather the evidence should be employed.

6. Analysis and interpretation of data need to be made.

7. Evaluation data needs to be used for the improvement of teaching-learning experiences and thus for the further attainment of educational goals.

Characteristics of Evaluation

Evaluation Should Be Comprehensive

Important goals should not be omitted in evaluation merely because progress toward them cannot be appraised with high objectivity. Evaluation is concerned with all objectives which the teacher hopes will be achieved.

Evaluation Should Be an Integral Part of All Educational Activity

Education is a continuous activity, and evaluation is an essential and interrelated aspect of the teaching-learning process. Effective evaluation is ongoing, constant, and continuous. It is not a terminal activity, and it is more than sporadic testing at weekly or monthly intervals.

Evaluation Should Utilize a Variety of Techniques

Evaluation is not limited to the use of paper-and-pencil tests; it includes all means of obtaining valid data concerning desired changes in pupil behavior. Many tools and procedures should be utilized. Some devices, like anecdotal records or observations, yield descriptive evidence; others, like standardized tests, yield quantitative results. An awareness of the limitations and advantages of both are essential to intelligent evaluation. Tests must be selected according to the purpose to be served.

Evaluation Should Be Concerned With All Aspects of Individual Development and Behavior

Evaluation needs to be concerned with more than intellectual development. Attitudes, interests, skills, abilities, action patterns, as well as knowledges and understandings, should be the concerns of the teacher.

Evaluation Should Be More Concerned With Growth Than it is With Where the Pupil Stands in Relation to His Peers or to National Norms

Evaluation stresses the progress the child makes in terms of his own aptitudes, interests, and goals rather than how well he compares with other children. National norms are helpful in interpreting how well a pupil is expected to do on a certain test and what his score means in terms of age or grade norms, but the emphasis should always be on a comparison of his score with his previous score in order to note the growth or progress that he has made. National norms, unrelated to specific situations, are not alone an adequate goal for evaluation.

Evaluation Should Be a Cooperative Process

All children should learn to make self-evaluations – to recognize their strengths and weaknesses, their successes and failures. Children should be encouraged to evaluate their growth in the objectives and standards they have helped establish. Greater progress is made when both teachers and pupils understand the objectives and when both work to achieve them.

Evaluation Data Should Be Put to Use

Data gathered by the teacher or the children through self-evaluation should be used to improve learning experiences. Results need to be skillfully interpreted. Evaluation should reveal next steps, needs for materials, improved standards for work, and improved use of methods. Conferences with parents and interpretation of the program are other illustrative uses of evaluative data. Evaluation data that is not interpreted or evaluation data that is not used is of little value.

EXTENDING YOUR LEARNING

1. Select a grade level and formulate the major objectives of a language-arts area. In addition, define each major objective briefly in terms of pupil behaviors that would indicate growth in the objective.

2. Set up a check list for a language-arts area, at a given grade level, which can be used for teacher-pupil evaluation.
3. In what different ways might a teacher use the information secured from test results administered in October of a school year? In what different ways might a teacher use the information secured from test results administered in April or May of a school year?
4. It has been stated that "to know an individual means to be able to describe him accurately and fully." What would be central in such a description for a fifth-grade girl having difficulty with spelling?
5. Assume that you are beginning to teach a new group of students. Make a list of the types of information you would like to have about the new class. For which could standardized tests contribute the information either wholly or in part? For which would informal procedures be used either wholly or in part?

BIBLIOGRAPHY

Anderson, Paul S., *Resource Materials for Teachers of Spelling*. Minneapolis, Minnesota: Burgess Publishing Company, 1963. 118 pages. A practical guide which includes teaching, remediation, and evaluation suggestions.

Baker, James F., *Elementary Evaluative Criteria*. Boston, Massachusetts: School of Education, 1954. 109 pages. This instrument and the criteria contained therein will provide a valid means for evaluating elementary schools and will furnish staff members with specific suggestions to bring about improvement.

Bauernfeind, Robert H., *Building A School Testing Program*. Boston, Massachusetts: Houghton-Mifflin Company, 1963. Chapter 7, "Testing in Grades K-3." Chapter 8, "Testing for Educational Developmental Grades 3-12." Chapter 13, "Using Subject-Matter Achievement Tests." Chapter 15, "What's Ahead in Educational Testing?" – projections by nine test specialists. An index of tests is included.

Buros, Oscar K., *Tests In Print*. Highland Park, New Jersey: Gryphon, 1961. A bibliography of tests currently available, and an index to the *Mental Measurements Yearbook Series*.

Burr, James B., Coffield, William, Jenson, Theodore J. and Neagley, Ross L. Boston, Massachusetts: Allyn and Bacon, Inc., 1963. Chapter 10, "Evaluation of Program and Staff." This chapter should be particularly helpful to a staff as they come together to consider the broad topic of evaluation. Among many other considerations, the chapter considers evaluation of pupil growth and evaluation of staff.

Burton, William H., *The Guidance of Learning Activities*. New York: Appleton-Century-Crofts, Inc., 1962. Chapter 20, "The Measurement and Evaluation of Learning Outcomes." Chapter 21, "The Diagnosis of Learning Difficulties." Chapter 22, "Marking and Reporting Progress."

Cincinnati Public Schools, *The Primary Manual: A Teachers Guide Kindergarten-Grade Three*. Cincinnati, Ohio: Board of Education, 1963. 412 pages. A comprehensive guide to sound educational practices based on research findings and on experimentation of many Cincinnati teachers, principals, and supervisors. Suggests content, procedures, and activities with adaptations suited for the average, slower-moving, and rapid-learning pupils.

Cincinnati Public Schools, *The Intermediate Manual: A Teachers Guide Grades Four, Five, Six.* Cincinnati, Ohio: Board of Education, 1962. 404 pages. This manual includes procedures for teaching, activities, diagnostic information, suggestions for corrections of difficulties, meeting individual needs, and appraisal suggestions.

Columbus Public Schools, *Agreements Booklet.* Columbus, Ohio: Board of Education. A sequential arrangement of goals for kindergarten through grade six. A product of experimentation, study, trial, evaluation, and revision involving many members of the professional staff. Not a "given pattern" to be followed but suggestive of the cooperative endeavors of one school system.

Commission on the English Curriculum, National Council of Teachers of English, *Language Arts for Today's Children.* New York: Appleton-Century-Crofts, Inc., 1954. Chapter 11, "Factors Which Facilitate a Good Language Arts Program." Chapter 13, "Evaluation of the Language Arts Program."

Denver Public Schools, *A Guide for Teaching the Language Arts.* Denver, Colorado: Board of Education., 1960. 402 pages. A practical guide for teaching and evaluating. A product of the efforts of an entire school system. Another example of what can be accomplished when a staff thinks together.

Durost, Walter N. and Prescott, George A., *Essentials of Measurement for Teaching.* New York: Harcourt, Brace, & World, Inc., 1962. A clear, concise measurement and evaluation text written for teachers. The doctrine is supported that evaluation is a part of the teaching task, not something added to or imposed upon the teacher. The authors set forth numerous workable suggestions. Chapter 9, "How to Tell Parents About Evaluation Results." Chapter 10, "What Constitutes an Adequate Evaluation Program."

Findley, Warren G., *The Impact and Improvement of School Testing Programs.* Sixty-second Yearbook of The National Society for the Study of Education, Part III, 1963. An up-to-date comprehension and practical statement of measurements and evaluation.

Freeman, Frank N., *What Research Says to the Teacher: Teaching Handwriting.* Washington: Department of Classrom Teachers and the American Educational Research Association of the National Education Association, 1954. 33 pages. Current research and evaluation suggestions about this all-important skill are made available to the classroom teacher.

Gates, Arthur I., and Russell, David H., *Diagnostic and Remedial Spelling Manual: A Handbook for Teachers.* New York: Bureau of Publications, Columbia University, 1940. 50 pages. This manual is designed as an aid to the discovery of the kinds of spelling difficulties encountered and their underlying causes, together with the procedures that can be used for overcoming them. Chapter VI especially helpful in suggesting devices for the remedial program.

Greene, Harry A., and Petty, Walter T., *Developing Language Skills in the Elementary Schools.* Boston: Allyn and Bacon, Inc., 1964. 572 pages. This text includes objectives for the language arts, specific teaching and remedial suggestions, and two chapters on measurement and evaluation of language outcomes. This comprehensive and useful text should be in every professional library.

Gerberich, J. Raymond, Greene, Harry A., and Jorgensen, A. N., *Measurement and Evaluation In the Modern School.* New York: David McKay Company, 1963. Chapter 15, "Reading, Vocabulary, and Listening: Measuring and Evaluating the School Subjects." Chapter 16, "English Language, Spelling, and Handwriting: Measuring and Evaluating the School Subjects." Chapter 3, "Characteristics of Good Educational Appraisal." Chapter 13, "Analyzing Results of Measurement and Evaluation." Chapter 14, Interpreting Results of Measurement and Evaluation."

Harris, Chester W., Editor, *Encyclopedia of Educational Research,* Third Edition. New York: Macmillan Company, 1960. Theodore Harris, "Handwriting" pp. 616-624. Ernest Horn, "Spelling" pp. 1337-1354. A current, concise discussion based on the findings of research.

Heltman, Harry Joseph, *Handbook for Remedial Speech.* Magnolia, Massachusetts, Expression Company Publishers, 202 pages. The primary purpose of the book is to help the elementary school teacher by giving practical suggestions for the improvement of speech difficulties.

Henry, Nelson B., Editor, *Teaching Language in the Elementary School,* Forty-third Yearbook of The National Society for the Study of Education, Part II, 1944. Chapter IX, "Evaluation in the Language Arts Program." Chapter XI, "Interpretation of the Language Arts Program to Parents and Community."

Henry, Nelson B., Editor. *The Measurement of Understanding.* The Forty-fifth Yearbook of the National Society for the Study of Education, Part 1, 1946. Chapter IX, "The Measurement of Understanding in the Language Arts."

Horn, Ernest, *What Research Says to the Teacher: Teaching Spelling.* Washington: Department of Classroom Teachers and The American Educational Research Association of the National Education Association, 1954. 32 pages. Theoretical and practical suggestions based on the results of research.

Kearney, Nolan C., *Objectives of Elementary Education.* New York: Russell Sage Foundation, 1953. Part II, "Recommended Goals for the Elementary School Years." This report is a study of goals for elementary education in America as they were outlined by a group of prominent educational authorities and criticized by an equally capable group of educators at work in the schools. The report was prepared by The Mid-Century Committee on Outcomes in Elementary Education.

Lindvall, C. M. *Testing and Evaluation: An Introduction.* New York: Harcourt, Brace, & World, Inc., 1961. Chapter 2, "The First Step: Defining Objectives." Chapter 3, "Selecting and Appraising an Evaluation Procedure." Chapter 7, "Constructing Tests for Use in the Elementary School." Chapter 10, "Standardized Achievement Tests." Chapter 11, "Improved Non-testing Evaluation Procedures." Chapter 13, "Planning the Total Program of Testing and Evaluation."

Minneapolis Public Schools, *Communication: A Guide to the Teaching of Speaking and Writing.* Minneapolis, Minnesota: Minneapolis Public Schools,

1959. 118 pages. This guide can be profitably used by teachers as they plan for teaching, evaluating, and remediation.

Myers, Emma Harrison. *The Whys and Hows of Teaching Handwriting.* Columbus, Ohio: Zaner-Bloser Company, 1963. Chapter 8, "Measurement, Evaluation, and Remediation." Chapter 9, "Individual Differences."

Nunnally, Jum C. *Educational Measurement and Evaluation.* New York: McGraw-Hill, Inc., 1964. Part II, "Construction and Use of Teacher-Made Tests." Part VI, "Development of Testing Programs."

Oklahoma Curriculum Improvement Commission. *Evaluation Manual for the Improvement of Elementary Schools.* Oklahoma: State Department of Education, 1958. 48 pages. A set of evaluative criteria to be used as a means of self-evaluation in the elementary schools. "Self" check lists provide helpful suggestions for in-service study and discussion.

San Diego County Schools, *Oral and Written Language.* San Diego, California: San Diego County Schools, 1957. Another suggestive guide for teaching, evaluating, and remediation.

Shange, Harold G., Mulry, June Grant, Reddin, Mary E., and Gillespie, Margaret C. *Improving Language Arts Instruction in the Elementary Schools.* Columbus, Ohio: Charles E. Merrill Books, Inc., 1962. 526 pages. Throughout the chapters, practical appraisal and remediation suggestions are given. Appendix 3, also useful for teachers: "Instructional Materials for Use In Language Instruction."

Shane, Harold G., and McSwain, E. T. *Evaluation and the Elementary Curriculum.* New York: Henry Holt and Company, 1958. Chapter 9, "Evaluating the Language Arts."

Sowards, G. Wesley, and Scobey, Mary-Margaret. *The Changing Curriculum and the Elementary Teacher.* San Francisco: Wadsworth Publishing Company, Inc., 1961. Chapter 3, "Educational Objectives: Direction for the Elementary School." Chapter 20, "Utilizing Evaluation: Determining Progress Toward Goals."

Taylor, Stanford E. *What Research Says to the Teacher: Listening.* Washington: Department of Classroom Teachers and the American Educational Research Association of the National Education Association, 1964. 32 pages. The most current research findings presented as a help to the everyday problems of the classroom teacher. Specific activities and evaluation suggestions given.

Thorndike, Robert L. and Hagen, Elizabeth. *Measurement and Evaluation in Psychology and Education.* New York: Wiley, 1961. Chapter 4, "Preparing Objective Tests." Chapter 7, "Qualities Desired in Any Measurement Procedure." Chapter 12, "Questionnaires and Inventories for Self-Appraisal." Chapter 16, "Planning a School Testing Program."

Wrightstone, J. Wayne, Justman, Joseph, and Robbins, Irving. *Evaluation in Modern Education.* New York: American Book Company, 1956. Chapter 1, "Origins and Trends in Measurement and Evaluation." Chapter 3, "Types, Uses, and Qualities of Major Evaluation Techniques." Chapter 4, "Administrative Aspects of an Evaluation Program." Chapter 9, "Checklists and Rating Scales." Chapter 14, "Evaluating Achievement in Language Arts." Chapter 23, "Evaluating School and Teaching Practices."

Index

A

Acuity, auditory, 121
Aesthetics, 54
Albright, D., cited, 76
American Handwriting Scale, 307
Anderson, Dan W., cited, 203
Anderson, Paul S., cited, 189, 200, 229, 233
Applegate, Mauree, cited, 152, 238, 249, 260
Arts, creative: *see* Creative arts
Arnstein, Flora J., cited, 167
Audio-visual aids in foreign language instruction, 284
"Auding," 121
Ayres, Leonard P., handwriting scale, 307

B

Baker, G. Derwood, cited, 165
Balance, artistic, 76
Barbara, Dominick A., cited, 133
Barghahn, Kenneth C., cited, 241
Barnett, Walter W., cited, 241
Beck, Harriet K., cited, 15
Behavior, expressive, 3
Benjamin, Harold: *Sabre Tooth Curriculum,* The, 66
Bernstein, Basil, cited, 20
Bezzi, Rocky, cited, 204
Binney, James, cited, 241
Birkmaier, Emma M., cited, 278
Bixler, H. H., cited, 334
Boleslavsky, Richard, cited, 76
Borgh, Enola, cited, 245, 252
Brink, Lauren L., cited, 105
Broening, Angela, cited, 105
Brown, Don Pardee, cited, 121
Burns, Paul C., cited, 186, 199
Butterfield, Blair J., cited, 241
Butterfield, Marguerite, cited, 155, 258

C

California Language Test, 324
Capitalization
  evaluation of, 355, 356
  skills, 148, 149
  skills: grade-placement practices, 263, 264
Carey, G. V., cited, 144
Carin, Arthur, cited, 16
Carlson, Ruth Kearney, cited 140
Carroll, John B., cited, 2
Cerebrum: intrinsic portions, 18
Chalkboard, use in handwriting instruction, 185
Chase, Naomi, C., cited, 106
Check lists, 295
  for evaluating handwriting,

312-316, 319, 320
for evaluating listening, 299, 300, 303
for evaluating oral language, 346
for evaluating spelling, 327, 330, 341, 342
for evaluating writing, 351
Clarity, 256
Coherence, artistic, 76
Combes, Arthur W., cited, 23, 25, 31
Communication
blocks to, 68, 69
early forms, 2-4
oral: foreign language, 280, 281
oral: *see also* Speaking and Speech
subjectivity and, 69
surmounting blocks to, 69, 70
transition from oral to written, 141-143
Comprehension, auditory, 121
Concepts, definition, 16
Conrad, Edith U.: *Conrad Manuscript Writing Standards,* 307
Consonants (English)
articulation of sounds of, 216, 217
letters, 217
phonemes, 214
sounds, 214-217
Cooing, 2,3
Creative arts, reasons for, 67
Creative expression, 54
Cultural deprivation, effect on language of children, 37, 38
Cultural insights, 275

D

Dawson, Mildred A., cited, 111, 232, 249
Definitions, memorized, 248, 249
Dennis, W., cited, 21
Dentals, 214, 216
Deprivation, cultural: effect on linguistic skill, 20,
Dialogue, use in dramatics, 89
Dictionaries, 232
Differences, individual, among children, 100-103
Discrimination, auditory, 121
Dramatic play, 80, 81
and language development, 45, 46
Dramatics, creative, 62-89
Dramatics, creative, 62-89
functions of, 73
nature of, 70, 71
and nature study, 74
processes, 79-83
requirements, 71-73
in social studies, 74, 75
uses in language arts, 75-77
Dramatization
of stories, 88, 89
use of dialogue in, 89

E

Education, utilitarian, 64-66
Elementary schools
daily schedule, 55, 56
Element representation (dramatics), 87
development of speech, 104, 105
foreign language in, 270-290
language arts program, 37-60
listening instruction in, 120, 121
punctuation uses to be taught in, 144-147
relation of foreign language to total curriculum, 277, 278
role of teacher in listening instruction, 133, 134
teaching of grammar in, 246, 247
teaching and improving handwriting in, 170-207
teaching of typing in, 200-202
weekly program, 56, 57
yearly program, 57
Elwell, Ardell, cited, 232
Emotional security, environments fostering, 30
Emotions, differences among children, 101
Emphasis, artistic, 75, 76
English, "good," 248-250
Enstrom, E. A., cited, 182, 188, 193
Environment, effect of, on sentence structure, 256
Eriksson, Marguerite, cited, 276
Experience charts, 142
Experience units, 106

Experiences
complex: ways of introducing, 84-85
language and, 19
Exploration, freedom for, 27, 28
Expression
ineptness, 69
oral, 58
written, 59-60
Evaluation, 294-361
characteristics of, 360, 361
of children's writing, 167, 168
criteria for, 359, 360
functions of, 359
of handwriting, 202-205
of oral expression, 112, 113
of writing, 140

F

Field trips, 96
Finocchiaro, Mary, cited, 283
Foreign language
criteria for judging instructional materials, 283, 284
in elementary school, 270-290
future trends in elementary school, 288-290
limitations likely to be encountered, 275, 276
objectives of study, 274-277
optimum age for beginning study of, 272-274
rationale for teaching, 270
relations to total curriculum, 277, 278
role of teacher, 287, 288
teaching techniques and materials, 279-287
time required to master, 271-274
Forest, Ilse, cited, 276
Francis, W. Nelson, cited, 238, 250
Freeman, F. N., cited, 203, 204
Freeman, Stephen A., cited, 271
Fries, Charles C., cited, 213, 244
Frogner, Ellen, cited, 241
Frost, Joe L., cited, 19, 22, 23,
Furness, Edna Lue, cited, 144

G

Games, use in spelling instruction, 233
Gardner, Bruce D., cited, 1, 3, 16
Gates, Arthur I., cited, 338
Gates-Russell Diagnostic Series, 335
Generalizations, definition, 16
Glanzer, M., cited, 244
Gleason, H. A., Jr., cited, 246, 261
Goldfarb, W., cited, 21
Graham, Martha, cited, 88
Grammar
definitions of, 238, 239
as editorial tool, 255-257
formal, 240, 241
functional, 241, 242
generative, 246
structural linguistic approach to teaching of, 242, 243
teaching of, in elementary school, 246, 247
teaching of, as structural framework, 250-255
transformational, 244-246
and usage, 237-267, 358, 359
grade-placement practices, 262, 263
viewpoints concerning teaching of, 240-244
Grapho-phonemes (English)
analyses, 220-225
consonant, 217
Greene, Harry A., cited, 148, 149, 249, 257, 334, 341
Grouping in speech instruction, 107-112
Growth, implications of modifiability, 5, 6
"Grunt and point," 4

H

Halstead, William P., cited, 76
Handwriting, 60
check lists for evaluating, 312-316, 319, 320
commercial systems, 174
content of beginning program, 191-194
cursive, 172

cursive: differences from manuscript, 195, 196
cursive: individual instruction, 198
cursive: prerequisites to emphasis on speed, 199
cursive: transition to, from manuscript, 194-200
evaluating quality through diagnostic and analytical scales, 308
evaluating through general merit scales, 306-308
evaluation of, 202-205
formal evaluation, 306-311
grade-level goals, 172-174
how to begin, 184
informal evaluation, 311-316
manuscript, 172
meaningful experiences in, 305
objectives, 304, 305
pupil self-evaluation, 319, 320
remediation suggestions, 316-318
teacher self-evaluation, 318, 319
teaching and improving in elementary schools, 170-207
typical programs, 171-181
Handwriting Evaluation Scales (Freeman and Zaner-Bloser Staff), 307, 308
Harris, Louis, cited, 65
Hatchett, Ethel, cited, 260
Hawkes, Glenn R., cited, 19, 23
Health, relation to language ability, 13
Heron, W., cited, 21
Herrick, Virgil, cited, 172, 174, 186, 203
Hildreth, Gertrude H., cited, 12, 20
Home, characteristics of poverty-stricken, 102
Hook, J. N., cited, 244
Horn, Ernest, cited, 335, 341
Hudelson English Composition Scale, 348, 349
Hughes, Vergil H., cited, 12, 260
Hunt, J. McVicker
assistance acknowledged, 19 (footnote)
cited, 18

I

Ideas, interchange in preprimary period, 95, 96
Images, definition, 16
Inexactness, linguistic, 68
Infancy, language development during, 2-4
Inflectional endings, 253, 254
Inflexion, 3
Information, listening to acquire, 130, 131
Inquiry, factors stifling, 30, 31
Inskeep, James, cited, 205
Intellectual capacity, differences among children, 100, 101
Intelligence
definition, 16
effect of stimulating environment on, 21, 22
potential, and linguistic skill, 20
relation to language power, 19
unchanging, 18
Interdentals, 215
Interest, 257
Intonation, 3
Iowa Language Abilities Tests, 323, 352
Iowa Every-Pupil Tests of Basic Skills, 323, 352

J

Jandoli, Russell, cited, 241
Johnson, Dorothy, cited, 233

K

Knowledge
acquisition of, and language arts, 51, 52
listening and, 116, 117
Kraus, Silvy, cited, 244

L

Labials, 214, 215
Laird, Charlton, cited, 149
Langer, Susanne K., cited, 37-39

Language
arranging sequence for learning, 265, 266
characteristics, 1, 2
changes in methods of teaching, 239
development in children, 1-35
development, and dramatic play, 45, 46
development, early, 37-39
development: listening and, 39, 40
development, nature of, 5
development: role of teacher in, 27-32
development: schema, 24
development: "whole child" approach to, 23-25
disability and emotional disorder, 14
evidences of growth in, 6
and experience, 19
foreign: *see* Foreign language
essential functions, 237, 238
guiding principles for building instructional programs in, 93, 94
interrelationships among aspects, 12, 13
learning related to opportunity, 264, 265
oral: *see* Oral language
patterns, 9
potential intelligence and skill in, 20
power: effect of social and culturally impoverished environments on, 37, 38
relation of health to ability in, 13
relation of intelligence to power in, 19
relation to thinking, 15, 16
socioeconomic status and development of, 19
speaking and, 40, 41
teachers as models, 29
teaching: principles influencing, 26, 27
teaching, 25-32
usage: evaluation, 353, 354
and writing, 137, 138
written: *see* Written language
Language arts
creative dramatics in, 75-77
elementary school program, 37-60
inseparability of, 43, 44
interrelationships among, 39-44, 129
Language arts
and other curricular areas, 44-45
planning for instruction in, 57-60
working with children in, 264-266
Larison, J., cited, 198
Leadership, education for, in group participation, 109
Lee, Doris May, cited, 41, 44
Lefevre, Carl, cited, 238, 243, 251, 261
Lefevre Helen, cited, 238, 243, 251 261
Legibility (handwriting), 311
Lessen, Sheldon, cited, 241
Letter formation (handwriting), 311, 312
Letters (of alphabet), introduction of, 187
Letters
business, 158, 159
friendly or social, 156, 157
Lewis, Edward R., cited, 188
Lewis, Helen P., cited, 188
Linguistics, structural: approach to teaching of grammar, 242- 243
Listening, 116-134
check lists for evaluating, 299, 300, 303
critical: skills involved in, 131, 132
critical: value formation through, 118
evaluation of, 296-304
formal evaluation, 299
goals of instruction program, 129
informal evaluation, 299
instruction in, in elementary school, 120, 121
and language development, 39, 40
meaningful experiences in, 298, 299
objectives, 297

pupil self-evaluation, 302, 303
remediation suggestions, 301, 302
skills, 296, 297
synthesis of skills, 130
teacher self-evaluation, 303, 304
theory of, 121-132
theory: basic premises of, 124-129
time involved in, 118, 119
Loban, Walter D., cited, 14, 244

M

Manuscript writing, 181-184
Martin, Clyde, cited, 12
Materials, teachers must provide, 29
Mathematics, language arts and, 49, 50
Matthews, E. G., cited, 244
McCarthy, D., cited, 3, 4, 8, 14
McDavid Raven I., Jr., cited, 238
Meaning enhanced by structure, 243, 244
Mearns, Hughes, cited, 167
Melzack, Ronald, cited, 21
Metropolitan Primary Manuscript Handwriting Scale, 308
Migrant laborers, language skill of children of, 22
Miller, C. G., cited, 241
Misinterpretations, 69
Mitchell, Lee, cited, 76
Mood, 79
development, 83-85
Morine, Greta, cited, 252
Morine, Harold, cited, 252
Morphology
considerations related to, 211-213
relations to semantics and syntax, 210-219
Morton-McCall Spelling Scale, 324
Motivation, intrinsic, for writing, 154, 155
Mulhausen, Ruth, cited, 276
Mulry, June G., cited, 190, 241

N

Nature
role in development of children, 19
study, creative dramatics and, 74
Needs
nonutilitarian, 67-70
utilitarian, 64-66
Nemec, Lois G., cited, 249
Nice, M. M., cited, 8
Nichols, Ralph G., cited, 133
Noble, J. Kendrick, cited, 170, 179
Nursery school, language development in, 9
Nurture, role in development of children, 19
Nutrition, 54

O

O'Brien, Robert, cited, 170
Olson, Willard C., cited, 5
Oral English
instruction in, in other subjects, 105-107
in preprimary years, 94-96
program for, 92-114
Oral expression
evaluation of, 112, 113
maintenance of social relations, 109
Oral language, 58
analytical and remedial suggestions, 351-357
check list for evaluating, 346
formal evaluation, 345
goals in primary years, 96-99
informal evaluation, 346, 347
interrelations with reading and writing, 14
levels of experience, 266, 267
meaning experiences in, 345
objectives, 343, 344
teacher self-evaluation, 358
Organization of presentations, 257
Orthography, 210

P

Painter, Margaret, cited, 105
Palatals, 214, 216
Paper
for beginning handwriting instruction, 184, 185
placement of, for handwriting instruction, 188, 189

Parents, role in development of linguistic skill, 4
Parker, William R., cited, 270
Parts of speech, 253-255, 261
Peabody Vocabulary Test, 22
Pens, ball-point, 186
Perception, visual and auditory, 122
Percepts, definition, 16
Personal development, relation of speech to, 14
Petty, Walter T., cited, 148, 149, 171, 190, 226, 249, 257, 341
Phonemes 215
Phonological units, 9
Phonology
  relation to reading instruction, 213, 214
  uses of, 211
Phrase structure, 210, 211
Piaget, Jean cited, 4, 17
Pitman, Sir James, cited, 220
Poetry writing
  children's, 165-167
  guides to performance expectancies, 166, 167
Pooley, Robert C. cited, 239, 247, 249
Postman, Neil, cited, 252, 261
Prefixes and suffixes, 253, 254
Preschool child, development of speech of, 94-96
Preschool period
  language development during, 4
  use of manipulative devices, 95
Principles, definition, 16
Problem solving, 24
  language arts and, 51, 52
Prose,
  poetic, 77, 78
Prose
  writing, techniques for motivating, 160-165
Punctuation
  evaluation of, 356, 357
  skills, 143-147
  skills: grade-placement practices, 263, 264
  suggestions for grade placement, 147, 148
Pupil criticism, organization of, 111, 112

Q

Qualifiers, characteristics of, 255

R

Randall, Earle S., cited, 286
Rankin, Paul T., cited, 119
Rasmussen, Carrie, cited, 105
Reading, 59
  interrelations with writing and oral language, 14
  relation to language arts, 42
  relation of phonology to instruction in, 213, 214
  talking and, 41
Reference material, use of, 46
"Relief," linguistic ability of children from families receiving, 20
Rhythm, 76
  variety in, 79
Rhythmic experiences, 81-83
Rice, J. M., cited, 226
Riesen, Austin H., cited, 21
Roberts, Paul E., cited, 237, 239, 245, 247, 253, 255, 261
Rose, Elizabeth, cited, 165
Rowland
  Monroe
Russell, David H., cited, 16, 122, 301, 338
Russell, Elizabeth F. cited, 122, 301

S

Schools, elementary: *see* Elementary schools
Science, language arts in, 46-49
Semantics, relations to syntax and morphology, 210-219
Sensations, definition, 16
Sense perception, 82, 83
Sentence
  definitions, 250
  patterns, 251
  of preschool child, 9
  sense, evaluation of, 354, 355
Shane, Harold G., cited, 190, 241
Shibles, Burleigh H., cited, 8

Skeels, Harold M., cited, 21
Skills, acquisition of, 52
Slang, 248
Sledd, James, cited, 250
Smith, Madorah E., cited 7
Smith, Mary K., cited, 7, 150
Social adaptation, listening facilitates, 118
Social relationships, maintenance through oral communication, 109
Social studies
creative dramatics and, 74, 75
language arts in, 45
Socioeconomic status
effect on educational policy, 101, 102
relation to linguistic development, 19
Soltis, Rosemary, cited, 186
Speaking, 58
and language development, 40
Speech
development at elementary school level, 104, 105
development in preprimary years, 94-96
egocentric, 4
fluency in, and written language, 43
parts of: *see Parts of speech*
objectives of instruction in, 103
relation to personal development, 14
socialized, 4
standard, 248
substandard, 248
units, 9
writing and, 138
Speed
in cursive writing, 199, 200
measurement, in handwriting, 309, 310
Spellers, inefficient, 229, 230
Spelling, 60
adjustments for individual differences, 227, 228
charts, 221-224
check lists for evaluating, 327-330, 341, 342
diagnostic and remedial chart, 336-338
evaluation through teacher-made tests, 332-334
guidelines, 340
linguistic approach to teaching of, 209-233
materials for instruction, 232, 233
meaningful experiences, 322
measuring through diagnostic tests, 334-335
measuring as part of regular teaching program, 324-326
Measuring through standardized achievement tests, 322-324
methods of teaching, 225-233
objectives, 320-322
remediation suggestions, 335
self-evaluation in, 341, 342
standards for, 231, 232
time allotments for instruction in, 226, 227
Sputnik, effect on utilitarian education, 65
Staiger, Ralph, cited, 244
Stanley, Julian C., cited, 202
STEP essay Tests, 349
Stevens, Leonard A., cited, 133
Stewart, James Reece, cited, 241
Story
creation, 85, 86
telling, 344
Stress patterns 255
Strickland, Ruth G., cited, 152, 249
Structural units (speech), 9
Sund, Robert H., cited, 16
Symonds, Percival M., cited, 241
Syntax, relations to semantics and morphology, 210-219

T

Talking, 3
Tape recorder, use in spelling instruction, 233
Taylor, Stanford E., cited, 296, 301, 302

Teachers
as diagnosticians, 31, 32
as good language models, 29
provision of environments fostering emotional security, 30
provision of materials, 29
provision for stimulating inquiry, 30, 31
role of, in language development, 27-32
Teaching
language and, 25-32
language: principles influencing, 26, 27
Television in foreign language instruction, 286, 287
Templin, Mildred, cited, 8
Tests, standard, 294
Thinking
creative, 25
critical, 25
relation of language to 15, 16
Thompson, William R., cited, 21
Thorndike, E. L., cited, 203
Thought, solitary: provision of time for, 28
Torrance, E. Paul, cited, 28
Trauger, Wilmer K., cited, 192, 238, 243, 249
Typewriter, use in elementary schools, 200-202

U

Understanding
factors essential to, 256, 257
value of, 68
Unity, artistic, 75, 257
Usage, English, 358, 359
categories, 247, 248
grammar and, 237-267
improving in elementary school, 258-260
motivation to correct, 258
persistence of habits, 259
procedure for attacking problems, 259-260

V

Van Allen, Roach, cited, 41, 44
Velars, 214, 216
Vocabulary
differences due to socioeconomic status, 103
effect of reading on, 42, 43
increase in childhood, 6, 7
reading and oral usage, 127
reading and understanding, 40
techniques for development of, 150, 151
written, 149, 150
Vocalization, 2
Vowels sounds, 218-222

W

Walter, Nina Willis, cited, 167
Ward, Winifred, cited, 74
Watts, A. F., cited, 3, 4, 8
West, Paul V.
cited, 204
American Handwriting Scale, 307
"Whole child"
approach to language development, 23-25
study, 330-332
Willing Scale for Measuring Written composition, 348
Wilt, Miriam E., cited, 119
Winter, Clotilda, cited, 13
Wood, Nancy E., cited, 15
Words
fascination of, 257
order of, 254
selection, 149, 150
Writing
children's, evaluation of, 167, 168
creative, 159-165
development of skills in, 143-145
function, 139, 140
function and purpose, 152-159
interrelations with reading and oral language, 14
as process, 141-152
as process and product, 139
providing purposes for, 153, 154

speech and, 138
teachers' and children's goals for, 152, 153
teaching to children, 137-167
types of, 138, 139
utilitarian, 155-159
Written language, 42, 59-61
analytical and remedial suggestions, 351-357
check list for evaluating, 351
formal evaluation, 348-350
informal evaluation of, 350
meaningful experiences in, 348
objectives, 346-348
teacher self-evaluation, 358

Y

Young, F. M., cited, 20

Z

Zollinger, Marian, cited, 232